BUSINESS AND CAPITALISM

GEORGE GISZE, GERMAN MERCHANT OF THE STEELYARD, LONDON, 1532

BUSINESS AND CAPITALISM

An Introduction to Business History

N. S. B. GRAS
Straus Professor of Business History
Graduate School of Business Administration
Harvard University

F. S. CROFTS & CO.

1939   New York

COPYRIGHT, 1939, BY F. S. CROFTS & CO., INC.

ALL RIGHTS RESERVED

No part of the material covered by this copyright may be reproduced in any form without permission in writing from the publisher.

MANUFACTURED IN THE UNITED STATES OF AMERICA
BY THE VAIL-BALLOU PRESS, INC., BINGHAMTON, N. Y.

TO
WALLACE BRETT DONHAM
WHO CALLED BUSINESS HISTORY
INTO ACADEMIC REALITY

INTRODUCTION

In so far as this volume deals with business history it is a mere introduction. I think of the present treatment as a synthesis of business history and business genesis. Hundreds of moot questions are passed over as if they hardly exist. In this book the interest lies in the stream of economic effort.

Capitalism is a system of getting a living through the use of capital, which in turn we may regard as goods or trained abilities used in producing other goods or services. In this system of capitalism there are three broad types—pre-business, private business, and public business. The great achievement of private business capitalism is (1) the effective use of capital in production and distribution and (2) the accelerating flow of capital, both goods and abilities, into production and distribution. So long as these two continue, men will save, invest, venture, plan, work, and achieve. All forces, social or political, which impair these productive operations threaten the material and therefore the intellectual welfare of mankind.

Chief attention is given in this book to types of *private* capitalism. These may be listed here: petty, mercantile, industrial, financial, and national. There may be some divergence of opinion as to the underlying concepts, but there is little doubt that some such analysis is a necessary prelude to progress in business history.

The ideas of others have been accepted or rejected with little explicit reference. They have not been rejected lightly. This one thought is taken to be basic, namely, that the term "capitalism," like "rheumatism" and "indigestion," must be abandoned or differentiated. To be sure, discrimination in the use of the term impairs its propaganda value. Our interest here, however, lies simply in a better understanding of the subject.

A study of the history of capitalism shows that major struggles do not occur between capitalism and some other order of society but between two rival forms of capitalism. If any social group wishes to win in the social-economic contest, it must teach itself how to use capital and how to make capital flow in its direction. One group of capitalists may win over another and the victory may be progressive or retrogressive, but some form of capitalism will remain triumphant. To be sure, force could be attempted, but a seizure of a capitalistic society without a preparation in the use and investment of capital is like an invasion of an orderly state by Huns and Vandals.

A set of concepts has been created here which, although possibly in need of revision, appears to provide a point of departure for business history. The field in general is so nearly universal that the broad outlines will probably be found to apply very generally; but, still, national variations of great significance are bound to occur. Perhaps these will reflect degree of maturity rather than national genius. Parallel effusion and constant diffusion have been playing their parts in evolving the most suitable business forms and policies.

In all probability, the figure in this book to which most objection will be taken is the sedentary merchant. Although passed over in economic history, he stands out as a major figure in business history. Much study of this type of merchant is still required. He will be found to hold the key to a long period in history. It would appear that the economic history of Europe from 1200 to 1800 must be rewritten, this time with a pattern.

The challenge to the business historian is in large part to discover the main lines of development in *business policy* and the chief results of *business management* through the centuries and to correlate the two.

The field of business history, bordering so many social estates and skirting so many cultural streams, is no narrow specialty. Already it is evident that if progress is to be made, the work must be separated into specialized subjects. There is great present need for special work in the history of the internal organization of business, marketing, accounting, private finance, profits, and secular and cyclical movements in business.

Business history has no patron saint, no matter how great

its need for one. Tradition points out the narrow grooves for men to follow and among scholars they lead not to thoughts of business or administration. Heavy spectacled scorn demands the old mental attitudes in the social sciences. Classical and ecclesiastical lore bears down with withering might upon efforts to understand the immediate and the useful, even though these lead ultimately to beauty, comfort, variety, security, and contemplation. No idealists or leaders of thought can do more for the intellectual and moral nature of man than the constructive materialists can do. None have obstructed human progress more than those who have seen heaven nearer than it is.

A bright-colored thread running through this book is the recognition of individuals as leaders. I know that this goes counter to a common view developed in the nineteenth century. In such leadership, however, has lain progress in business and general culture. Obviously the leader needs reward in every field. In business, after a certain competence has been gained, the chief reward that is emphasized by the executive of larger mold is satisfaction in meeting administrative challenges. To be sure, there are devotees of mammon in business as elsewhere. To those who really think about the matter, the profit motive is as wide in application and ambiguous in meaning as it is potent in operation.

Among men there are many types and groups. At the risk of over-simplification we may isolate three of these groups, first among workers—devotees of amusement, misfits, and lovers of work. The members of the first group regard work as a means of getting support for play. Finding no satisfaction in work, they live for the evenings, the holidays, and the vacations. At work, they can be depended on chiefly to watch the clock. To this *permanent* journeyman class, work presents no challenge except to endurance. Complaisant mediocrity prevents the members of this class from becoming creatively useful in business, even though the individuals who compose the group be likable persons and good citizens. The members of the second group are poor workmen. They soon develop hostility to their labor and begin to think of how to change their work or how to get out of it entirely. It is difficult to decide what makes these persons, who really represent various levels of ability, incapable of sustained effort on a normal plane. Physical ills, especially glandular malfunctioning, play their parts and should be discovered and remedied. More and more, however, it is becoming apparent that maladjustment at home or on the job is really at the bottom of the trouble. Employers should help these persons to remove their maladjustments on a wholesale scale as a great and good investment in men. Some of such misfits become active in sabotage, some in trade unions, and some in municipal politics. Often it is difficult to determine whether such persons lose their jobs because of poor work or because of their political activity, but for whichever reason they are the first to be fired when a depression arrives. The third group is made up of those who love work—it may be repetitive labor or individual creative work. They find a challenge in their jobs. They may invent new processes or new machinery. Everywhere these look out for a chance to save time or material. Members of this group become foremen and even superintendents, managers, and top executives. They are *temporary* journeymen whose ancestors had training as farmers, master artisans, and storekeepers. As long as this class is numerous and untrammeled, business will be so strongly rooted in the soil that storms will not destroy it. This class is needed in the ranks of capitalist entrepreneurs and capitalist investors: it provides the yeast without which the bread does not rise. It is the germinating, creative force with which all human progress is directly or indirectly associated.

A little reflection will show that a similar three-fold classification is found among business men. First, there are the playboys of business who disport themselves in various ways—chorus girls, race horses, stamps, airplanes—anything but business. Of course, I am thinking not of the modest hobbies or avocations of business men but of the struggle for profits to buy distracting toys. The members of this group find no engrossing challenge in business but just hard uninteresting work. Seeking quick profits, they often violate obvious rules of good conduct. They may be as selfish in their work as they are frivolous in their play. They give business a bad reputation and make reforms necessary. Second, there is a class of misfits among executives that is not generally suspected. The individuals who make up the group have been born into business or married into it or have grown sour in administration. They may make sundry unpromising experiments in their business or branch out to invest in other enterprises. Rather logically, they end by impairing the financial position of the very business that they should nourish and cherish. The third group, however, is made up of those who love business administration—doing the big job in the way that helps most people at the time and looks to results that last longest. They are not good administrators because they seek profits, but they earn profits because they are good administrators. If their firm needs their earnings, it gets them. Their business is their masterpiece: society will profit from it. The creative business man, artist, scholar, and philosopher are fashioned from the same vital clay: finally, they perish and the work of their hands crumbles, but their influence becomes human heritage.

There have been in history various movements of a humanistic nature. In the fourteenth and fifteenth centuries, to go no farther back, there was a strong movement against supernaturalism and the Church and in favor of the classics, particularly the Greek. In this, the business men of Italy played a genuine part. Farther north, a similar manifestation occurred in the Protestant Revolution, in which business men were stalwart champions. In a second humanistic movement, this time of the eighteenth century, business men participated because they favored freedom from political and social restraint which bound the human spirit and curbed business. The emancipation of the intellect and the individual was to aid the industrial capitalist in his pioneering changes in business. In the philosophical movement of the late nineteenth century, which bore the name of pragmatism (or humanism), the business man played no part, though the new philosophy was nothing if not his own approach to life and work. In the humanitarian movement of the nineteenth century the business man did his share in emancipating mankind from cruelty, disease, ignorance, and slavery. Unfortunately, business men did not always see the application of the movement to the treatment of their own employees. Now, in our time, however, the new study of the adjustment of the individual, carried on under the auspices of business firms and business educational institutions, promises to advance the cause to an extent not dreamed of by its earlier leaders.

In the recent humanistic movement which opposes materialism and vocationalism, the business man can take no part because he knows that materialism is the basis of general progress, though it is not the goal of man. He believes also that the preparation for work is a primary duty of every individual who would be a free man and a free citizen among men. And in the sixth, and last, humanistic movement which is pertinent here the business man could also play no part. This is the movement against economic competition and biological evolution, which runs off into communism. Although the philosophy of the business man is emphatically against the demoralizing submergence of the individual in the group, still the business man is ever ready to modify competition in favor of mutual aid, agreement, and group action.

Thus, out of these six humanistic movements the business man has been in sympathy with four, has participated in three, and has opposed two, one of which is a false humanism and the other degenerate. When these most recent humanistic movements coalesce, they conspire against the health of the very men they would assist. In our day they have plumbed the depths of sentimentalism and reached down into the dregs to glorify the biologically unfit. For years we have been unconsciously building up a culture for worms, not men; breeding a degenerate society to be swept away by more virile peoples from the hills.

Examples of the opinions that have grown up in our degenerate humanism are found in the views that the visiting nurse performs more social service than the factory owner, that the postman is more useful socially than the banker, and that the professor has to face intellectual challenges the like of which never come to the business executive. Such ideas, which rule emotionally in many homes, reflect a misunderstanding of essentials. Much of the basis for the befuddled viewpoint comes down from certain classic traditions of ancient days, nurtured in the supernaturalism of the mediaeval Church, and now fanned into flames that at times threaten to fuse the social order. Every politician, every professional man, and every voter should pass a test on the meaning of "social service."

Let us not create an antithesis of humanism vs. private business capitalism, but rather consider the relation between the two, the extent to which private business capitalism has advanced virile humanism. Such opinions as this and others that I have been expressing are not to be taken as encroaching in any way upon facts and generalizations from facts found in the body of this book. I hold to the ideal of the separation of facts, generalizations, and opinions. I would burn no man for errors in any one of them.

It should be pointed out here that owing to the dovetailed and integrated pattern of the evolution of capitalism, as here presented, no one can read all that I have written, for instance, about industrial capitalism until he has read other parts, in this case about financial capitalism and even national capitalism. Anyone reading just a part of this book can only misunderstand it all.

Since this book was written in the summer of 1938, it reflects somewhat the emphasis of that season. A few parts were later added before going to press in March 1939. During this interim I was able to profit by consultation with friends and colleagues.

Helpful as many scholars have been, I hasten to absolve men and institutions from all responsibility for the generalizations and opinions herein expressed.

My obligations to colleagues and fellow scholars are very real. For years I have drawn upon the fund of knowledge of Dr. Henrietta M. Larson who has read the whole manuscript and given invaluable advice at many crucial points. Dr. Ralph M. Hower has read parts of the manuscript and made critical and constructive suggestions of great value. Mr. and Mrs. Raymond de Roover have been generous in sharing their knowledge of mediaeval business history.

To Miss Frances Carpenter I owe help in tracing many a point and in verifying many a fact. To my son, Alfred E. Gras, I am under obligation for a complete reading of the text and for suggestions from the point of view of the student. To my wife I am indebted for aid in typing and in formulating conclusions at every stage of composition.

Widener Library and Baker Library have been mines of information which could not be exhausted. Life itself—the market place, the class room, the tea party, talks on a farmer's verandah, and the political contest—has offered a rich array of facts. Many a field has been surveyed only to be left unplowed. It is fitting that other scholars should go much farther along the lines of endeavor here sketched. Scientific work is a relay race in which each runner hands on the flag to a fresh contestant.

N. S. B. Gras

CONTENTS

I. PRE-BUSINESS CAPITALISM
The Dominance of Status

1. Capitalism before private business — 1
2. The earliest stages of economic activity — 3
3. The capitalism of the pastoral nomads — 7
4. Coöperation in the settled village — 13
5. Administration of the large estate and manor — 18
6. Civilization of pre-business capitalism — 23

II. PETTY CAPITALISM
The Birth of Private Business

1. The nature of private business — 27
2. Rise and nature of petty capitalism — 30
3. Sedentary petty capitalists — 33
4. Traveling petty capitalists: traveling merchants — 37
5. Traveling petty capitalists: pedlars — 44
6. Agents and auxiliaries in petty capitalism — 48
7. Forces at work — 51
8. Accumulation and flow of capital — 52
9. Strength and weakness of petty capitalism — 58
10. Survival and revival of petty capitalists in our day — 62

III. MERCANTILE CAPITALISM
Birth of Control in Private Business

1. Rise of the sedentary merchant — 67
2. Policy and management of the sedentary merchants — 74
3. Partnership flourishes — 81
4. The flow of capital — 85

5. Control	88
6. The mercantile capitalist and industry	92
7. Joint stock companies	103
8. Bookkeeping as a business device	114

IV. MERCANTILE CAPITALISM
Maturity with a Tendency to Disintegrate

1. Merchants' policies and mercantilism	120
2. Metropolitan economy	127
3. Managers, contractors, promoters, and speculators	132
4. Credit instruments and merchant bankers	141
5. Sedentary merchants and commercial banks	148
6. Forces at work	151
7. Strength and weakness of mercantile capitalism	157
8. Development within mercantile capitalism: various types	165
9. End of the sedentary merchant and mercantile capitalism	169

V. INDUSTRIAL CAPITALISM
The Triumph of Firm Specialization in Big Business

1. The rise of industrial capitalism	175
2. The new transportation	181
3. Commercial banking and its relation to business	186
4. Three phases of industrial capitalism	189
5. Marketing in industrial capitalism	195
6. Business agents and auxiliaries	207
7. Secular trends in prices and profits	215
8. Flow of capital under industrial capitalism	218
9. Effect of industrial capitalism on internal organization	224
10. Social engineers	227
11. Strength and weakness of industrial capitalism	234

VI. FINANCIAL CAPITALISM
The Money Middleman Influences or Controls Business

1. Search for profits by turning away from specialization	238
2. Financial capitalists	246

3. Flow of capital 259
4. Industrial integration and diversification under financial capitalism 266
5. Transportation and communication 272
6. Public utilities 279
7. Merchandising under financial capitalism 288
8. Use of agents, auxiliaries, and business tools 293
9. Secular trends and financial capitalism 297
10. Mistakes and crimes in business 304
11. Strength and weakness of financial capitalism 316

VII. NATIONAL CAPITALISM
Political instead of Financial Control of Private Capital

1. Meaning of national capitalism 323
2. Early adumbration of national capitalism 332
3. Forces making for national capitalism 337
4. Fascism 339
5. Naziism 343
6. The American New Deal 348
7. The secular trend in business and the growth of national capitalism 359
8. Flow of capital under national capitalism 362
9. Strength and weakness of national capitalism 365
10. The philosophy of capitalism 368

Readings 373

Suggested Studies 386

Index 393

LIST OF CHARTS AND ILLUSTRATIONS

George Gisze, German Merchant of the Steelyard. London, 1532. Photograph of a portrait by Hans Holbein the Younger, now in the Kaiser Fried. Museum, Berlin. From the original photograph by Franz Hanfstaengl, Munich. Frontispiece

Horses and Cart. England, fourteenth century. A. Parmentier, *Album Historique,* vol. II (Armand Colin & Cie, Paris, 1897), p. 43. *facing* 8

Farm Equipment in Use. France, thirteenth century. Parmentier, *op. cit.,* vol. I (1896), p. 157. *facing* 8

Oxen and Wheel Plow in Use. England, eleventh century. Parmentier, *op. cit.,* vol. I, p. 170. *facing* 8

Haider Khan Points the Way to Fresh Summer Pastures. The headmen leave the "directors' meeting." Persia, 1924. Film "Grass," Paramount Pictures, Inc. *facing* 9

Sheep—Black and White—Crossing a Mountain River on the Way to Fresh Pastures. Persia, 1924. Film "Grass," Paramount Pictures, Inc. *facing* 10

A Fortune in Rugs. The journey is over the mountains to summer pastures. Persia, 1924. Film "Grass," Paramount Pictures, Inc. *facing* 11

Mediaeval Tally. England, thirteenth century. Amount — £11 18s. 2½d. The amounts were determined by the position and width of the notches. Taken from *Introduction to the Study of the Pipe Rolls* (London, 1884), p. 64. *facing* 28

Interior of Shops (Shoemaker's, Draper's, and Goldsmith's). France, fifteenth century. Parmentier, *op. cit.,* vol. II, p. 38. *facing* 28

Lübeck Marketplace, about 1580. G. Steinhausen, *Der Kaufmann in der deutschen Vergangenheit* (Eugen Diederichs, Leipzig, 1899), Beilage 7. *facing* 29

Interior of a Store. Germany, fifteenth century. Parmentier, *op. cit.,* vol. II, p. 66. *facing* 32

Huckster Calling Out "Apples, Ladies." Ancient Gaul. Parmentier, *op. cit.*, vol. I, p. 15. *facing* 33

A Turkoman Traveling Merchant. Merv, Russian Turkestan, about 1918. Photograph by Dr. M. O. Williams. Copyright by, and published in the *National Geographic Magazine*, Nov., 1919, p. 422. *facing* 36

Dutch Ship, fifteenth century. Steinhausen, *op. cit.*, no. 44.
facing 40

American Rural Pedlar, nineteenth century. *Harper's Weekly*, June 20, 1868. *facing* 41

Golden Bezant. *Solidus* of Theophilus, Emperor (829–842) of the Byzantine Empire. British Museum. The bezant was worth about half a sovereign and circulated widely among commercial peoples for over eight centuries and a half until about 1260 and even later. *facing* 60

Exterior of a Retailer's Store and Dwelling. France, sixteenth century. Parmentier, *op. cit.*, vol. III (1900), p. 17. *facing* 60

Hall and Court of a Merchant. Augsburg, 1539. Woodcut from Steinhausen, *op. cit.*, no. 68. *facing* 61

Luca Pacioli and a Young Nobleman. Naples, late fifteenth century. Portrait by Jacopo de' Barbari (?), in Musea Nazionale, Naples. Photograph by Fratelli Alinari, Naples. *facing* 72

Merchant's Counting House Interior. Berlin, seventeenth century. Engraving from Steinhausen, *op. cit.*, no. 116. *facing* 73

Merchant's Counting House Interior. Nürnberg, seventeenth century. Engraving from Steinhausen, *op. cit.*, no. 115.
facing 74

Three Balls—Sign of the Pawnbroker's Shop. Engraving from a section of a picture drawn by Hogarth in 1751 as a caricature of a London street, "Gin Lane." *facing* 74

Venetian Galley, 1486. Parmentier, *op. cit.*, vol. II, p. 86. *facing* 75

Groups Controlled by the Sedentary Merchant. 90

Apprentices Learning Arithmetic. Nürnberg, 1518. Steinhausen, *op. cit.*, no. 84. *facing* 90

Sir Thomas Smythe, London, about 1610. From an engraving published by W. Richardson, London, 1797. *facing* 106

LIST OF CHARTS AND ILLUSTRATIONS xxi

A Sedentary Merchant at Work. The merchant discusses matters with customers, the bookkeeper writes entries in the Journal, and the first assistant cashier keeps the cash and a record thereof. On the upper left, goods are carefully weighed. Germany, late sixteenth century. Woodcut by Jost Amman. From Steinhausen, *op. cit.*, Beilage 6. *facing* 107

Part of the (Same) Sedentary Merchant's Establishment. A bookkeeper transfers entries from Journal to Ledger. Assistant cashiers count and test the money. Packers prepare outgoing freight. On the left, allegorical figures stand for plenty, quiet, and integrity. Germany, late sixteenth century. Woodcut by Jost Amman. From Steinhausen, *op. cit.*, no. 56. *facing* 122

Part of the (Same) Sedentary Merchant's Counting House. On the left is the writing room where the chief cashier keeps his records and stows away the cash. On the right, plate and jewels are carefully listed. Germany, late sixteenth century. Woodcut by Jost Amman. From Steinhausen, *op. cit.*, no. 57. *facing* 123

Plan of the Second Royal Exchange. London, 1837. From W. Thornbury, *Old and New London*, vol. I (Cassell and Co., Ltd., London, 1897), p. 497. 130

Inner Court, Gresham's Royal Exchange. London, late sixteenth century. From W. Thornbury, *op. cit.*, vol. I (1897), p. 492. *facing* 138

Office in the Fugger Bank, Augsburg, 1516. Parmentier, *op. cit.*, vol. III, p. 31. 144

Conrad Peutinger. Augsburg, 1465–1547. Engraving by Johann Jacob Haid, about 1750. *facing* 154

Jacob Fugger. Augsburg, early sixteenth century. Woodcut from Steinhausen, *op. cit.*, no. 89. *facing* 155

Changes in Mercantile Capitalism: Types of Sedentary Merchants. 168

Sir Richard Arkwright. Engraving by J. Jenkins from a painting by Joseph Wright, R.A. Published by Fisher, Son and Co. London, 1833. *facing* 186

Cornelius Vanderbilt, about 1850. Engraving by the American Bank Note Company, from a photograph. *facing* 187

Andrew Carnegie, about 1899. Photograph (by Peter A. Juley and Son) of a portrait by W. W. Ouless, R.A. Provided by Mrs. Andrew Carnegie. *facing* 202

John D. Rockefeller, Sr., 1895. Photograph of a portrait by Eastman Johnson, now in the University of Chicago. *facing* 203

The Claflin Merchandising Empire in 1914. 205

John Pierpont Morgan, Sr., in the 1890's. Engraving from W. T. E. Hardenbrook, *Financial New York* (Franklin Publishing Co., Chicago, 1897), p. 328. *facing* 251

Two Dominating Combinations in American Business, 1904. Based on ideas and facts presented by John Moody in his *Truth about the Trusts* (Moody Publishing Co., New York and Chicago, 1904). First chart. 252

Diffusion of Business and Capital. 260

Mistakes and Crimes Especially in Business. 306

Recent Political and Economic Changes in National Régimes. 329

The National Capitalistic Pyramid. 331

Italian Fasces. 339

Nazi Swastika. Ancient and widespread symbol of good luck. 343

American Blue Eagle. Designed overnight by C. T. Coiner, of Philadelphia. Symbol of the National Recovery Administration and American New Deal. Business firms advertised their membership in the NRA by displaying the Blue Eagle. 351

The American National Administration. Based on a chart distributed by the United States Information Service and dated September, 1938. 353

The Flow of Capital under Financial Capitalism. 362

The Flow of Capital under National Capitalism. 363

Chapter I

PRE-BUSINESS CAPITALISM

The Dominance of Status

Migration has charms, settlement greater income;
Freedom is desirable but unnecessary.
Free contract is indulgence, for status is the rule;
Exchange of goods and services is between users.
Capital without business has little future.

1. CAPITALISM BEFORE PRIVATE BUSINESS

The old-time analysis of the factors of production still holds. Land (natural resources), labor, capital, and management have been the historic ingredients of economic activity. Land and labor change but little in fundamentals. The key to strategic shifts in the history of man's efforts to get a living is found in capital and management, not separate but in conjunction. These two are woven together into a line of events by a system which we may call "capitalism." To the historian, capitalism is simply a system of getting a living through the use or investment of capital.

Whether there was ever a pre-capitalistic stage in human history, we do not need to stop to inquire. If so, it lay in that dim past connected with the missing link. It may have existed in the days when man was hardly man—a time for which we have no precise evidence, historical or anthropological. Certainly, it would have been of a low and somewhat animal order, in no way idyllic as the poets have dreamed. It was not a golden age in which man walked with God and God provided a high plane of living.

We are more interested in the stages through which the capitalistic system has gone. There are at least two broad stages with a possible third. First, there is capitalism before private business comes upon the scene. Second, there is capitalism under a régime of private business. And, third, there is a possible and developing capitalism under a régime of public business. The first is the interest of this first chapter, the second of substantially all of the rest of the book. The third leads right into communistic capitalism such as Lenin established in Russia—a system which under Stalin is being changed.

It is obvious that the concept of capitalism used here is very broad. The historian can handle no other. The view of Marx and his followers that capitalism is a system of exploitation is useful only for propaganda. Capitalism may involve control and even exploitation, but, as we shall see, it may not.

Capitalism is, as we have observed, a system which combines (a) capital (only goods at first but later also a capital fund) and (b) management of capital. We may also call these (1) the accumulation and flow and (2) the use of capital. These have gone through a long series of changes. Just now, in this chapter, we are interested in the system of capitalism which existed before private business came upon the scene. By this I mean that early system of using capital before there was a class of business men, that is, before any individuals gained their living by providing goods or services for sale. Some might say that this must have been in the days of self-sufficiency. To be sure, there was a suggestion of this but it was not complete.

On the negative side, the chief characteristic of the earliest stage of capitalism was the lack of business, or specialized production for sale or specialized exchange for a money profit. On the positive side, there were four principal characteristics. First, the individual was fixed in society by his status in the group to which he belonged or in reference to land-holding, a status that was largely a matter of unwritten custom. An independent contractual position, or even existence apart from the group, was inconceivable. Second, such exchange of goods or services as took place was with users, not middlemen or specialized men of business, for there were no business men. Third, there was approximate self-sufficiency (until private business capitalists from elsewhere entered the picture). Fourth, there was a lack of a spirit of change. This does not mean an absence of change but a lack of rapidity and a lack of conscious aiming at improvement.

In this early stage there were considerable, though varying, amounts of capital, as we shall see, and elements that later went into the fabric of business. Some of these elements were a gradually growing division of labor, an unfolding organization for management, and a system of control, which, however, was associated with status rather than contract. In other words, though capitalism existed, it was primitive. At its height, it might be called agrarian capitalism. (This should not be identified with the later capitalistic agriculture, which is something very different.)

Like all beginnings, this first stage of capitalism was feeble. Some persons might say that it was the cloud on the horizon, not the storm. We should miss a lot, however, if we did not see the capitalistic elements involved. But let us get on into the details, or inner reality, of this early segment of man's economic experience, out of which will come a clearer realization of the essentials of what has been said than can be briefly expressed by way of generalization.

2. THE EARLIEST STAGES OF ECONOMIC ACTIVITY

It is an amazing fact that the longest periods of human existence were the earliest. We might argue that they were also the most important for man.

The pre-business era of capitalism, in which capital accumulations grew in size and management grew in strength, was probably at least a hundred times longer than the private business era of capitalism. In other words the type of capitalism dealt with in this chapter was that much longer in development than the type dealt with in the rest of this book.

Fortunately, the long era of pre-business capitalism can be cut up into segments for examination. In other books I have called these collectional economy, cultural nomadic economy, and settled village economy. In all probability these economies grew shorter as one followed the other. Perhaps we may make this happy observation that everything points to an acceleration of man's power to advance, though at times we may individually have doubts about the continuation of the advance.

In the stage of collectional economy man appropriates nature's gifts. This has been called the hunting and fishing stage. In truth, the economic activity of primitive man was much wider than either hunting or fishing. It included the collecting of fruits, nuts, tubers, wild honey, and the like. It was strongest in the provision of commodities, weaker in manufacture, still weaker in storage, and at its lowest point in transportation. Exchange was all but non-existent.

Capital goods were in a process of being born in the collectional stage. They were of the simplest type, such as the bow and arrow, the grubbing stick, the boomerang, the bone fishhook and line of twisted fiber, and the fire drill. Since the animal possessed none of these, man could do very well in competition with it. On the side of the management of these capital goods, there is little to be said, because in collectional economy management was almost non-existent. There was labor—the obvious direct, simple use of the tools and weapons—and little or nothing more.

The second stage was cultural nomadic economy. This is the stage in which man moved over wider areas and developed a greater mastery over nature. Instead of just appropriating what was at hand, man added to his attainments the cultivation of animals and to some extent in some instances the slight cultivation of plants. What he cultivated, he could control. When he controlled, he could be sure of supplies. Security was an early pursuit of man.

The capital goods of some of the great nomadic tribes were very extensive. Some scholars have regarded this as a great capitalistic era which in due time went into decline. So important is this aspect that a whole section will be devoted to it in this chapter. Not only were the capital goods extensive, but the management involved in their use was considerable and promising for man's future. To be sure, the management was essentially on a kinship basis. It was primarily a matter of patriarchal organization. Of course, the family was the old-time large group of patriarchal head, sons and their wives, grandchildren, and cousins of varying degrees. Such a form of organization prevailed in early biblical days—in the time of Abraham, Isaac, and Jacob. Coöperation on such a family basis grew up without plan and rested on custom rather than on any rules such as a modern coöperative society draws up for its governance. One step forward was taken when kinship groups acted in common not only in war but in peace. Such tribal grouping was and is found in the pasturing of animals.

The Arabs stand out among nomadic peoples for their high qualities and power to advance somewhat beyond the nomadic stage. In their pre-Islamic days they wrote poems of war, feasting, and love—fierce yet tender, barbarous yet cadent. The hero is mounted on a she-camel or horse, with sword, spear, and armor. The haircloth tent is his only home, the desert his world. The sea he beholds in the distance—it may be a mirage; the stars are night lamps to guide him. He shivers by night and sizzles by day. Tall, lean, and swarthy, he is both rheumatic and romantic. To kinsmen and guests he is the prince of hospitality; to enemies he is the demon of blood and plunder. He murders his love's kinsmen and carries off the fair one. The rosind juice of the grape, the liver and hump of the camel, the fresh milk and curds are delicacies reserved for loved ones. The four-footed creatures of the sand-hills are his friends. The howls of beasts are known in every tone. Shadows and darkness of the night are haunted by no fear. Poor in coin and credit, he is rich in yonder flocks and herds; strong in his armor and courage, he is conspicuous for his action, his song, and his love.

Some of the Arabs (and other nomads, too) have been great traders. Living in semi-arid regions, they have had to move long distances to pasture their flocks and herds. Some of their number have become traveling merchants crossing vast deserts in camel caravans or crossing the southern seas even to the far Orient. But this business development belongs to a later phase. It came when the Arabs found that some peoples in both the west and the east had settled down in towns and had established markets for goods which they were well located to supply. The traveling merchant of Arabic and other nomadic groups really belonged more to the town life of other more advanced peoples. We shall study the rise of this traveling merchant class in the next chapter.

The third of the early stages is settled village economy. The nomads commonly, if not invariably, found need for settling down to a more intensive use of the soil. Whereas the nomads had used hundreds or thousands of acres to support a single human being, the settled villagers could get sustenance for one person from a very few acres. A common reason for settling down is thought to be the pressure of population on subsistence. Certainly we can see this process at work in parts of Africa even in recent times.

A shift occurred in the capitalism of the era. The amount of capital goods per acre of land increased, as we pass from the second to the third stage. At the same time the degree of management rose.

The nomad, especially the pastoral nomads with their flocks and herds, had been rich in livestock, horses, camels, and so on. While there was little change in kind, that is, the flocks and herds remained, still animals were relatively less important in the settled village economy than they had been in the previous stage. Along with animal husbandry went plant cultivation on a much more intensive scale than the fast-moving nomad could engage in. And these two—animal and plant culture—were increasingly integrated in farm management. They were managed so that one would help the other. The animals would manure and help cultivate the fields, while the fields would provide grain for both beast and man. Since we are dealing with the special aspect of management in the settled village in a subsequent section, we may leave it at this point.

We have expressed the opinion that capital accumulations were less in the settled village stage per acre of land than in the cultural nomadic stage. At the same time, the capital accumulation was probably greater per person when men shifted from nomadism to settled villages. We cannot help thinking of the barns, stables, granaries, cook-houses, dairy-houses, carts, harness, the plows, harrows, spades, forks, and flails that had not existed at all in the earlier stage or only to a very limited extent.

Throughout these three stages, however, there was no business and no business man. There was capitalism, and it was important. When the era is viewed as a whole, it appears as a time when capitalism was growing, though it had not attained the quickening pace that business was to provide.

It should be noted that, in these three stages and in the prebusiness era of capitalism generally, capital had to be used by the possessor in order to yield an income. In other words, it was a usucapital system. Later, a great improvement was to be introduced when the possessor of capital could put it out or invest it in order to derive an income from it. This second mode of using capital was an invention of the later days of town economy, as we shall see later.

3. THE CAPITALISM OF THE PASTORAL NOMADS

The capitalism of the pastoral nomads is worthy of special consideration because it was so well developed. Some of the great and early peoples of history would bear careful examination in this connection, notably the Vandals, Goths, Huns, Arabs, and Berbers.

On the side of capital goods we find a notable array of commodities. Of course I omit from consideration articles in finished form and ready for consumption and only thus used—such as milk, butter, cheese, clothing of leather and cloth, and ornaments.

The central group of capital goods was made up of cattle, sheep, or goats, or a combination of these. How large the flocks and herds were, we have no precise information. We may be sure that in the case of those peoples, for instance, in Asia Minor who migrated hundreds of miles over swollen rivers and across snow-covered mountains that the numbers tended to be kept down by the accidents of travel and the quality impaired by the strenuous labors involved. And yet the animals in question yielded milk and its derivatives, and also flesh, hides, and horns.

At the other extreme were the tents and other household equipment which had to be moved with the grazing animals. Commonly these were piled on the backs of horses or camels or drawn in carts or wagons by horses or oxen. We may see in our mind's eye in well-developed groups on the plains long trains of carts wending their way along the trail and packed with goods, women, and children. Here and there a covered wagon, with banners flying in case the group had warlike ambitions, might give variety to the procession.

Other capital goods were manufactured articles. Rugs constitute a well-known example because they are so highly prized in advanced nations. The quaint designs, the soft colors (originally from vegetable dyes), and the skillful weaving have created a living memorial to the life of the nomads, even though most of such rugs are not now made by nomadic peoples. About the early trade in such rugs little or nothing is known. Whether one nomadic tribe exchanged rugs with another is not clear. When towns arose within reach of the nomads, traveling merchants came to offer for sale one of the few things which the

HORSES AND CART, ENGLAND, FOURTEENTH CENTURY

OXEN AND WHEEL PLOW IN USE, ENGLAND, ELEVENTH CENTURY

FARM EQUIPMENT IN USE, FRANCE, THIRTEENTH CENTURY

HAIDER KHAN POINTS THE WAY TO FRESH SUMMER PASTURES, PERSIA, 1924

nomads had that others wanted. But all this belongs to the private business era of capitalism which came later.

A second group of manufactured articles consists of metallic wares, as found among peoples well located for procuring supplies of metal, particularly iron and steel. Nomads, even Gypsies, are great blacksmiths. Their skill makes up for their lack of equipment. Swords, knives, and parts for carts and wagons are their chief products. To what extent such articles are traded is not clear.

It is a matter of dispute as to whether nomadic peoples kept slaves in view of the difficulties involved in retaining and using them. To be sure, they supplied peoples who had settled down, with such slaves as they could capture or buy. Central and North Africa is one of the areas in which this trade has flourished even as late as the nineteenth century, but all this is beyond our present interest, which is confined to pre-business capitalism.

Apart from slaves, which were capital, there was free or half-free labor but no labor problem in this stage. The men had plenty to do, aided by their sons and dogs, in tending and defending the flocks and the herds, and the women had the many tasks involved in cooking, making clothing, repairing tents, and the like.

In this stage there was control and power. Many persons in our day think that business is responsible for the introduction of control—the pressure that one man puts upon another. In truth, in all stages except in the first—collectional economy, the one nearest the animals—it has been found necessary to have control for the welfare of the group. The reason is that, in practice, there are always at least a few idle, incompetent, and recalcitrant who will shirk their duties. If these are to share in the benefits, they must be controlled. Among the pastoral nomads, control and power lay in the hands of the patriarchs or chiefs, who might also be arbitrary and exacting, who in fact had to be high-handed in times of great stress such as in warfare.

A great silent film was made by Paramount Pictures in 1924

to illustrate the life of a nomadic people. The scene is in northwestern Persia. The people—one small group of the Bakhtiári—are shown facing exhausted winter pastures, as usual at certain seasons, and confronted with the problem of moving a long distance eastward through swollen rivers (especially the Karun) and over the snow-capped Taurus mountains to the rich summer pastures at the foot of the Kardeh Kuh Pass. The chief holds a council of migration. The decision is clear: the time for movement (April) is at hand. Each headman knows what is to be done and what route to follow. So, down with the heavy-blanketed tents which have been made from the wool of the sheep. Then, load onto the donkeys' backs the black tents—and also the poles. Conceal some of these tents, for others are waiting in the eastern pastures. Assemble all that must be packed or carried—women with babies, household utensils, chickens, and so on. Drive the herds of cows and flocks of sheep and goats. At the rivers the goats, women, and children must be ferried across on rafts made of inflated skins. Horses, cattle, and sheep must swim or sink. For six days the swarthy men battle heroically on their inflated goat skins to save the sinking or winded animals. Some men cross the river six or seven times to help the animals. Then, when dry again, up the mountains, through the snow, ever higher and higher. A girl carries a sick calf, a man shoulders a young donkey that can go no farther. At night, each family group builds its camp around the animals so that neither thieves nor wild beasts can reach them. At last, after nearly seven weeks, the valley lies below—with plenty of rich grass. For these capitalists, the depression is over and good times have come again.

Here is a struggle—seasonally enacted—that has been repeated perhaps two thousand years. The larger group of about 50,000 persons possess perhaps 500,000 head of livestock of various kinds. It is a contest for capital, first to produce it on rich pastures, then to guard and preserve it during migration. Shall we call this the original type of migration of capital or flight of capital? Not a sheep or goat, horse or dog, must be lost, if

SHEEP CROSSING A MOUNTAIN RIVER ON THE WAY TO FRESH PASTURES, PERSIA, 1924

A FORTUNE IN RUGS, PERSIA, 1924

CAPITALISM OF PASTORAL NOMADS

vigilant men, boys, and women can prevent loss. Each animal is useful for both production and consumption. With the best of efforts, however, the losses are heavy. In such a situation, there is no great labor problem, though, for long stretches of time and travel, the labors of men and young women are herculean. One quarter of life is spent in this migration. When labor is mixed with danger and adventure, few shirk it. There is no problem of money value but a keen sense of utility value. There is no organization chart, though each man knows what to do and where to get his orders. His rights and obligations are fixed by his status as a tribesman. Each head of a family owns tents, utensils, animals, and weapons. Great inequality of possessions exists, as disaster, mismanagement, or sometimes gambling eats into the family fortune, which the women do their best to guard. The struggle is primarily economic, but warriors are armed and mounted, ready to do battle on the slightest provocation. The few outside needs can be met by exchanging the few surplus goods, such as woolen rugs and blankets for arms and ammunition and sheep for rice. The tribesman's prize possession—his capital—is livestock. It is the livestock not the land that he cultivates. This living capital is used (in production and consumption) not invested. The capital moves but it does not flow. Such a system of capital use provides a living but affords no basis for progress or change.

It was the pastoral nomads who were located on reasonably fertile lands that tended to settle down first, probably induced to do so by an increasing population. Those located on less fertile lands might remain nomadic, as many still do in Africa, Asia, and Asia Minor. But there was an interesting situation that arose when pastoral nomads bordered settled villages. At least from the shepherd people of ancient Egypt called the Hyksos, who produced an early dynasty for the Nile peoples, down to the wandering Teutonic, Magyar, and Tartar groups of the Middle Ages, these pastoral nomads have been in conflict with settled villagers. At first they raided the settled villages, then collected regular tribute for not raiding, at the same time keeping off other disturbers. Then they settled down in or among the villages as lords of the land and gradually intermarried. The Northman wanderers of the tenth and eleventh centuries somewhat exemplify this process, and the story of Robin Hood is the romantic flowering of the opposition of the conquered to the conquerors. Anyone interested in this theory of the origin of the state in conquest by nomads should read Franz Oppenheimer's *The State*.

Whether Oppenheimer's theory of the origin of the state has universal or wide application, we need not stop to inquire. One aspect of the theory, however, belongs very much to our interest; that is, that the nomads, particularly the pastoral nomads, possessed great power. This power arose from several factors. One is the diet of the nomads—milk, butter, cheese, and meat—which tended to give vitality to the children and strength to the adults. Moving long distances and the frequent breaking of camp were very favorable to sanitary living. The stimulus that comes from movement in family groups is very real—it provides an awareness to new circumstances that keeps individuals alive to the world in which they live. And then there was the concentration of power, political power in the patriarchal head who held sway over the producing unit of kinsmen. In the case of a whole nation of nomads, the head of the nation would be one of the patriarchs chosen for his strength or from the fact that he was head of the group or clan that had seniority among the group. A nomadic group of men well fed, well armed, and well led was a formidable foe to settled village groups, which by their very nature were scattered, isolated, and immobile.

On the other hand, this capitalistic group of pastoral nomads in the pre-business stage had weaknesses that were noteworthy. Disease among the animals or a drying up of the main pastures would undermine the capital resources and the health of the people. This is to be compared with a severe business depression in modern times. A second weakness lay in a competitive situation: once some of the nomads began to settle, the amount of land available for pasture was progressively limited. This was the beginning of the end in many cases. We might also list as other factors lack of deep knowledge of animal husbandry, lack of adequate cereal supply, and absence of a regular dependable exchange of goods. Outstanding in the long run must have been the general unbalance between expanding capital goods on the one hand and a stationary amount of land on the other. The settling down of the peoples sometimes led to a scramble on the part of nomads for lands. Consider the wanderings of the Teutonic tribes in the early centuries of the Christian era. Compare European families in later centuries migrating to America. And nowadays we seem to find that too large a percentage of our people live in large cities—that is, they are once again too dependent upon capital goods which may fail them. A healthy civilization seems to require a ratio of capital to land, changing from era to era, but one which cannot be violated with impunity.

4. COÖPERATION IN THE SETTLED VILLAGE

The nomads who settled down soon learned that they had a fresh set of problems to meet. They had to develop field cultivation, which, according to the newly rising plan, had to be undertaken by the men of the group. The land had to be cultivated in such a way that field cultivation and animal husbandry were integrated and in such a way that the fertility and fitness of the soil would be maintained. A system of ownership and inheritance of land had to be developed. The universal rule arose that the valuable land—that is, the part prepared for permanent pasture, meadow, or arable—belonged to the family that cleared it. Among many peoples, particularly in northern Europe, there was no thought that each family should hold enclosed fields. The idea was rather coöwnership of scattered strips; that is, each family owned a definite proportion of the whole but not single identical parts. To be sure, the homestead was owned outright and in severalty, but that was about all the landed property so possessed.

The inheritance of land presented a problem that was difficult and variously solved. Some peoples divided their holdings among all the children while others handed down each estate intact to the oldest or youngest child. The widow of the deceased head of the family and the non-inheriting children had to adjust themselves in such cases as best they could. It is a plausible inference that there was a widespread tendency for the coöwnership of arable lands in many parts of Europe to give way to the ownership of definite and specific pieces of land, scattered about the village.

With settlement went a slow change from the large to the small family. In mediaeval England this is thought to be marked by the shift from the hide of 120 acres to the yardland of 30 acres. At any rate, it was a further move toward individual or small family ownership. This was a move of great import for the social and economic welfare of man. Consider the pros and cons of this situation for yourself.

As to when social classes arose in human society, we have no exact knowledge. We may infer that we are witnessing the birth of groups that will become classes as the centuries roll along. The full-fledged large families that originally settled a village got each, say, one-tenth or one-twentieth of the various kinds of land. Children who did not inherit estates and persons who drifted in had to be provided for. Out of such a situation came four rural classes of considerable fixity. First, there were the full-fledged citizens, in England called the "yardlanders," then, a partially landed group with smaller holdings, third, a cottager class with little or no land, and, fourth, a half-outcast group of squatters on the waste lands who had little and expected little. In all probability, there was a tendency during the ages for the abilities of families to reflect the size of their holdings, for able men could add gradually small bits of land to their estates, though the process was difficult. At any rate, social inequality arose through a process of settling the land. The families that labored to clear the land and build the houses, barns, and stables insisted on ownership and made acquisition difficult for other persons. In recent generations in the new world we see the same kind of process going on. The old families obtained the best lands and tried to hold on. The pioneer families formed a kind of aristocracy: the new-comers might be welcomed economically but not always socially.

Many old problems held over in the settled village from nomadic days. There was the ever-present problem of control, at least following the collectional economic stage. Much as we dislike control, we must submit to it if we are to enjoy the advantages of social grouping. To escape, we must become hoboes, hermits, or pocket farmers. And so, in the settled village, the control of the patriarchal head had to be exercised if production was to continue efficient. The substitute for the patriarch of nomadic days was the headman of the village, an office still hereditary in some parts of the world. It is a plausible surmise that among some peoples, especially the Teutonic, there was a tendency for the office of headman to become elective. The reeve of the mediaeval English village seems to have been the successor to the headman. Aiding the headman or reeve was a small group of top men, heads of the pioneer families, who with the headman or reeve formed the local court which at once enforced the old customs of the village and created new customs. Later in England, the reeve and four men represented the village in county courts and might be summoned by the king to meet any emergency.

Surviving on into the settled village stage was the community feeling. Just as one nomadic tribe enjoyed a fight with another, so did the settled village group accumulate a feeling of animosity to another group which could be worked off only in a game (for example, of football) or by a free-for-all fight followed by mutual withdrawal.

Outstanding in the settled village was the coöperation of the various classes of villagers in carrying on the production of the village. The coöperative task of caring for flocks and herds was a hang-over from the nomadic stage. In the settled village stage, however, the tasks were delegated to cowherds, shepherds, swineherds, and so on; and these persons who combined labor and management received for their services not only holdings of land but also rights to so many calves, lambs, and so on.

The new coöperation lay in the cultivation of the fields, particularly plowing. The scattered condition of the family holdings invited this, but the poverty of the rank and file made coöperation necessary. One family head could provide a plow, another oxen, and still another only labor. By combining the abilities of all, a plow-team, for instance, of four or eight oxen could be brought together and fully manned.

Exceptional coöperation occurred when new land had to be cleared or a house or barn had to be erected. Such has been the normal course in America and, I suppose, in the world generally.

All work and especially coöperation among early peoples was routinized and integrated with the seasons and the festive occasions which the seasons brought about. It was fun for some to work when plenty of ale would soon flow or when licence between the sexes would be permitted. No matter whether it was the spring's return or the harvest's gathering, the peasants would celebrate by dancing and music, eating and drinking.

In the far-off times before the towns came into existence, certainly in the Middle Ages and probably also in the ancient period, work and recreation were closely interwoven as we have indicated. Perhaps it is unfortunate that we have lost this, for nowadays when we work we work and when we play we play. This is perhaps inevitable in an age which requires the more complicated entertainments and recreations involving skill and the service of specialists. In early times, however, not only were work and recreation mixed up effectively, but magic and religion came in to play their parts in such a way that control was easy. There was a community sanction given to every kind of work. Imps, fairies, witches, and the like were interwoven with the Virgin Mary, Jesus Christ, God, the saints, and the rest of those who helped good men or damned the bad. Thus was the group integrated economically, socially, and religiously.

The Church had a hard time to Christianize barbaric Europe from the second century of our era onward. It offered a great bribe to the underman—to give him in heaven all he lacked on earth. Then it fitted itself into the customs of the people, accepting, modifying, and supplementing them till it had created a civilization of fear and hope. This made it possible for an organized Church to grow and engraft itself upon the people. For services rendered, its priests, bishops, and monks would receive part of the land, much overlordship, rents, and dues in great numbers. A great advance was involved in the succession from the earlier medicine man, soothsayer, or druid to the Christian priest. The love of Christ, however, had in practice to be entwined with the fear of God before the unruly passions of pagan peoples could be brought under the effective control of the organized Church.

The Church, representing property and clan interests, soon became conservative. It assisted in maintaining the coöperative order which helped produce the year's supply of meat, grain, wool, hides, honey, and eggs. It sanctioned obedience to those officials in the lay world, as it expected obedience to its own officials in the ecclesiastical world. It helped to soften and humanize customs that were crude and ruthless. In due time, it sponsored better methods of production, learning, and the arts. Generally speaking, the Church stood for the smaller people, those who attended the services and paid Church dues. Its services and ritual were adapted to what it found. It had no desire to spread the good things in theology, the arts, and philosophy among more than a select number of the people. Its leaders knew that this would have been a waste of effort. The Church sponsored the development of control in the village, power in the hands of kings, and strength of ecclesiastical and other princes. It had become a power in the land. It believed in coöperation in agriculture and in non-agricultural pursuits wherein each played his part according to well-tried rules and slowly developing customs.

5. ADMINISTRATION OF THE LARGE ESTATE AND MANOR

The settled village was at first normally free and was, as we have seen, cultivated under a system of coöperative management, with control vested in a village governing body that might be called democratic in the sense of representing the chief group or groups of villagers. So far as we can discover, the social order resulting was fairly stable but the economic system was weak and the military position merely defensive, quite exposed, and very uncertain. There was a tendency to produce for a normal year, since anything beyond normal needs was mere waste in view of the absence of a market. In years of scarcity there was famine and, following this, disease. When enemies came along, for instance, viking bands along the coasts, the village was more or less helpless. The villagers could flee but on returning found their movables carried off and their homes destroyed. On the borderlands between settled and nomadic peoples, regular raids of nomads resulted in the theft of goods and women. The settled villagers as such could not survive. They could easily provide plenty but there was little inducement to do so; in no case could they give themselves military security.

One of two developments could occur. Outside peoples, such as pastoral nomads, might enter into the situation and reduce the villages to dependence. As we have seen, this infiltration would not occur suddenly, but it would reduce the villagers to a condition of subordination more or less complete. The new nomadic conquerors might just regard themselves as landlords and collect a tribute in the form of commodity rents. They might go farther and, in order to insure the payment of the rent, force the villagers to cultivate a piece of land—the home farm— which they would carve out of the village for themselves. When this was done, we have the essentials of the manor. The loss of freedom might occur in another way. The villagers might seek strong men to whom they might commend and subordinate themselves in return for protection in case of attack or food in case of famine. The strong man might be a bishop or an abbot and either of these might be also a warrior. In such ways did the villagers give up freedom for security. Later, they were to revolt against their lords in order to substitute freedom for security when they saw opportunities for themselves or their children in the towns.

A large estate might arise in a wholly different way, namely, by the creation of a villa or plantation by a powerful leader who would settle his followers or work his land by means of slaves secured in war. If the slaves should be changed into serfs, that is, tenants who cultivated small holdings for their own support and also gave part of their time to help cultivate the lord's farm, the result of the process would be a manor, just as in the case of the free village reduced to dependence.

As time went on, vast aggregations of dependent villages or manors were built up to support a lay or ecclesiastical potentate. Or, from another point of view, these potentates came to the rescue of helpless villagers and provided for them the security they needed. But here was an administrative problem which is as challenging to us to understand as it was to the leaders to solve. It was hard enough to develop a means of administering a single manor or plantation. It was more difficult to administer a group of thirty to sixty. Such a problem was millennia-old, for ancient temples had to face it and obviously not without success.

On a certain large estate in Lower Egypt in the sixth century A. D. there were many officials. The chief of these were the head agent (or seneschal), agents of subordinate estates, collectors of dues, bookkeeper, cashier or treasurer, butler or winekeeper, and keeper of the general stores. Although we know the very names of some of these officials, we have no exact knowledge of their duties. How we wish that ancient and mediaeval artists had been interested in drawing, painting, and carving some of these functionaries who made the wheels of affairs go round. But then artists, like scholars, had and still have no appreciation of administration and only of necessity give it attention.

In the individual manor of the Middle Ages there was a chief official—whether a new bailiff or the old village reeve made over for a new purpose. Since such a man of affairs would ordinarily not be a scholar, a scribe had to be found to do the work of recording the accounts. A local rector or vicar would be a likely person. In the case of a group of manors there had to be an administrative head who would have general supervision. This was ordinarily a seneschal. The lord's personal or official treasurer would receive the products yielded by all the manors. A special auditor (or controller) would be required to examine and report on the accounts individually and collectively.

Here was a kind of big business which both in ancient and mediaeval times must have challenged the best brains as it does today. Unfortunately, little was written about the challenge or the administration adopted. In Greece, where so much good administration probably occurred, Xenophon wrote an excellent treatise which has survived, called *Oeconomicus*. It sets forth in a humorous way the problems that a landholder with many slaves and only one wife had to meet. Mago the Carthaginian wrote a treatise on agricultural administration which the Romans read and perhaps imitated in their treatises. We might all stop to read Cato, Varro, and Columella of the ancient Roman world and the Italian compiler who owed so much to these Romans, Petrus Crescentius, who lived and wrote about 1300. In England the prize treatises were compiled in the thirteenth century. These deal directly with manorial problems of the day. Walter of Henley's *Husbandry,* the anonymous *Seseschaucie,* and Bishop Grosseteste's *Rules of Managing an Estate* can all be profitably studied in this connection. An earlier treatise of a somewhat different type might also be studied to see how seriously administration was taken in twelfth-century England, namely, Roger Fitz Neal's *Dialogue of the Exchequer* which shows how the royal treasury of England met its fiscal problem.

Let us go at once to one of the main devices used in rural estate administration, that is, accounting. By means of surveys and customals, the lord knew what was his due from his estates —how much rent and what services were due to him. Then, once a year, an account was turned in for each manor. The bailiff (or reeve) was responsible for the account, no matter who actually wrote it down. The account was in single entry, being divided into two general parts: Income and Outgo. Then, a statement at the end indicated the balance due to the lord. In addition, there was a physical inventory of the lord's goods, roughly, his capital goods on the manor.

Although these accounts were very adequate for the purpose at hand, still we may note the fact that there was no cost accounting and no double entry. There would be no point to either. There was no thought of increasing the income by reducing costs. And there were no creditors, partners, or nonresident agents to require such checks as double entry provides.

Judging from the uniformity of such mediaeval accounts, for example in England, we may safely conclude that a model was worked out and widely adopted. Where it came from is still unknown—from the practices of monasteries or perhaps the Frankish court of the eighth century, possibly farther back from the ancient world through Constantinople.

Let us look at some general aspects of the administration of the large estate or manor. Unfortunately, we can find neither treatise nor account that does not come from a later stage—from the time when town economy was extending its sway over rural communities. We run the risk of putting town influences into earlier rural situations, but there is no alternative.

First and foremost, then as now, there was the element of control—that compulsion that one man puts on another in order to get results. One man says "if you are to eat, you must work." This has never become popular. This control was based upon knowledge found in the surveys, customals, accounts, and inventories. In peasant uprisings from the fourteenth to the nineteenth century, many such documents were destroyed. The second part of the control came through officials who from seneschal and bailiff to the lowest oxherd and swineherd had duties which were mingled with rights, interwoven with a feeling of security involved in the general situation and all sanctified by the Church. Recreation, magic, and religion helped to cement the peasant in his position in the manor and to keep him there. We shall never know how effective the discipline through officials really was. We know that there were thefts and bad work but we also know that the lord received his income.

Besides such knowledge and disciplines, there was division of employment from the hayward to the dairymaid and from the bailiff to the shepherd. Techniques were worked out both for animal husbandry and field cultivation. Although we must label these techniques as adequate, we cannot find that they contained many progressive elements. Efforts were made to secure efficiency and they attained success. From our standpoint they were not outstanding. One of the great difficulties lay in the immobile peasant mass that could not be moved along any ordinary road to progress. Another fault lay in the fact that the landlords commonly delegated to administrators or officials the whole of the duty of management so that only routine and no new policies were feasible.

The chief policy of the administration was to get each year what had been obtained last year. This involved the more elemental policy of always spending less than was taken in; that is, not allowing the bailiff to incur expenses beyond the income. Cato understood this, yet modern statesmen choose to forget. Actually, it was a wise policy of coördination of production that leads to success and the avoidance of disaster.

One of the many lacks of the stage of village economy in its pure form was trade as a major occupation. While exchange of goods took place in a minor way, there was no business and there were no business men. This was the fault of no one: business had not yet been born.

There had come upon the world, however, something of great value—administration. It was understood as necessary but not otherwise important. Its significance or usefulness was not intimately understood. The business of a landlord was honorable but the work of the underlings was not. A man became an official not because of the distinction but because of his love of gain or desire to exercise power. The Church produced great administrators as well as many bad ones, and yet it never produced, so far as I know, a treatise recognizing the importance of the calling. Lay lords themselves did no better. Except in very recent times, scholars have risen to no greater heights along this line. Administration has been vital, but, like many other things, has had to wait a long time for recognition of its importance in history. In our day, the great stumbling block is the recalcitrance of the laborer who will not see in administration any task of importance, perhaps because it closes in on him to force him to work when he would go fishing or motoring. In communistic Russia, the problem of administration has proven to be both important and difficult. Communistic states, like chain stores, may go to pieces on the administrative rock.

6. CIVILIZATION OF PRE-BUSINESS CAPITALISM

Man's civilization of a high order is commonly identified with the rise of towns. In this chapter we do not reach this stage in human genesis. Nevertheless, there was a something social, economic, and cultural attained in village or manorial economy which was superior to conditions under collectional economy. The evolution had been in the direction of larger amounts of capital goods per person. It had been first toward plenty and then toward economic and political security. Changing from a mere labor system to a management system involved great strides. The progress that man made came to be closely connected in the course of time with his permanent settlement on the land. From the perfect economic equality of the stage of collectional economy, man had gone a long way to the class distinctions of the manorial-feudal system in which substantially all the classes of today were represented except the business classes.

The pre-business capitalistic stage reached its height in manorialism and feudalism. The manor was the unit of economic production based on coöperative agriculture carried on under the lord's control. The feudal holding of a lord, made up of various manors, was a unit of political power. At the top of the feudal holding of duke, baron, or knight was the feudal king. Cutting right across this nascent national statehood was the feudal Catholic Church of Rome. Long as the struggle between the state and the Church has continued, however, there is still no clear-cut indication of final victory.

Both the state and the Church developed their ideals of what is important in society from the manorial-feudalism on which both were founded. In other words, the original emphasis was upon the interest and well-being of the landed elements. Since these were to oppose the system of charging usury for the use of money and to the market-price policy of town civilizations, so the Church, and with less emphasis the state, was to oppose usury and market price. Always the rural classes found themselves debtors and therefore sought every defensive advantage in dealing with their creditors.

The manorial lord—the controller of agricultural production—was interested in war, whether in mortal combat on the field of battle or at play on the gaudy field of chivalry. This lord was a great hunter. After the hunt, he sought the feast and after the feast the songs of minstrelsy celebrating the deeds of war and of the chase and depicting the beauty of a lady love. In romantic Europe love was often unattained and unsatisfied, while among the peoples of the Near East no love was worth the lord's while that did not reach physical consummation. But both in East and West the day's pleasure was put before the day's work. The lord labored only vicariously through his bailiff or seneschal or treasurer. He insisted only on such routine management as was required to maintain his holdings. This at least came to be the case in the later days of the manorial-feudal system, even by the late thirteenth century.

The chief aim of the feudal lord was to secure an income from his estates and secondly to keep up the estates for the sake of his family or Church organization. Maintaining the property involved benefits to his peasant tenantry but these were incidental. The masses sought and obtained security, the lords sought and retained power. There was no widespread demand for plenty or liberty. These came with the town and business capitalism: they came slowly but they came.

In the progression of stages of economic activity, indicated in this chapter, there was real progress in evidence. There was developed regular work, division of employments, administration of production, and close control through supervision and through accounting. There was also an increasing amount of capital used per person. And yet there was no business capitalism because certain essential ingredients were missing. First, the guiding plan of social existence was according to the status of the individual, not according to contracts. This meant that work and life itself were carried on in accordance with custom and not according to fresh undertakings and arrangements. Second, there was little or no production for exchange. Third, there were no specialized business men. Fourth, there was no emphasis on progressive yield or income, no policy of advancing in material affairs. No men planned to sell better and better things to their fellows in return for a greater income for themselves.

In collectional, cultural nomadic, and settled village economy the dominant aspect of life and work was status, as we have indicated. In the last analysis, this means lack of freedom for the individual. Throughout the long stretch of time covered by these stages, men were not individuals but units in a group. Some classes on the manor, for instance, might be called "freemen" in distinction to serfs or slaves, but they were really free in name only. Legally they might move about as they would, marry off their daughters without restraint, and so on. Actually, they could imagine no existence apart from the group to which they belonged. Because of the great use of capital goods, they lived in a world of capitalism; but because of the lack of certain business attributes they lived in a system of pre-business capitalism.

After a long experience with business, that is, private-business capitalism, chiefly from the twelfth century to the present, men are again crying out for security. Weary and winded by a free competitive system of individual effort, many persons want protection—the protection of the group: they would return to status again. Those that do feel this way may withdraw from private-business capitalism; indeed, they may drag down the whole business structure upon their heads. What they seek may for the moment be called social security, national capitalism, or communistic capitalism. Pessimists see the pendulum slowly swinging back to something resembling pre-business capitalism. Optimists, however, think the demands for security and the drift toward status are but the growing pains of our still-evolving civilization, intensified by the deep depressions of downward secular trends in business.

Chapter II

PETTY CAPITALISM

The Birth of Private Business

Work well and continuously, count costs, trade;
Be content with a restricted market.
Unite in gilds when you can;
Avoid the control of stronger men.

1. THE NATURE OF PRIVATE BUSINESS

In most of man's history there has been no business. In fact, business is such a late-comer that whole groups of men have never become adjusted to it. We may infer that it arose in the East—whether in India or China, on the one hand, or in Babylonia or Egypt on the other, we do not know. Certainly, Europeans have thought of Phoenicians and Carthaginians, Jews and Greeks, all near to Babylonia or Egypt, as the pioneers in business and as the keenest of the devotees of business. The Armenians (townsmen) of the same general district have similar aptitudes. It is the Jews who have gone out bravely among the non-business peoples and helped these peoples learn to carry on business. For their pains they have been rewarded by scorn and contempt, cuffs and kicks, robbery and death. Perhaps we should jump ahead and study the diagram which shows the historic Diffusion of Business and Capital (see p. 261).

It is highly significant that some nations have no word for business. The English commonly use trade, commerce, and traffic. Only recently are they reluctantly turning to the generic term of business. Of course, the word is old enough, but it has had other meanings. At first, it meant simply busy-ness or industriousness. Then, it meant occupation and that remains its chief use in England. The third meaning is the special kind of occupation that we are dealing with.

Our problem at this point is to define business. To me, business is the administration of labor and natural resources, in partnership with capital, in a process which leads to the sale of goods or services, with other activities in a subordinate position. In the pre-business capitalistic era we find commodity production, place production, form production, and time-utility production dominant. In business capitalism, the chief kind is possession production, the others being contributory. Those who now oppose what they call "capitalism" mean that they want to go back to the era of "production for use" (without any possession or exchange being involved). Of course, in the pre-business capitalism—in the cultural nomadic and settled village stages— there really was production for the managers and controllers of management. No production exclusively for use has ever occurred, except in the first stage of human existence—that nearest to the animal. The preponderating emphasis upon labor in human history is accurate only for the most primitive stage and even then natural resources were on a par with labor. Perhaps we should go back and re-read Adam Smith and Karl Marx and see whether we really agree with their emphasis on labor.

Business is administration that looks towards exchange. Private business expects a profit for its service; public business would pretend to offer a service without profits.

The private business man is the dynamic person, born late into the world, who has used his energy to serve others that he may receive a profit, always through the avenue of exchange. We may sum up many of his essential activities and attitudes. In doing this, we may assume that no brief statement can do justice to an actor in life's varied activities as complicated as those in which the business leader must play his part. What the future will bring we can see but darkly.

MEDIAEVAL TALLY, ENGLAND, THIRTEENTH CENTURY

INTERIOR OF SHOPS (SHOEMAKER'S, DRAPER'S
AND GOLDSMITH'S), FRANCE, FIFTEENTH CENTURY

LÜBECK MARKETPLACE, ABOUT 1580

The Private Business Man

With incomplete information I take risks;
  For service rendered I expect profits.
Capital is my sword and price my shield;
  Competition and monopoly are but shifting fields of strife.
When I make contracts, I must have control;
  Land and labor are the team I drive to market.

It is interesting to raise the question why so many persons in the world cannot succeed in business. Perhaps there is something to the view that some groups have so recently emerged from pre-business capitalism that they produce very few individuals with an aptitude for business. Spaniards and Russians, Negroes and American Indians are not good business men. On the other hand, Italians and French, Dutch and English, Germans and Scandinavians produce a large number of able business men. Of course, we must take climate into account as well as social development; if so, the southern peoples—those near the equator—would produce fewest men of business. Perhaps we may conclude that tough-minded men in temperate climates are the best business men, soft-minded in tropical climates the worst.

When we come to the group of persons around about us, we find that there are certain categories of individuals who cannot understand the value of business. There are some farmers, craftsmen, artists, and thinkers, who are for varying reasons incapable of appreciating the contributions of business men. Not being able to manage themselves, they see no value in business. They and others coming under the influence of business sometimes find themselves injured by business. They and others may live in a fool's paradise of believing that the world owes them a living, in which case business management is superfluous in their thinking. Of course, each person must think these things out for himself. Just now we are interested chiefly in isolating the phenomenon of business. Much of the rest of our task lies in an analysis of the different types of business that have arisen for better or for worse.

2. RISE AND NATURE OF PETTY CAPITALISM

When business came into the system of capitalism, private business capitalism was born. The first type of private business capitalism may be called "petty capitalism," its sponsors "petty capitalists" or "bourgeois." Such were apparently the first business men and at this point business history takes its beginning.

Petty capitalism wrote the first chapter in business history. Its rise created the economic town and town economy. It was petty capitalism that planted oases in the desert of rural society. This was probably as true of the ancient as of the mediaeval period, of the East as of the West. Just why petty capitalists grew up in one particular place or another, we do not need to consider at any length. It might be a matter of a ford in a river, a firm gravel landing place on the bank of a deep river, a protected harbor on the seacoast or island used by fishermen, crossroads or trails, or a castle, monastery, or temple. And so the economic towns arose along the trail of history—ancient Ur and Babylon, Memphis and Thebes, Tyre and Carthage, Athens and Delos, and Rome and Capua; and mediaeval London and York, Paris and Rouen, Cologne and Bremen, Bruges and Antwerp; and Rotterdam and Amsterdam. It has been the achievement of the Chinese to have created innumerable towns and the most stable citizens—petty capitalists—on record.

In the towns, we witness the birth of the middle class, the bourgeois, the fat and greasy burghers of market places and walled towns. Here are the people to the fore who have made history, created what we call "civilization." These are the men and women who in their pride of achievement are called "smug" by other classes that lack their nervous energy, willingness to venture, and phenomenal persistence. Fairly successful in war, they have been unrivalled in peace. Appreciating land, they have seen that the future lies in capital goods. Working through profits, under the spell of the golden calf and the golden apple, they have created the fastest moving order of men. Damn the middle class if you will, but not till you have seen the achievement that lies behind the class. Whether the future belongs to the middle class or whether the recent past must remain its peculiar field of glory, remains to be seen.

The various kinds of petty capitalists (pedlars, shopkeepers, and so on) had three avenues of trade open to them. First, there was the oldest and most essential trade with the immediate countryside of about fifteen or twenty miles. This trade though primary was always limited by the fact that the countrymen were not very progressive, not commercially minded, and unable to break through the shackles of the rural system—the feudal-manorial in the Middle Ages. Second, there was the trade between townsman and townsman. This was an increasingly progressive exchange that tended toward finer goods and more artistic design, in the development of which the nobility played an important part. Third, there was the extended trade between towns, far and near. Here the traveling merchant played a vital part. And here wholesaling was the most distinctive feature. The products peculiar to distant lands engrossed this third type of trade.

Within the town itself, whether ancient Athens or mediaeval London, ancient Rome or mediaeval Florence, there was a set of associations called "gilds" which have received a great deal of attention. In fact, gilds have been studied almost to the neglect of the real business of the men who established them. The reason for this is that gild records have been readily available for study. It requires but little reflection to see that the petty capitalists—butcher, mercer, draper, vintner, and fishmonger—could operate without gilds of any kind. Indeed, many petty towns had no gilds or at most one big gild for the whole town. In earliest town experience this general gild, or merchant gild, was uppermost. It arose in mediaeval England not later than the eleventh century. It was made up of storekeepers, shopkeepers, traveling merchants, house-builders, and even local manorial lords. Following this, sometimes supplanting it, came the craft gilds, or one-craft gilds, each (theoretically) being made up of persons engaged in the one occupation represented by the gild. Weavers, fullers, bakers, and shoemakers had gilds in English towns of the twelfth century.

The general spirit of the gild was that equals should control all in the group and keep the individual hewing to a line of mediocrity in exchange but superiority in manufacture. In general, there were two groups of craft gilds: those to which considerable powers of regulation were entrusted by the town government and those to which less authority was given. The latter were chiefly the provision trades, which, to say the least, the town magistrates never felt they could trust fully.

The equality of the craft gilds, never complete, tended to disappear as the generations went by. Those crafts or trades that found themselves in strategic positions with reference to the market, for example, those which handled the finished product, tended to grow into positions of wealth and dominance, while the others sank into positions of impotence and poverty.

For more details about gilds, go to other books. Business would have been less smooth and less fair without them, but business would have developed pretty much as it did, had they never been heard of. Their chief value was to set up standards (often violated) and to provide materials for historians. Their records have value for the light thrown upon the activities of their members, but historians have commonly emphasized the gild organization to the neglect of the living business men who made and unmade the gilds themselves.

The petty capitalists operated primarily on their own capital, earned and saved, plowed back into their business, autogenous capital if you will. They also carried on a certain part of their business with borrowed capital—goods or money borrowed directly from the owner. We shall note more about this in a later section.

To us, the chief interest lies in the business administration of the petty capitalists. This consists of (a) policy and (b) man-

INTERIOR OF A STORE, GERMANY, FIFTEENTH CENTURY

HUCKSTER
CALLING OUT
"APPLES, LADIES,"
ANCIENT GAUL

agement. I know of no contemporary statement of policy as such, but policy may be inferred from action and from gild and municipal regulations. One conception of that policy is to be found in the verse that heads this chapter. Analyze this statement, criticize and rewrite it to your own satisfaction: it is but a first effort. The difficulty in framing a policy for the divergent groups of petty capitalists is considerable. The value of the effort to summarize the policy of any group may be greater than the resulting statement.

In the actual management of business within the policies already indicated we find a number of interests. First, control was of the most elemental kind. The small master—and all the masters were relatively small—had direct contact with his customers and employees. He kept accounts of what he owed and what was owing to him. Second, he used partners for special occasions where risks were high or the need for capital beyond his means. Third, he used agents, where necessary, especially brokers and notaries. Fourth, he was always close to the heart of his business and was himself chief workman, foreman, and master, all in one.

3. SEDENTARY PETTY CAPITALISTS

Some years ago, economic historians were much occupied with the more or less speculative consideration of petty capitalism when they considered the beginning of early town life. There would be one good reason for our leaving the matter alone, namely, that the records are very vague or missing. Business historians, however, cannot dodge the issue because it concerns the effective beginning of their subject. We must use the surviving sources of evidence, analogy from later (particularly American colonial) records, and inference from the logic of events.

It would seem worth while to divide the stage of petty capitalism into two phases. The first is characterized by the existence of a general storekeeper (*mercator* or *mercer*), a few shopkeepers (such as a blacksmith, a shoemaker, and a fuller), and a market place for peasants. Supplementing these would be traveling merchants who would bring in the most needed commodities, such as iron, spices, drugs, and salt. The traveling merchants would take in return the chief products of the locality such as wax, verdigris, copper, goat skins, and wine. Doubtless, goods were exchanged for goods in terms of money, but without the use of money, or at least with little use of it. In all probability there was no coined money at all in the early part of pure town economy. To be sure, coins might come in from more advanced areas. At any rate, the traveling merchant may be regarded as the kingpin of the whole structure. Without him there would be only local and casual exchange of goods for goods between producers, an exchange which does not ordinarily lead to the growth of business at all.

It is doubtful whether the market place was to be found in this first phase of petty capitalism, that is, at the dawn of town economy. Here the shades of certain historical economists will hover over our heads, for many of them have seen in the market place the very origin of towns. A thousand years of the exchange of goods among producers in Africa and the South Sea Islands have occasioned no economic towns. There is no great difference in this matter, however, for markets (open and frequent) did come in during the second phase of petty capitalism, at least, so it seems.

Before going to the second phase, however, we cannot avoid raising the question as to the classes from which have been recruited the different kinds of petty capitalists, such as general storekeeper, specialized shopkeeper (blacksmith, etc.), and traveling merchant. Again, explicit evidence fails us, but we may infer that free peasants independently in some places and unfree peasants under the guidance and with the sanctions of their lords in other places arose to perform the new functions. No matter what the origin, free or servile, freedom soon came to prevail. The motto "town air makes free" was real and operative.

SEDENTARY PETTY CAPITALISTS

If this analysis is correct, then the earliest business men or petty capitalists were not pedlars, as I and others had thought, but general storekeepers, specialized shopkeepers, and traveling merchants.

In the second sub-stage or phase of petty capitalism the general store was supplanted by more specialized stores such as those of mercers, grocers, drapers, vintners, ironmongers, salters, and taverners. In addition, the number of shopkeepers or artisans increased by scores. The market place became a lively center where a peasant could bring his products and find enough customers to make his coming worth while. By this time, there were arising other classes, such as notaries, scribes, brokers (who also acted as hosts to traveling merchants), and priests.

Working toward the same goal of civilization—or town life—were business, the Church, and the political (feudal) power. Those who are accounting for the rise of towns need to weave all three together.

Our interest at the moment lies in the rise and development of petty capitalists who were resident in the town—the storekeepers and the shopkeepers. House-builders at this time were probably largely casual peasant laborers to be recruited when needed or just piece-wage workmen who did such work as was offered to them. Since there were no contracts or profits in their work, there was no business involved.

It is not without interest to note that so far we have not had to emphasize gilds. But somewhere in this second phase the merchant gild, including all classes buying and selling goods, and the craft gilds of various trades, did arise. The amounts of capital involved in business were small, but tended to be greater in the case of storekeepers than shopkeepers, though there were exceptions to this rule. The tendency was common for townspeople to seek autonomy—to buy a charter guaranteeing the rights of freemen and of free trade without which the risks of business would have no goal.

Of greater interest to us are the special managerial problems of storekeepers and shopkeepers. During the first phase of petty capitalism, when the town was little more than an embryo, the storekeeper had one paramount problem of getting from the peasants the goods which traveling merchants would take in return for the wares they imported. These local products would be exchanged for imported goods in terms of the unit of money that prevailed—a deerskin, a cow, a pound of copper, or some other such unit. In the second phase one of the problems was for one storekeeper to learn to carry on his fast-growing specialty without undue competition with other retailing specialists. This problem was not wholly solvable. Indeed, in the stage following petty capitalism there remained the same kind of jurisdictional problem.

The special managerial problem of the shopkeeper or handicraftsman, such as the blacksmith, the shoemaker, and the dyer, during the first phase of petty capitalism was to obtain raw material. This shopkeeper had to depend either upon the local peasantry or, in case of goods from a distance, upon the storekeepers or the traveling merchants. Often petty shopkeepers joined forces in buying supplies from traveling merchants. For instance, London shoemakers bought leather from Spanish merchants in the late thirteenth century, whether wholly for use in the making of shoes or also to help them become dealers in leather is not clear. In the second phase of petty capitalism the special problem was to develop a high quality of workmanship to meet the rising standards of townsmen, clergy, and feudal lords.

In the business of the storekeeper and shopkeeper the training of workers was, of course, by means of apprenticeship. The apprentice, whether a son or outsider, lived with the master's family. In due time he became a journeyman, that is, a workman receiving a time wage—so much a day. After a period of work for a master, the journeyman had accumulated a little capital with which to become a partner with another person or to set up a small store or shop of his own. Since this system opened the doors of opportunity to all who were able and industrious, there could be little serious opposition to it as a system. Even such

Photograph by Maynard Owen Williams, Copyright National Geographic Magazine.

A TURKOMAN TRAVELING MERCHANT,
MERV, RUSSIAN TURKESTAN, ABOUT 1918

elements of exploitation as might have been involved in the payment of low wages were endured with the thought that the temporary victim would in due time have the same advantage over other workmen.

4. TRAVELING PETTY CAPITALISTS: TRAVELING MERCHANTS

We have already had occasion to note the existence of the traveling merchant. Two other petty capitalists who moved about were the pedlars, whom we shall consider in the next section, and the hucksters, whom we shall dispose of here so as to get rid of them.

The hucksters sold on the streets and at the doors of the homes within the town. They were retailers. Their wares were purchased on the market place or in shops or stores. They were much regulated by the town magistrates and were hated by the storekeepers because they short-circuited some of the trade of the storekeepers. In ancient Rome, shopkeepers met competition by sending out their own hucksters to sell their wares, particularly at the baths. To the consumer hucksters were obviously a convenience rather than a necessity.

The traveling merchant, whom we have regarded as the kingpin of early town economy, rose with the town and participated in the birth of business. He has a long history in the ancient, mediaeval, and modern periods. In the ancient period his patron deity was Mercury, later he prayed to St. Nicholas. He has been much noted but his operations have been too little analyzed, the possible exception being the traveling merchant of twelfth-century Genoa.

Pirenne thought that pirates were the progenitors of mediaeval traveling merchants. Such a view reflects little knowledge of the business of this class or of what is required by business. It is doubtless just a thoughtless guess. There seems no other origin except peasants or fishermen with an aptitude for exchange (some early peasants were nicknamed merchants) who turned to specialize in trade. It would be the peasant located on a river or seacoast and accustomed to use and possess a boat, and not the inland tiller of the soil, who would be most likely to become a merchant. This is a very prosaic origin but I see no other possibility. Of course, I am not forgetting the Jewish and Arabic traveling merchants and also a long line of such merchants going back to the Cretans and Phoenicians of the ancient period. In the slowly developing Western Europe such strangers, notably the Jews, would be helpful models for natives, nothing more.

A Traveling Merchant of Norway

A remarkable prose treatise (the *King's Mirror*) written in Norway not much before 1260 describes the profession of the merchant and of the king's service. The anonymous author had intended to include also the clergy and the peasants. If he had, then his little book would have been a rounded sociological exposition of unique value. As it is, the part dealing with merchants is for our purpose indispensable. Before noting details, we should observe that the kind of merchant that the author knew was the traveling merchant, a type that was still the only one in far northern countries. Let us synopsize some major points.

1. Although the author belongs to the king's service, he admits that "often the best of men" enter the ranks of merchants.
2. A merchant must expect to encounter perils at sea and in heathen lands.
3. He should be "polite and agreeable" but should examine goods before he buys them and in the presence of witnesses. If by chance he has purchased inferior goods, let him resell them for what they are and, taking his losses, deceive no one as he has been deceived.
4. When abroad, the merchant should live well but carefully and with restraint of speech and passion.
5. He should study especially the local law books, when he has time. He should master the customs of the place he is trading in.

6. He should shun drinking, chess, harlots, quarreling, and gambling.

7. He should study the sky, directions, and the sea so as to be able to navigate. All merchants have great need of arithmetic.

8. Let him cultivate the friendship of the officials of the country in which he trades and pay the dues that are required. Let him see to it that none of the government's property gets into his cargo.

9. He should sell quickly if he can get suitable prices and then be off, for a quick turnover is the life of trade.

10. If he owns his own ship, he should have it thoroughly coated with tar. It should be kept in good shape so as to attract capable men. He should equip it with the best materials.

11. He should always buy shares in a good ship or in none at all.

12. *If he acquires wealth rapidly,* then he should invest part of his wealth in a partnership trade with others doing the traveling, but he should be cautious in selecting partners.

13. *If he acquires a great deal of wealth in trade,* let him divide it into three parts. Let him invest one-third in partnership with experienced and reliable men who are permanently located in towns ("market boroughs"). The other two-thirds may then be invested in various business ventures for the sake of the safety that lies in diversity.

14. If he acquires very great wealth, persumably near old age, he should invest two-thirds in good farm land and the other third at his will—either in trade or in more land. The land will be a source of security for him or his descendents.

15. When the traveling merchant has attained sufficient trading capital and when he has satisfied himself that he has a good working knowledge of foreign commercial conditions, he should discontinue his own journeys at sea and substitute therefor the investment of his funds in the ventures of other merchants. Although he has become an investing merchant, staying at home, he still has ample opportunity for utilizing his knowledge of foreign lands and foreign trade.

It is clear that there were two groups of traveling merchants. One was active and the other an investing (sleeping) partner.

The active traveling merchant traded on his own account or as a partner but he was always the manager and adventurer. He risked his money if he had any to invest; he always risked his life on the voyages. He might act as a factor for one or more other traveling merchants. He might own a ship or a share in one, or might charter a vessel for a voyage. If luck favored him and if his business sense was of a high order, he might prosper. If he gained wealth, he would probably shift to the second class—the class of investing traveling merchants.

The investing traveling merchant was the middle-aged or old merchant who had attained success. He had grown conscious that each voyage might be his last: he had run enough physical risks. Subsequent success lay in conserving what he had earned. One way of doing this in early town economy as today was to give up the actual management of trade and turn to investment —in lands and in trade managed by others. In addition, he might loan money to princes or churchmen, as did William Cade, a twelfth-century merchant of St. Omer. Or as a "banker" (money lender) he might make loans to active merchants. Doubtless in this way the clergy and nobility added to their jealousy of merchants the hatred that debtors feel of creditors. The opposition of the Church to trade was not based wholly on spiritual considerations.

At this point we are witnessing a social change. The merchant family invests in trade, loans money, and owns land. The son or grandson may continue to invest whether in St. Omer or in Genoa. Failure is likely to attend commercial investments because of a lack of the first-hand knowledge of the founder. This would dry up the surplus cash and put an end to money-lending. Thus, we are left with just a landed family, doing pretty well if lands in a flourishing town had been purchased but just holding its own if the estates were purely rural. So far as business is concerned, this is a dead end. This traveling merchant class does not recruit the later and more promising class of sedentary merchants whom we shall consider in the next chapter.

Sombart, the pioneering and journalistic historical economist

DUTCH SHIP, FIFTEENTH CENTURY

AMERICAN RURAL PEDLAR, NINETEENTH CENTURY

who has fertilized so many arable strips of economic history, has maintained that capital accumulations originated in the urban rents of landlords on whose lands towns arose. The rents from such lands, Sombart thought, were entrusted to traveling merchants. We have already learned the true explanation: the active merchants retired and invested in both land and trade managed by others. Critics of Sombart could not swallow the thought of a purely landed class having a surplus for investment. Such a class buys more land if it comes into the possession of ready money, or embarks upon some venture such as the crusades, or endows sons and daughters, or spends its cash on living. The spirit of the landed aristocrat is more holding on to than acquiring, spending than venturing.

There are many ramifications of the trade and experience of traveling merchants. One of their great achievements in Western Europe was the formation of regulated trading companies, such as the Flemish Hanse of London and the men of Cologne trading in London, both in the twelfth century. Such companies, whether operating by land or sea, had a regular organization both financial and military. A treasury provided for the expenses of travel, locating abroad, securing privileges, providing defence, and so on. Officials were elected to head the company, care for the treasury, and command the military or naval forces. Of course, such companies were mere associations of individual merchants living in one town or in a group of adjacent towns. Each merchant traded in person or through an active partner at his own profit or loss. Certain groups of such merchants—of Cologne, Brunswick, Bremen, Lübeck, and so on—might be regarded as the progenitors of the great Hanseatic League of towns in the fourteenth and following centuries.

The caravan trade of Asia, Asia Minor, and North and Central Africa illustrate the operations of traveling merchants. Ships of the desert plowed their dusty way through the sands that separated distant cities and seaports. A strong caravan leader with an effective backing of armed clansmen was hired to beat back the Bedouins or other pirates of the inland. Subsidies were paid to the racketeers of the district—the nomads who would otherwise plunder or destroy. A caravan of four camels would be small, of two thousand to four thousand camels would be very large and would require as careful administration as the European regulated company. The large seventh-century caravan of Mecca was operated by a syndicate or gigantic partnership of merchants, shopkeepers, landlords, tenants, and so on. Capital would be pooled and further money borrowed with this capital as a pledge, or as we should put it, a loan was floated with stock as collateral. At the end of the venture, profits, if any, would be divided according to the amount invested. Thus did gold, drugs, spices, slaves, ivory, grain, olive oil, wine, silks, arms, and chinaware reach remote and otherwise inaccessible parts.

In Western Europe a few principles of trade arose that were important at the time and directly or indirectly ever since. When a transaction was completed, witnesses should be present. The exchange of God's penny was the common seal of a deal. Disputes concerning trade were referred to a hastily gathered jury of merchants and others who were familiar with the facts or the type of issue at hand. Standing in the dust of the road in the heat of the day men arrived at a judgment from which there was no appeal. The law enforced was the common law of merchants, the *lex mercatoria* that came to be incorporated into the common law of England at least in part. The courts were called piés poudres (*pieds poudreux*) or dusty-footed. They may be compared with the courts of arbitration of the present time. No lawyers were involved and no technicalities of procedure. The traveling merchant had to be on his way: delay to him would be the major injury.

We have thought of the traveling merchants as operating everywhere individually and in some areas in companies. We have assumed they were trading between towns. In fact, traveling merchants frequented the great fairs, buying and selling there as in inland towns and seaports. Above all, at these fairs they settled their accounts both receivable and payable. Bills of exchange were paid at the last days of the fairs, notably of Champagne where merchants from south and north, east and west met to settle their obligations.

The administrative policies of traveling merchants deserve more attention than we can give to them. Their chief policy was to sell by wholesale, but many a town forced them to sell for two weeks or forty days to all comers before disposing of their wares to the trade. This was particularly important in the wine, salt, and corn trade: rich lords, storekeepers, shopkeepers, and others of means provided for their family or trade needs. A second policy, after they had sold their imports, was to pick up goods for export so as to make the next call or at least take advantage of the favorable seasons for the onward or perhaps homeward voyage. A third policy was to prefer cash but to accept good credit. A fourth policy was to diversify as much as possible. The merchant should own only a part of the ship, invest in the trade of other traveling merchants, ask other traveling merchants going to some other town or at another season to sell and buy goods for him, and finally invest in land if fortune provided clear profits. A fifth policy was to avoid the control of other men unless it be for a single venture.

Special managerial problems in great plenty arose in the trade of the traveling merchant. A careful selection of wares for sale had to be made, always in the light of the destination and the season. The seasons had to be followed carefully, for some were safe sailing whilst others were not. Only a stout ship was to be used and a trustworthy crew. Easy to say this but hard to be sure. Diplomacy and tact had to be used in foreign parts. If partners were taken on or other merchants commissioned as factors, the greatest care had to be exercised to secure a combination of honesty and ability.

Those interested in the traveling merchant might read some of the narrations of merchants' voyages, such as the fifteenth-century ventures of the Russian Nikitin, the Genoese Santo Stefano, and the Venetian Nicolò Conti, all to India. In such, we get an indelible impression of countless delays under the blistering sun or during the prolonged monsoons. Ships lie in ports for weeks, then ride the seas becalmed for many weary days. Robbers carry off goods and records and snatch bags of gems and coins from the heart of the merchant. Officials open their palms for bribes or draw their swords for booty. Inns charm the weary traveler and then prove to be brothels. Sickness and heartache bring back the scenes of childhood. Yes, the homeward voyage must be attempted. A horse will be bought and ridden to port. The horse sold, passage will be hired on an open boat that makes only one lap of the journey. The rains fill the hold and silks and spices are ruined. Never mind, there are still a few rubies and jewels. At last, luck brings the weary traveler home, richer in experience than in profit.

It was the supreme duty of the traveling merchant actually to arrive home in person. He must avoid dying abroad because of the common rule that the property of a dead alien reverted to the king. We know this under the French term *droit d'aubaine,* but it prevailed widely in Europe and also in the Orient.

I am so impressed with the work and the contributions of the traveling merchant that I feel like recommending studies of his life and culture. His work was as creative as his hazards were many. For the spread of goods and ideas he has been a winged ship and messenger. Seeking his profit, he served the world. Although a few of his number in favorably located centers such as Genoa, Venice, Marseilles, Bordeaux, Bruges, and London attained wealth, most were rewarded with violent deaths and bankruptcy. As petty capitalists they began and petty capitalists they remained, except in the most unusual cases and in these instances they left their rank of trade for the safer halls of landlords.

5. TRAVELING PETTY CAPITALISTS: PEDLARS

Like the traveling merchant, the pedlar was somewhat of an adventurer. Strange are the drives that send men on to their vocations in life. It is hard to tell whether a missionary goes out into the field to save heathen souls or to attain a life of respectful retirement; whether a soldier joins the army to fight for his country or to get away from home; and whether a scholar becomes a teacher in order to earn a living at congenial work or to display the vanity of his learning before less sophisticated minds. And so with the pedlar, was it merchandising or was it a continuous change of scene?

Pedlars are typically retailers and operate characteristically in the country. An old English name is "rural chapmen." Without the frequency of hucksters, they may have a certain regularity of operation over a longer period. In some cases they may be not unconnected with traveling artisans such as tinkers and shoemakers. Many Continental workmen, before becoming masters, put in a few years of travel, and, for their benefit, brotherhoods of workers made special provision in certain towns. In America there has been since colonial times a small army of hoboes who are workers, often skilled, liking work but not too much of it, who stay here for a month and there for a week and then pass on, neglecting or ignoring responsibilities to others.

It is worth noting that the pedlar was one who carried his wares in a bag or basket (that is, in a ped or pad). The word has nothing necessarily to do with walking. The pedlar might go afoot, on horseback, by cart, wagon, or boat. If careful and efficient, he might graduate from the more laborious to the more congenial mode of travel.

It is a plausible inference that there were two classes of pedlars—the ordinary group that made only a bare living and the successful. The successful might, if ambitious, join the ranks of the traveling merchants, as did St. Godric in the twelfth century; or he might retire to a position of an investor or loaner of small amounts of capital, as was apparently the case of Peter Chapman, of St. Ives, in 1296. This Peter loaned to John Spicer, a traveling merchant going to Scotland with a packload of wares on his horse, a small sum of money for which he expected a reward. The case, going to court, turned on the issue whether the money in question had been given by way of a loan or a partnership investment.

In 1568 we find a pedlar of Frankfort depicted as carrying through the countryside an open basket of mercery—made up of breeches, flutes, bangles, spices, sugar, brandy, mirrors, bells, combs, needles, hair bands, cookies, lace, and gloves. These things were said to have been made by the pedlar's father the preceding year.

Doubtless this pedlar's father was a small-scale artisan, a wholesale handicraftsman. This suggests one of the chief sources of pedlars' goods—the small workers who made the various wares of cloth, metal, or leather. A second source was the traveling merchant who could be found in large seaports in the right seasons. A third source in both Europe and America was the retail store. A fourth was the pedlar's own customers who bartered skins, woolen cloth, or any commodity which they themselves made by hand.

In England in the sixteenth century the pedlar and tinker were an object of concern to the government because they belonged to that growing band of vagabonds whose activities alarmed the authorities. They were regarded as sturdy beggars and annoying thieves whose women folk tended to corrupt the districts they visited. Sometimes the tinker's wife would be a peddling woman, perhaps a "baudy basket." The pedlars were said to sell from horse-packs or foot-packs, on holy days and Sundays on the church porches, and daily in the abbeys. In 1598 an English law ordered that all pedlars or petty chapmen, resident in any township and brought up to their trade, might go to the usual markets and fairs but without opening or showing their wares on the way. We may be sure that such a regulation could not be enforced.

In America pedlars were at work within about one generation of settlement. Generally, the northerners operated southward and westward. Connecticut and perhaps Pennsylvania produced more than their share of pedlars. Some operated among white folks on the fringe of settlement, while others traded with Indians. In either case, it was customary to trade trinkets for furs, home-made cloth, food, and so on. The Indians would give valuable furs for cheap scalping knives and whisky. Pedlars from Connecticut were famous for their tinware and clocks. As the pedlar prospered, he gave up travel by foot, even by horseback, in favor of the horse and wagon stocked with a wide array of kitchen and personal goods. At times, the pedlar even took his wife and children with him. In the nineteenth century, Jews became active and successful pedlars and in this way often got a start toward bigger things.

Storekeepers sometimes sent out wagons with sundry goods for sale in the country roundabout. In Vermont this was common and, even today, there as elsewhere, storekeepers send auto-trucks with meats, bread, fruits, and vegetables for sale to farmers and summer residents.

The wholesale pedlar was developed in Vermont in the nineteenth century. One large store would send out several wagons of goods for sale to retailers scattered over a wide area. In the present century large firms have undertaken to sell from delivery trucks tobacco products and also groceries. This sale is by wholesale both to urban and rural retailers.

In America, besides the pedlars of tinware and clocks and so on, there were the pedlars of printed matter and the pedlars of patent medicines. Both classes played important rôles in rural districts. Much of the early literature that reached the rural homesteads came via the pedlar's pack or wagon. Among the printed books and pamphlets were the Bible, almanacs, contemporary novels, primers, and the like. Much of the early peddling of patent medicines was finally taken over by rather large firms sending out scores of wagons for long periods selling cathartics, cures for rheumatism, and concoctions to take the kinks out of negroes' hair.

In spite of the fact that pedlars probably frequently took advantage of the ignorance of consumers and charged too much for their wares, there is no doubt as to their great service, particularly to country people. Their very visit was itself a welcome novelty and the news they brought was as a cool breeze on a hot day.

Obviously, the average pedlar never accumulated much capital, though a few were graduated into the ranks of traveling merchants where they could still find adventure or into the sedentary retail business where they might prosper. Often the pedlar was a ne'er-do-well who drank or gambled away his accumulations. Peddling had no great future but it was attractive to its devotees and useful to others. Like the services of most petty capitalists, those of the pedlars were expensive to their patrons because inherently inefficient.

6. AGENTS AND AUXILIARIES IN PETTY CAPITALISM

The business man operates on the basis of the lowest costs. Accordingly, he employs the smallest number of workmen, foremen, and managers so as to avoid costs in the production of goods and services. If he were not careful in this way, he would not be able to sell his output, so high would be his costs. One of the means which the petty capitalists, particularly the traveling merchants, employed, was the agent. A business agent received not a salary for time put in but a commission fee for service rendered. Here was the minimum waste and therefore the maximum gain.

Perhaps the earliest agents were brokers. These persons arose privately to gain a living by performing a service, namely, bringing buyer and seller together. They became semi-public functionaries when their services were regulated by the town magistrates. The broker might set out to bring a visiting traveling merchant and local storekeeper or shopkeeper together, or it might be two visiting traveling merchants; but he was sorely tempted to step in and make a deal on his own account. As soon as he became a trader himself, his services would be prejudiced, for he would seek first of all to sell his own wares. The towns had to prohibit this. Their efforts were in vain, for periodically renewed attempts had to be made to prevent brokers from becoming principals.

Brokers, particularly in early days and in undeveloped towns, tended to be hosts to incoming merchants. In other words, they were innkeepers. This additional occupation had also to be regulated, for the broker-host sometimes was dishonest and this dishonesty was serious for the stranger whose money, papers, and goods were ordinarily stored where he lodged. Normal growth tended to take care of this, however, for specialized taverns and inns arose in all prosperous towns. Moreover, regulated companies of traveling merchants established special houses to accommodate both merchants and their wares. The Steelyard of the German merchants in London is a notable example of this.

A second type of agent was the notary to whom merchants and other petty capitalists went to have documents drawn up and recorded in their books. The notarial records of Giovanni Scriba, of Genoa, are among the most important sources for business history because they contain so many partnership contracts between active traveling merchants and their investing partners. There was a tendency for the towns to use these notaries in a semi-official capacity by requiring that all commercial contracts must be enrolled by some notary before they could be binding. One copy of the contract would go to each of the principals and a third would be found in the notary's book.

A third type was the scribe. He was primarily a writer. It is a safe inference that petty capitalists were not adept in reading and writing nor in keeping accounts. A resident scribe who could be hired on occasion could perform all the literary work required. For certain occasions it was necessary to employ traveling scribes. This was true of ships carrying the goods of many merchants, along with the cargo belonging to the captain of the vessel and to the crew. On large caravan ventures a similar person had to be employed. How much more than a traveling shipping clerk he was, would depend upon the scribe himself.

Certainly there would be sundry jobs that he might perform: for instance, on a return voyage he might put together the tallies and other fragments of records into a connected financial statement for a traveling merchant who would find it necessary to make some kind of an account for his investing partner in the home port.

Protective agents (comparable to those we have frequently to employ in America to guard property, notably railroad property, against thieving by sundry persons of the lower middle and working classes) had to be used in ancient and mediaeval times. It was found convenient to hire a captain to lead a band of soldiers whether in Western Europe or on the caravan routes to Mecca. A similar situation existed on board ship when pirates or war threatened peaceful traffic.

Finally, we mention an important kind of non-specialized agent easily overlooked. This was the traveling merchant who agreed to act on a specified voyage as the agent or factor of another traveling merchant who could not embark on that particular enterprise. Such a factor would sell the goods consigned to him for a commission fee and, it might be, make purchases from the proceeds for a similar fee. This practice has lasted down from the early days of town economy to the nineteenth century and, of course, in other forms down to the present.

While the agent performs routine service, the auxiliary, to whom we now turn, merely gives advice and maintains the irresponsibility of an outsider. This class has grown to considerable proportions at the present day, but was in the time of petty capitalism very immature. There were no lawyers or specialized accountants to be consulted. Lawyers, we should remember, did not enter the field of business as such until modern times. Persons resembling accountants were brought into disputes which came before municipal courts. These were called "auditors" and were simply other petty capitalists who, being in the same business, might be expected to aid the courts largely as expert witnesses. It is not much of a stretch of the imagination to regard the hastily improvised witnesses to a deal as business auxiliaries, for they gave aid to the business man though they might receive no more fee than a drink of ale or wine.

7. FORCES AT WORK

It is a nice but difficult exercise to explain why business capitalism, in the form of petty capitalism, came into existence. In the form of the question "why did towns arise?" the problem is not new.

Unless villages continued to take in new land, the sons of cultivators who could not inherit land at all or not enough to live on were constantly being invited to get out. They might marry an heiress in their own village or in a neighboring community, or they might go off to join a robber band, or they might enter the Church. The town offered another opportunity. Moreover, the town and petty capitalism offered a chance for those with aptitudes not given full play in the country—for trade and for manufacture. This is one of the most impelling forces known to man—the drive to adjust himself so that he may get the most out of himself and for himself.

In the case of towns that had charters, and especially in the case of towns that had liberal charters of autonomy, a real inducement was probably the freedom that was involved. As we have seen, it was no idle rule or boast that "town air makes free." By the late thirteenth and fourteenth centuries in Western Europe the demand for freedom had become a major factor in economic and social existence.

As a force of accretion very generally, and as quite elemental in the case of a few towns, was the presence of a Church institution or a castle. In those towns where there were monasteries (congregations, schools, and hospitals) and judicial courts, perhaps also courts of princes, there were many inducements for men to come to try their fortunes or, if already in the town, to devise services to sell to their fellow townsmen.

Here, in social differentiation, is a power for civilization. It is not diffused from far-off lands so much as it is effused from the soil of a fairly mature people. It is what a people does next when it approaches a mature phase of settled village economy. An effective way of expressing the situation is to say that a new opportunity for income or profit has arisen. Be it noted that this income was individual. The individuals obtaining the income had thereby created a new social income of material goods, security in capital goods behind strong walls, and satisfaction in opportunities of a wide range. The opportunities during the stage of petty capitalism were wide open—up the ladder of apprentice, journeyman, and small master.

Some persons will be disappointed on learning that we cannot find some mechanical device that started the processes of petty capitalism. To be sure, there was the abacus that aided in reckoning and there was the mariner's compass that assisted the traveling merchant—apparently first the Chinese, then the Arabian, and then the Western European. Spinning wheels, hand looms, and water wheels lay in the background but cannot be regarded as factors in the rise of petty capitalism, though they may have been minor factors in the development of the system.

8. ACCUMULATION AND FLOW OF CAPITAL

The process of nature creates both natural resources and the laborer. It is management, however, which creates capital, accumulates it, and makes it to flow. At first, this capital was created and accumulated (but not made to flow) in a pre-business world. Later, it was created, accumulated, and made to flow in an era of private business. The first stage of this private business was, as we have seen, petty capitalism. It is this petty capitalistic system that concerns us at the present moment.

The creation of capital involves production and, beyond this, saving for further production. Man has found the first process easier than the second. The accumulation involves increased saving far beyond the chances of immediate use and indeed for the remote contingencies of partial disaster, display, or power over fellow men. Much as this accumulation has been denounced by moralists, intellectuals, and reformers, it has been the means whereby those very persons have been kept alive and nourished, for it is the great reservoir in time of famine and disease and the source of power to resist the foe in time of attack. A danger to the individual accumulator, it is a boon to society. This fact was discovered even before the days of business when a strong man's fortress and granary were a refuge for the democrats of the whole district. In our period of petty capitalism there was accumulation but it was fairly even and widespread. Great wealth was the exception as was great poverty. The capital accumulated was in the form of shops and ships, tools and goods, money and plate, improvements in real estate in town and country.

In this stage of petty capitalism a new circumstance was the flow of capital. In earlier times a man might lend a horse or a hoe but he got no advantage, except the chance to borrow in a similar way. In other words, capital was for use and could yield a return—a profit—in no other way. This may be called the usucapital system which, of course, lives on into the present and must continue as long as private business prevails. But now, in petty capitalism, a direct putting-out system was fashioned whereby the owners of capital could derive an income from their accumulation or their inheritance.

By the direct putting-out system of capitalism I mean a way whereby the possessor of capital puts out directly to the user a certain amount of capital goods or money in return for a promise to pay interest or dividends. This is a creation of business in the stage of petty capitalism during the early part of town economy. By this device it was possible for an active business man, a retired business man, a clergyman, a widow, or an orphan to derive an income from the simple process of putting otherwise surplus capital out to work in the business of someone else. That individuals should object to this new device for mutual advantage is difficult for anyone to believe except the worshippers of bad management. That the system worked hardship for the landlord, libertine abbot, or spendthrift heir who contracted consumptive loans is clear enough. And yet they would have been in an even worse situation, had they not received the loan. And, unless rewards for loans were the order of the day, there would be little or no capital to come to the relief of either the good or the bad managers.

There were three principal methods of getting an income by putting out capital directly to the user during the stage of petty capitalism:

1. Selling goods on credit but at a charge
2. Loaning goods or money
3. Investing in a partnership

Selling at credit is probably almost as old as selling goods by business men. It is a means of facilitating exchange, dangerous but useful. If only small sums are involved and spread over many customers, the hazards are limited. One of the chief difficulties was making the obligation clear so that the borrower or his heir would be forced to pay. Registration before a town court or official was a first-rate device. In thirteenth-century London the chamberlain recorded a great many such obligations, incurred by shopkeepers and storekeepers when buying imported wares from traveling merchants and apparently by one traveling merchant purchasing from another. The promissory notes given often specify in the case of one traveling merchant dealing with another that payments were to be made at certain fairs where, of course, both merchants or their servants might be. The credit arrangements between business men seem to have involved a terminal date as well as a plan of payment. What we do not know is how far interest was involved in a deferred payment and how far further interest was involved in case of a failure to pay on time. The probability is that both were commonly but not always implied, but this is a special question which need not detain us long. Certainly, the Church was dead against any price that was above the just price for a commodity. A market price which it objected to might be the just price of the commodity, plus an addition for deferred payment.

We may note that the bill of exchange arose in the system being dealt with. At first—not later than the thirteenth century in Western Europe—it was a promise to pay, given by the purchaser of goods to the seller. Later it became a draft drawn by the seller on the purchaser and to this day it retains that form. The outstanding situation was for international traveling merchants to give bills or to accept them, to be paid at one of the fairs of Champagne, just east of Paris. There, on one of the closing days, the merchants got together and liquidated their debts. Up to this time, the bills of exchange in question might have circulated as money, each holder endorsing the same.

The regular loans of the ancient and mediaeval periods were of three principal types, at least in the case of sea traffic, about which we have most information.

1. Bottomry
2. Respondentia
3. Sea loan (*foenus nauticum*)

The first two are well known and exist today, as they did in ancient Greece. If a ship required repairs or refitting in a strange port, the captain might make a bottomry loan on the ship and a respondentia loan on the cargo. If the ship and cargo reached home, then the principal and interest were due. If the ship was lost with the cargo nothing was due. The ordinary sea loan was quite different. A merchant, being short of capital, borrowed a sum of money at a specified rate of interest in order to buy merchandise with which to trade. He owed both principal and interest regardless of the income. Disputes went to court for decision. If the borrower lost money, he sometimes claimed that the lender was really an investing partner and should share the loss. Of course, the lender would insist that he be paid both principal and interest. There is some question as to what the Church law was on this subject but certainly the spirit of that law was to allow interest (or what was then called usury) on a loan that involved clear risk. There were variations in these types of loan and, in spite of its name, the sea loan was found in land transactions as well as in sea traffic.

There were other loans both for business and non-business purposes. The attitude of the Church to these loans was troublesome, complicated, and to the modern mind not very logical. To be sure, the Church was in a tight corner: it had made pronouncements on the subject of loans (and prices) in a non-business period and found it difficult to change. If laws are given divine sanction, then it is only brave men who will ask the divinity to change its mind. Fresh interpretations could be made, however, and that was what was done. Various special allowances were made so as to cause the least difficulty. Jews could loan money to Christians because the Jews were damned anyway. Strange to say, Christians could borrow from them without themselves losing all chance of heaven. Since many of the consumptive loans were made by Jews, a large number of the total is accounted for. In the case of productive loans a special arrangement had to be made. Usury might not be charged but interest might. The distinction arose in this fashion. A lender made his loan to the borrower, for instance, an investing traveling merchant to an active traveling merchant, for a certain period, say one month, with the understanding that, if the principal was not returned at that time, the borrower would pay interest to the lender as a kind of recompense for loss which the lender would suffer or for the gains which the lender would be unable to make. While Jews were allowed $43\frac{1}{3}$ per cent for their (consumptive) loans, the loans (many productive) made by others (Lombards) in the thirteenth century were at a higher rate. The Church would allow interest when risk was obvious as in the case of sea traffic. It also allowed for other special circumstances.

The flow of capital from hand to hand was greatly facilitated by the system of partnerships, first used by petty capitalists and continued in later stages. The basis was commonly for a single venture on land or on sea. For instance, a traveling merchant, whether still active or retired, would put out so much goods or money for a venture, say, from Genoa to Alexandria in the eleventh century. There were two principal types and many variations of the two. First, there was the ordinary partnership in which the investor put two-thirds of the total capital and the active merchant the other third. Then both shared equally in profit or loss. In addition, the active merchant might be allowed a venture on his own account, but in this case he paid a *pro rata* share of the expense. This partnership was fair to both parties and tolerably flexible so far as the two parties were concerned.

The second type of partnership was called the commendation. The active merchant might accept from various investors a sum of money or an amount of goods for sale on a certain voyage. The investor supplied all the capital of the particular partnership, while the active merchant supplied the management and took all the physical risks. The investor received three-quarters of the profits and the active merchant one-quarter. Each bore his share of the expenses. Often the investors were widows or orphans or any other who had goods or money to put out for an income. While we learn not a little about the sums put out in these commendation partnerships, we learn very little about the private ventures of the active merchant, which went unrecorded because one active merchant was alone concerned and entered into no contract that might be left behind for our benefit.

There has been a theory, propagated by Sombart, that capital flowed from landlords to merchants or from rent rolls to commercial ventures. The thought is that the lord of the land on which a town had grown up came to have a large income in the form of money rents which he turned into foreign or extended trade in order to increase his income. To some scholars this is a favorite theory, for, as it is put, capital has a base origin —unearned urban rents. Base in origin, in use, and in growth, capital should be early exterminated. This is pretty much like saying that women should be eliminated from society. But let this part of the idea of the flow of capital pass. Other scholars have found that Sombart's theories did not apply to Venice, Augsburg, and so on. More than one scholar holds to the view that, in the case of Genoa, capital was invested by neighboring rural landlords in oversea trade. Documents prove this as early as the twelfth century. To some extent such investment was probably the work of younger sons who so used their patrimony. And probably it was most common among families that had come, either through the male or female side, from that very trade at an earlier date. On the whole, there is much more likelihood that capital flowed from commerce into agriculture on a balance than from agriculture into commerce. Of course, we must not rule out the gains of feudal nobles made in wars as possible investment capital, but these would be occasional rather than continuous.

This direct putting-out system of using capital was the creation of petty capitalism but it has survived that stage. For instance, pawnbroking, practised by Lombards and Jews in the Middle Ages, and now by Jews and Gentiles alike in some countries, is a good example of a form that has come down to us almost unchanged.

It was the business man who invested and urged the direct putting-out system in its most useful parts. The system blessed him who loaned or invested and him who received the loan or the investment. The Church saw the point only darkly, if at all, but it compromised with necessity. The Church took the stand of preferring risk to certainty; we should say that it took up the cause of common stocks (often dangerously near speculation) in preference to bonds.

9. STRENGTH AND WEAKNESS OF PETTY CAPITALISM

We early acquire the knowledge that there is something strong and something weak in every social order, something socially good and bad in every system devised by man. Gradually, a better system is worked out that corrects the evils and also, be it noted, loses some of the good of the old system. Realization of this fact gives to the conservative a talking point but awards the weight of the argument to the progressives when they succeed in introducing a new system that has more good points than bad. Let us examine petty capitalism, put it into the balance so as to form some opinion as to whether we would have kept it, had we lived at the time it flourished, or whether we would not now restore it. In most of China it still reigns supreme. There are elements of petty capitalism in small towns everywhere today. Indeed, the system has had its powerful champions in the classroom, the pulpit, and the rostrum. Just what do we individually think of the system?

Many of us would say that one of the sources of strength lay in the widespread ownership and use of capital. Coupled with this was the fact that no one person owned enough capital to exert any great control over his fellow man. If all persons had been equally able and coöperatively disposed, this would have had much in its favor. But it is right here where we find an element of weakness. A third point of strength lay in the invention and adoption of the direct putting-out system of capital flow. A fourth lay in the individualism that was developed to the point that each person felt that he had only himself to blame if he did not prosper. All could freely make contracts so long as they maintained their reputation for probity and ability. Fifth, the "law merchant" or mercantile law which the petty capitalists invented, was a speedy, efficient, and flexible system of settling difficulties between business men in which lawyers had no place and in which Church rules would receive the minimum of attention. Sixth, there was the tremendously important form of business combination invented called the "partnership" which in later times developed right into the joint stock company incorporated. Some scholars would emphasize the associations known as gilds and regulated companies. I should not rule them out. Some would urge the claims of handicraftsmanship and I should not deny them, but this skill had been growing in earlier stages and actually became such an obsession that centuries were required to force artisans to learn to make what people wanted rather than what they themselves had learned and liked to make.

In the working out of urban mercantilism there were probably two phases, not always separable and yet different. First, there was early urban mercantilism created by petty capitalists. This was a policy of "the town for townsmen." Under this policy much of the actual regulation of economic activity was delegated to the gilds. Business that concerned the food supply of townsmen, however, was not wholly delegated. The town as a community would not tolerate the engrossing of foodstuffs, the forestalling of supplies, or the complete regrating of provisions from the countryside or from outside the district. In accordance with the deep feeling of petty capitalists the gild ordinances looked forward to high quality of work and to economic equality in the fraternity of business men and the régime of petty capitalism. It is true that early urban mercantilism was much changed by mercantile capitalists, especially in the fifteenth century and later, but that is another story.

I recognize, without emphasis, a sturdy culture that petty capitalists started on the road to higher things. Much of the attainment in sculpture, painting, architecture, poetry, and music that flowered in the later era of mercantile capitalism, sprang from seeds planted by petty capitalists. The town, indeed the world, was the gainer when craftsmanship went over into art. When to the security and well-being of the town was added leisurely specialization in the arts, then attainments ran high. Ancient Athens and mediaeval Florence have had few peers, but in each case the ripe fruit came only after the petty capitalist had yielded to the mercantile capitalist. Also, on lower levels of cultural attainment there is something to be said. Much of the creative work of petty capitalists we have not seen fit to admire or to preserve with care. When a shoemaker wrote songs, composed music, and propounded philosophy, the result was more important for him than for us. And, then, going on down

GOLDEN BEZANT, EARLY NINTH CENTURY

EXTERIOR OF A RETAILER'S
STORE AND DWELLING,
FRANCE, SIXTEENTH CENTURY

HALL AND COURT OF A MERCHANT, AUGSBURG, 1539

to the lowest level—the mere enjoyment of things beautiful and true—we can observe an astonishingly large percentage of townsmen—petty capitalists—getting satisfactions that the cultivators of the soil under village economy never knew. From the creative standpoint, consumption is always at a low level of effort, but at the same time it is the social realization of the individual's highest effort. The next stage—mercantile capitalism—saw civilization reach a higher level, but also it saw the enjoyment by the rank and file begin to recede. Such is the seesaw of creation and enjoyment, production and consumption.

These elements of strength are impressive in kind and in number. The items of weakness are not so numerous but they were sufficiently potent to change the system of petty capitalism into a system of mercantile capitalism. First, in petty capitalism there was a tendency to multiply the number of small masters to the danger point. True, this system of opportunity for all to become masters worked itself out more extensively in the next stage but the movement of over-crowding in business was well under way in petty capitalism. The reason was that so little capital was required to set up a shop or a store or become a pedlar or huckster or even a traveling merchant that too many entered the various fields. Everything in the system encouraged over-competition which sooner or later would be ruinous to all concerned. Secondly, there was an ingrained tendency to produce for a narrow market and in accordance with locally developed and locally inherited tastes and traditions. Up to a point this was advantageous, but such a system could never allow a town to grow very large or develop an extensive distant or foreign trade. As soon as merchants came along to organize a wider market, these petty capitalists receded into the background as independent business men. Great expansion, such as was suggested by the very increase in the number of small masters, required catering to the market, that is, giving up some of the local ways of working and meeting the needs of distant peoples. We shall meet this situation in the next chapter. There is no doubt that there was a lack of high commercial technique when every merchant, for instance, had to use up so much of his energy in traveling and every industrial master and storekeeper in acting as his own foreman and chief workman. In other words, management was severely limited in its possibilities of growth. Accounting control was feeble, though adequate for limited transactions. And, finally, there were few great fortunes to remain in business and give vigorous leadership to business men in formulating commercial policies and carrying through political and military action. Just as in the country strong leaders were required, so also in the towns—in order to extend business, maintain local defence, and encourage art, letters, and philosophy. The leadership that was necessary was provided by the sedentary merchants of the next stage.

When the petty capitalist loses a point in his fight, he raises loud lamentations, whilst the big fellows of later systems just fold up their tents and slip away into oblivion. Whether this is an element of weakness or contemptible strength on the part of the petty capitalist, we do not need to debate. When the petty capitalist cries out, the thinkers or writers do not stop to consider whether the squeal indicates any social loss or whether it points to anything beyond a shift in the career of one who is an innate conservative.

10. SURVIVAL AND REVIVAL OF PETTY CAPITALISTS IN OUR DAY

Petty capitalism was followed by another system and that by another, and so on. This means not that the old forms disappeared necessarily but that one new form dominated in some striking way. Petty capitalism died but not petty capitalists.

Petty capitalists have lived on and have kept growing with the increase in population. They have thrived in modern towns, just such as the original centers in which they took their start and reached their height in the ancient and mediaeval periods. Driven out in one industry, they have risen in another. Threatened, buffeted, and decimated by rivals, especially in manufacturing, they have been submerged only to rise again.

In agriculture they have made their greatest conquests in modern times. In Europe, as manorialism and feudalism declined, the peasants became tenant farmers or proprietors carrying on production on at least a partially commercial basis. The farmer class in America and in other new countries illustrate a revival of the small capitalist class. Many of the new farmers were old artisans. Many of them remained skilled in craftsmanship while they learned the technique of agricultural production. The millions of modern farms normally above the subsistence level and below the level of agricultural factories may be regarded as belonging to the group of petty capitalists.

In the metropolitan centers, petty capitalists have been pressed hard but have shifted their activities. Some have become ancillary to other and larger units, for instance, in manufacture. Others have increased in kind and in number beyond all precedents and experience, especially in providing consumers' goods and services.

The automobile industry has built up big manufacturing plants producing cars, parts, tires, gas, oil, and so on. But for every big plant there have probably been created a thousand small undertakings, such as repair shops, service stations, stores selling automobile parts, road-stands, tourist houses, and the like.

During prohibition in America, that is, from 1919 to 1933, the manufacture of beer, ale, whisky, rum, and brandy almost ceased in large plants. In place of big units there arose, under cover, innumerable illicit breweries and distilleries which have left behind no statistical record.

One of the largest and most strategically located groups of petty capitalists is made up of professional people—doctors, dentists, lawyers, and business auxiliaries. These persons have sunk large amounts of capital in the training of their abilities, they are independent in their business, and they amass considerable amounts of wealth, much of which is for investment.

The group of petty capitalists is open at both ends. It is open to the capable and ambitious workman. It is a training and proving ground for those who have the ability to rise to higher things. For instance, the owner of a small store may start a second and a third and even develop a chain. It was thus that Woolworth grew.

During the first years of the New Deal, there was much agitation in America against big business and in favor of small units. In many States, laws were passed crushing out the large and favoring the small. Regardless of the merits of any particular piece of legislation, the small man has been able to look after himself. To be sure, he has had to shift, to yield, to alter his work. But so do large units. I am not impressed with his defeats —in spite of the lamentations of would-be friends—but with his victories.

Following are groups of petty capitalists now in America. The list is obviously incomplete.

1. Specialized factories: shoes, tools, cosmetics, etc.
2. Shops producing new products: tailors, shoeshops, printers, photographers, etc.
3. Repair shops: autos, clothes, machine, furniture, etc.
4. Mills: grist, saw, spice.
5. Builders and repairers: boats, houses.
6. Service shops: laundries, cleaners, barbers, restaurants, garages, shoe-shine parlors, funeral parlors, etc.
7. Unit stores: grocery, dry goods, hardware, etc.
8. Pawnbrokers.
9. Hostelries: hotels, tourist houses.
10. Specialized farms: gardeners, chicken farms, duck farms, mushroom farms, fur farms, etc.
11. General farms.
12. Fishermen: fish, oysters, clams, lobsters.
13. Amusement places: theatres, night clubs, music halls, etc.
14. Hucksters.
15. Pedlars.
16. Tinkers.
17. Teamsters.
18. Taxis (independent).

SURVIVAL AND REVIVAL

19. Agencies: insurance, real estate, advertising, employment, etc.
20. Professional: doctors, dentists, lawyers, business auxiliaries.

Many of the current small capitalists, sooner or later, form corporations. Read the weekly lists of newly incorporated business units. These point to great virility. Most of these corporations are little more than incorporated partnerships.

No statistics of the size of business units are more than approximations. Such as these are, they tell a story that is clear-cut: namely, that petty capitalists still find an outlet for their entrepreneurial abilities. Take as one illustration the following figures for 1928.

Business Units in the United States, 1928 *
(*Number of units*)

	Corporations	Non-corporations
Agriculture	10,265	6,264,855
Trade	129,766	1,508,761
Professional service	36,829	1,157,138
Total	495,892	9,997,000

* R. R. Doane, *The Measurement of American Wealth*, 1933, p. 53.

Of course, since many of the corporations are essentially small partnership units, the total number of petty capitalists is even larger than is indicated by the figures. And, then, the number of units is not the only comparison of large and small business. We have no figures on the subject of the percentage of business transactions carried out by small units, but we might guess 75 per cent—and be wrong. In any estimate, we should include goods sold and services contracted for (apart from regular wage-earners).

Someone may express the view that a few corporations are large and a smaller number very large; in fact, that it is these large units that are proletarianizing the people of the country.

This may be the case, but it is at least a partial answer that those who become permanent workmen *tend* to be the ones who are unfit to be petty capitalists. I cannot prove this but I believe it. Petty capitalists are being squeezed out, like inefficient larger units in more advanced systems, by individuals and firms better able to do their work and serve society. Our first example of this is the sedentary merchant's rise to wealth and power at the expense of petty capitalists in early towns. Although the petty capitalists have been edged out of their economic positions, still many retain the necessary virility to rise again when opportunity shows its head. This is part of the seesaw of large and small that weaves strange patterns through history.

Chapter III

MERCANTILE CAPITALISM

Birth of Control in Private Business

Increase your capital and build up your credit;
Leave travel to servants and agents;
Multiply your ventures; integrate your functions.
Control through factors and partners;
Demand free trade at home and privilege abroad.

1. RISE OF THE SEDENTARY MERCHANT

The sedentary merchant was the dominant figure in mercantile capitalism. In fact, the system of mercantile capitalism began and ended with him. I do not mean that he was the first merchant capitalist, for we remember notably the traveling merchant before his time. The traveling merchant, however, never succeeded in gaining dominance over other classes: though a merchant capitalist, he helped create only a petty capitalism.

The sedentary merchant differed from the traveling merchant in a number of respects. While the traveling merchant spent his best energies in moving from place to place, the sedentary merchant used his abilities in the administration of his business. While the traveling merchant was largely subject to a single great risk (though he tried to remedy this), the sedentary merchant diversified his risks over a wide front. While the traveling merchant apparently arose out of the peasant class, the sedentary merchant probably descended from the storekeeping and shopkeeping classes. While the traveling merchant belonged to the declining régime of international fairs, the sedentary merchant belonged to the period of fast-growing industrial towns and metropolitan centers.

It is not easy to determine which merchant was traveling and which was sedentary during the period of the thirteenth century in Italy and Flanders and the fourteenth century in England and North Germany. Of course, the sedentary merchant would not be found in the records to be traveling, at least not ordinarily; but he might be off on a visit to old clients or to open new connections. The sedentary merchant would employ many agents (supercargoes and other factors), but then again the traveling merchant sometimes employed another traveling merchant as his factor. There could be no final method of determining the class to which a merchant belonged, short of examining his accounts and other records. It is the failure to do this that has kept economic historians from dividing mediaeval (and we may add ancient) merchants into these two classes of traveling and sedentary which are radically different in so many respects.

There were two general types of sedentary merchants, based on an analysis of goods handled. First, there was the merchant who traded in an area, for instance a London sedentary merchant might send out his ships to the Baltic area and make that trade his life's work. As a youth he had gone out as a clerk for a traveling merchant and learned the customs and goods of the area. Henceforth, he found this business fully occupied his powers. The second type was the one who, originally at least, specialized not in the trade of an area but in a line of goods. Such were the mercers, drapers, grocers, haberdashers, ironmongers, and so on. These sedentary merchants specialized in their own line of wares, but they had commonly to accept other commodities in the exigencies of trade.

There were two principal classes from which sedentary merchants arose. Traveling merchants as a class did not constitute one of them because that class reached a dead end in turning to investments in foreign trade and land—at the very time that sedentary merchants were getting a start. No, the two classes are, as we have seen, storekeepers and a certain section of the shopkeepers. In various industries some groups were strategically located for marketing, either buying the raw product or selling the finished goods, or both. These shopkeepers, or small master handicraftsmen, tended to turn to employ the other trades in their industry. A good example is found in the saddlers of London who in the fourteenth and fifteenth centuries came to dominate the other workers in the saddle industry, such as the lorimers, the joiners, and the painters. Their original interest was doubtless selling saddles to local consumers, saddles on which they had done the leatherwork and other workers other parts, but as the saddlers succeeded in getting control of the other masters they turned their attention to the wholesale trade. Whereas the storekeepers developed chiefly out of their need to *import* wares, the shopkeepers developed often from the need to import raw products but more commonly from the need to *export* the finished product. Thus, it mattered little whether the original drive was to import or to export, the result was a combination of the two. We need many studies of developing mercantile trades made from the records of individual merchants.

Most revolutions are largely silent in their essential workings but few occur without leaving behind some evidence of hard feeling, strife, and bloodshed. In the earliest towns there was a struggle between the old urban landlords and the petty capitalists. The latter won. Now, as mercantile capitalists aspire to dominate the scene, the petty capitalists are on the defensive, and they finally lose. It is possible that some of the opposition to Jews in the period 1250–1350 was due to the mercantile activities of some of their numbers, quite apart from money-lending. This merits further study. I know of no evidence of opposition from traveling merchants or storekeepers. The situation was different, however, in the case of many of the shopkeepers, or small industrial masters, the retail handicraftsmen who saw their independence threatened. We have noted the case of the saddlers of London. In 1327 rioting broke out on the streets and blood was shed. The saddlers who themselves did the leatherwork on a saddle had bought wooden and metal parts and employed painters at a piece wage. The complaint of 1327 was that the saddlers were trying to reduce the small masters (lorimers, joiners, and painters) serving the industry of saddlery to a position of serving them alone and no other persons in London. The lorimers, joiners, and painters got together and fought back, as did the journeymen of the saddlers at a later date. This was a common story on the Continent—in Italy, France, Flanders, and so on. Blood flowed freely but the victory remained with the ambitious capitalists who reached out to control the small handicraftsman.

At this point, we need to turn for a moment to see what was happening in the general field of industry or manufacture. In the early towns, as we have seen, the shopkeepers, or small industrial masters, or handicraftsmen, as we may choose to call them, were part and parcel of petty capitalism. We may fittingly call the system prevailing "retail handicraft." The small master bought his raw materials and sold his finished products normally to the local consumer in the town or in the country. Increasingly, he sold his wares to the traveling merchant, or at least some of the masters did this, thereby increasing their volume. At this point, the retail handicraft system gives way to the wholesale handicraft system. As long as the wholesale handicraftsman sold to the traveling merchant, he maintained his independence, for the traveling merchant was in no position to do aught but buy what was available. With the advent of the sedentary merchant, however, the situation became quite otherwise. He set about to control the hitherto independent wholesale handicraftsmen, that is, to reduce them to economic subordination. If this theory is generally true, then we have a correlation of first-rate importance.

It was a bitter pill for the petty capitalists in the industrial field to swallow—to see themselves reduced from full-fledged freemen in their community, that is, independent petty capitalists to a position of journeymen working in their own little shops at a piece wage for a certain master or perhaps several certain masters. On the Continent in the thirteenth century and in England in the fourteenth century this struggle was marked. One set of gild ordinances after another indicates an effort of the dying petty capitalism to hold its own. Frequently, this took the form of checking some ambitious individuals in the trade—small masters who wanted to get ahead. Their fellows feared that, if the ambitious masters should get ahead, they themselves would be subordinated or reduced to a position of dependent wholesale handicraftsmen. To obviate this, the gilds which still remained in the control of small masters prohibited various practices which have been misunderstood by modern investigators. They prohibited working at night, ostensibly because bad work would result and fires would be started in the town, but really so that no one master would get ahead of his fellows. They prohibited a master from having more than a few apprentices or journeymen or working them on Saturday afternoons. They prohibited masters from exposing wares on Sunday instead of just hanging out their signs.

Now, let it be made clear at this point, very briefly, that not all the dominating figures that were arising to plague the small masters were mercantile capitalists; some of them were industrial entrepreneurs who had the small masters work for them and who sold the finished product to the sedentary merchants. In many cases, however, the sedentary merchants were directly responsible for this economic situation of handicraftsmen.

The central figure of the new system was the sedentary merchant. If you wished to be cynical, you might say that he was the arch spider who crouched low within his artful web to engulf all the helpless small masters and workmen who came his way. The metaphor is extreme and unfair. He was the master mind that saw a new opportunity of getting rich, if only he could extend the market and make the town grow. This work was done in or from his counting-house. This was the accounting house or office where the new master merchant had his account books not under his hat but on tables and well bound and labelled. The Medici accounts and others exist in considerable numbers for the fifteenth century. Perhaps with the accounts was a treatise on double-entry bookkeeping—the merchant's Bible, whether by Pacioli or some other compiler—but at any rate in the best style of Venice. Besides the books there was an iron chest containing ready cash and a balance with a set of weights to weigh the coins. There were a few merchants' guides and treatises dating from the late thirteenth century. An occasional map was found upon the wall. A few samples of a new commodity might be spread out for examination. Such was the heart of the new system, the center of the new power. Into this counting-room came not only local handicraftsmen and storekeepers but ships' captains and supercargoes and factors about to lie abroad for their masters' benefit.

A new era was dawning for business, one in which administration was a primary consideration. The sedentary merchant amassed wealth and that was a source of strength, but by far the greater reliance was on knowledge, supervision, planning, and directing. This new business administration supplanted the old petty capitalism because of its superiority in policy and management. Put it another way: it offered more to society than the old system had provided. Poor old agriculture had to wait until the eighteenth century, when Norfolk husbandry introduced a new planned technique which has been the basis of modern commercial agriculture that has neither skimmed nor mined the soil.

The pages of mediaeval history are full of the deeds of sedentary merchants. We know them all too often, however, when they perform some unusual service. Marco Polo belonged to a sedentary merchant family of Venice which traded with the East through its branch in Constantinople. His travels to China and back were not made as a merchant. But such service we shall not stop to consider. In Douai there was Jehan Boinebroke, in Hull Sir William de la Pole, King's Merchant and farmer of the customs revenue, in Bristol William Canynges, in Florence the Medici, and in Augsburg the Fuggers and Wel-

LUCA PACIOLI AND A YOUNG NOBLEMAN,
NAPLES, LATE FIFTEENTH CENTURY

MERCHANT'S COUNTING HOUSE INTERIOR,
BERLIN, SEVENTEENTH CENTURY

sers. Those who remember their nursery stories and are not too violently anti-bourgeois will be pleased to learn that Dick Whittington was among the worthies of this class. The author of *The Libel of English Policy* called him "That lodestar and chief chosen flower," and urged a truism that, when such merchants flourished, the whole realm prospered. Further examples are the great London merchants and colonizers of America, Sir Thomas Smythe and Matthew Cradock. In America itself among the best known are John Hancock, John Jacob Astor, and Stephen Girard.

Whatever we may think of the system of mercantile capitalism we must admit its power of endurance. No other system of business capitalism has flourished so long—about six centuries.

On both sides of the Atlantic objection has been made to the term sedentary merchant. Objections to new words are common, for we do not like to have to start over again to learn new terms. It may be that someone can find a better term, such as general merchant, though to this one the objection of ambiguity can be urged.

Why has the sedentary merchant not been recognized before? Actually his existence has been felt but not clearly seen, as in Pirenne's writings. The reasons for his remaining unidentified are several in number. First, the word "merchant" (or its equivalent) is applied continuously, alike to traveling and sedentary merchant. Second, the sedentary merchant often got his apprenticeship through acting as a factor or clerk abroad. Third, the sedentary merchant frequently went abroad to inspect his old markets or to discover new ones. Fourth, traveling merchants lingered on long after the sedentary merchants gained dominance. Jacques Savary, writing about the 'perfect merchant' in the seventeenth century, gave a wholly false description of the important merchant of his own time. Actually, he described the petty traveling merchant still lingering on, especially in the provinces, and particularly in France, one who 'should be strong and robust so as to stand the fatigue of traveling, attending fairs, and visiting foreign lands. He should be able to bale goods and easily carry bulky merchandise without difficulty.' Such a merchant was doubtless found but he was the old-time typical traveling merchant. Fifth, many sedentary merchants were called drapers, mercers, haberdashers, grocers, vintners, and salters after the gild or livery company to which they belonged. Their affiliation with such an association might or might not mean connection with the trade in question, but certainly it did not mean that the man was not a merchant; and from other sources we know that some of the outstanding merchants belonged to the very gilds mentioned. Sixth, and most important, the records, especially the accounts of the two classes of merchants, have been but little studied. They alone give the inside story of the work of the two classes.

2. POLICY AND MANAGEMENT OF THE SEDENTARY MERCHANTS

A whole volume might profitably be written about this subject partly because of the importance of the subject at any one time and partly because of the long period covered—from the late thirteenth to the early nineteenth century. The volume in question can profitably wait until the accounts of more sedentary merchants have been studied.

The primary policy of the sedentary merchant was not to waste time in travel. The substitutes that were adopted by him were agents and partners, and many were the disputes as to whether a man was agent or partner. The sedentary merchant constantly had in mind the problem of risk. He met the problem in part by a system of partnerships and by mutual insurance. He believed in joint action not only in insurance but in trade associations, such as regulated companies, and later in the sixteenth and following centuries he went so far as to form joint stock companies for distant trade. His high strategy was to control others without the full responsibilities involved, for instance in trade, manufacture, fishing, lumbering, and mining. He sought special privileges, particularly in distant trade, and would go far to get a monopoly through a regulated company

MERCHANT'S COUNTING HOUSE INTERIOR,
NÜRNBERG, SEVENTEENTH CENTURY

THREE BALLS — SIGN OF THE
PAWNBROKER'S SHOP, LONDON, 1751

VENETIAN GALLEY, 1486

as against his fellow countrymen who did not join the company. In general, he preferred an enlightened despot to the feudal-Catholic powers of the slowly declining Middle Ages.

The sedentary merchant, sitting in the counting-house, like the pilot in the steering house of a ship, had to estimate hazards; charts, glasses, chronometer, and sextant were not in themselves enough. He had to have a great number of channels and courses open to him. In other words, the sedentary merchant, sitting in his control room, planned to meet danger by diversification, but this diversification was to be in such a form that he could handle it. This means integration of functions. Moreover, the business man who organizes his business in such a way that he can devote himself to administration, such as policy-formulation and the control side of management, has during certain seasons time on his hands and he has developed abilities that can function mightily and smoothly if given a chance.

The upshot of this situation was that the sedentary merchant gradually found it profitable to perform from six to a dozen functions. First, he was primarily an importer or exporter and soon found himself forced to be both. Second, he was by the nature of his foreign or extended trade forced to be a wholesaler and this doubtless would have remained his preference. Through the centuries, he worked himself over to the position of more nearly disposing of his goods to the trade by wholesale. Third, the sedentary merchant was forced by circumstances to perform the task of retailing. Mediaeval town laws had compelled the traveling merchant to sell to consumers for so many days after the arrival of his ship. The same laws forced the sedentary merchant's agents to sell to consumers in the ship or elsewhere. This did not ordinarily mean to break bulk and sell in small quantities. It did mean that corn, wine, salt, and the like were sold to consumers who could buy in as large quantities as the local retailers. Thus, a nobleman, a bishop, a draper, and a mercer would buy a cask of wine pretty much as a vintner or taverner would. The poor man would still have to patronize the retailer. There were reasons other than legal, however, why the sedentary merchant engaged in retailing. He found that he often could profitably dispose of his imports to consumers in a store of his own. Moreover, he found that this was necessary in case he had goods left over, which he could not sell to the specialized retailers of his own town. In addition, he often found that a retail store helped him accumulate products for export—products of the district in which he lived which he could buy through the same retail organization as he used to sell his wares. This was particularly the case in smaller towns and seaports where trade with countrymen was essentially a matter of money-barter, that is, the exchange of goods for goods in terms of money but without the actual use of money.

A fourth economic function was transportation. The sedentary merchant might own one ship or scores of ships. He might own outright or just a share, for instance, one-sixteenth or two-sixteenths. In case of the ownership of only a small share, the merchant in question might have general control of the ship; or such control might be vested in the captain, if he owned a share. The merchant might not be much interested in transportation but he was anxious to secure cargo space so that his shipments would not be delayed. Often he or his factor would have to hurry around to find another merchant to take up vacant cargo space in his ship. Or, he might instruct his captain or supercargo to sell his ship at the other end of the voyage. We do not know what responsibilities for the men he assumed in case of such a sale. Of course there were some merchants like William Canynges, of Bristol, in the fifteenth century and William Gray, of Salem and Boston, in the early nineteenth who never seemed to have too many ships. In short, some sedentary merchants were skillful not only in using their ships themselves but also in getting freight to carry. Here is an adumbration of the large-scale common carrier.

A fifth function was storage. Even the traveling merchant had a warehouse. It remained for the sedentary merchant to develop the function of storage not only for himself but for those who wished to hire space. Here was a development in common warehousing. Storage has a long history but it awaits a chronicler. Often the merchant's warehouse was part of his dwelling; just as often it was on his dock or on a rented wharf. At any rate, it was used in part to facilitate wholesaling, for instance, in the display and inspection of the goods as well as in storage and breaking bulk.

Closely related to transportation was a sixth function—communication. The sedentary merchant was a great letter writer. He had to send instructions to his agents in many parts. After these agents had left the home port, they were supposed to write to the merchant who sent them out and he in turn found it necessary to change instructions or wanted to impart fresh information as to events at home. Of course, the agents abroad were constantly writing to headquarters. The chief means of communication was by ship captains who took bundles of letters from their masters and from other merchants. By the eighteenth century at least, some captains, doubtless acting under instructions from the merchant, would not accept letters unless the same were left open for them to read. Customers and friends used the merchant's mail bag as their means of sending letters to distant points.

A seventh set of activities may be grouped as banking. As the sedentary merchant gradually gave up sending his agents to fairs to liquidate bills of exchange, he must, of course, pay the bills drawn against him at home. In his counting-house he not only paid bills of exchange drawn upon him but wrote others for his own trade and for customers and friends who wished to carry funds in this manner. In his counting-house he was his own money-changer. His strong box held coins of many nations, not only his own coins but those of his friends and neighbors who left their money with him for investment or just for safe-keeping. Thus did deposits come, and beyond this did they grow, as we shall see. The issuance of circulating notes against these deposits was an easy step. Banking was being born.

Pawnbroking was a function performed by some sedentary merchants where the laws permitted. In the thirteenth and fourteenth centuries Italian merchants, also called "Lombards," not only carried on trade in English and other towns but loaned money on pawns. The borrowers were bishops, lay nobles, princes, and others. Jewels were the common pledges put up. The rates were high and the complaints loud. It is said that the symbol used on the stores of some of these merchant-pawnbrokers was three golden bezants on a dark background and that this finally became three golden balls. In time, this came to be accepted as the traditional sign of pawnbrokers' "shops," including those of petty capitalistic Jews, and is still used in England, the United States, and Canada. First in Italy, in the fifteenth century, and later elsewhere, charitable pawnbroking establishments, often municipal, were set up especially to aid the poorer people in the community. From the private business point of view the chief interest in pawnbroking lies simply in the flow of capital into consumptive channels.

Insurance was the ninth function. When a merchant wanted someone to help him bear a risk, he might take a temporary partner in the venture. Increasingly, it would seem, the merchant made use of mutual marine insurance in his business. This began not later than the fourteenth century, probably in Italy, and may be an innovation of the sedentary merchant class. The method was for a merchant planning a venture to let it be known among his fellow merchants that he would welcome their participation in underwriting insurance to the extent of £100 or £500, as the case might be. Perhaps five would come into his counting-house and write down their names at the foot of a policy, each for so much money. I have seen policies in New England that insured molasses in terms of molasses, that is, guaranteed to provide 1,000 or 2,000 gallons of molasses if the ship was lost. By the sixteenth and seventeenth centuries brokers of insurance kept the books for many merchants' policies, found underwriters, paid premiums, and collected the principal in case of losses, all for a commission fee. In Boston in the eighteenth century there was a tendency for the merchants to be grouped around two or three insurance brokers and to insure all acceptable risks not just for mutual benefit but for the premiums. Of course, specialized marine insurance was under way also, reaching its greatest height in Lloyd's association which in the eighteenth century attained a strong feeling of group consciousness though it did not incorporate till 1870. Early in the eighteenth century marine insurance began to be written by incorporated companies in London. But, before such efforts as these, the merchants themselves had devised and carried through a system of mutual insurance.

Even now we have not exhausted the functions performed by the sedentary merchant. Whereas he managed the functions already listed, he chiefly controlled those that follow. Instead of waiting for manufactured goods, fish, minerals, furs, and lumber to come to him, the sedentary merchant undertook to arrange for their production. A somewhat more remote business activity he promoted when he helped finance expeditions of exploration and discovery. Later, he aided in colonization but on a commercial or profit basis in most instances.

A further function lay in investment in commercial companies, incorporated, and in lands. The sedentary merchant might or might not be interested in the management of these concerns. In case he bought a manor, he might carry on cultivation of the home farm through a bailiff or he might lease the land to a farmer. In case he cultivated the land through a bailiff, his influence and control extended to the tenants of the manor who owed him service.

Before the sedentary merchant could function, he had to build up an organization of a few employees in his counting-house and many more agents in various parts of the world. The employees of a sizable firm were an accountant, a cashier, and a clerk. The agents were of various kinds. First, there were the merchant's own agents. The supercargo was the most elemental of these. In lieu of a supercargo the agent might require that the captain, aided by a clerk, should do the work of the supercargo. This, however, was generally ill-advised, for the navigation of a ship and buying and selling required separate abilities.

Other agents of the merchant were resident abroad either living singly or collectively in the factory of some regulated company. The topmost factor might be such a one as Pegolotti who was entrusted by the company of the Bardi with most important commissions. During four years he was the director of the Bardi branch in London where he carried on trade and made loans to both king and nobles—a true Lombard on Lombard Street. Pegolotti's great distinction was not only to have been a clever well-paid factor but to have written a considerable treatise on mercantile affairs about the year 1340. As we have seen, the sedentary merchant might employ other merchants to act as factors in selling goods sent to them on consignment or to buy goods according to orders given to them. Their commission fee was commonly about five per cent.

All these factors were commercial. There were others who got certain things made or otherwise produced. The most notable examples of this in the Middle Ages were factors who were employed in putting out wool for spinning, yarn for weaving, and cloth in the gray for dyeing and finishing.

As to the actual day-to-day management of the business of the sedentary merchant, only a few points can be made here. The merchant wrote out elaborate instructions for his captains and supercargoes and then told them to do whatever they found best, if circumstances changed. This was wise because, during a few weeks, and much more during a voyage of two or three years in later centuries, conditions might change radically and old plans be ineffective. Before instructions could be given, news had to be gathered at the docks, at the exchanges, at the inns or coffee houses or through correspondence and the reports of returning captains and supercargoes. This news had to be digested and policies of action formulated. In busy seasons the merchant worked late at night and began early in the morning. He personally or through partners did all the office work with the help of one or more of the employees named—accountant, cashier, and clerk. Increasingly, it was necessary to get far behind the mere buying of goods for sale by seeing to it that certain workers

—commonly small masters—made wares needed for distant markets. I wish we had more information about this. From the fourteenth century to the early nineteenth I conceive it to have been one of the important duties of the sedentary merchant to learn what the market abroad required and then to try to have the commodities in demand produced at home. Often this involved changing the quality of work and the design of the commodity used locally. This was hard work and required real management. In the seventeenth century it was absurd to send cloth, clothing, and shoes that Englishmen made for themselves to be used by slaves in Virginia. Another comparable problem was to force the home workers to produce on time for the sailing of the ships. Many a merchant must have wished he could drive the scattered small masters of the towns and villages to work in a central workshop where they would be forced to produce goods when and as they were required. That was precisely one of the events that happened.

3. PARTNERSHIP FLOURISHES

We recall the traveling merchant's partnerships. They were on the basis of a single voyage, though occasionally they might run over a period of from three to five years before being terminated. The accommodation form of partnership was the highest that the traveling merchant knew. Under this form any number of investors might contribute money or goods—the whole amount of each venture—and receive one-quarter of the profits. The active merchant managed the transactions and received three-quarters of the profits. The active merchant also had ventures which were exclusively his own.

The sedentary merchant was doubtless much influenced by prevailing partnership customs of the traveling merchants but in time he developed his own practices. He made up his trading venture with route, season, destination, ship, captain, and supercargo in mind. Then he might take the whole risk himself or might take in partners for $\frac{1}{16}$th, $\frac{1}{8}$th, $\frac{1}{4}$th, and so on. Just what determined the number of shares he would offer to others would depend upon a variety of personal and general conditions. That he could not be wholly selfish in the matter is clear enough; that is, he could not take the whole risk when trade conditions were promising and find merchants to join him when conditions were unfavorable. There was a certain amount of mutuality in these ventures that baffles precise analysis. We might almost speak of coöperative trading companies on a one-venture basis. In this connection we should also think about the mutual marine underwriting that was done by sedentary merchants. It is a plausible surmise that there were some extremely individualistic merchants who plowed lone furrows through the ocean of traffic and trade while the rank and file preferred to work in groups both in underwriting insurance and in forming temporary partnerships.

Like the traveling merchant, the sedentary merchant might own ships jointly with others. The more successful sedentary merchants owned their ships outright and owned many of them, large and small. Indeed, it is at the time when the rich sedentary merchant was the dominant factor in shipping that most progress was made in early modern ship-construction, particularly from the sixteenth century onward in Western Europe. This was essentially the wholesale handicraft system in its dependent phase. This was probably because the merchant took his requirements to the ship-builder and insisted that they be met—requirements that involved economy of operation and safety of cargo. Ships grew in size, in the number of decks used, and in the equipment used. Freight was the main consideration, but passengers were taken, and by the middle of the eighteenth century even transatlantic sailing vessels approximated some regularity of accommodation, for instance, from Rotterdam to Philadelphia, stopping at some English port such as Cowes or Southampton on the way. Not only that, but the money was advanced to some of the passengers to pay their way across, for which the merchant owner of the ship was compensated by selling the services of the passenger for a period of years after

PARTNERSHIP FLOURISHES

arrival in America. In such cases the captain of the vessel, perhaps aided by a clerk, could do the work of the supercargo.

If we were writing a history of ship-building, especially in the early modern period, we should have to include the work and influence of at least two groups besides the sedentary merchants. Certainly the developing ship-building entrepreneurs —individuals and partners—built ships for sale or for charter to the merchants and also for sale to the various governments interested. From earliest times, governments have played an important part in the improvement of ship-construction in their endeavor to conquer their neighbor or to prevent him from conquering them. While governments have wanted to carry many persons (sailors and soldiers), sedentary merchants have been anxious to transport the greatest amount of freight. The ship-building entrepreneurs have catered to the needs of both.

The chief interest in partnerships which the sedentary merchant has for us lies not in the one-venture partnerships nor in the joint ownership of vessels but in the terminal general partnerships. These commonly ran for one, three, or five years. The outstanding examples are the partnerships of two or three members of the same family getting together to carry on importation, exportation, and wholesaling, these primarily, with other functions in the background. The senior partner would contribute most of the capital and also most of the formulation of policies. A junior partner might also contribute capital. The operating partner would contribute largely or only his managerial ability and his energy. A double-entry system of bookkeeping would be employed. The junior partner might be the cashier of the partnership. At the end of the partnership a balance sheet would be drawn up and an inventory prepared. Then the assets would be divided. Often the articles of partnership would state not only what percentage of the profits each partner should receive but what proportion of the assets on dissolution. In the case of the Medici family we have scores of examples of such partnerships in existing records. The Fuggers found it convenient to use the partnership form of combining business men into one unit particularly because they had so many branch houses all the way from Naples to Bruges. As far as possible, there was a real point in having a kinsman in a distant office or branch, for, whether he was able or not, at least he could be trusted.

In order to carry on the retail trade a sedentary merchant often took a junior partner. It was doubtless found better to employ a man with greater interest than a mere store assistant would have, particularly in view of the fact that the one in charge of the store would be so much on his own in selling goods and in many cases in taking wares in exchange. Chain stores in our day sometimes give a share in the business to their branch managers.

In order to get control of manufacturing it was found effective by the Medici in the fifteenth and sixteenth centuries to take a partner who would manage the production of goods, for instance, give out wool to be spun and yarn to be woven. Wage books would be kept and also commodity accounts prepared. It is probable that this form of partnership was generally entered into with someone outside the family, someone who knew the industry well.

Complicated arrangements were made in case of the fishing industry. For instance, Samuel Sewell, of Boston, owned a share in a fishing boat and extended a line of credit to enable the fishermen to buy at his store hooks, lines, nets, rum, salt, and so on. The fishermen promised to sell to him all their "merchantable" fish and oil. Doubtless in these fishing partnerships, as probably in those for mining and lumbering, the partnership was not confined to members of the same family.

In general, we may say, by way of conclusion, that the whole partnership system was most flexible. The strong sedentary merchant could enter into partnerships very easily to suit his convenience and without great risk to himself, because they lasted for but a voyage, a season, or a term of a few years. Terminal partnership reached the place where it was substantially an opportunity for an investment by a senior partner of wealth and experience and for a salary by an able and active junior or executive partner. Incorporation was unthought of and would have had no value. One-venture partnerships had offered divisible and transferable shares to the partners but the period in question was too short to lead to any development of promise in business.

The study of early terminal partnerships points to the special position occupied by the senior partner—the owner of capital, the possessor of administrative abilities, and the recipient of widespread public confidence. His position of growing dominance in commerce and finance was cut short by the change in world trade following oversea discoveries and colonization. His type was to attain success only in the financial capitalism of the late nineteenth and early twentieth centuries.

4. THE FLOW OF CAPITAL

Capital is created, preserved, and put to use largely by business men. The coarse clay of the soil and the fine clay of men are molded to the purposes of creation and accumulation. This capital is directed to flow into one channel or another. Here it proves to be a profitable channel, there it is lost in a sieve or a sink. Gain or loss, the process goes on. Rarely quiescent for long, capital is induced again to do its work—induced by those who expect an income from it. Just whose capital is being used is of less importance to the business man than whether a net income or profit results. To society the profit is of equal importance in the long run and the source of flow of the capital is important for society at every turn.

In tracing the genesis of the flow of capital we should consider three stages. First, there is the usucapital system wherein capital, to produce an income, must be used by the possessor or owner. This is the oldest system and it is still of major importance, though it is threatened in part by socialistic and communistic schemes. Second, there is the direct putting-out system wherein the possessor or owner may derive an income from his capital by putting it out to someone who will use it for him. Third, there is the indirect putting out system wherein the possessor or owner of capital entrusts his capital to an intermediary, a money middleman, commonly a banker or bank, which in turn puts the money out to the user, directly or indirectly. There are ramifications to this system of the deepest business and social import, as we shall see later.

The mercantile capitalist, that is, the sedentary merchant, played an important part in using the first system, in expanding the second, and in creating the third. The sedentary merchant did business primarily on his own inherited or accumulated capital. Losses were frequent and large, and few there were who amassed great fortunes. As usual, society was the chief beneficiary of the efforts of the business man. This self-evident truth will be generally understood by few, for our ability to learn from observation and experience is clouded by idealistic philosophies that began before Plato and will continue after Trotsky.

The sedentary merchant put out capital directly to form partnerships with other merchants. Merchants and others put out money for him to use under partnership arrangement. But so had the traveling merchants. The sedentary merchant's contribution to the direct putting-out system of capital lay at several points and these we may deal with exclusively. Capital was put out directly to form terminal partnerships, as we have already noted, and capital was invested in joint stock companies for which the sedentary merchants were responsible, as we shall see later. We may seem to be making too much of partnership but the importance of that form of business organization for the late Middle Ages and early modern period is hard to overemphasize. Many economic historians hardly mention it.

Productive loans were made to individuals as in the stage of petty capitalism. Terminal partners were recipients of loans for the first time in the stage of mercantile capitalism, as were joint stock companies. When a joint stock company had exhausted its capital, as was the case with the Virginia Company, it was necessary for the treasurer to secure loans for the carrying on of further trade and colonization.

We cannot stop to consider at great length the individuals who loaned the capital. Clearly there was a great variety. Among them must be listed merchants (active and retired), widows and orphans, gilds, and banks loaning their own capital (rather than deposits).

In the indirect putting-out system there was a money middleman who stood between the owner and the user of the capital. The two outstanding examples in mercantile capitalism are, first, the sedentary merchant who became a merchant banker like the Peruzzi and the Bardi of Florence, the Fuggers of Augsburg, and the goldsmiths of London, and, second, the commercial banks doing a deposit and loan business, such as the Bank of St. George in Genoa, the Bank of England, and the Bank of North America in Philadelphia. We shall consider both types separately, noting that they are creations of sedentary merchants and well integrated with the business which these merchants carried on.

We may note certain results arising in these developments in the systems of capital flow. Clearly, more people were getting incomes than would otherwise have been the case. Widows, for instance, and especially orphans, could not ordinarily use their capital, but they could put it out. Also, individuals with a leaning toward art, letters, and philosophy could invest inherited or earned capital. The perfection of a means of getting an income from capital induced more people to accumulate and to save because of the advantages involved. The coming of a class of money middlemen who could safely be trusted to handle funds engendered greater certainty in loans. One result of this was a tendency toward a lower rate of interest. In the fourteenth century in Western Europe the rate had been about 15 per cent for productive loans, in the fifteenth century about 10 per cent, in the sixteenth century about 8 per cent, and in the seventeenth century about 6 per cent. For the sedentary merchant the new mechanisms for making easier the flow of capital meant greater opportunity for profit or loss, according to circumstances, and certainly greater flexibility.

Although the sedentary merchants played a strategic part in developing new methods of making capital flow, still much was left for later business men and others to do. The new systems that were devised we shall study in the chapters on Financial Capitalism and National Capitalism.

5. CONTROL

A dear old professor of English leaned across the table at an unimportant meeting of a committee to ask the writer what is meant by that word "control." "I hear people using it," he said, "and I never know what it means." Being interested in the drama, he should have known, for he constantly sees the dramatist controlling his puppets or his actors.

In pre-business capitalism the individual experienced a good deal of control, except in collectional economy. He was controlled by the patriarchal family, by the village coöperative group, and finally by the manorial lord. When he broke loose and joined a robber band or viking group, he was controlled by a personal leader. In business capitalism, control shifted to other channels. In petty capitalism, it was at a minimum. It was notable in the regulation of affairs by gilds, that is, by the producing group. The rank and file felt but little restraint though ambitious able leaders of great energy doubtless felt that business had few satisfactions for them. Of course, there was a measure of Church control in business, as we have observed. There also was the "law merchant," a mercantile law which imposed on each the customs sanctioned by all. The town government and the incipient national government passed new regulations and these presented an element of control.

It was in mercantile capitalism that control in the potent but subtle sense of private compulsion was born into business capitalism. Now and henceforth the possessor of capital in large amounts and the administrator of ability could put pressure upon an increasing number of his fellow beings. A new influence, a potent force for good or evil, was born into the world.

In contemplating the system of control set up by the sedentary merchant over various groups of his fellow men, we must not think that he was himself free from the system. Like the owner of slaves and serfs he had to play the game of compulsion. This always works both ways. The owner or administrator becomes part of the discipline he imposes on other persons. The sedentary merchant was lord of a business system but servant of a nexus of his own creation. He had responsibilities and ran risks. His head was never free to lie on a bed of ease with untroubled thoughts. He could not freely retire from business because his business had got the better of him, as Jacob Fugger found. We do not pity him, for he had satisfactions for the enjoyment of which a law of nature says he must pay a price.

We can gain not a little insight into the meaning of control by noting some of the chief examples. First, the sedentary merchant controlled his own employees including those in his office, warehouse, retail store, ships, and landed estates. This type of situation was, of course, very old. Only rich merchants would employ very many men—such as usher, information clerk, porters, packers, weighers, accountants and assistants, clerks, cashier and assistants, interpreter, captains, sailors, and so on. In this group should be included one or two apprentices accepted by the merchant only on the payment of a fat fee. Second, there were factors, both traveling and resident abroad, who commonly received a fee rather than a wage. This was a new situation. The control of those resident abroad often came under the regulated companies of which the sedentary merchants were members. In such cases, elaborate regulations were made, in some instances the factors being kept from marrying and being forced to be inside at nights by a certain hour, and so on. Third, the junior partners were under the control of senior partners; even though the junior partners might have some independence in management, the policies were formulated by the senior partners. Fourth, there was a measure of control which one merchant had over another in the business of mutual insurance, as we have seen. Fifth, the handicraftsmen of the dependent wholesale system came under the control of the sedentary merchant in a variety of ways, but notably in the quality of the goods made, the styles used, and the time of

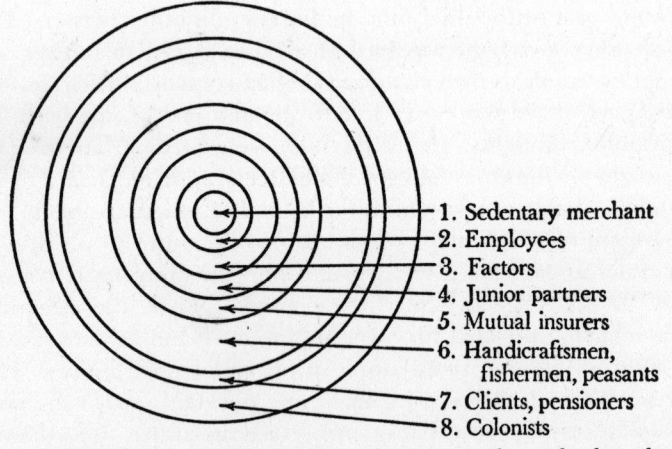

1. Sedentary merchant
2. Employees
3. Factors
4. Junior partners
5. Mutual insurers
6. Handicraftsmen, fishermen, peasants
7. Clients, pensioners
8. Colonists

Note: The farther away from the sedentary merchant the less the control exercised by that merchant.

GROUPS CONTROLLED BY THE SEDENTARY MERCHANT

completion of the articles in question. Sixth, the sedentary merchants of wealth had clients or pensioners who were given *largesse* that they might write, paint, carve, and so on, or that they might travel to unknown parts to discover new channels of shipping and new markets for goods. It would be interesting to study the sources of support which the navigators and explorers had during the period of the late fifteenth to the late eighteenth century. Sir Thomas Smythe would be an example of a sedentary merchant in London who more than did his share in promoting new routes and new trades. Seventh, there was

APPRENTICES LEARNING ARITHMETIC,
NÜRNBERG, 1518

control over colonists sent out by trading companies managed by sedentary merchants. In these cases the persons controlled could fairly easily shake off the control because they were aided by distance and natural conditions. Part of the history of colonies lies in the effort to get free from mercantile capitalists.

The power of the mercantile capitalists lay partly in their capital accumulations but more especially in their administrative ability. Many are the scholars and social reconstructionists who treat such a statement cynically. Just a little examination of facts, however, indicates that economic power under the circumstances we are considering went to those who in the long run had ability and character. Wealth was more of a result than a factor.

The instruments of control in the hands of the sedentary merchant were first his own eyes and direct supervision. Second, he had servants and agents who did his bidding. Third, he got information in various ways, particularly through correspondence. Fourth, he developed an effective system of double-entry bookkeeping. Whether this was the work of the merchants of Genoa or the City of Genoa which used it before 1340, is not clear. Probably it was the merchants, for instance those in the group that founded the Bank of St. George which had larger projects at hand, that were the innovators.

The significance of this control of men by sedentary merchants is far-reaching. More intelligent direction was given to the work if not the life of many a man. There was some evil in this but probably much more good. Challenge and disprove this if you will. Natural man dislikes control and resists it in his own ways. He wants to go fishing, or would like to disport himself on a feast day; he resents being driven to continuous work by the industrial factor of a sedentary merchant even if it is to produce goods in Durham which must catch the summer ships if they are to be sold for use in Virginia. No matter what our opinion of the merits of the situation may be, at least we have to see that this kind of control has helped lay the economic foundation for social unrest and social agitation.

Through such control as we have dealt with, the sedentary merchant and many of his successors have really created work for reformers. This is a class that mankind always has in plenty: it must not be left with nothing to do. Pre-business capitalism created conditions that needed reform; so did private-business capitalism; and so would public-business capitalism; in fact, it has done so in Russia.

The principle became well established that "he who will not work, shall not eat." This goes back to the very beginning of group life. Its origin antedates business capitalism by thousands of years. All that the sedentary merchant did was to establish the custom that all persons who do not or will not play the game of business or who will not coöperate with business men to produce an income, shall be neglected or pushed out of the group as drones, criminals, or otherwise useless and harmful members of the group. The great crime was fundamentally non-coöperation. Society breeds the type with great ease and the individuals of the type devise ideologies to defend their case. Unfortunately, there are many abuses in every business system that lend credence to wholesale denunciations and schemes for revolutionary changes. The task of the student, the thinker, and the citizen is to distinguish between the use and the abuse of each system. This is an old formula more honored in the breach than in the observance.

6. THE MERCANTILE CAPITALIST AND INDUSTRY

In the manufacture that followed petty capitalism, there were industrial capitalists on a small scale but there was no system of industrial capitalism. Even the cloth industry of the late Middle Ages and the early modern period was subordinate to mercantile capitalists. True, there was to come a system of industrial capitalism in the late eighteenth and early nineteenth centuries, but that is far ahead of our story.

It will be our task here to show the different kinds of relationship that existed between the sedentary merchant and those who were concerned with manufacture. In tracing this relationship we shall see that the sedentary merchant was *generally* the dynamic factor: he was the hammer, while the others were the anvil. The products hammered out constituted the social justification. *At other times,* and less often, the sedentary merchant trailed behind and merely sought to profit where he could not lead. Right at the beginning we should note a major point: the sedentary merchant was far removed from mechanical things. He was an office man, a manager of industrial processes only by remote control. His strength lay in his knowledge of consuming and producing markets. In this commercial field he was a dynamic factor, but apart from this he could make but little headway. What his industrial relations were we shall now see.

For the purpose of clear exposition let us note what the framework of industrial development was.

Stages in Industry or Manufacture

1. Usufacture (chiefly in the home for home use)
2. Retail handicraft (in early town economy)
   a. Order phase
   b. Chance-sale phase
3. Wholesale handicraft (in later town and early metropolitan economy)
   a. Independent phase
   b. Dependent phase
4. Centralized manufacture (in metropolitan economy)
   a. Central workshop
   b. Factory

When the retail handicraftsman turned to make goods for chance sale to consumers and to traveling merchants, he was driving a wedge into his business that was changing the very nature of it—from a retail handicraft industry to a wholesale handicraft. Perhaps we should say that it was the traveling merchant that was driving the wedge and that, as the sedentary merchant followed his practice of buying manufactured wares from the handicraftsman, he was widening the crack. The wholesale handicraftsman retained the economic independence that he had originally possessed as a retail handicraftsman: he might buy from anyone and sell to anyone. In many towns an increasing number of handicraftsmen had to rely upon raw products brought in by the traveling merchant and then by the sedentary merchant; for instance, in London in the case of workers in iron, pewter, and wool. As the trade of the town grew, dependence on ever wider markets increased, that is, dependence on the merchants.

As the small masters of the town—the handicraftsmen of the wholesale stage—came to sell more and more to the sedentary merchants, we wonder whether they began to fear the new position they were coming to occupy. Later, they were to be very conscious of the danger of their position. At first, however, the chief cloud on the horizon was that the wholesale merchants were tending to patronize the country masters, those just learning to devote much time to manufacture. We should recall that the cultivator of the soil is normally a manufacturer of many goods and rather skilled in the production of a few wares. Here was a fruitful field for the sedentary merchant to draw upon, and many goods did he buy up for sale at a distance—goods produced by small masters working in their own homes or shops in town or country.

The haberdashers of London present a rather interesting case that parallels the development just indicated. Originally they were retailers and got their supply of goods from artisans in their own locality—such wares as hats, girdles, purses, bows, arrows, chains, and the like. Increasingly they came to buy from merchants, bringing in from foreign lands trinkets, novelties, and miscellaneous wares, such as mercers and grocers had sometimes handled. At the same time, they began to grow into sedentary merchants themselves, trading in distant parts and wholesaling locally. They were merely going through at a late date the processes which the mercers, grocers, drapers, ironmongers and others had gone through at an earlier time. Like the others the haberdashers made over their craft gild into a livery company.

The problem of the sedentary merchant was not only to sell his goods at a remunerative price but to buy them well made and at a low cost in the first instance. Times then were very different from the present, for there was no automatic machine that could be set to work and no three-shift day, in fact very little division of labor and almost no discipline in manufacture. In solving the problem of the supply of manufactured wares the sedentary merchant had two principal alternatives. He might send a servant or a factor out to buy for him goods already made up, or he might encourage independent industrial entrepreneurs to procure the goods for him. The latter proved to be a very satisfactory arrangement.

The case of Thomas Paycocke (died 1518), of Coggeshall, Essex, illustrates the type of industrial entrepreneur that arose to meet the sedentary merchant's needs. For a study of this clothier's business we have his old homestead surviving in fair condition, a brass plate to his memory in the village church, and his last will and testament. A few points are clear. Paycocke employed a number of workers in his neighborhood and his relations with them were smilingly friendly. He seems to have given out wool to be combed, carded, and spun into yarn, doubtless largely by women and children. The yarn he then gave out to weavers who worked in their own homes and probably got a good deal of their living from their garden, cow, and chickens. The cloth in the gray, that is, unfinished cloth, was put out to a fuller, and finally to a dyer. The last processes of pressing, inspecting, and packing were carried on in Paycocke's own large home. How many processes were carried on right under the one roof and in sheds is not clear. Often, in similar cases, weaving, fulling, and dyeing were done on the clothier's own premises. Clearly, Paycocke was not in a mature stage of the development he illustrates and he was not so full of ambition as many clothiers proved to be. At any rate, the bolts of cloth were finally ready and were duly carted off to London for sale to the sedentary merchant. The sedentary merchant, called a draper, might sell the cloth to a consumer in his retail store or he might sell it at wholesale to a tailor of London or export it to another English town or abroad. If he was a member of the Merchant Adventurers' Company, the cloth would go to the Low Countries where the Company had a staple or factory or, if we wish, a Company warehouse.

Now, let us note in passing that Thomas Paycocke, with good humor and tact, was reducing the small peasant masters of his village to the position of dependent wholesale handicraftsmen. He was supplying them with the goods they worked on, he was paying them a piece wage, and he was coming more and more to be their sole means of industrial support. Here was a little industrial control system growing up afresh in answer to the developing needs of the sedentary merchant and the widening market which he was creating.

But here is another development which the sedentary merchant was himself *directly* responsible for. In many areas and in many industries, but notably in the woolen cloth industry, he was reducing the small independent master to a position of dependence. This was happening in both town and country. In Italy and Flanders it was in the thirteenth century, in England in the fourteenth, fifteenth, and sixteenth centuries, and in America in the seventeenth, eighteenth, and early nineteenth centuries. The town was harder to handle than the country, for the town masters had gilds to help and they were able to get together. We have seen the struggle against the saddlers. But one group could be played against the other and the result was finally the same in town as in the country. The small masters went down together. This was serious for both groups, but the country masters were deeply disturbed and in many instances completely uprooted where they lost their little holdings of land through inclosure or their chance to work in the fields in season or their right to pasture a cow in the common pastures. We may weep at their misfortunes but we should recognize that it is of such stuff that social progress is made.

The sedentary merchant might be content to reduce hitherto independent masters to dependence upon himself. On the other hand, he might go far beyond this and establish a central workshop for a few industrial processes. The Medici accounts of the fifteenth and sixteenth centuries illustrate this development in Florence. At this point let us consider an even earlier example —Jehan Boinebroke.

Jehan Boinebroke was a sedentary merchant who flourished in Douai at the end of the thirteenth century. His chief business lay in importing English wool, having it made up into cloth, and exporting it abroad. How much trade he carried on apart from wool, dyes, alum, and the finished cloth, is not clear. Since he seems to have sent his cloth long distances, for instance, for sale at the fairs of Champagne (whence it was shipped even farther probably to such Italian towns as Genoa and Florence), we may infer that he was primarily a merchant. On the other hand, the kind of information which has survived emphasizes the manufacture of cloth: this information arises out of testamentary claims brought by many small industrial masters and others after his death about the year 1286. From his central warehouse he apparently sent out wool to be washed, spun, and woven into cloth. The small masters who did this work came to be hopelessly dependent upon him, for he provided them with tools and machines such as looms, he owned their homes, and he gave them jobs which provided an income. To some he had loaned money, exacting apparently a promise that they would work for him alone. He did not hesitate to pay wages in truck—either in wool or cloth—when trade was not brisk. Perhaps we should point out that the evidence surviving is by its very nature damaging to Boinebroke. Claimants appeared on his death like buzzards over a corpse. Although valuable when used with care, the depositions are no more credible than a partisan government report.

These small industrial masters themselves might employ journeymen—a relic of the days of their independence. How far their misfortune came from their own incompetence, how far from the grasping character of Boinebroke, and how far simply from the competitive situation of the time is not clear. The most probable explanation is that all three conditions were required to produce the result of helpless dependence. Perhaps if Boinebroke had not organized the cloth industry and trade on this basis and paid low wages, he could not have competed with other merchants at home or abroad; and perhaps Douai could not have competed with rural English industry or the urban industry of Florence on any other basis; and perhaps without this organization Douai would have again become a village and the artisans at best but cottagers working on the land of others. It should be noted, however, that in Douai there were no gilds to protect the small masters and that Boinebroke was a magistrate who sided with the patrician class to which he himself belonged. What distinguishes Boinebroke's type is that he not only subordinated small masters to himself but carried on part of the work in his central workshop. Just how much work was done there and by how many employees, is not clear. Probably the cloth was dyed, stretched, sheared, fulled, and finished in one or two central shops, under the discipline and division of labor arranged by Boinebroke.

Boinebroke is an example of a type of sedentary merchant described below (on p. 166) as "later mature." That maturity, however, was early attained because Flemish industry was very advanced. Living in an inland town situated on an unimportant river, he possessed no ships. Clearly, his factors arranged for carriage, by land and sea, as it was required. This points to a certain amount of specialization in common carriage, both by wagon (or horse-pack) and by ship, a situation which we also know from other sources existed.

As a magistrate, Boinebroke had helped put down a revolt of workers in Douai in 1280. At his death he was hated. After his death (in 1311) his two sons, seeking safety in flight, were banished from Douai. The degree of social justice involved in this action, we shall probably never know.

A further type of relationship of the sedentary merchant to

MERCANTILE CAPITALIST AND INDUSTRY

industry is found in the merchant's purchase of the output of a larger independent industrial entrepreneur who has gone far beyond Thomas Paycocke and driven his workers into a central workshop to labor under discipline and under a system of division of labor. I do not refer to the Boinebroke type which combined the dependent system of wholesale handicraft with the central workshop but to the specialized industrial entrepreneur who carried on all or most of the processes of manufacture under one establishment and sold his output to sedentary merchants. The London merchants buying cloth from John Winchcombe, the owner and operator of a central workshop up to his death in 1519, illustrate this type.

We may briefly note the Winchcombe example. Unfortunately the facts are mixed with romance and only the underlying situation is to be accepted whole cloth. John Winchcombe, the rich and successful clothier of Newbury near London, was noted for having married a girl for her intrinsic merits rather than for her father's wealth and for the large central workshop which he operated. It is the latter situation to which we forcibly address our interest.

In this much referred to example of a central workshop, often wrongly called a factory, we find an amazing array of workers and equipment, all for the production of woolen cloth. Although the facts given about the central workshop are in ostensibly poetic form, we may prosaically list the statistical details as follows:

Class of Workers	Numbers	
Pickers of wool	150	children
Carders	100	women
Rovers	80	
Spinners	200	maidens
Weavers	200	men
	100	boys
Shearmen	50	men
Dyers	40	men
Fullers	20	men
Total	940	

It is nothing to us that this clothier of Newbury had a gigantic household and entertained lavishly, but it is significant that he was an employer on a large scale and turned out a great amount of cloth for merchants to handle. Whether his contemporaries More, Erasmus, Luther, or Columbus ever heard of him, would be as interesting a question as whether he ever heard of them. That Thomas Paycocke and the Cabots, who sailed from Bristol to explore America, and Jacob Fugger knew about him is quite likely.

Another extraordinary industrial entrepreneur—prototype of the industrial capitalist—was Sir Ambrose Crowley (1659–1713) and, we may add, his son John Crowley. Sir Ambrose was born the son of a blacksmith and may himself have been a blacksmith for a short time. Then, about 1682, we find him an ironmonger in Durham County, North England. Soon thereafter he was operating an ironworks in Sunderland. By 1688 he had his main office in London and his "factory" in Sunderland. He was then advertising for Belgian ironworkers. By 1690 he had two plants on the River Derwent, near Newcastle. In one he made heavy iron wares and in the other (consisting of two mills) he did the lighter work such as slitting iron and making files. In all, the firm came to employ 9 water wheels and, at his height, perhaps 1,500 men. The small master artisans who had been induced to come in from various parts of England and from Belgium had their own houses and shops—many ranged round "The Square"—for which they paid a small rent. In their shops they had their own tools and employed their own workmen. From the Crowley firm these small masters received iron to be fashioned as specified—nails, hoes, shovels, latches, bolts, bits, hoops, and the like. There seems to have been a clear-cut division between the heavy work performed by water wheels, for instance, in operating forge hammers and shears, and the lighter handwork of the small master artisans. The Crowley concern looks like a transition from the early wholesale handicraft system to the factory.

Crowley did not smelt iron and probably did not do all his

forging from pig iron. He and his son made hardware out of English, Swedish, and American iron. They probably had ships to carry it to London where it was sold to sedentary merchants for use in England and increasingly in the colonies.

Success came to Crowley in business and in the official life of the metropolis. He was a member of the Drapers' Company, not the Ironmongers' Company for reasons of no import, for the companies had been largely divorced from their industries. He was elected alderman and sheriff and was knighted. He was also elected as a member of Parliament and would have been Lord Mayor of London, had he not died so young. He was worth £100,000 at his death, part of his capital being invested in securities such as Treasury tallies to the extent of £8,000 and South Sea Company stock to the amount of £16,000.

Joseph Addison, the essayist and poet, undertook to satirize Crowley. Perhaps he had been reading Petronius' satire on the Roman merchant Trimalchio. However this may be, in doing so, Addison was calling attention to his own incompetence in business and politics. Of no power himself, except with the pen, he could see no merit in those who could do what lay beyond his shy and unimpressive personality.

Some will find Crowley's title to remembrance in his social engineering—his fair treatment of his workers. In his own day and in his son's and indeed down to about 1843 there was a board of arbitration that met weekly to settle difficulties in the plant. It was made up of the chaplain, two representatives of the workers, and two of the management. It entertained complaints from either side. Hard were its problems in the face of poor work, theft of materials and tools, and drunkenness. In addition to this sharing of management, there was a system of pensions for workers and their widows, provision of medical care, and a system for loaning small sums of money to the workers when in need.

And what an array of managers and foremen had been provided to look after production, while the Crowleys themselves managed the marketing and financing in London! We learn in the Crowley Book of Rules about a treasurer, an accountant, a cashier, a toolkeeper, a coalkeeper, a doctor, a monitor, and a surveyor. The surveyor was charged with the duty of supervising the quality of the work done and of destroying bad products. The monitor had to check up on the use of time. The workers were employed eighty hours a week in the mills and the monitor had to see to it that none of these hours were wasted. To be sure, since payment was by piecework rather than by the hour, the monitor was serving the men as well as the firm.

As time went on, power machinery was installed in most parts of the central workshop in England, thereby creating the full-fledged factory in the modern sense. By the new technique masses of goods were turned out for merchants to handle, as their predecessors had for centuries longed to do. These goods were cheaper, more uniform, and, all in all, of much higher quality for the price than anything known before. Here was an opportunity for both the factory entrepreneur and the sedentary merchant. And so the silks of Lombe, the cottons of Arkwright, and the brass wares and steam engines of Boulton and Watt reached the expanding markets of England and the rest of the world.

The factory owner was in an advantageous position, even ahead of the clothiers who were employing dependent masters and those operating central workshops. He found that he could sell his output not only to sedentary merchants but through his own factors and through commission merchants. Many sedentary merchants saw the writing on the wall—saw that much of the cream was being skimmed off their business. In order to save themselves, some sedentary merchants turned to factory production. In America Almy and Brown, of Providence, sought some mechanic who knew the new technique. At last they found Slater and the result was a number of industrial partnerships and several cotton-spinning mills. On the other hand, some merchants became factory operators themselves. Patrick Tracy Jackson is a good example. He turned from trade with

India and elsewhere to setting up the Boston Manufacturing Company which operated at Waltham from 1814 to 1929 selling its output almost wholly through factors in New York. It is clear that another dynamic force had arrived—power machinery production—and that the old advantage of the sedentary merchant was receding. A new era was developing in the wake of the Industrial Revolution.

7. JOINT STOCK COMPANIES

Throughout the life of mercantile capitalism there were regulated companies to which the sedentary merchant might belong. If he joined such companies—the Flemish Hanse of London, the Staplers, the Merchant Adventurers, the Levant Company, and so on, he would trade as a private merchant but under the rules and protection of the company to which he belonged. Thus, as we have seen, the regulated company was like the merchant gild, the craft gild, and the livery company, and existed parallel to and contemporary with them all. While they were associations of business men trading locally, it was an association of merchants engaged in extended or foreign trade.

The greatest of these associations of merchants became a confederation of towns—the Hanseatic League. As early as the twelfth century, the merchants of Köln were given the privileges of a counter or factory in London. Gradually the merchants of other towns in North Germany were added. By the late fourteenth century this North German merchants' association had become a league of over seventy towns, with Lübeck at their head. They were so powerful that they could and did wage wars against their enemies and secured valuable commercial privileges abroad, particularly in London, Bruges, Bergen (Norway), and Novgorod (Russia). At first the unit of trade was the traveling merchant. Later, gradually, it came to be the sedentary merchant who sent to London and to other counters his factor or junior partner. Through such a person, he carried on trade in his own ships or in those that were from time to time available. The counters (for instance, the Steelyard in London) were made up of a group of men (generally young) with their officials and a group of buildings used for storing, weighing, and packing goods. It was Hans Holbein the Younger who painted in exquisite line and delicate color a number of the Steelyard merchants. George Gisze, whose portrait at the age of thirty-five is reproduced as a frontispiece to this book, is an example of the type of young German merchant (and official) of the London Steelyard of the League.

Here, in this Hanseatic League, business men made the biggest bid for power since the days of the Phoenicians. Their enemies were the growing national states, particularly England and Holland. Had they succeeded and been imitated elsewhere, we should have had an urban capitalistic system and a predominantly bourgeois civilization; we should have had a triumph of political economics over economic politics, an empire of sedentary merchants, an enthronement of mercantile capitalism. But instead of such victories we find defeat, loss of trading privileges, and slow extinction.

A very different kind of organization was the joint stock company. It belongs to the genus "business combination" rather than "business association." These two types of organization did not exclude but supplemented one another. A sedentary merchant might be a member of regulated companies and also of joint stock companies. For instance, a London mercer might be a Stapler and export wool and a Merchant Adventurer and import millinery and fine cloths and silks. He might also be a stockholder in the Russia Company and as such invest in foreign trade only indirectly. With the joint stock company should be compared the individual merchant, and the various kinds of partnership. It might seem that the joint stock company was essentially the rival of the merchant, while the regulated company was his tool. The latter is true, but the former is not true of companies as they actually developed. In reality, the joint stock company was confined to enterprises different in kind from the work of the sedentary merchant or it engaged in trade of a nature which the individual merchant would not run the risk of entering. Moreover, the risk and the amount of capital required for one line of trade that the joint stock company might enter would be so much greater than his policy would permit.

Joint stock companies have assisted in the development of a long-time policy and point of view in business, which is of great importance in many kinds of activity, including foreign trade, transportation, and public utilities. The petty capitalist operated from day to day. The sedentary merchant entered into partnerships for a single venture or for a period of two or three years. The sedentary merchant could at best plan for the remaining years of his life. The joint stock company incorporated, however, could look forward to an indefinitely long existence, even though its charter were for but twenty years, because of the likelihood of renewal. Some types of business can be carried on by no other means than through a corporation, as for instance life insurance.

Joint stock companies, incorporated, were used in a succession of types of industries, the order of which is in itself interesting.

Banking (in Barcelona and Genoa in 1401 and 1407, respectively)
Mining (in central Europe, 1415)
Foreign trade (in England, Netherlands, late 16th century)
Public utilities (water, wharves, etc., 17th century)
Insurance companies (early 18th century)
Turnpikes (late 18th century)
Canals (18th century)
Manufacturing (late 18th century)
Railroads (about 1830)
Wholesale firms (late 19th century)
Large retail stores (late 19th century)
Investment banks (20th century)

The sedentary merchant was interested in the formation of all of such types down to and including railroads, without giving up his main business. Thereafter, he invested in the business of others when he abandoned his mercantile pursuits. We shall note later his activities in forming banks; at this point we may concentrate on early trading companies.

One of the earliest trading companies, joint stock and incorporated, was the Russia Company, formed in England about 1555. For a long stretch, England had no further experience of just this kind. The Russia Company was so unsuccessful that it was changed into a regulated company for a further effort. The scene next shifts to the Netherlands where the progenitors of the Dutch East India Company were formed in 1598. The English were fired with hopes of gain in the eastern trade and fraught with fear that another people would get ahead of them. They formed their East India Company in 1599, chartered it in 1600, and saw it send out its first trading fleet in 1601. In 1607 came the Virginia Company, in 1620 the Plymouth Company, and in 1629 the Massachusetts Bay Company.

In the establishment and operation of such joint stock companies sedentary merchants had certain advantages. They knew the background of foreign trade. They had managerial ability of a high order. They had experience with partnerships, and some of the accommodation partnerships for one venture were very much like the early efforts of joint stock companies: there were many persons holding shares and the unit of enterprise was the voyage. In the provision of capital the merchant had the advantage of having ready cash. He might not subscribe to many shares but he could pay up. Kings, nobles, gentlemen, and politicians would subscribe large amounts but find difficulty in meeting payments on time. Much of the capital that came in from the country was probably mercantile in origin. A generation or so previously a landed gentleman had married the daughter of a draper or a mercer. Perhaps some funds still remained with the family for commercial investment which otherwise would have been sunk in the morass of land and fine homes.

We are somewhat more interested in the mercantile capitalists

SIR THOMAS SMYTHE, LONDON, ABOUT 1610

A SEDENTARY MERCHANT AT WORK,
GERMANY, LATE SIXTEENTH CENTURY

who formed joint stock companies than in the companies themselves. Certainly the companies have come in for a good deal of attention on the part of economic historians. Let us consider Sir Thomas Smythe and the Virginia Company, John Peirce and the Plymouth Company, and Matthew Cradock and the Massachusetts Bay Company, all of London, and Willem Usselinx and the Dutch West India Company. In the last section we noted that the mercantile capitalists ran right into the Industrial Revolution and their own destruction; in this section we shall see that they ran right into problems of empire and religion that first challenged and then baffled them.

Sir Thomas Smythe was a member of the Haberdashers' Company and also of the Skinners' Company, both of London. He was the outstanding sedentary merchant of his time that turned to joint stock company affairs. So great did his reputation become that, when a new English company was formed to trade overseas, something seemed wrong if he were not the head of it or at least high placed in its management. The Russia Company, East India Company, Virginia Company, and Bermuda Company all came under his influence or dominance. These concerns were held together by family connections, religious ties, business association, and political support. Here was a mercantile compact of the first water. Why has no sleuth risen to discover an arch conspiracy against the human race? Surely where wealth and power sit under one tree, no matter how fruitful, there must be a serpent entwined among the boughs.

Although the Virginia Company was formed in 1606, Smythe did not become the head or treasurer until 1609. For the next decade he seems to have been the central administrator in the headquarters in London. Whether he was responsible for the drawing up of the new charter of 1609 under which he operated is not known to me, but his was the hand that guided affairs under that charter. He was largely responsible for the choice of governors sent out, captains despatched, settlers chosen, goods selected, and orders given for the settlement and the trade to be carried on. He was only indirectly responsible for the lack of coöperation and idleness of the settlers who for seven years were to be servants of the Company and only thereafter the owners of their own estates. Many of these early settlers were the sweepings of London and no greater good did the Indians ever do to American civilization than to destroy them. Smythe and his fellow directors and officers knew nothing about the qualities required of a settler who must till the soil and fight, plan for the future, and ultimately govern his district. One of the hardest jobs in business as in government is to find and select able subordinates of the small master and efficient servant type.

The chief policy of Smythe and the hundreds of other stockholders of the Virginia Company was to make money, first by tapping the resources of the fabulously rich far off land and then, when that mirage faded, to get a net income from agricultural production and trade. The latter centered in tobacco for which a sensuous civilization eagerly sat in wait. Starting out for gold, the Company discovered tobacco which would yield gold. But the pioneering processes both on the side of settlement and of trade were slow, wasteful, and exhausting. No one in the Company or perhaps in London had originally any idea of the developmental difficulties. The assumption was that trade with America was like trade with India which had already begun. That is, it was expected that there were peoples of a high order with whom the Company could trade in America as in India. Instead, a few scattered and shifting bands of half-painted savages were found who desired nothing except a few beads and bits of colored cloth. To be sure, the time came when the savages would hunt deer in return for guns and ammunition, scalping knives, and rum. Along with these objects the whites were to give without charge both Christianity and civilization and to throw in for good measure smallpox, tuberculosis, and syphilis. The plans of everybody seemed to go wrong everywhere.

In spite of the fact that the Company's servants did go out, plant gardens and build forts, and in spite of the fact that interest was rising in England to the extent of arousing the ambitions of men of means to carve out plantations or manors for themselves in Virginia, still there were no profits for the trading company. The whole organization was in danger of going onto the rocks during the process of development. Such is precisely what happens in our own day and what has always been happening in big business. It is hard to get enough capital to start a business; it is still harder to get additional capital to carry on the promotional work. This has been true of our railroads, airplane industry, and so on. Smythe had a herculean task. On the whole, he measured up well on the financial side. In the first place, he borrowed money on the Company's credit and apparently also on his own. This reminds us of Robert Morris' efforts at a later date on behalf of the struggling American Republic. Secondly, he formed subsidiary companies to perform certain special tasks which held out great promise of profit. Only the stockholders of the Company were allowed to participate in this preferred business. And, yet, apparently only one of these special enterprises succeeded in making money, namely, the sending out of one hundred women for wives who were picked up by the settlers at so much per head. No inference concerning the character of these women can be based on known facts. Perhaps we may say that Smythe had before him the three kinds of situations that have since become common to us. First, there was the position of the common stockholders, then of the preferred stockholders, and finally of the bondholders.

Of course, we have been considering only the Company's own plantation. In addition to it, there were the smaller plantations of well-to-do members of the Company and on these plantations there were varying degrees of success. Also, there were the servants of the Company, who, beginning in 1616, commenced to receive assignments of land in accordance with their original agreement of service. However, it is the Jamestown inner core that interests us here—the Company's trading post and storehouse, protected by a fort and skirting the tide waters which were a means of getting supplies in and might be a means of escape in case of attack.

At Jamestown the first English-American business man—Thomas Studley—established himself for a few months. For him, events moved fast—landing, settlement, trading, and death, all in 1607. He was the "cape-merchant" (or head merchant) of the Virginia Company. It would be more accurate to call him the Company's "resident factor." Studley combined in the one office trader, colonial treasurer, and keeper of stores. He was aided by two bookkeepers, who like himself, were chosen for one year.

As usual under the circumstances of Company management, there was loud growling and open demands for a change—both in Virginia and in London. In a semi-public activity, when the business man fails or seems to fail, a politician arises to lead the opposition and to give the people a new deal. In this case the person was Edwin Sandys, a lawyer, member of Parliament, and all-round would-be leader of something, preferably of the people. To him it was not enough to say that Smythe had not made profits, had not kept his accounts in good condition, and so on. To him it was more important to work out a policy that would meet the situation in Virginia. There is little question that this is just what Smythe would have done if allowed a little more time and given more support. In truth, Smythe was learning the shortcomings of his early policy and the possibilities of the colony. The upshot was, however, that Sandys was made treasurer in Smythe's place in 1619, and from then on to the end of the Company in 1624 he or his friends were in command.

Sandys brought fresh energies into the enterprise, emphasized colonization in preference to immediate profits, and saw the need for giving the colonists more liberty and somewhat more autonomy. Perhaps he is credited with too much, but there is no doubt of the general direction of his policies. More settlers were sent out, but the new with the old were massacred in wholesale fashion by the Indians in 1622. Let this be noted here, however, that Sandy's policy was fundamentally a profit motive as was Smythe's. The difference lay in the degree of emphasis upon building up a strong base in colonization.

The second merchant to play a vital rôle in American colonization was John Peirce and the second company the Plymouth Company. Peirce was a member of the Clothworkers' Company (gild) of London and a sedentary merchant. It was he who got the patent for the Company and helped finance it at the start and manage its affairs for several years. There were two groups of members in this Company, such London capitalists as Peirce, James Sherley of the Goldsmiths' Company, and members of the Merchant Taylors', Salters', and other livery companies or gilds on the one hand and the settlers on the other hand. The settlers were the Pilgrims who had tried their luck in Holland but found that, although they were respected and trusted there, they could not compete with the Dutch. They wanted a home in a land where life would be easier than in Holland and where worship would be freer than in England. They were petty capitalists or small artisans who were honest but not strong in management. The sedentary merchants had what these artisan settlers lacked—capital and managerial ability. Those capitalists who came into the Company sought two things—profits first and foremost and the satisfaction of helping fellow religionists as a close second.

Disgusted with the failure of the Plymouth Company to yield profits and with the obvious slowness of the Pilgrims to adjust themselves to their commercial opportunities, John Peirce was anxious to withdraw about 1624 or 1625. How far he was influenced by the impending withdrawal of the charter of the Virginia Company is not clear. But just as the Virginia Company had its Sandys, so did the Plymouth Company have its Sherley. It was the latter who stayed by the Company through its second trying period. Like Peirce, he waited for profits and loaned his own money with sympathetic understanding of the difficulties of pioneers.

When Peirce withdrew, the old London group of capitalists

broke up. Since it had never been incorporated as the Virginia Company had, the Plymouth Company's dissolution would have been easy. In fact, the Company's period of life had lapsed. In 1627 a second Company was formed of London capitalists and Plymouth settlers. Progress was slow. Misunderstandings arose. The Pilgrims showed signs of moral weakening but regained their strength. Sherley withdrew in 1637. By 1642 the London capitalists seem to have been paid off; whether they received anything more than their original investment is unknown.

Matthew Cradock was a member of the Skinners' Company of London and doubtless often thought of the profits to be made in trading in furs and skins from America. At any rate, he became a founder and the first governor of the Massachusetts Bay Company which was chartered in 1629. He went down to the sea to bid the ships farewell and was apparently responsible for the sending of the charter over from England to America. This Company, although including quite a number of well-to-do Puritans, had difficulty in getting together enough capital. All it could muster was sunk in equipment—ships, arms, foodstuffs, and the like. As usual, no sooner were the settlers confronted with their own peculiar problems than they forgot their financial backers in London. Some thought more about converting the Indians than they did about meeting their moral obligations in their old homeland.

In order to help meet obligations incurred and in order to raise more money for supplies, the London capitalists (themselves Puritans) and the settlers in America formed a second company with preferred rights—issued preferred stock, so to speak. This company was given certain monopolies in trade and traffic for seven years. But the period 1630-37 brought no more success than had the first. More capital was lost.

A few of the London merchants, such as George Harwood, haberdasher, had probably made money out of the equipping of the settlers. Doubtless Harwood sold them stockings. On the other hand, Cradock was principally interested in the furs and deerskins which might be attained through trade at his

JOINT STOCK COMPANIES

three posts, the most important of which was at Medford where his fine brick house still stands. Never in America himself, he carried on trade, fishing, and ship-building through agents. If he made any money, it was here. His widow was more impressed with his losses than any gains.

Willem Usselinx is the fourth sedentary merchant whom we shall consider. Born in Antwerp in 1567, he entered foreign trade apparently in the Azores where he probably became first factor and then partner in a mercantile establishment. Relatively early in life, he amassed some capital and with it went to the Netherlands to carry on business (in Amsterdam) and to plan commercial expansion for the Dutch people. Like many of the sedentary merchants he had two chief interests: one was private business and the other religion. His religious ambition as a Protestant was to thwart Catholic Spain. His means of bringing this about was to induce Protestant countries, first the Netherlands and then Sweden, to form companies to trade in America, thus short-circuiting the Spanish West India trade. In furtherance of his plans, he became a pamphleteer, an advertiser of America, and a company promotor.

Usselinx had no silly notions about the ease of making money in America. He expected hard-earned profits from hazardous trade. He set out to put his ideas into effect. Going from city to city and provincial government to provincial government in the Netherlands, he argued persuasively for the establishment of a Dutch West India Company to match the Dutch East India Company which had already attained considerable success. He found the Dutch hard to persuade and hard to move. His task became all the more difficult when his private business failed. It is probable that Dutch capitalists had less faith in a bankrupt leader than they had in a successful merchant. The first Dutch West India Company was formed in 1607, the second in 1618. The second charter, like the first, reflects Usselinx's ideas, but the second particularly stresses the welfare of the settlers. Perhaps this change was partly a result of the personal misfortunes of Usselinx. At any rate, we wonder whether it did not suggest to Sandys the policy which he advocated for Virginia. It was this Dutch Company, however, that was responsible for the founding of New Netherlands or New York.

Next, Usselinx went to Sweden where he persuaded King Gustavus Adolphus to charter a Swedish West India Company in 1626 (the South Company) to undertake trade and colonization in America. At this point, we recall the settlement resulting on the Delaware River in 1638. But Sweden was the worst country to go to for capital. Poor by nature, it was being impoverished by the Thirty Years' War. A private business venture (draining a lake) in Sweden brought only failure to Usselinx. Old, broken, and bankrupt, he went from court to court, counting-house to counting-house, trying to form companies to trade and to curb Spain. He did much good for everybody except himself.

What a group of forgotten benefactors of America—Smythe, Peirce, Cradock, and Usselinx! I doubt whether a monument is to be found to any one of them anywhere. Mingled in their efforts were business, politics, and religion. Little or no profits came from business. But no matter; seeking profits for themselves, they did much for others. It is often thus; if the business man succeeds in his business, he must benefit others; if he fails, he may still assist society and civilization.

8. BOOKKEEPING AS A BUSINESS DEVICE

The keeping of accounts is at least four thousand years old. It is a device for controlling or managing one's affairs in business and outside of business. Just where bookkeeping made its earliest progress is beyond our present interest. The two possibilities are, on the one hand, institutions such as temples, monasteries, villas, and manors and, on the other hand, the petty capitalists of early towns.

Institutional accounts which have survived in great numbers may be briefly described. Let us take mediaeval manorial records as our guide. There were five principal records. The chief one was the Codex or Ledger of customary receipts and payments presented as simple income and outgo. These were commonly equal; when this was not so, the official usually owed the lord a stated amount. The second was the Memorandum Book or original entry book which I have myself never seen. The third was the *physical* Inventory of such goods as grain, cattle, and tools. The fourth was the Customal which contained a list of customary sources of income, that were normally and regularly forthcoming, especially dues in money or in kind. The fifth was the Survey of land from which revenues might be derived.

The records of petty capitalism, although possibly genetically older than institutional records, are more simple. In this description I am piecing together fragmentary bits of information. The most indispensable was the Memorandum Book which contained transactions as they occurred. The entries might be very miscellaneous. An early example from Florence is dated 1211. The second book is the Ledger or Codex which, like the principal record of the institutional system, was the main account book. It was also kept on a single-entry (or paragraph) basis and contained items of receivables and payables. The principal reason for its existence was to keep track of debts incurred almost wholly in sales and purchases. Two principal types of transactions had to be recorded. The one was the common purchase and sale of goods and services, chiefly or exclusively on credit. The other was the single-venture accounts of traveling merchants who conducted a great deal of their business on the basis of temporary partnerships. The single-venture accounts were mere paragraphs setting forth sometimes a part of the contract but chiefly the amounts of goods or cash involved in the outgoing venture and then in the incoming venture. The difference between the costs of the goods and the total receipts constituted the net profit to be divided among the partners according to the contract.

Although the petty capitalists had a system of bookkeeping that was adequate for their needs, still there was no means of maintaining adequate records if the business should become large or complicated. The pressure that was put on accounting methods came from sedentary merchants or mercantile capitalists who arose in Italy in the thirteenth century, and in Western Europe in the fourteenth century, and in America about 1700. In ways not now known to us, single entry (or paragraph) accounting was changed to double entry, new classes of records were introduced, and the summary financial Statement was developed. It is to be concluded that one or two generations of sedentary merchants had been operating before these changes occurred. The improvements that the merchants developed were taken over by municipalities, notably in Genoa according to a decree of 1327. In time, outsiders wrote about the new system. Probably about 1458 Benedetto Cotrugli, of Ragusa, wrote a merchant's manual in which he briefly described the double-entry system of bookkeeping and the different books used therein. A Franciscan friar, Luca Pacioli, wrote his treatise, published in Venice 1494, much longer than Cotrugli's but still intended only as a part of a larger work on mathematics. In 1534 the first treatise on double entry, written by a bookkeeper, was printed. The author was a teacher of penmanship, the abacus, and bookkeeping in Venice. Thus was begun that effective stream of publications, by men who were wrestling with accounting problems, for the benefit of outsiders who at a very much later date were to make their own contributions to the art, as economists and others joined in an effort to solve problems of overhead, depreciation, obsolescence, and joint costs.

Valuable as the treatises on bookkeeping are, we must not make the common error of regarding them apart from the actual business which bookkeeping was designed to help control. The key to the new system of double entry lies in the business of sedentary merchants in the régime of mercantile capitalism. There are three situations which we need to keep in mind in this connection—the individual sedentary merchant, mercantile partnerships, and early joint stock companies (incorporated or unincorporated). Adequate treatment of these three would cover the period from the fourteenth to the late eighteenth or early nineteenth century.

The individual sedentary merchant had two principal kinds of situations to meet. He wanted an accurate picture of receivables and payables and full information about the individual tasks or ventures upon which his *agents* embarked. The first part had long been common to all petty capitalists and the second was comparable to the single ventures of the temporary partners of traveling merchants (one group of petty capitalists).

The most distinctive feature of mercantile capitalism is the use of agents. These went out as supercargoes or resided in distant ports as representatives of their master. They rode through the country buying up supplies. They put out raw materials to be made up into finished goods. Accordingly, we may safely draw the conclusion that the chief accounting problem of the sedentary merchant was keeping track of the tasks performed by his numerous agents at home and abroad, on the sea and on the land, in commerce and in industry. It may well have been that it was right at this point that the double-entry system of more nearly complete control came into being in some Italian city.

After the individual sedentary merchant came the mercantile partnership. Reference is here made to terminal partnerships of from three to five years, so common in Florence from at least about 1400 onwards. The partners had the old need for (1) information about receivables and payables in a general way. In addition, they wanted on record (2) *all* transactions whether cash or credit. They also required (3) exact records of the work of their agents, more numerous than ever. And, in addition, they had (4) the positions and equities of the partners themselves to keep before them. Sometimes these positions involved regular allowances for expenses and always periodic division of profits. When partners were located in other cities, in charge of branches, then the problem became very much like the control of agents, and should be regarded as of this general type. I can see no new classes of accounting records needed for partnerships except a book of agreements, a book of partners' expenses or allowances, and summary periodic profit and loss statements. When we find a subsidiary ledger in use in the early sixteenth century by Medici partners engaged in having cloth manufactured for their business, with a controlling account in the general ledger, we may feel that the Italians were just about reaching the height of accounting procedure under mercantile capitalism.

The third type of situation under mercantile capitalism is the joint stock company formed by sedentary merchants for such purposes as commercial banking (1401), mining (1415), and foreign trade (1555). How much special accounting would here be required should be made the object of further study. When the stockholders became alarmed at some action on the part of the directors, a demand for an independent audit would occur. This is largely a nineteenth-century development and belongs to the régime of industrial rather than mercantile capitalism. It is true that outside auditors were used under mercantile capitalism but chiefly in case of disputes between partners or in case of a law suit when an independent opinion was required. The auditors were then likely to be fellow merchants well acquainted with the type of accounts and difficulties in question.

The key to the origin of double entry lies in the business of the sedentary merchant. We should not emphasize the single-venture problem, for that was very much with the traveling merchant of petty capitalism, but the activities of the sedentary merchant's agents both in mercantile and industrial pursuits. We should not emphasize just partnerships because the richest experience of this type lay in the one-venture partnerships of traveling merchants recorded in single entry, but rather the terminal partnerships of sedentary merchants such as the Frescobaldi, Bardi, and Peruzzi of Florence. These terminal partnerships involved three important developments, all of which put pressure on the merchants concerned for an improved system of accounting control. First, the terminal partnerships tended to create a larger volume of business. Second, they gave rise to a need for a complete record of transactions, cash as well as credit, as a check against the operating partner. Third, they required a periodic financial Statement that would be satisfactory to the partners as an accurate basis for the division of profits.

By 1500 the double-entry method of bookkeeping was well known in Italy and by 1600 in Western Europe. A set of three books was commonly used. They were the Memorandum Book of original entry, the Journal made up from the Memorandum Book, and the Ledger posted from the Journal. Sometimes there were separate accounts for different situations, for example, when banking was combined with merchandising and when the merchant had goods made to order for his business. There were also Letter Books in which were copied by hand the most important correspondence. Medici Letter Books are rich sources of business information. Finally, there are financial statements in the form of profit and loss summaries and true balance sheets of assets and liabilities.

Whether double entry had been used in ancient Tyre, Carthage, Antioch, Smyrna, Syracuse, Alexandria, and other commercial cities is unknown. At least we can say that the system, as we have it, seems to have taken root in some Italian city about 1300 and arose out of the needs of sedentary merchants. That it came from the Arabs is unlikely because the Arab merchants were of the traveling variety. That it came down from antiquity through Byzantium is possible—as an inheritance from Syria or Asia Minor or Greece, not from Rome.

Chapter IV

MERCANTILE CAPITALISM

Maturity with a Tendency to Disintegrate

Guide public opinion, serve the state.
Control not only trade but industry and fishing.
Let the senior partner formulate policy;
Banking is a logical step to power and profit.

1. MERCHANTS' POLICIES AND MERCANTILISM

During the period of mercantile capitalism, that is, from the thirteenth century to the late eighteenth century, the central economic figure was the sedentary merchant. During the period of unimpaired Church dominance but little recognition seems to have been given to this merchant for the part he played. In the sixteenth and seventeenth centuries, however, the merchant's position was recognized, for instance, in England by Hales, Misselden, Mun, and others. To be sure, most of the appreciative writers were themselves merchants, but still others, such as Hume in the eighteenth century, accepted the judgment and placed the mercantile capitalist above the landed gentleman and farmer. The reason for the recognition was *not* that many of the writers were merchants but that the sedentary merchant, the mercantile capitalist, was the truly great organizer of trade, traffic, and labor. Without political power, he held the reins of economic power.

The height of recognition came when the basis of public wealth was seen to be private wealth, when the chief source of all wealth was thought to be foreign trade, and when the nation was held to the same limitations of policy as the merchant—to prosper the treasury must have more coming in than was going out. This was the acceptance of the merchants' point of view in affairs of state.

The key to public policy lies in private policy—the policy of the sedentary merchant. We have written something about this already but the subject will bear repetition, especially from a different angle. The primary policy of the sedentary merchant was to settle down and emphasize skill in administration. The national courts of administration and justice had already done this in the interest of efficiency in England in the thirteenth century. A second policy was concerned with the procurement of supplies with which to trade. This was solved partly by establishing retail stores that would take local goods in return for wares brought in from elsewhere. It was solved also by the development of controls, particularly over small industrial masters. The solution through power-machine production lay far in the future. It is a curious fact that historians in contemplating this development of control—the shift from the dependent phase to the independent phase of the wholesale handicraftsman—think of the master who lost position and not of the consumer who gained greater supply at lower prices. Let us not forget that the small master was also a consumer.

A third policy of the sedentary merchant was the sale of goods. Although this subject merits investigation, it has received but little. Certainly, the student of the sixteenth and seventeenth centuries gets the impression that the merchant had increasing difficulty in avoiding over-supply and glutting of the market. Take, for example, spices in the sixteenth and early seventeenth centuries and tobacco in the late seventeenth century. The solution, in so far as it came at all, lay in a general rise in European prices caused by the increase in the supply of precious metals, an increase in monopoly and the rise of protection, and the controlled limitation on colonial production as engineered from Amsterdam and London. Very close to this policy was the merchants' emphasis on foreign trade, either export or import. This we may label a fourth. Of course, we know that wholesaling was ancillary to this trade and that the merchant took it to be part and parcel of foreign trade. The retail trade, so high in petty capitalism, was falling into disrepute. Some thought there were too many retailers in the seventeenth century and were prepared to limit their numbers by law.

The grand coördinating policy in business is often called "financial." In the case of the sedentary merchant this was a point of strength. We may regard this as a fifth policy. The merchant would diversify his functions for safety as well as profits. He would integrate many of these functions so as to control supply and sales. In doing this, he established what we may call, not without challenge, "the natural order of business." Our merchant believed in keeping ready cash on hand, even though he might borrow at the same time. In addition, he saw the use to which he could put his credit—far beyond the actual capital at his command. This was a regular practice in the case of marine insurance underwriting. It led to speculative undertakings in good times which invited disaster as depressions swept the land.

There is a sixth policy which might have been considered along with the second, though it is not the same. This is the ever-present business man's policy of low costs. In the case of the sedentary merchant, the two outstanding sources of high costs were high wages and high interest rates. Legislation was procured to limit the rate of interest. High rates of interest, it is true, were often concealed in bills of exchange, as Malynes pointed out early in the seventeenth century, and could not easily be legislated out of existence. At a much later time, these items of cost appeared as elements in the distribution of the total income.

A seventh policy was market price as against just price. The Catholic position was that prices should be just to the consumer but not to the producer (including the merchant). The theory was that no man should charge more than the original

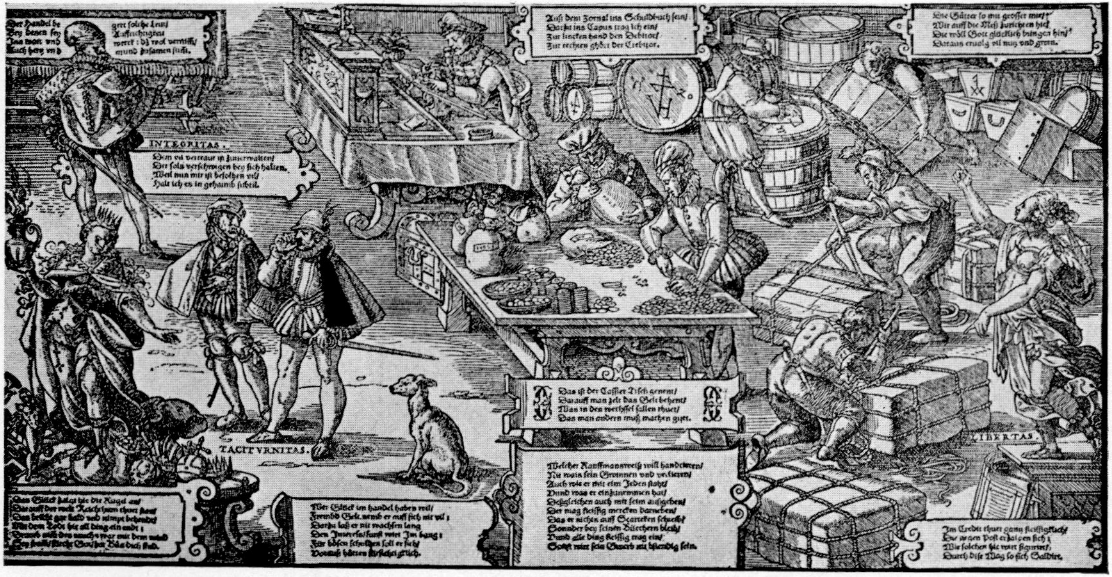

PART OF THE SEDENTARY MERCHANT'S ESTABLISHMENT,
GERMANY, LATE SIXTEENTH CENTURY

PART OF THE SEDENTARY MERCHANT'S COUNTING HOUSE, GERMANY, LATE SIXTEENTH CENTURY

cost of production, plus expenses and a reasonable profit to maintain the standard of living. This looks fair enough but it was not at all what it seemed because of the fact that each transaction was considered separately. The producer or merchant could not force the consumer to pay a remunerative price in time of over-supply and low price. He must, therefore, stand the loss. When there was a scarcity, he could not make up the earlier loss. To the producer or merchant, what counted was the total net income. Price to him was to be fixed to maintain this. And, of course, there was and is now no other way of operation. The merchant wanted to have this market price accepted and openly recognized. He got it in the early part of the sixteenth century and then, unsatisfied, he went on to secure for certain products a monopoly price. This situation has been considered by Ehrenberg, Strieder, and others but should be made the object of further special study.

We might now stop to consider public policy as advocated by the merchants—Malynes, Misselden, Mun, North, Child, King, and others. This we would label "mercantilism." We should find it first worked out for the towns, as Sieveking has pointed out, and then for the province, the nation, and the empire, as Schmoller and others have shown. This mercantilism was the earliest non-ecclesiastical system of economics that has come down to us in uninterrupted growth. It was indeed the childhood or adolescence of economics. True, it was faulty. It over-emphasized production, dealt with consumption in an arbitrary fashion, and neglected sharing-distribution as a branch of economics. Clearly, many mercantilists over-emphasized money and none gave a very satisfactory account of capital. Mun made real progress when he distinguished between natural wealth and artificial wealth. The latter was close to capital. Recently, Professor Johnson has discerned in the early use of the word "art" a measure of capital and of business enterprise.

Our main thesis here is that the policy of the sedentary merchant was the basis of national mercantilism and of the later imperial mercantilism. The sedentary merchant emphasized foreign trade, a favorable balance in his income and outgo, the possession of a strong box of hard money, and navigation. He sought low costs, as we have seen. English public policy in the sixteenth and seventeenth centuries reflects his thoughts about costs. Interest was given a maximum rate, wages were fixed in accordance with the price of provisions (a subsistence wage?), and the people were to be taxed to support the poor only on condition that they work in poorhouses (a policy not consistently followed). A large number of sedentary merchants regarded the domestic market as of less importance than the foreign market. In fact, the home people were thought of as producers of goods to be sold abroad, rather than as consumers of goods. Industrial artisans and others were to produce cheaply. Their capacity to purchase was but little considered. They were not thought of as a potentially expanding element in marketing. National mercantilists generally accepted this view and only at a later date was it changed, and then under very different circumstances. Perhaps above all these considerations was enthroned the ancient thought (now challenged but not overthrown) that the nation cannot safely do what individuals cannot safely do in their economic affairs.

We should note particularly that this national economic policy is called mercantilism. It is rather well named—the system of mercantile capitalism, the system of the sedentary merchant. The merchant is the central dominating, dynamic figure. Adam Smith made his own reputation partly through misunderstanding mercantilism. He thought of it as an over-emphasis on gold and silver rather than national economic policy comprehending a well-rounded development of national resources. To be sure, in some countries the system might become lopsided. An example of this is found in French Colbertism which tended to develop foreign trade at the expense of agriculture. English mercantilism did not make this mistake.

There is some conflict in thought as to what the ultimate objective of mercantilism was. Let us consider only national mercantilism. One extreme view is that national mercantilism was political in objective and the other that it was economic. The fact is that the objective was both, at one and the same time. The sedentary merchant, the key man in business, regarded national mercantilism as the embodiment of his policy. To him national mercantilism was the policy of sedentary merchants writ large—accepted by the national government. To him both the goal and the means were essentially his own—first and last, economic. To others, particularly to statesmen, the goal of national mercantilism was political while the means was economic. By adopting for the nation the policy and even the managerial methods of the sedentary merchant, the statesman could make his nation rich, powerful, and cultured.

Of the three leading contributions of the sedentary merchant, namely, the destruction of petty capitalism, the beginning of the transformation of town economy into metropolitan economy, and the creation of mercantilism, many persons would say that the last was the most important—because, besides being the policy of a nation, mercantilism became part of the fabric of man's thinking. Let this issue of importance pass, so that we may be free to note how the sedentary merchant had the influence necessary to promote and create national mercantilism.

In considering how the sedentary merchant exercised such influence upon national policy we are forced to rely largely upon inference. As magistrates of growing towns during the late Middle Ages, sedentary merchants had helped create late urban mercantilism which in England and other countries stood as a model in miniature for the national mercantilism of the sixteenth and following centuries. The early urban mercantilism, which we have already noted, was greatly changed by sedentary merchants. The town still existed for townsmen, but exceptions were made which made possible, even provided for, the further growth of business. For instance, manufacture was no longer kept as a monopoly of urban artisans: rural workers (half peasants, half artisans) who could produce more cheaply, were encouraged to manufacture goods for sale in the towns and, of course, through the sedentary merchants. Limitations on ambitious masters within the town were nullified. The old-time monopolies of gilds and early regulated companies in the matter of regulation and right to grant exclusive privileges to their members were paralleled by the sedentary merchant's organization and administration of the later regulated companies and joint stock companies.

As servants and creditors of the chief governments of Western Europe, sedentary merchants had a chance to unfold the beneficial influences of their own policy if and when applied to the whole nation. As examples of successful leaders in society, the merchants must have stood high, particularly when churchmen and lay nobles were losing their claims to public acceptance: the Church was weakening from within and the lay nobility was giving up the manorial system in favor of mere landlordship or was tending to live more at the national court rather than remaining at home to provide local leadership. Finally, in the seventeenth century the merchants themselves, as we have seen, were coming to the front as pamphleteers and authors of treatises on trade, money, and economics. All in all, the case for the influence of sedentary merchants is impressive: the conclusive evidence is the product—national mercantilism.

One of the great needs of a community, local, national, or imperial, is to think about fundamental matters. The Church had generally frowned on heterodoxy as heresy. Sedentary merchants and mercantilist writers brought their subject to the front in public controversies. In England in the 1620's there was the dispute between Malynes, on the one hand, and Misselden and Mun, on the other hand, concerning foreign exchange. During a depression in business, Malynes urged that the government should control the purchase and sale of foreign exchange, while his opponents denied the necessity or value of this procedure. Also, at the same time, there arose a controversy that lasted over a century in England as to whether we should think of a favorable balance of trade in a general way or apply it to each individual country. In 1713 one group of controversialists issued the penny paper called the *Mercator*. The chief contributor was Daniel Defoe. The rival journal was *The British Merchant* in which contributors, notably merchants, maintained that a nation should avoid trading with another nation if the result was an unfavorable balance. An example was England's trade with France. From the way in which business and national interests, economic and political considerations, were woven together, we may regard this as a controversy in political economy and distinctly modern.

2. METROPOLITAN ECONOMY

We have seen how close the policies of the sedentary merchant and of the mercantilistic state became. We have now to examine the semi-public organization which stood in between the merchant and the state or nation, that is, metropolitan economy.

Metropolitan economy was the organization of producers and consumers who worked out their material needs through the agency of a group of business men in a large commercial city. The producers and consumers in question lived in the central city and also in the wide hinterland dependent upon the city. The inner core of business men was made up of sedentary merchants.

The explanation why metropolitan economy stands in between sedentary merchants and national mercantilism lies in the fact that the whole metropolitan group became so large that the difference between it and the nation was not seen. This was notably true of such a country as England in which the London area was relatively large and strategically situated. The chief early rival of London—Bristol—was off to one side, with an economy largely its own and commercial connections to the north, west, and south quite different from those of London, and quite inferior.

The idea is that the sedentary merchants developed interests and policies for the business section of society in accordance with their own interest, that these interests involved the wide metropolitan area as well as the center, and that this large agglomeration in early days in smaller nations came to be accepted as the nation. Of course, in a nation so large as the United States, Canada, and Russia no such confusion could arise, at least not for long nor in any important way.

Mercantile capitalism may be regarded as developing in Florence in the thirteenth century and reaching its height in the fifteenth; and as developing in London in the fourteenth century and reaching its height there in the period 1550–1750. In a sense, one of the greatest triumphs of mercantile capitalism was metropolitan economy; another was the governmental policy of mercantilism. In neither case did the triumph come immediately or without long and hard work.

The medium in which the *petty* capitalist lived and operated was the town and its dependent limited hinterland with commercial connections, far and near. The medium in which the *mercantile* capitalist operated was first the town (in its later days) and then the metropolis and its wide dependent hinterland and numerous commercial connections, far and near. Before the town economy of petty capitalistic days had been broken down, the mercantile capitalists began to create a late urban mercantilism. Roughly this was about the fifteenth century in Western Europe. Under this system of late town economy we find that economic equality was a lost ideal. Independence was fading from the realm of possibilities for the rank and file of the small masters. Merchants were becoming dominant over manufacturers. The leaders of commerce were settled and not traveling about. Their techniques of management and control were worked out largely through agency, terminal partnership, and accounting methods (chiefly double entry).

In the metropolis itself, that is, a city that had grown large and was dominated by sedentary merchants, there were two principal groups of business men. The older was the petty capitalist group of business men who were fast losing, if they had not completely lost, their independence. The other group was made up of the sedentary merchants and their employees, agents, and dependents. Among these dependents were, as we have often seen, the shopkeepers, or small industrial masters, who received their raw materials from sedentary merchants and worked for sedentary merchants. Many of the storekeepers were junior partners of the sedentary merchants. Even the traveling merchants came to depend more or less upon the new master merchants sitting in their counting-houses. Wool dealers collected wool and sold it at central marts or in metropolitan centers for sedentary merchants to handle. Cloth dealers collected cloth in the countryside and sold it to the retailers and sedentary merchants. Thus were the two groups of business men—petty capitalists and mercantile capitalists—fused into a single system of mercantile capitalism in metropolitan economy.

In the metropolis there were institutions that stood out as typical of events happening beneath the service. The gilds of the petty capitalists were made over into the livery companies of the sedentary merchants, not all of them, but those in industries or trade capable of expansion under existing conditions, such as mercers, grocers, drapers, cloth workers, ironmongers, salters, and the like. In London, the term used was "livery companies"; in Continental towns, other terms indicative of power and wealth were adopted.

A second institution was the mercantile exchange or bourse. In the late fifteenth and early sixteenth centuries such exchanges grew up in Bruges, Antwerp, Lyons, and so on. In London, the Royal Exchange was founded by Sir Thomas Gresham in 1564, and formally opened in 1570. To these exchanges came the sedentary merchants of the city in question and the representatives (agents and partners) of sedentary merchants of other towns, as well as traveling merchants and retailers of the older régime. In an open space or in an enclosed hall, transactions were begun which might be completed in the sedentary merchant's counting-house. At first, these exchanges were confined

130　　MERCANTILE CAPITALISM

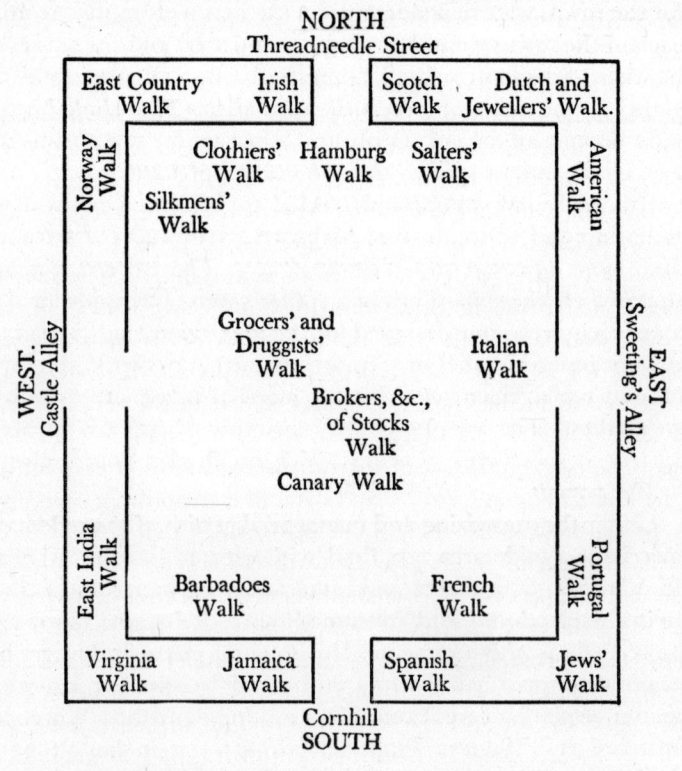

```
                        NORTH
                   Threadneedle Street
    ┌──────────────────────────┬──────────────────────────┐
    │  East Country    Irish   │   Scotch    Dutch and    │
    │     Walk         Walk    │    Walk    Jewellers' Walk.│
    │ ┌────────────────────────┴──────────────────────┐   │
    │N│  Clothiers'   Hamburg    Salters'             │A  │
    │o│    Walk        Walk       Walk                │m  │
    │r│  Silkmens'                                    │e  │
    │w│    Walk                                       │r E│
    │a│                                               │i A│
    │y│                                               │c S│
    │ │                                               │a T│
    │W│  Grocers' and                                 │n  │
    │a│   Druggists'              Italian             │W S│
    │l│     Walk                   Walk               │a w│
    │k│         Brokers, &c.,                         │l e│
    │ │         of Stocks                             │k e│
    │ │           Walk                                │  t│
    │ │        Canary Walk                            │  i│
    │ │                                               │  n│
WEST.│                                               │  g│EAST
Castle│ E                                            │P '│
Alley │ a                                            │o s│
    │ s  Barbadoes              French               │r  │
    │ t    Walk                  Walk                │t A│
    │ I                                              │u l│
    │ n                                              │g l│
    │ d                                              │a e│
    │ i                                              │l y│
    │ a                                              │   │
    │ │ ┌───────────────────────┬──────────────────┐ │W  │
    │W│ │                       │                  │ │a  │
    │a│ │ Virginia   Jamaica    │ Spanish   Jews'  │ │l  │
    │l│ │  Walk       Walk      │  Walk     Walk   │ │k  │
    │k│ │                       │                  │ │   │
    └─┴─┴───────────────────────┴──────────────────┴─┴───┘
                         Cornhill
                          SOUTH
```

PLAN OF THE SECOND ROYAL EXCHANGE, LONDON 1837

to dealings in commodities, but later they also witnessed the purchase and sale of what we should call stocks and bonds. In due time the two functions were separated into district organizations—commodity exchanges and stock exchanges.

A third institution was the old-time open market place. The general market of the town in the days of town economy became a whole group of specialized markets in the metropolis—all devoted to the retail trades, such as corn, fish, and poultry.

Off in the background is the hinterland of agricultural, fishing, and mining villages. Towns existed but not town economy, for the towns were dependent upon the new metropolis. Around each of the towns were the villages mentioned and the scattered hamlets and often isolated homesteads. But all were held together by the nexus of mercantile capitalism. The whole hinterland became an area of supply and a market for sale. It was the web of the master spider—the sedentary merchant.

Gradually, the hinterland tended to become a network of radiating and concentrating highways, river and coast routes, and, later, of canal and railroad routes. The pattern was not that of a checker-board but of a spider's web. The spider makes an efficient web—one designed for the maximum load carried by the minimum number of supports. In such a network, the capital and management of sedentary merchants and others would go farthest. The people would be supplied with the greatest variety of goods and at prices which no checker-board scheme would permit.

Under the organizing and managerial genius of the sedentary merchant a wide area was fired with greater commercial zeal. In other words, it was brought into active exchange and higher living. It produced and consumed more. It became more and more tied up with a price mechanism; and prices and wages became less a matter of custom and social "justice" and more a matter of market conditions. Here mining flourished. There, in Brittany and Western England, fishing even in far off Newfoundland was promoted and carried on. In Norfolk a new agricultural technique was perfected that became the model for both the Old and the New World. The gentlemen farmers of Norfolk, the sons of gentlemen but the grandsons of drapers, mercers, and the like, put capital and managerial ability into the sandy soil of Norfolk and took out a harvest of gold and glory. The agricultural capitalism of old days was made over into the capitalistic agriculture of the modern period.

Out from the central group of sedentary merchants ready to buy and sell and to finance and promote new activities came a thousand and one influences. The greatest was the demand for more foodstuffs that led to the Norfolk system and the agricultural revolution and the demand for more manufactured wares that led to the Industrial Revolution.

It would be a nice exercise to work out a score of first-class influences of sedentary merchants operating through the new metropolitan economic organization. In any list we should have to put the rise of a market price, an emphasis on speculation and promotion, and the gradual decay of international fairs which found part of their business drained off by the new metropolitan organization.

If we were to try to give a complete statement of the forces and factors at work, we should have a hard job. The will to wealth and power on the part of the sedentary merchant would deserve primary emphasis. There was the long continued search for economic opportunity which the metropolis offered even beyond the capacities of the town. Into the metropolis the discontented countrymen poured in great numbers, some to rise and some to sink. The cultural possibilities of the very large city appealed to the nobles, in varying degrees, to persons who would be artists and lawyers, and to a large group of nondescripts of more or less cultural importance. The metropolis had some political administration as well as business administration. At times, it is difficult to determine which was primary and which secondary. Commonly, the two administrative influences went hand in hand.

3. MANAGERS, CONTRACTORS, PROMOTERS, AND SPECULATORS

In the history of institutions and practices we observe that a new form or type has hardly become dominant before it begins to develop rivals or begins to show signs of decay. The system of mercantile capitalism was no exception. Although the sedentary merchant remained the kingpin and although his policies and management continued to prevail, there were other figures in the picture or there were sedentary merchants who displayed variations from the normal.

Managers or executives came into existence who contributed

only managerial ability. For instance, there were officials of gilds and regulated companies. Minor gilds and companies might employ only part of the time of members in executive posts, but important organizations had salaried officials. This subject might be given further study. A late example is Edward Misselden, who was a deputy-governor of the Merchant Adventurers about 1623. He was employed also by the East India Company. We recall that it was this Misselden who entered into controversy with Malynes on the subject of foreign exchange and early used the phrase "balance of trade," and pointed out that national wealth arises from private wealth. Of course, the governors, deputy-governors, and treasurers of joint stock companies might also be salaried managers; probably it was even more likely that the managers sent abroad or to the colonies would be salaried and wholly devoted to their company duties.

Partnerships produced two types of illustrations. There was the very skillful servant who was put on a salary basis and given such important duties, whether stationed in offices or required to travel, that we may regard him as a manager, that is, one who had discretion of action within the broad policies of the firm and whose conduct was a source of profit or loss. Such a person was Pegolotti, the distinguished manager of the Bardi firm of Florence in the fourteenth century.

A slightly different situation is found in those partnerships into which a manager is taken because he possesses not capital but ability and experience. The Medici partnerships of the fifteenth century illustrate this. For instance, we find a sedentary merchant, anxious to engage in trade or industry beyond his capacity of personal management, associating with himself an able manager who contributes no capital but who will draw an annual salary and receive a share of the profits. Perhaps some would call this share a bonus. Certainly this managerial class was later to develop into a very important group of business men. No matter how relatively insignificant this group of business men was in the days of mercantile capitalism, it did stand as a memorial that, in business capitalism, management (which includes ability, experience, and integrity) was an ingredient that could stand alongside of, even if not quite measure up to, capital ownership. And, of course, we know that in the long run it is management that creates capital accumulations and makes them grow.

We are very much in need of information about the history of contractors. I suspect that in early times this story would not loom so large in construction as it does today. Rather would it assume large proportions in performing fiscal services, meeting emergencies in time of dearth and famine, and especially in warfare. The Church had a gigantic problem of transferring contributions from widely separated parts of Europe to Rome without depleting the supply of local pennies and without glutting the Roman market. In the twelfth century, Sienese merchants performed this service with distinction. In the early sixteenth century Jacob Fugger, of Augsburg, helped finance the sale of indulgences in Germany. This included the transfer of the receipts to Rome for the building of the Church of St. Peter. The states and empires of the ancient and mediaeval and early modern periods required the assistance of mercantile capitalists. In the Roman Empire a class of publicans arose who more or less specialized in the loaning of money and administration of estates and provinces. I suspect that this class was an offshoot from the merchant class.

To many a mediaeval and early modern monarch the resources and abilities of sedentary merchants were invaluable. When a king wanted to make war, he required cash in a hurry. This was just the thing that a feudal sovereign, with the typical impecunity of a landlord, utterly lacked. Edward I borrowed from the Frescobaldi, of Florence, and gave in return the right to farm certain customs revenues. This borrowing was a developing habit which ultimately led to commercial disaster about 1345 when Edward III did not meet his obligations to the Bardi and Peruzzi, also of Florence. International bankruptcies in great numbers resulted.

When sovereigns got into deep difficulties in finance and

could no longer rely upon the routine results of civil servants recruited from the nobility, Church, or courtier group, they often turned to business men. From 1436 to 1451 Jacques Cœur, sedentary merchant of Bourges in Central France, was in the service of Charles VII, who was waging a desperate struggle against the English in the last phase of the Hundred Years' War. Cœur had gained wealth in trade in Southern France and across the Mediterranean. He succeeded in trade, operating largely through partnerships and to the point of becoming a power in the land. Of tremendous energy and without any refined scruples, Cœur might be expected to serve the Crown effectively. His ships were operating everywhere in the south, his agents were found in the chief towns, his profits flowed in from every quarter. Such a man was made master of the mint and sent on various important diplomatic ventures. His cash was at the command of the king as was his sword. As he fought at the king's side, his kinsmen were given important positions or married under happy circumstances. His credit, like Robert Morris' standing during the American Revolution, was better than that of his country. The end was not far off, however, for Cœur was but the instrument of a political chief. Put not your faith in princes or politicians, for they seek only their own advantage. But then Cœur was doing about the same thing. At least we can say that he and his sovereign alike won a place in the history of France. On the side of private business, Cœur has left us not only the record of his success which in all healthy times is a matter of applaud but his motto which still has value in the world of action. This motto is "Dire, faire, et taire." We may translate it as "Make your position clear, act decisively, and then shut up."

Another interesting example of a sedentary merchant undertaking an important job for the nation—contracting to bring about a result in a general way—is Sir Thomas Gresham, the fiscal agent of the English throne at a time of great hazard. Gresham was the son of one mercer and nephew of another, both knights and both lord mayors of London. A merchant himself, probably slightly tending to the financial and landed phase of a sedentary merchant's career, he became a useful servant of the Crown in Antwerp as financial agent and part of the time as ambassador, 1552-74. He assisted in getting a foreign loan for his government, in securing valuable information abroad, and in providing much needed munitions. He established a paper mill for his own profit at the same time that he was planning the Royal Exchange for his fellow merchants.

In times of dearth, famine, and war, sedentary merchants were called upon to perform certain services largely or wholly on a profit basis that otherwise would have been beyond attainment. English history, during the period about 1275-1350, illustrates this abundantly. The merchants in question may not have all been sedentary merchants, a sprinkling of traveling merchants perhaps being found in the group, but they were given the special status of King's Merchants in recognition of their importance. A notable example is William de la Pole, of Hull, who served Edward III in many ways. He loaned his cash and dangerously pledged his credit to finance the war against the French. He received the farm of part of the customs revenues. He was knighted and made a baron of the Exchequer. In spite of all his services he fell faster than he rose. Being a King's Merchant was somewhat like being a royal cow: the cow might only be milked, but then it might be slaughtered.

It is to be noted that during this period 1275-1350 the lower house, or house of commons, came into existence and that in this house the merchants had a place. In England and elsewhere there was gradually being recognized a third estate—a class of business men which, however, included both mercantile and petty capitalists.

While the group of business men, roughly called contractors, undertook to do work and produce results indicated to them in advance, the class of *promoters* sought out and planned the undertakings themselves. Moreover, while the contractors were certain of a reward, the promoters could never be sure that their gains would exceed their losses. In considering the class of promoters, I am not forgetting, of course, that the chief examples are the sedentary merchants themselves in their several capacities already considered. Their promotion reached its height in the formation of joint stock companies, already considered, and commercial banks, still to be examined. I am thinking rather of that class of business men who conceive of new undertakings, set them going, and then pass on to other challenges. They are not good administrators but excellent planners. Some of their schemes succeed but many of them fail. On the whole, society is the gainer. Perhaps it is this class rather than the merchants that are temperamentally descended from pirates and vikings. And yet they aim at constructive not destructive results.

Gilbert van Schoonbeke, of Antwerp, went far beyond his contemporaries of the sixteenth century in promoting and carrying out new enterprises. Besides speculation in trade and farming taxes, he built a vast array of houses in Antwerp, a chain of breweries, and forts, docks, and canals.

Sir Bevis Bulmer was an English promoter about whose ventures we have scattered bits of information for the period 1566 to his death in 1615. His chief interest lay in promoting mining schemes—tin, lead, silver, gold, and coal. He even made salt and fished for pearls. He was ingenious in contriving a machine for pumping water out of mines and also for supplying part of the population of London with water. He sought special concessions from the English sovereign and often offered large sums of money for them—not only for mining but also for farming the taxes on the coal trade. Earning much in a short time, he was prodigal in gifts and living. He was daring, vain, and ambitious. Though he forged ahead in fortune and rank, he died in debt. He cut a wide swath through the half-exhausted mining fields of Britain. He dared and gained, he dared again and lost.

An unimportant but still interesting example of a promoter is Charles Povey (1660?–1743). He was a coal dealer in Wapping, England. He founded the Sun Fire Office, published a commercial journal, 1705-10, which was supported by advertisements, maintained a penny post in London, and planned a parcel post. That he was also a Whig pamphleteer is of less importance here.

The period beginning with the sixteenth century is replete with promoters. There was always somebody ready with a scheme—to make starch, soap, or gunpowder; to build a dock, water supply system, or canal; to mine lead or transmute copper into gold; and to form a company to drain a swamp, to trade or colonize, to insure lives, or to milk wild cows in the Argentine. Much of this creative effort came to a ludicrous and disastrous head in the speculative crises of 1720 in both Paris and London, and to a less extent in Amsterdam. One might almost conclude that society was becoming impatient with the slow processes of the sedentary merchants and sought new leaders. To be sure, some of these sedentary merchants were willing enough to join the group but they cannot be said to have led the more speculative ventures of the period 1558–1720 which witnessed so many commercial disasters.

William Paterson was a Scotsman who followed the trail into England for a full meal, wealth, and power. On the way, the peasant boy acted as a pedlar. In London he became a successful sedentary merchant. His brain was full of plans in that period (1680–1720) when many persons devised more schemes for business than the rest could execute. Paterson planned the Bank of England and became a director for a year. Then, he devised the Darien Company to trade at the Isthmus of Panama. It was backed by Scotsmen and was to enrich the Northern kingdom. One year, 1698–99, saw its rise and fall. Paterson then planned another and similar company but he had lost prestige. It was significant that he died in 1719, one year before the blowing up of the big bubble which in a sense he had helped to create.

Just what speculation is has never been satisfactorily explained. Certainly one aspect is brevity of interest in a business or in a phase of a business. A man who goes into a business or venture with the thought of making a profit and then getting

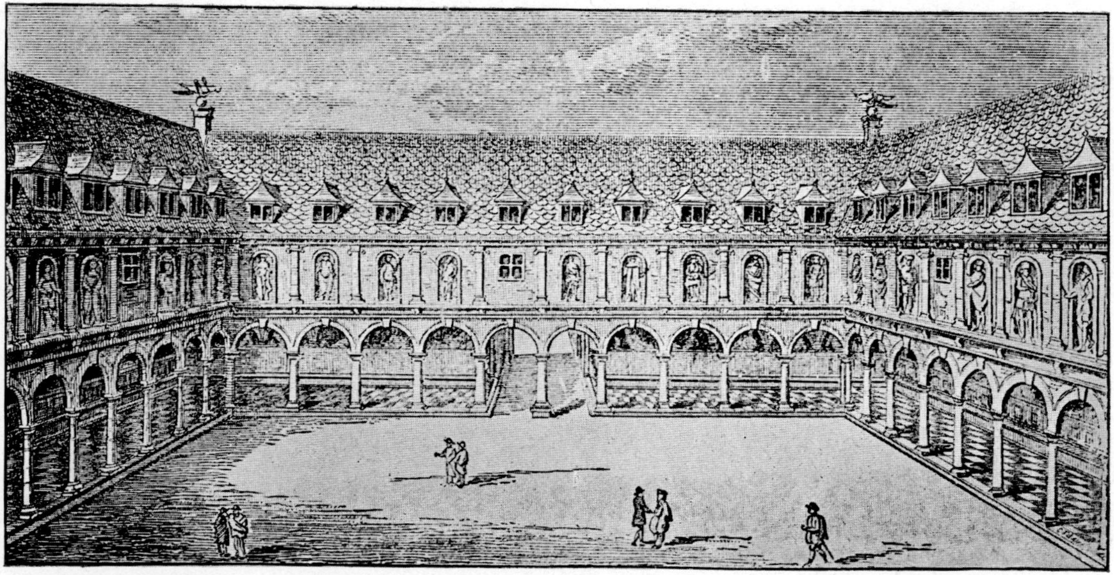

INNER COURT, GRESHAM'S ROYAL EXCHANGE, LONDON, LATE SIXTEENTH CENTURY

out is a speculator. To be sure, he may be very useful. In our period, from the thirteenth to the late eighteenth century, there were various groups of speculators, only a few of whom can be mentioned here. We have already noted the speculative promoter of a new process or business. There was also the less conservative, or more speculatively inclined, sedentary merchant. And then there was the out-and-out specialized speculator—the pure risk-taker of business.

The speculative sedentary merchant needs more study. He was a nimble dealer, during the Middle Ages, chiefly in corn and salt—necessities the supply of which weather or war might deplete. The history of the corn trade shows operations of such dealers. The uncritical would regard them as buzzards feeding on the necessities of the people. The critical would see in them the entrepreneurs who took risks for profits which they could earn in meeting the pressing needs of large groups of persons. In the early seventeenth century the merchant Gerald Malynes was an occasional dealer in corn and salt, though his fame if not his fortune was made through his writings.

Adam Smith had two types of merchants in mind when in his *Wealth of Nations* he wrote of the speculative and the nonspeculative. He pointed out that the conservative merchant rarely makes a fortune even in a large town except through "a long life of industry, frugality, and attention." Today we should say that the fortune would come through wise policies, careful management, and a measure of favorable external circumstances. The "speculative merchant" shifted from corn to wine to sugar to tobacco or tea according to conditions of the market. The gains of one venture, Smith thought, were likely to be lost in another. Such a speculative business, he pointed out, could be carried on only in great towns—our metropolitan centers.

There was another speculator of great significance coming onto the scene—the pure risk-taker, the business man who did not handle goods or provide general services, but confined himself to the business of taking risks and profiting or losing therefrom. His task was oiling the machinery of business. It is one that has rarely been understood by the public and never appreciated by the public or by politicians, except in one form of insurance underwriting. By the seventeenth and eighteenth centuries in London there had arisen a group of persons who as individuals underwrote marine insurance and might do nothing else. Their trade association was and is called "Lloyd's," from the coffee house in which the underwriters originally gathered.

There is one example of a risk-taker that merits special attention. This is William Braund, of London, whose life spanned the years 1695-1774. Thus we see he lived during the disintegrating period of mercantile capitalism. A bachelor, connected with many business firms in London and inclined to stay pretty much in the metropolis and the neighboring countryside, Braund was a successful operator and highly interesting example of a growing but minor variation of mercantile capitalist.

The account books of Braund show that he traded briskly with Portugal during the period 1741-63. He had no warehouse and no store, only a counting-house or office. Indeed, he handled no goods physically. He procured English woolen cloth through intermediaries such as packers, factors, warehousemen, local merchants, and so on, and had his exports sent on ships that carried freight for all-comers to his agent in Lisbon. There, Portuguese colonial gold was procured for export to London, and ultimately to Amsterdam.

At the same time as Braund was carrying on this trade, he was doing three other types of work. First, he was an investor in stocks and bonds. He held securities of the South Sea Company, the Bank of England, the East India Company, and the Sun Fire Office. In the latter two, he was a director. Second, he was a partner in ship-operation. Ships would be built or bought for chartering to a merchant, especially the East India Company. One of the partners, commonly Braund's brother, was the ship's husband or managing partner. Third, he underwrote marine insurance as a member of Lloyd's association. This was a type of business which he could carry on even in the later years of retirement almost to the time of his death. When this insuring was arranged by a broker in Lloyd's, then Braund's share was that of a pure risk-taker.

Here we find a highly specialized business of financing ventures, arranging ventures, but not managing things. Controls were more often in the background than actually in use. An analogy is found in the work of the Medici senior partners in the fifteenth century and of Jacob Fugger in the early sixteenth century. From the business standpoint England was even more advanced in 1750 than Florence had been in 1450.

It was not to be expected that the sedentary merchant would occupy the whole field of business. Do as we may, however, we cannot find many groups of unrelated rivals and none that were very serious. Members of his own class might branch off from the central functions and others might come into the fringes of business, but still the sedentary merchant of some type stood dominant at the center. Mercantile capitalism remained the ruling system of business.

4. CREDIT INSTRUMENTS AND MERCHANT BANKERS

At this point we turn to a specialization of the sedentary merchant, namely, his development of banking. Before doing this, however, we must examine the credit instruments that the merchant banker handled.

In studying the development of the exchange of goods we seem to find that man devised various methods or, as we may say, passed through various stages. First, goods were exchanged free, gift for gift. Then, goods changed hands with a keener sense of valuation, the expectation being that the values were equal. Next came a measure of exchange—a beaver skin, a shell, a wedge of salt, a large circular stone, or a weight of metal, such as copper, silver, or gold. These commodities measured the values in the exchange of goods for goods and might be used to make up differences. This was money barter. Then, when metals were made into coins, it was possible to exchange goods for money and money for goods, freely and smoothly, in a system of money economy. In the stages of money barter economy and money economy goods were often sold on credit.

The instrument that recorded the indebtedness of one man to another, whether in the sale of goods or the loaning of money, has received some attention from scholars but too often from the legalistic point of view. We may note only a few points here. Probably the earliest form of credit instrument was the tally or short stick notched so as to show amounts of money and with writing on the side indicating dates or any other matter. The stick would be split in the middle lengthwise, the creditor keeping one part and the debtor receiving the other. Probably because the tally was clumsy and could easily be tampered with, it was abandoned early by merchants—in England during the fourteenth century but by the government of England not until the nineteenth century. The substitute was, of course, parchment or paper. These instruments—wooden tallies, slips of parchment, or pieces of paper were recognitions of debts for goods or loans. When re-payment was made, they might be made into receipts.

Similar to this recognition of debt in the form of a bill were the promissory note and the bond which went farther in guaranteeing payment. The bond might be made payable to the creditor only, or to his order, or to the bearer. Whether issued by private merchants or by cities and princes, these bonds were transferable under the merchant law of nations and in England under the developing common law.

The promissory note, for instance, as written in Mediterranean cities in the thirteenth century, simply stated that one merchant owed another so much money to be paid in such and such currency at a certain fair or at a certain place. There was no statement of usury: the element of usury was buried in the amount of the note, either for the sake of simplicity or in order to evade the canon law against usury. It is common for scholars to regard this note to pay as an early form of the bill of exchange.

There are two schools of thought in the field of origins. One is the diffusionist school. According to the diffusionists the bill of exchange flowed from some place to some other place. In this case it lived on from the ancient period in Byzantium and thence spread to Italy where it was nourished and, like missionaries of the Church, sent to various parts of Europe. Others hold that it was developed by the Arabs, possibly taken over from the Chinese, and either in direct contact or through Jewish traders passed on to European merchants. To me the effusionist explanation is much more effective: man may devise ways and means of accomplishing results without having to copy. In the history of man in earlier times this explanation has great potency. In this instance, the theory means that Italian merchants devised the simple instrument for their own use. Be it noted that this early form of the bill of exchange was the creation of the traveling merchant who was going to the distant fair or town himself. It continued into the period of the sedentary merchant who sent a factor in his stead to collect debts due and to pay debts owing. By and large, the bills of exchange receivable equalled bills of exchange payable.

The peculiar creation of the sedentary merchant was the draft form of the bill of exchange. The seller of goods ordered the buyer to pay so much for goods received. It is a plausible view that this draft form of the bill of exchange was devised by Italian sedentary merchants who had offices in various countries, beginning in the fourteenth century, and who were adding banking functions to their ordinary commercial functions. Frequently, this bill of exchange would be issued to a traveler going to Lyons, or to London, simply to obviate the necessity of the traveler's taking cash with him. Thus, it would be like a draft which one bank today would draw up payable at a branch or at the office of a correspondent bank.

Since we are dealing with uses, not abuses, we may pass over the inevitable unethical practices involved. Some bills of exchange were sold at high rates, thus concealing excessive rates of usury. Others were mere drafts of convenience of one office of a firm on another office, whether perpetrated by a Fugger or a Strozzi. Modern branch banks have done similar things.

At this point we must note a growth of considerable significance. International sedentary merchants tended ever toward banking. Some of them kept up their trade in goods and their

**OFFICE IN THE FUGGER BANK
AUGSBURG, 1516**

trade in money. Others went over wholly to the trade in money, particularly in Western Europe about the middle of the sixteenth century. At this time the papal prestige and the canon law were at a low point and hence trading in money (at usury) was not dangerous. Also, there had developed great fresh centers of finance at Lyons and Antwerp, later at London and Amsterdam, where on the exchanges or in the counting-houses the credit instruments of commerce as well as cash could be handled freely.

Scratch an early private banker and you find a merchant. He was a senior partner of a commercial house of a second or third generation of a family that had attained success in trade. Trade in money offered less trouble and less risk than trade in commodities. The great houses of Florence, the Bardi, the Peruzzi, the Medici, and the Strozzi pointed the way. The Fuggers and the Welsers of Augsburg followed. By the first half of the sixteenth century there were many firms with from six to twenty offices or branches from Naples to Antwerp, and from Hungary to Portugal.

It is interesting to note how the Fuggers who were weavers in the fourteenth century and merchants of cloth in the fifteenth became dealers in money and credit in the sixteenth. And so with the goldsmiths of London. Families which had actually hammered out plate and fashioned jewels came to employ small masters working in their own shops, they themselves managing only the commercial aspects of the business. Then, by 1622, at least some of these goldsmiths had become merchant bankers.

Two London goldsmith bankers are sufficiently outstanding, not in priority but in importance, to justify special emphasis. The first of these is Sir Francis Child (1642–1713). Son of a clothier in Wiltshire, Child was apprenticed to a goldsmith in London. Eight years later he was admitted to the Goldsmiths' Company (or gild). Then he married the daughter of the last male in a goldsmith family on Fleet Street. About 1671 he entered partnership with his wife's stepfather. At this time he was a full-fledged goldsmith. Up to 1680 his accounts show his business to have embraced the goldsmith's trade, pawnbroking, and banking. After this date he was probably only a banker. The second goldsmith is Sir Richard Hoare (1648–1718). The son of a yeoman and horse dealer of London, he was apprenticed to a goldsmith and in due time admitted to the Goldsmiths' Company. About 1673 he began his business as goldsmith and later added banking. He issued demand notes, accepted cheques, and invested funds in the stock of the East India Company and Hudson's Bay Company. In 1690 he located at 37 Fleet Street where the firm still carries on.

The careers of these goldsmith twins run strangely parallel. Both were commercial goldsmiths and then bankers on Fleet Street. Both were members of the Goldsmiths' Company, lord mayors, members of Parliament, and knights. Both loaned large sums of money to the government. Both escaped the fire and plague of London. But, while the second had seventeen children in his family, the first had only fifteen.

We have had no adequate studies made of merchant bankers either in England or on the Continent. Such studies would have to be based on the records of the bankers themselves. We should probably find something like the following. The merchant bankers had their policies formulated by a senior partner, such as Jacob Fugger. The junior partners, many of them heading branch offices, would actually do the managing of affairs. Some firms preferred salaried officials but that is just an important variation. Capital would be contributed by the partners, active and silent, and by friends and clients by way of deposits. These deposits would bear interest when business justified it—normally five per cent or more in the sixteenth century.

These funds would be invested in goods such as pepper, cloth, quicksilver, and copper, if the firm was still partly commercial. They might also be partly invested in lands, including mines. They would be loaned to princes and towns in round amounts at usury. They would be loaned to individual merchants in the form of discount loans on promissory notes. Some of the funds would be devoted to the buying and selling of bills of exchange and bonds payable to the bearer. Such was the operation of the merchant bank which developed in Italy in the fourteenth century and spread to France, Germany, Flanders, and the Dutch Netherlands in the sixteenth century, and to London in the seventeenth century.

These merchant bankers came to use two other instruments of great importance, namely, the cheque and the demand or circulating note. By the latter half of the seventeenth century both were in use. Whether these two instruments were invented by merchant bankers or by commercial banks is another matter. Whether directly or indirectly, however, they were the creations of sedentary merchants in so far as these merchants were themselves prime movers in the affairs of commercial banks.

There was another type of private banker, which we need to consider in passing. This was the Jewish money-lender (and pawnbroker) who came to receive deposits. This story is unwritten, perhaps unrecorded, for Jews tended to obscure or destroy their records to escape unfair treatment from Christians. At that point where a Jewish money-changer and money-lender began to take deposits from his co-religionists (chiefly), he would be a banker. We might expect this in Amsterdam in the seventeenth century. We know about the Rothschilds of Frankfort in the late eighteenth century and the Rothschilds of entrenched power in London, Paris, Vienna, and Naples in the nineteenth century.

The United States of America has little or no story to record of merchant bankers, though a sizable one of Jewish bankers. There is the case of the merchant Stephen Girard, however, which should be noted in passing. Girard turned to banking toward the end of his life and established a bank which still exists. This institution, however, was of the nature of a chartered public rather than a private bank.

This story of the transition of many sedentary merchants to the position and work of merchant bankers (a term still used in financial London) constitutes an important chapter in the history of the flow of capital. The capacity and experience of the sedentary merchant in the exchange of goods prepared him for the business of handling money and credit. This handling of money and credit was facilitated by accumulations of families which were anxious to get out of active trade and derive an income from deposited (loaned) capital, families which perhaps had partly invested in lands, and partly in mercantile partnerships. Socially and culturally we can see the service of the merchant bankers in making retirement and leisure possible. The assumption, however, is that the freedom from routine and worry was used in creative work of a cultural nature. Unfortunately we have no information that justifies much argument in favor of or against this sequence. But we can be certain that the service of the loans of merchant bankers was very great when they put out their cash or credit to those younger business men who were coming to the front.

Ehrenberg has written two volumes which show how important these merchant bankers were in financing the military operations and political schemes of France, Spain, England, and so on. Merchant bankers were constantly confronted with the decision whether to buy merchant paper or government bonds. Thus was begun in a small way the alternative possibilities of investment in private and public enterprises. In our day this issue has become so important that we wonder whether the public will not engulf the private.

The immediate result of the rise of merchant bankers who were infinitely more important than commercial banks until the nineteenth century was that a class of experienced business men was making an income from usury which the Church had so long prohibited under most circumstances. They borrowed money at a low rate and loaned it at six or eight per cent. Everybody was served except those whose credit was so bad that they could get no loan. Also, the rising business man could get a boost at the right time if he had ability and good character. And, thirdly, the owners of capital could put out their funds indirectly—through the hands of experienced persons—and receive an income with greater assurance than ever before.

5. SEDENTARY MERCHANTS AND COMMERCIAL BANKS

We must not think that merchant bankers were always successful. In fact, few of them were. Their chief danger arose from loans to princes who failed to meet their obligations. This may be a warning to those who are nowadays rushing into national capitalism. At any rate, as the merchant bankers went down like grain before a storm, the commercial banks rose, not in great numbers but with longer life. No country illustrates this better than the Venetian Republic in the sixteenth century. And no more interesting episodes occurred than the financial crises which swept Europe as a plague. One had occurred about 1345, but that was conspicuous by its isolation. In the sixteenth century—a time of creation and destruction—one crisis after another, beginning in 1557–58, happened in Western Europe. How far these were matters of commercial finance and how far national finance it is not now possible to say, but they were severe and international.

The commercial banks that were established during the régime of mercantile capitalism, whether following a crisis and the downfall of merchant banking houses or not, divide themselves into two principal groups—one the loan bank and the other the transfer bank. Examples of the loan bank are the Bank of St. George established in Genoa in 1407 or earlier, the Bank of England founded in London in 1694, and the Bank of North America set up in Philadelphia in 1781. Such banks had capitals which were loaned and received deposits which were also loaned. They bought and sold coins, bullion, and bills of exchange. They came to discount promissory notes as a regular part of their business. By the second half of the seventeenth century they were issuing demand notes.

The transfer bank was not originally designed as a bank of loan but a bank of transfer. Without paid-in capital, the bank received deposits and transferred credits. Examples are the Bank of Barcelona dating from 1401 and the Bank of Amsterdam dating from 1609. Some of these banks, notably that of Amsterdam, issued notes to any depositors who wished to draw out their funds in this way. The practice of loaning deposits developed, ordinarily first to cities and princes and then to companies and individuals.

No matter which road the old-time commercial bank started on, it sooner or later came to perform about the same round as the commercial bank performs today. Noted for their long lives, many of these early banks, for instance, in Venice and Genoa, were mowed down by Napoleon and by French expansion. Except for English and American institutions, the existing commercial banks are commonly products of the nineteenth century. The Bank of Sweden is a notable exception.

In the formation and development of these early commercial banks the sedentary merchants played a strategic part. Probably an investigation would discover that almost all early commercial banks, John Law's bank 1716–20, of course, excepted, had sedentary merchants behind them. These merchants made at least six outstanding contributions to the early commercial banks. They promoted them in the first place, for instance, the Bank of St. George, to look after and follow up the special position of the creditors (of the City of Genoa), and the Bank of Amsterdam to receive on deposit the sundry foreign and local coins that came into the coffers of the merchants and to transfer credit therefor to other merchants. Secondly, they bought stock in the loan banks, in other words provided part of the capital. Thirdly, they provided much of the policy formulation through the members of the board to which they as major stockholders were elected. Fourthly, they provided much of the management, for merchants were commonly the topmost real executives, and frequently a minor merchant took a subordinate part such as that of cashier. Fifthly, they became the chief depositors. And, sixthly, they were the principal borrowers. Their notes and bills constituted the most dependable self-liquidating form of asset that the banks ever knew. To be sure, in a stable state like England the government's pledge to pay eight per cent for a loan was ahead of the commercial paper but then there were few governments like that of England.

For mercantile capitalism these commercial banks were of great significance. The commercial bank was expected to be and proved to be a more stable institution than the merchant banking house. Its incorporation and official position in the community pointed this way. More numerous and more staple outlets were provided for commercial paper. A new agency was created for the collection of debts and the general inculcation of promptness of payment rather than neglect or refloating of debts. Assistance was given to the borrowers at the banks in keeping down the rates of interest. A commercial bank was of great assistance to the local merchants in so far as it enabled them to deal more independently with merchants of older centers. In America, Boston wanted a bank in the 1680's, 1713, and 1739 partly to provide itself with currency but partly also to enable local merchants to be in a better bargaining position when dealing with London merchants. Nevertheless, Boston did not get its bank until 1784.

There were in fact two circumstances that drove sedentary merchants to establish commercial banks. Perhaps the older was to provide a mutual service in their own business. Herein the banks were part and parcel of mercantile capitalism. The other circumstance was to obtain an additional outlet for investment, particularly for the benefit of retiring sedentary merchants. This second drive became the dominant factor and fairly early led the banks in the direction of industrial capitalism, that is, specialized capitalistic enterprise.

6. FORCES AT WORK

It is difficult to isolate forces, factors, or influences in social and economic changes. It is particularly difficult to do so in the case of mercantile capitalism because the system was so many sided and continued to change in its long period of growth.

Sombart has been the leading exponent of the rise and development of capitalism. His works have been stimulating, popular, and influential. Probably his thories will be discovered to be almost all wrong. At any rate, one of his main contributions, namely, that capitalism arose out of the spirit of exploitation, is probably entirely aside the point. Brentano once said that capitalism is "born in the heart of man." If he meant simply that individuals seek their own advantage, he was right. The essential of mercantile capitalism was not exploitation but control. Such exploitation as arose was the abuse of the system and not the system itself. No one would say that laxity of life was the basis of monasticism just because laxity periodically arose and had to be checked.

Religion has been regarded as a factor in business. Certainly Catholicism did about as much as it could officially to check mercantile capitalism, but its efforts were about as effective as when it tried to substitute saints for fairies, and devils for imps and witches. On the other hand, some of the Church's necessities really aided mercantile capitalism. Church officials needed incense, vestments, jewels, and the like and patronized the merchants who would furnish them. The Church needed to transport money to Rome and employed merchants, traveling and later sedentary, for the purpose. And then, where missionaries had gone to convert, merchants could later go to trade. This aided the earlier traveling merchants as it did the later sedentary merchants. Through its ethical teaching, the mediaeval Church tended to aid business. When it condemned sloth or idleness, it helped petty capitalism. When it denounced covetousness, it took a stand against mercantile capitalism, but it made up for this by praising prudence, temperance, and fortitude.

The Jews have certainly been regarded as influential. There is no question about the fact, though in the period we are considering the Jews were not always allowed to be merchants. They had helped spread Arabic ideas and thus aided petty capitalism. They did hustle, they did set the example of international trade, and they did ignore the petty local and ecclesiastical restriction on trade whenever possible. They were highly competitive, impersonal, and rational.

Protestantism, especially Calvinism, had much in common with Judaism. Artisans in Catholic France commonly became Protestants. Sedentary merchants in English towns commonly were early in accepting the new religion. While the artisans in France may have turned Protestant in opposition to the sedentary merchants who exploited them and who were in France more likely to be Catholics than Protestants, the sedentary merchants in England, Holland, and elsewhere early became Protestant to further the nationalistic aims of their class as against all outsiders—priests or merchants—who sought advantages within the nation. Once a merchant had become a Protestant, he might become more active, pioneering, and through religious bigotry more persevering and revengeful, as in the case of the Antwerper Usselinx.

It is rather difficult to have clear-cut ideas about religious influences when the ecclesiastical expression of religion is so devious and fluctuating. Certainly the Christian Churches have always been either turning to Christ or away from him. If Christ was in favor of petty capitalism, then the Churches were alternately for or against petty capitalism. If Christ was opposed to mercantile capitalism, then the Churches were alternately against it or indifferent to it. All comparative evidence shows that religion is, over the long run, more a derivative from economic and social necessities than a fundamental factor in them. During a short period, however, religion through its theology or other Church influence may be a potent though confused factor in economic and general social existence.

The Renaissance was thought by Sombart to have furthered the growth of capitalism. It seems to me that the Renaissance and capitalism were parts of the same movement to express individualism and to win income and satisfaction. Once developed, however, the Renaissance would aid in the further growth of mercantile capitalism, because it was worldly, rational, and planning. It gave rise to new needs for trade and it helped to extend the imagination of men beyond old confines and to devise new instruments for navigation, including maps, which indirectly aided mercantile capitalism in the last half of its existence.

No better illustration of the influence of the Renaissance of pagan law and learning could be found than the life and work of Conrad Peutinger, of Augsburg. Born in 1465, Peutinger was a young man when the Jews were expelled from Spain and when

America was discovered. He saw Spain and the Empire united. He witnessed the Protestant Revolution. Above all, he became part of the Italian Renaissance. He is ever remembered for his publication of a thirteenth-century map of Roman roads as they existed in the third century A. D. Learned in Roman law, intrigued by the mediaeval history of Germany, he espoused the cause of humanism as against the supernaturalism of the Church. It was easy for the descendant of sedentary merchants to be sympathetic with the financial phase of mercantile capitalism—already attained in Italy. That his city of Augsburg, where he was clerk, and his people of the Empire, in which he was a trusted adviser and diplomat, should go over to this advanced form of mercantile capitalism seemed to him natural and praiseworthy. Accordingly, he developed a policy to bring this about. In this policy he included three principal parts. First, there was to be no limit put upon the capital or the number of branches which a mercantile house or a merchant banker should have. Doubtless he had his friends the Fuggers and Welsers chiefly in mind. Second, he championed the market price against the just price of the Church. Third, he favored special concessions and monopolies for mercantile capitalists. From one standpoint, we may call Peutinger a liberal Catholic who, though a layman, was fifty years ahead of the official Church leaders. From another standpoint, we may call him the champion of mercantile capitalism against petty capitalism. Learned, luxurious, and lifeloving, he appreciated wealth and power. Active in his own life, he could appreciate the administrative accomplishments of others in both business and politics. What ripe enjoyment Conrad Peutinger and Alexander Hamilton would have together, could they but meet in ghostly banquet!

War has been laid at the doorstep of business as a bastard child of its own creation. The charge is only partly correct and therein lies the danger. War is a biological survival that is kept alive by many influences, including history, literature, and the amenities of family life. War is the flowering of nursery ambitions. It is a deep-seated ingredient of our animal selves. It has

CONRAD PEUTINGER, AUGSBURG, 1465-1547

JACOB FUGGER, AUGSBURG, EARLY SIXTEENTH CENTURY

become a function of our racialism, nationalism, culture, and business. It is no part of the *rationale* of business capitalism, but it is part of the abuse of business capitalism, and of mercantile capitalism. But warfare did not beget mercantile capitalism. In truth, warfare kept it back. It is true that a few merchants and a few merchant bankers profited but not the mercantile capitalists in general.

I would give an important place to the growth of double-entry bookkeeping as part of the technique of control used by the sedentary merchant, but I should put it down as a result of mercantile capitalism rather than a cause. In all probability the new accounting arose to meet the needs of the sedentary merchant. Similarly, in the fourteenth and fifteenth centuries the sedentary merchant (especially Italian) used Arabic (as well as Roman) numerals in his accounts, whilst municipal and national administrations generally clung to the Roman numerals.

Political development—in the direction of strong sovereigns, the enlightened despots—probably aided business. To me this political change was conditioned by the rise of mercantile capitalism without which there could have been no enlightened despots able to cut the heads off feudal barons or wage long wars against rival powers. Sedentary merchants provided them with goods and ships and merchant bankers provided them with cash or credits. Without these no great political power could have arisen on a national basis. It is a little bit helpful in this connection to remember that some of the new despots were themselves the heads of sedentary merchant, or merchant banking, families, as in the case of the Medici of Florence. Edward IV of England reversed the process and went into business himself to entrench his position in a feudal state.

Laws helping to create, extend, or prolong subsistence wages have been thought of as a conspiracy on the part of the capitalist employer in the towns and the landlords in the country against the workman and the laborer. The sedentary merchant has been thought of as specially encouraged by low costs resulting from low wages. The idea is that his profits were all the greater for this reason. If wages were kept down in one country and allowed to find their own level in other countries, the point would be well taken. But, if one country, such as England, kept wages down to a point near subsistence just to be able to compete with other countries, there would be little point to the argument. Of course we now know that keeping wages too low impairs the market for goods and injures all concerned. I can see no great general influence in wage legislation over a long period.

The incoming of Spanish gold and then silver raised prices and encouraged normal business and speculative business. The rise of metropolitan economy with its unprecedently large market and corresponding opportunities for trade tended in the same direction. Such factors were accelerating, nothing more.

The great and potent force underlying mercantile capitalism, as it seems to me, lies in the opportunity for gain which certain able administrators came to see as petty capitalism grew mature and old and then as mercantile capitalism discovered one type of enterprise after another. It is a fact that in life certain men have ability to hold things together, to make ends meet, to profit and help others to profit. Scholars, clergymen, artists, and reformers are notoriously deficient in this respect. Marginal and submarginal peasants and farmers are in the same condition. On the other hand, administrative ability was evident in several of the earliest popes, in occasional episcopal and monastic leaders, and in some lay lords. In mercantile capitalism there was an additional opportunity for people of administrative ability.

Just as petty capitalism had invited men of certain aptitudes to leave the farm, so did mercantile capitalism invite petty capitalists to abandon their pursuits for the new type of business—the kind that involved the performance of many functions at the same time and the control of many people for the general good. All this—control and power—was to come through the subtle process of impersonal relationship—that no man should eat who would not play a useful part in business or in his chosen occupation in life.

The great force was, in truth, not religious, military, cultural, political, or technological. It was the exercise of pagan, local, "vernacular," human opportunity to do something new that would profit society and that society would pay for. It was beyond the Church and beyond supernaturalism. It was worldly, rational, and planful. Blind trust in an external power—"one step enough for me"—was no part of the system of mercantile capitalism.

Here is a lesson in causation. Systems do not always arise out of other systems. They may grow out of their own past. To be sure, one potent force in human evaluation is the cross-fertilization of one system by another. We shall see this in the case of industrial capitalism, the birth of which was the result of the marriage of mercantile capitalism and applied science. In the rise of mercantile capitalism, however, we discern no technological forces and no supernatural or other external factor.

7. STRENGTH AND WEAKNESS OF MERCANTILE CAPITALISM

Before beginning an appraisal of the work of sedentary merchants, we should do well to note that there were really several types. They varied in respect to the lines of goods which they emphasized in their dealings. They varied in the degree of coöperation with other merchants, some playing almost a lone hand and others joining their fellows in all kinds of commercial activities. They varied in respect to the degree of risk taken: some were speculatively inclined, while others preferred to carry on a conservative business and at times to emphasize commission work for other merchants. They varied in the degree to which they emphasized transportation, the ownership of vessels, and the carriage of goods for other merchants. They differed in the amount of banking which they undertook. Accordingly, any appraisal which is attempted must concern the general work of mercantile capitalism without regard to special types of mercantile capitalists.

The first element of strength to be accorded the sedentary merchant or mercantile capitalist is his system of control over other men, regardless of the fact that those other men may at times have disliked that control. In a sense, the new order of business was comparable to the manorial-feudal system which did much for the rank and file of cultivators, though at times those cultivators did not relish the servitude to which they were subjected. The merchants, however, never attempted to follow up their economic control by any direct legal bondage. Indeed, their success with workers depended upon the existence of a large measure of freedom.

What was needed in early town economy was economic power and control in the hands of a few, so as to create a business system that would cater more to possible developments in production and marketing. Petty capitalists had done their utmost in small commercial towns. Further progress lay beyond their static satisfied condition. Not power machinery but business administration on a larger scale was needed. It is true that new business administration would reach out and control small men who wanted to be economically free. It is also true that the new administration would provide small masters in industry, fishing, and mining with both capital and a market far beyond their own command. The difference in market is the difference between town economy and metropolitan economy.

The sedentary merchant scoured the late town and the early metropolitan market for goods to sell. He also took orders from afar for goods to be made in his own region. The business of the Van der Molens in Antwerp in the early sixteenth century illustrates this very well and some persons would think it really important because art objects were involved. The four brothers of the Van der Molen family had their main office in Antwerp and another office in Venice where one of the four was in charge. They exported and imported on their own account and bought and sold on commission, particularly for Italian merchants.

They were commissioned to buy not only woolen and linen cloth but tapestries of special design and quality. Factors bought the goods in question or had them manufactured. The goods were then sent by common carriers who served the sedentary merchants by overland routes to Italy. Here we have Italians seeking Flemish tapestries, as well as Dutch paintings, which illustrated themes and events that appealed to them. The cultural import of this kind of organization must have been considerable.

The system and the administrative abilities of the sedentary merchants led to great flexibility and to a measure of stability. The sedentary merchant could lay up his ships, keep his factors at home, and tighten his belt while waiting for better times. To be sure, workmen and fishermen and colonial planters would suffer but they had other means of livelihood which could support them for two or three years. At the end of that period, business would begin again and all would return to prosperity. Now, this is not an even keel, not stability in any sense of perfection; and yet the periods of distress were usually not very long and, when long—due to warfare, we may say that they would have been longer without the sedentary merchant's flexibility.

The administrative ability developed by the sedentary merchant and merchant banker was available for the management of joint stock companies and for the organization, management, and reorganization of national finance as occasion served. The work of Jacques Cœur in France, Sir Thomas Gresham in England, and Robert Morris in America illustrate this point.

The chief strength of sedentary merchants lay in their day-to-day administration of private business—doing the World's work in commerce. In passing, we may note that some sedentary merchants also contributed to the formulation of economic policy and even theory. Malynes, Misselden, Mun, North, and Child may be cited in England and Pelatiah Webster, Tench Coxe, and Henry Lee, Jr., in America. In many cases the poorer the merchant the greater the theorizer, but let that pass.

During the period of the régime of the sedentary merchant there occurred a growth of wealth, well-being, and culture both in the ancient and the late mediaeval and early modern periods that are unparalleled, except for recent times. More goods for more people at lower prices; but, of course, not enough goods for enough people at sufficiently low prices—from the standpoint of the consumer and without reference to general conditions.

The sedentary merchant was not without a cultural position in the world of his day. I pass over as unimportant the fact that some merchants were more successful in amassing wealth than in learning how to use it. Both ancient and modern writers have been eloquent on this subject. It has an interesting analogy in the conspicuous display of learning by some journalistic scholars. There is an unwritten chapter on the sedentary merchant's contribution to humanism. The rank and file of sedentary merchants everywhere occupied a dignified position in their community. Their standards of consumption were frequently imitated by the rural nobles and the urban professional classes. They are noted for their support of art, philosophy, letters, and exploration. The books of history are not lacking in information of this sort. A few of the merchants developed fine critical tastes and a handful even displayed creative abilities. All in all, the beautiful houses and splendid palaces of the merchants compare favorably with rural residences of landed gentlemen and nobles. Merchants' houses led the way in size and comfort, light and air, and gardens and green fields. To many of the merchants, such buildings were the avenues to alliances with noble families or the visible signs of nobility which they themselves secured by purchase or by force in many a land in Western Europe.

The weakness of sedentary merchants lay just around the corner. The control exercised through junior partners, factors, and a few servants was essentially weak because the operations were so spread out that effective guidance was impossible. A major problem then, as now, was to find able and reliable business lieutenants. The joint stock company helped to concentrate management, for instance, in the case of English companies in Russia, India, and Hudson's Bay. At distant points, trained officials of the company could operate according to instructions and according to fresh circumstances with a higher degree of success than could the ordinary person on whom the sedentary merchant had to rely. In our day, we find a comparable problem in discovering satisfactory managers for branch factories, distributing plants, and retail stores. Whether this source of weakness would have proved fatal to mercantile capitalism is, however, quite another matter.

Along the same line was an accounting difficulty. With a dozen or more ventures afloat, the merchant could not feel sure of what his exact position was. To be sure, this very diversity was a source of strength, unless there was an unusual series of disasters coupled with a depression at home. It was the habit of many sedentary merchants to use their credit to the limit. In other words, they would embark upon the maximum number of adventures and at the same time underwrite the adventures of others. Often marine disasters were followed by widespread bankruptcies when overextended merchants were called upon to meet their obligations. Although this was a weakness of individual merchants and of individual groups, the system itself would probably not have fallen for this reason.

We get the impression that mercantile capitalists had succeeded rather too well and weakened the position of the business structure and therefore of society also. By the sixteenth and seventeenth centuries they had changed Europe from a land of chronic undersupply to a land of normal oversupply. There are no statistical evidences of this, just unprecedented complaints of gluts, low prices for certain goods, and losses and bankruptcies of dealers, both merchants and retailers. The oversupply lay not in manufactured goods but in raw products which were pouring in from colonial and oriental sources and from an improved agriculture at home. Continued oversupply would have ruined business in the long run and therefore undermine the economic base of society. There were two possible remedies: one was to improve, even to revolutionize, manufacturing processes which would use up the raw materials and increase the supply of cheap industrial products and at the same time give employment to idle persons at home and raise the general plane of living; the other was monopoly and restraint and protection in the interest of high prices in the face of plenty. Such rival systems come constantly into conflict. The New Deal in America introduced the system of monopoly, scarcity, and high prices in 1933, but the Supreme Court killed it two years later. The early New Deal in the colonies and the sedentary merchants at home had much in common. Monopoly and restriction were as popular with big business (sedentary merchants) in England as with small farmers in colonial Virginia and Maryland.

There was a chronic tendency for mercantile families to dry up. If successful, the experience and capital of such families were removed to some other pursuit, such as investment in real estate, merchant banking, or gentleman farming. From the standpoint of business, and therefore the society which business serves, the draining off into cultural pursuits is unfortunate, especially if the culture is but assimilative and critical without being constructive. But, at this point, we get into difficulty, namely, the thought that enjoyment is really the end of life and retirement to enjoy is an acceptable goal. In the last analysis, however, this is a highly individualistic point of view and somewhat anti-social. I leave the issue for others to follow out. At any rate, while this withdrawal, or it might be minor specialization in business, would weaken mercantile capitalism, it would hardly have destroyed it.

About 1750 Postlethwayt pointed out that there was a lack of mercantile colleges in which to train young men entering business. Hardly any type of business needed more equipment on the part of the young man. Apprenticeship and marriage with a merchant's daughter were normal means of getting into business. There were local schools in the chief towns and seaports where arithmetic, bookkeeping, Latin, and vernacular languages were taught, but while such instruction was helpful it did not go far. Business had to wait till the latter half of last century before its needs were considered by those concerned with education, and then it was found that the chief task was to learn from business men what the best methods were and to hand on to learners what could be culled from outstanding and significant examples.

There was also a weakness on the side of the flow of capital—as distinct from the use. While the mechanism for the putting out of capital, from the hands of the owner to the hands of the ultimate user, had been improved, and improved chiefly by sedentary merchants as we have seen, still the rate of interest required to make the capital flow remained high. It had fallen in the sixteenth century to eight per cent and in the seventeenth to six, but still in highly competitive lands, as old countries were apt to be, this rate put a heavy burden on business by raising costs to a point where only the most efficient were likely to succeed. Perhaps it was high interest rates that forced the sedentary merchant to try to keep down labor costs or wages, thereby restricting his own market.

From the public or social point of view the sedentary merchant was in an exposed position. A few of the thoughtful citizens might appreciate the abundance of wares and the low price of the same, but the rank and file were more impressed with the low wages which were paid to workers. Sentimentalists swung into line. The sedentary merchant was depending upon the middle classes, not the laboring classes, for a market to a large extent. Even in the thirteenth and fourteenth centuries artisans rose up and attacked the servants and the persons of the merchants in one town after another. In England in 1649 the Levellers cried out against commercial monopolies, especially of the merchants operating in regulated companies, and sought a reform of debtor laws. Both of the grievances in question were of long standing but had not been much remedied.

Opposition to a type of business may be widespread and deep seated without any change following in its wake. Indeed, there is probably no social institution that does not engender strong antagonism. Opposition is normal; it challenges and embarrasses but does not kill.

There was a weakness in the heel of the sedentary merchant that long went unnoted. He was so occupied with multiple functions that he could not take on one more, especially if that function happened to involve technological skill or knowledge. The Lombes, silk dealers of London, succeeded in setting up silk mills, Sir Dudley North had a chemical laboratory for experimentation, and so on, but business administration did not generally leave time for attention to mechanical problems. The helplessness of the sedentary merchant is seen in the case of Almy and Brown who in Providence, Rhode Island, sought to adopt the new technique of power machinery to the manufacture of cotton yarn. Their letters show a pathetic helplessness, born of inability to grasp or control the technological problems at hand. A few sedentary merchants had the necessary skill or feeling for mechanics or had the sense to hire those who had and accordingly could enter into the Industrial Revolution. But, as they made the necessary adjustments, they had to take steps that killed the system of mercantile capitalism: such sedentary merchants became industrial capitalists. Much of the actual capital accumulated under the régime of mercantile capitalism was turned into enterprises undertaken under the new order of industrial capitalism or was invested in land. The gentleman farmers of Norfolk perfected technique of agricultural production that spread around the civilized world. In other words the actual capital amassed in mercantile capitalism financed much of the Industrial and the Agricultural Revolution, especially in England.

8. DEVELOPMENT WITHIN MERCANTILE CAPITALISM: VARIOUS TYPES OF SEDENTARY MERCHANTS

The sedentary merchant held sway for about five hundred years. During this long period, however, he was growing in functions, wealth, and control. Unfortunately we have no adequate information about these changes. The effort to sketch, largely by way of a résumé, the changes in the development of the sedentary merchant and his system of mercantile capitalism is tentative. And it is to be remembered that individuals and firms do not necessarily conform exactly to any one type.

The first type was the *beginner*. He was a storekeeper or shopkeeper who in the fulness of his ambition was becoming a merchant. He developed a set of functions which provided him with a restricted but integrated business. He imported, wholesaled, retailed, and perhaps exported. The goods he imported, he preferred to wholesale to retailers in his own town or in adjoining towns. Some of his imports he would himself sell by retail. In undeveloped colonial towns of the seventeenth and eighteenth centuries, he would take in country produce for the goods he sold by retail. These products he would sell locally or export abroad, along with other goods in steady demand abroad—such as furs, pork, grain, and rice. True, he might not send exports abroad to pay for imports: he might pay for them by bills of exchange as early as the thirteenth century in Western Europe. Such a merchant might charter a ship, rent cargo space, or own shares in a vessel. His lack of capital would not permit him to invest much in transportation.

These beginners slipped over into the status of *early mature merchants* when they invested in ships, operated considerable warehousing plants, and carried on some banking. They transported their own goods and those of other merchants, stored their own goods and those of other merchants, and did their own banking and in addition some for their clients and friends. Frequently they entered into temporary partnerships with other merchants in order to make export and import less risky.

Or they might enter into informal groups of merchants for the purpose of mutually insuring cargoes and ships. This type would be found in fourteenth-century Europe and eighteenth-century America. John Hancock and Robert Morris are examples in America. The success that came to a sedentary merchant at this stage of his growth encouraged friends and acquaintances to entrust their surplus capital to him for investment in trade.

Later mature merchants, performing the various functions already enumerated, were distinguished by the development of control over other business men, such as petty capitalists or workmen. These might be engaged in manufacture, fishing, mining, or trapping. In Europe they would be found in the fifteenth and sixteenth centuries (earlier in Italy and Flanders) and in America in the eighteenth. As opportunities came their way, they would invest in joint stock trading ventures or indeed form companies on their own initiative. Sir Thomas Smythe is an outstanding illustration in London.

The *financial type* of sedentary merchant with branch houses grew up in Italy and Southern Germany largely in the fifteenth and sixteenth centuries but never was developed by Englishmen and never reached American shores at all. Rich families of sedentary merchants formed terminal partnerships for trade, manufacture, and so on. The senior partner provided capital and formulated policies. The operating partner took care of management. Here we find an adumbration of the financial capitalism that grew up in Europe and America in the late nineteenth century. The type is illustrated by the Medici of Florence and the Fuggers of Augsburg. Such merchants had many branches extending from Naples to London and Portugal to Hungary. These branches were in the charge of junior partners, whether members of the family or not. In these branches were carried on both trade and banking. The trade was in such staples as cloth, spices, and copper. The banking consisted in receiving deposits, in making loans to private persons and to governments, exchanging coins, and handling bills of exchange for merchants, travelers, and others.

The fair promise of mercantile capitalism reached its height in this phase of growth, that is, in the merchant banker. The rise of an oversea trade in the Southern hemisphere and Western World, however, first put this form of capitalism under a cloud and then killed it. The new geographical discoveries, trade routes, and colonization started a kind of trade that the late mature merchant could best flourish in. The high hopes of establishing a régime of financial dominance centering in Florence, Venice, or Augsburg gave way to the rising prominence of Lisbon and Antwerp and then Amsterdam and London. This advanced type of mercantile capitalism missed its destiny with the shift of dominance from Southern to Western Europe.

Decline and decay seem to be an inescapable part of the social as of the natural order. Within the circle of mercantile capitalism decay is marked by the shift to *disintegrating specialists*. For instance, some sedentary merchants invested their capital in land and joint stock companies which carried on a banking or commercial business. The investment involved little or no management and a minimum of risk. It represented the decline of enterprise in mercantile families and a shift to other than business pursuits—the idle life of the landed gentleman. Other sedentary merchants might maintain their enterprise but shift from the hazardous trade to the more secure operations of the specialized merchant banker. The London goldsmiths provide an excellent example of this growth. They gave up the business of a commercial goldsmith in order to specialize in banking. William Braund illustrates a high degree of specialization in the financing of London's foreign trade in the eighteenth century. In America, Stephen Girard shifted from the early mature phase to the disintegrating specialization of banking. Less venturesome souls in America stayed in foreign trade but shifted the major risks to others by specializing in commission agency, in which they received goods on consignment and obtained their own reward from a fee which was a percentage of the goods sold. Henry Lee, Jr., of Boston, illustrates this type.

The following diagram shows the growth of the various types in various areas down to the disintegration of the system.

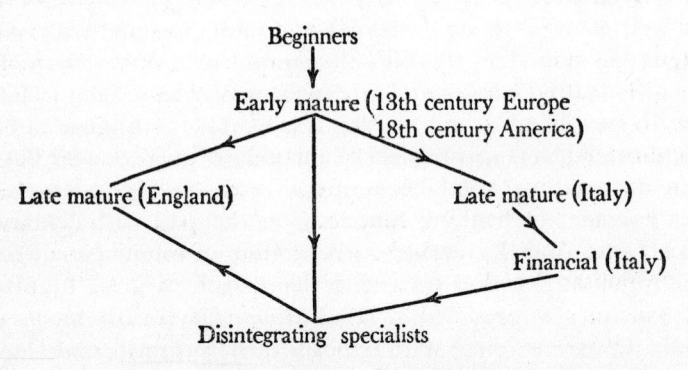

```
                          Beginners
                              │
                              ▼
                  Early mature (13th century Europe
                              ╲   18th century America)
                  ╱                           ╲
    Late mature (England)          Late mature (Italy)
                                              ╲
                                        Financial (Italy)
                  ╲           │           ╱
                   Disintegrating specialists
```

CHANGES IN MERCANTILE CAPITALISM: TYPES OF SEDENTARY MERCHANTS

All who are interested in the sedentary merchant are invited to study such forms as can be found in Europe, America, and the Orient. Obviously only part of the story is told in the diagram above. Outstanding in the picture, however, is a threefold variation. In Italy and, we may add, Southern Germany, the system of mercantile capitalism displayed a financial phase that marks off Southern from Northern Europe. In the incipient metropolitan centers of the Italian nursery of business men (and of scholars and artists) the mercantile system reached perhaps a logical phase in which the capital accumulations and administrative experience of merchants were used for the control of economic life. The money power of the great merchant banking families of Italy went over into the arena even of political control and dominance. At this point, mercantile capitalism was exposed to turmoil and destruction. The system as a whole was saved by the alternative development of England, Holland, and France, where the highest type was the late mature sedentary merchant who played so strategic a part in opening up world trade and distant colonization.

In America there was time only for development of the first two phases. Even if there had been more time, conditions would have sorely hampered further growth. London merchants were so well entrenched that colonial and early national progress along the same lines was difficult. Control over others, such as small industrial masters and fishermen, was practised but could hardly be carried far in a country possessing so much free land. Commercial banks arising in Philadelphia, New York, and Boston during the period beginning in 1781–84 precluded the development of banking functions on the part of sedentary merchants. And the marked concentration of colonial trade in metropolitan London precluded the growth of great branch systems such as prevailed in late mediaeval and early modern Italy. Of course, there were opportunities for great wealth in American trade but within the undeveloped form of the early mature system, as exemplified by the lives of Thomas Hancock, Stephen Girard, and John Jacob Astor. It is profitable to reflect why merchants, living at so late a date, were so undeveloped in functions. We may note two rather obvious facts: in America it was not possible to carry very far the dependent wholesale handicraft system (control of handicraftsmen) nor to build up a merchant banking system, first, because of a lack of capital and, later (1781 onwards), because of the competition of commercial banks.

9. END OF THE SEDENTARY MERCHANT AND MERCANTILE CAPITALISM

The sedentary merchant and mercantile capitalism were killed not by the opposition of the Church, by the criticisms of Adam Smith, by the antagonism of the Physiocrats, nor yet by more popular and less vocal discontent and opposition, but rather by specialization from within and by the Industrial Revolution (at least partly) from without.

MERCANTILE CAPITALISM

The sedentary merchant and mercantile capitalism have actually lived on in less advanced parts of the world and is found even yet in the Orient and in other parts where specialization and the Industrial Revolution have failed to arrive. In those parts of China away from the seacoast and away from occidental influence there have been, and still are, two types of capitalism —the petty and the mercantile. The genius of the Chinese has known how to use petty capitalism to the fullest extent. Chinese storekeepers, shopkeepers, pedlars, and traveling merchants have played a dominant part. Of these the greatest were unquestionably the shopkeepers or small master artisans who have produced objects of art and utility of fine taste and rare beauty. It is doubtful whether the Chinese traveling merchants left the confines of China much before the twelfth century. Up to that time, for several centuries, foreigners, such as Jews and Arabs, had visited the Flowery Kingdom, but the Chinese were slow in paying a return visit. From the twelfth to the seventeenth century Chinese traveling merchants were venturing farther and farther afield in southern seas and even on to India. At home, sedentary merchants were beginning to arise in the larger cities and seaports. By the seventeenth century the merchants of the gild or Hong were well entrenched in the city of Canton where they had a monopoly of all trading with British merchants. In advanced provinces such as Shansi some of these sedentary merchants were becoming merchant bankers. In spite of the sharp practices of Chinese business men generally, there is unanimity of applause for the integrity of the sedentary merchant when operating on his honor. The dealings of the East India Company in Canton illustrate this. It may be a fairly accurate statement to say that China as a whole will pass from petty capitalism to industrial capitalism, without having developed mercantile capitalism as a dominant system. It is hard to avoid the reflection that the Chinese, the most economic (and least political) of peoples, have made but little progress in the higher reaches of business.

A brilliant Chinese student of economic history, Mr. Lien

Shihsheng, has generously responded to my request for information about mercantile capitalism in China. His statement, made at Hongkong, November 30, 1938, runs as follows.

In the early Han dynasty [3d cent. B. C. to 1st cent. A. D.], big merchants lived on high interest, while small tradesmen were doing a retail business. Neither of them ever missed a chance of selling their goods at a price several times higher than usual, whenever a political crisis occurred. In this way, these merchants were able to keep themselves free from manual work and their wives and daughters free from spinning and weaving. At the same time, they and their family enjoyed the most beautifully embroidered clothes and the most delicious food. By virtue of their financial power, they gradually came into close contact with high officials who in turn gave them all sorts of advantages in doing business. Moreover, these merchants kept a number of scholars and writers as their *protégés* who could speak and act on their behalf.

In the North Sung dynasty [10th to 12th cent.], the capital Pi'enliang, now Kaifeng, Honan, was the political and commercial center of the country. The biggest monastery in the capital was used as a fair and was open five times a month. All sorts of business were transacted in the monastery. The tea houses and restaurants, being very well equipped, became places of great temptation to business men who came to prefer to take their meals there rather than eat at home. No big shop closed till midnight and each opened early the next morning. Some crowded places would carry on their business day and night without intermission of any kind.

After the fall of the North Sung dynasty, the capital was moved to Linan, now Hangchow, Chekiang. This city became the center of trade both by land and by sea. It had 440 gilds, and within and without the city there were at least a dozen pawnshops.

Now, let me turn from historical development to current conditions. I shall pass over Shanghai, Tientsin, Canton, and Hankow as highly industrialized cities, more or less under the influence of foreign capital. Rather let me speak of Peiping, Foochow, and Chentu. I have direct knowledge of the first two and rely upon a recent survey of the third made by my friend Professor Tao Hsisheng.

Peiping, Foochow, and Chentu are at bottom unaffected by the Industrial Revolution. In fact, business men in these cities operate just as their ancestors did a thousand years ago. Examples are the merchants dealing in rugs and enamelware in Peiping, those handling tea, oil, and lacquer in Foochow, and those selling medicines and silk in Chentu. Their scale of production is so small, their technique of manufacturing so antiquated, and their methods of marketing so slow that they should be identified with mercantile capitalism, pure and simple.

In my native city of Fukien, the tea merchants are generally the richest people; at least their financial power is unrivalled by that of the small industrial workers. Early in the spring, they form partnerships with their friends and relatives or absorb the limited savings of widows and small business men. Then, they open workshops in their own mansions or in their ancestral halls, or in shrines and temples. They stay at home as the managers of their business and send their agents into the neighboring villages to buy tea leaves. When the tea leaves are ready, they are sent to outworkers, generally women and children, to be sorted. Payment is in piece wages. When the tea has been well roasted, finished, and properly packed in wooden cases by workmen who have acquired the technique, it is sent by water to Foochow where the tea merchants have their representatives, generally their brothers or older sons or other close relatives who can bargain with foreign customers or agents. Since Foochow has been blockaded this present year (1938), many agents of the merchants are coming down to Hongkong to trade.

The formulation of policy and the management of business are the chief distinguishing marks of the tea merchants. They do not necessarily carry on the same business each year. They may close their shops for one or two years, for they must balance the supply of good tea with the foreign demand for the same. If they are expert in policy formulation, they will make a lot of money; otherwise, they may lose all. The merchant of moderate means and of no great calibre will always hesitate to embark upon the tea business.

The chief source of information which the tea merchants use is not the telegraph or press but the tea house. This is a Chinese institution of great importance for the dissemination of many kinds of information of concern to business. It is in the tea house that wholesale dealers and big importers and exporters meet and it is here that all disputes among merchants of the same trade are settled. Unless the mechanism of state control is put into force, the tea merchants with their traditional methods of production and distribution will remain the best survival of mercantile capitalism in Modern China. Thus ends the statement by Mr. Lien Shihsheng.

The tradition of the merchant prince lives on in literature and nursery stories to say nothing of history. His ideas, embodied in mercantilism, continued to be championed by former sedentary merchants such as Tench Coxe in America and by others who had never engaged in trade. His policies went over into industrial capitalism but only in fragments. For instance, in the Boston type of textile manufactures the carefully balanced and coördinated financial policy which began in 1813 still continues though badly shattered. In accordance with this policy, production, marketing and finance are kept separate. The financier—treasurer or president of the company—gives but little attention to production or marketing, leaving the first to a mill agent and the second to a selling agent. His supreme task is to keep financially solvent and to secure a net income. He closes his plant when profits are not in sight. If one of his factories needs help, he may draw upon resources from another factory and so on.

Of course, our whole private investment policy of diversification is reminiscent of mercantile capitalism. It is a device for securing an income with a minimum of risk. Some measure of control may be involved but not much. Flexibility is a major concern. Social responsibilities do not loom large. In the later financial capitalistic system there are interesting analogies, as we shall see.

The several functions performed by the sedentary merchants were taken over by specialists. Some of the new specialists might be former sedentary merchants. Some of these merchants devoted themselves to the export or import trade, while some became purely commission merchants taking few risks under the new régime. Some entered manufacture, some transportation. Some took office as administrators under their governments. Others, such as J. P. Cushing, of Boston, who had been a merchant in Canton, retired to more leisurely tasks of investment in bridge and turnpike companies, factories, insurance companies, railroads, and so on. When mercantile capitalism burst asunder, the parts flew in many directions.

The sedentary merchant gave way before the industrialist, and mercantile capitalism before industrial capitalism. The world lost its most stable type of capitalism and one of its most dignified and useful servants in high places.

Chapter V

INDUSTRIAL CAPITALISM

The Triumph of Firm Specialization in Big Business

Put your eggs into one basket, then watch the basket;
Compete with rivals, drive your men.
Make and sell; finance takes second place.
Your firm is your monument, a corporation your exit.

1. THE RISE OF INDUSTRIAL CAPITALISM

The new type of capitalism was very different from the old. On the surface, the new was less dignified and more hurried, fighting, and grasping. Below the surface, both forms were alike in that they were driving toward profits through social service. Society will pay its capitalists like its laborers, musicians, preachers, and soldiers, only in case they serve. Below the surface, of course, there were fundamental differences. Industrial capitalists were specialists who, wherever possible, used power machinery, drove their employees hard, and preferred paid workers to agents and, gradually, corporations to partnerships. The tendency toward specialization, however, was the underlying characteristic. This was a change in the policy of business capitalists. It was along the lines that had been followed by petty capitalists in town economy and was in keeping with the cultural and general scientific growth of the times.

The period of this new system of industrial capitalism might be put down roughly as 1790–1890. At both ends, there was, as is usual under such circumstances, a good deal of overlapping. And the movement as such began in England and spread to Europe, America, and the rest of the world of advanced civilization.

When such a fundamental change occurs in the social order as a transfer from mercantile to industrial capitalism, we discover the need for studying the weakening of the old system as well as the strengthening of the new. In other words, we want to know what preparation there was for the return to the specialization of the petty capitalists but, of course, the return in the field of big and not petty business, not in a town market but in a metropolitan market.

We have already noted that some sedentary merchants tended to emphasize ship-operation. An early example is William Canynges, of Bristol, and a late example William Gray, of Salem and later Boston, Massachusetts. Now, just as some merchants might have more ships than they could use in their own trade, so must others have had less shipping than they needed. Smaller sedentary merchants could save on capital by hiring freight on the ships of other merchants. This was as true of Merchant Staplers in fifteenth-century England as of minor colonial merchants such as William Trotter in Philadelphia, 1803-15. When regular liners were established, first of sailing vessels and then of steamships, there was a further invitation to the sedentary merchant to rely upon others for transportation.

When the bill of exchange became a recognized instrument and was in common use, not only payable at fairs but in large centers, then there was a further invitation to specialize. A merchant who wished chiefly or exclusively to export might do so and import bills of exchange. Similarly a merchant, such as Trotter above mentioned, who wished to import might pay his London or Liverpool or Leeds commission merchant by sending him bills of exchange. Be it noted, that such one-sided traders would commonly have no ships.

Manufacturers who arose in the iron industry and in the textiles to sell their output chiefly to sedentary merchants were specializing in an important way. The importance grew in the industrial capitalistic stage. And so with merchant bankers and specialized marine insurance underwriters like Angerstein. Promoters appeared in mining and in house construction. And pure risk-takers, like William Braund, arose in metropolitan centers.

In time, these leaks in the ship of mercantile capitalism might have been disastrous. Actually, it was a major event that precipitated the end of mercantile capitalism and introduced industrial capitalism in a hurry. This was the movement of the Industrial Revolution which the system of mercantile capitalism had itself called into being.

The Industrial Revolution added power machinery to man's productive equipment. The sedentary merchant had been putting pressure upon specialized artisans and farmer-artisans for centuries to hurry up and produce, and to make goods that could be sold in markets other than their own. About all that could be done under existing circumstances was done in changing over from the independent to the dependent form of the wholesale handicraft system and in introducing the central workshop with its discipline and division of labor. Still, there were not enough goods of high quality, uniformity, and low price to meet the obvious needs of the growing market which the sedentary merchant had partly discovered and partly created.

So much for the demand side. The supply of manufactured goods, low in price and high in quality, was met by at least three groups—sedentary merchants, industrial entrepreneurs who had long supplied sedentary merchants with goods, and petty capitalists. There may have been a fourth class—laborers—who could be put here on the supply side of the Industrial Revolution. That they should have contributed labor on jobs making new machines and even ideas in the process of inventions is not to be denied. To identify the blacksmiths, carpenters, and wheelwrights of the Industrial Revolution with the modern permanent laboring class, however, is simply inviting confusion and mixing elements that do not belong together.

Sedentary merchants contributed capital, policy, and management to the power-machine industry introduced during the Industrial Revolution. While they were in no position to qualify as experts along lines of mechanical engineering, they did direct processes, influence procedures, and procure machines and the inventors of machines. Sir Thomas Lombe (1685–1735) had been apprenticed to a mercer of London, was admitted to membership in the Mercers' Company, and became a mercer in the metropolis that was fast becoming a center for the silk trade. Trading in silks and other wares, doubtless from France and Italy, he conceived the idea of making silk thread by machinery as it was being made in Italy. He sent his half-brother, John, who had mechanical ability, to learn the secrets of silk-throwing in Italy. Then, after 1718, he set up a silk-throwing mill on the River Derwent. Lombe himself remained in London where he was more concerned with the marketing of the product than with superintending the technical processes. How much of his large fortune was made from manufacturing and how much from merchandising is unknown. Because of the fact that Lombe stood more or less alone, we must conclude that, as far as England was concerned, he was the morning star, not the rising sun, of the Industrial Revolution. Many other sedentary merchants had made and were to make efforts to produce goods in mills, to be sure, with simple power arrangements. Paper mills are an example.

Almy and Brown, sedentary merchants of Providence, Rhode Island, made similar contributions, only, instead of sending somebody to steal ideas and plans abroad, they found someone —Samuel Slater—who had already stolen them in England and had arrived in America with them. The merchants, entering into partnership with the mechanic—a skilled spinner, a master of power-machine technique, and an ambitious man—started a stream of industrial capitalism that still continues—the textile industry of the Blackstone River. On the Charles River, and later on the Merrimack, other merchants began another course of development and another branch of industrial capitalism. Francis Cabot Lowell stole from England, as Lombe had from Italy, ideas, patterns, and designs for manufacturing—cotton weaving, however, rather than silk-throwing. Another merchant —Patrick Tracy Jackson—contributed capital, policy, and management which he could do without stint, since he had abandoned the business of a sedentary merchant. He and his fellows in the Boston Manufacturing Company hired a skilled blacksmith to make machines, for one of which Lowell had the designs.

The second group of leaders in providing the new revolutionary technique of manufacture were the industrial entrepreneurs. The ironmasters provide a good illustration. Among these the Crowleys and their partners are outstanding. Another example is Matthew Boulton and his son.

The third group, the petty capitalists, are the most intriguing of all. Aiming at rising in the world of business, they bent every effort toward success. The blacksmith, the carpenter, and the wheelwright are examples of petty capitalists who could turn to a power-machine technique of production. None of these, however, equalled the barber, Arkwright.

The most gigantic figure in the Industrial Revolution in England was Sir Richard Arkwright. Born in an impoverished family, he early became a master barber. In this trade, he invented a dyeing process for human hair. This hair he bought chiefly from young girls and sold it, when dyed, to wigmakers at great profit to himself. In an atmosphere of textile invention, he turned his attention to improving spinning machinery in 1767. Taking out a patent in 1769 for a spinning frame, he set up his factory. His frame would spin more cotton threads than any other machine and, above all, finer and stronger threads, so that the warp yarn could be spun by machine as well as the woof yarn. His first power was horse, then in 1771 water, and, finally in 1790, a Boulton and Watt steam engine. In 1775 a patent was extended to include carding, drawing, roving, and spinning. When Arkwright needed capital, a local banker recommended him to go to Jedediah Strutt, the improver of the stocking frame and later the employer of Samuel Slater. A partnership solved Arkwright's pressing need for equipment. His fundamental contribution was to make the central workshop into a factory. Throwing many small master spinners out of employment, he gave jobs to many more. That he offered work did not prevent the mob from destroying one of his big mills.

Arkwright was an asthmatic giant, a prolific inventor and adopter of other men's ideas, an able promoter, and, above all, a business administrator. He had confidence, drive, persistence, organizing power, and capacity to coördinate production and distribution. His genius lay in his ability to make mechanical processes practical and to administer the business he created. He combined Boulton and Watt in one person. He was Grand Marshal in the field of industrial capitalism.

For our purposes it is a matter of minor importance that economists, also, were changing their emphasis. During mercantile capitalism the anonymous author of the *Discourse of the Common Weal,* also Misselden, Mun, Child, North, and so on, emphasized trade, especially foreign trade. Then came a turn away from an emphasis on mercantilism to production. Petty (1623–87) was much concerned with this aspect of economic activity. Adam Smith more definitely headed a school of industrial economists with an emphasis upon labor using land, particularly among primitive peoples. Although Petty stressed labor value, he included under labor the administration of business men. Such cannot be said of all later industrial economists. Out of the theory of labor value, elaborated by Marx, have come socialism and communism. Until central workshops, and then factories, came into being, labor had not been emphasized much since the days of petty capitalism. And now, with the supremacy of the factory, we have less real need for emphasis on labor's contribution than ever, because the increasingly important factors are machinery (capital) and business administration. A formula for the laborer and workman that arises out of the evolution of business is as follows: (1) work, (2) coöperate with other classes, and (3) build up a combination of productive capacity, importance in consumption, and general citizenship in war and peace.

2. THE NEW TRANSPORTATION

If the first victory of the Industrial Revolution was in manufacture, the second lay in transportation. Moreover, there was the same kind of preparation for the big changes in transportation (railroad and steamship) as occurred in the case of manufacture. There was an existing demand for better transportation and there had been as much response to the demand as was possible without the steam engine. The response to the demand was of various sorts. There were improved devices in land vehicles and sailing vessels. There were advances in the art of navigation. There were regular services for passengers and freight. Monthly sailings between Liverpool and America rivalled the old services from and to London in the spring and the autumn. And, for centuries, there had been specialization in transportation on the part of petty carriers—waggoners and horse-train operators. Indeed, there was some evidence of a capacity for big business in land transportation such as was found in the organization of the carrying trade between Antwerp and Venice and other Italian cities in the sixteenth century.

On the side of improved avenues of land transportation, something had been done before the nineteenth century. The bridges had been improved and more had been constructed. Highways had been broadened and paved. Canals had been built in strategic places but their numbers were not large. However, canals passing through or radiating from Birmingham had been built in time to facilitate the distribution of Boulton and Watt steam engines.

Not only freight and passengers but also letters were being

182   INDUSTRIAL CAPITALISM

carried more or less regularly between the chief towns and cities before the Industrial Revolution and the revolution in transportation took place. Stage coaches were more vitalizing in their economic and cultural effects than has been commonly realized.

The great early contribution in transportation was the railroad, which increased the volume of trade with the seaports and opened up and intensified the economic life of the inland everywhere. The coming of the railroad was like the resurrection of the dead to the fulfillment of the promised life in plenty.

About the history of the railroads we know a great deal and yet our knowledge is largely centered in routes, personalities, equipment, and financing. The vital story of railroad administration is almost unknown, except at a few scattered spots. We need many studies of the policies of railroad executives and of the management of the railroads under those policies. Probably we should find that the first period in the history of railroads, particularly in America, covered the period about 1830–69. During this time the dominant effort was to produce the service of transportation in the area in question. The stockholders were concerned with the organization of the company and the choice of executives. The executives formulated policies for the construction and operation of the line. Securing effective equipment taxed the best energies of many boards of directors and officials. At first, the lines were separate local stretches of rails between two towns. Later several of such lines were amalgamated to form district lines and finally these district lines were in turn put together to constitute inter-metropolitan or regional systems. In America, unlike Belgium, France, and Germany, there was no unified plan for a national network, only a set of plans for many systems. By 1869 railroads had been built from Atlantic to Pacific. But, even more, a system that was to have great weight had been formed—the New York Central, extending from New York to Chicago, both north and south of Lake Erie, under the leadership of a remarkable executive, Cornelius Vanderbilt I. At last, the all-water route was formed, not singly by the extension of rails—that was completed in outline by 1852—but by the effective building up of a regional and inter-metropolitan system.

Vanderbilt was only one of several distinguished railroad leaders of the 1860's and later, but he was a leader of the leaders. His administration was to close the first phase of the new transportation and introduce a new one. The second phase was one of severe competition from 1869 to 1893. This was wholly American and, by and large, popular. Inter-metropolitan systems competed with one another for big business and long hauls. Agreements were made with customers to allow rebates and one town was discriminated against in favor of another. The people of America liked competition but this was becoming too hot.

Unfortunately for the railroads, and for business in general, the period from 1866 to 1897 experienced a downward trend of prices and of profits. The country was young, however, and goods in plenty had to be hauled. But while this trade provided enough income to meet most expenses, it did not provide for all. Accordingly, many of the railroads went into bankruptcy. Governments were not moved to help them. Indeed, unfriendly legislation had marked the period 1873-87.

The great issue was to reorganize the railroads on a basis that would enable them to meet expenses and to pay dividends so as to do justice to customers, stockholders, and creditors. There are two ways of doing this. One is for the railroad itself, or through some individual railroad man who buys his way into a bankrupt railroad, to reorganize its management so as to coördinate production and distribution, or expenses and income, in the interest of a net profit. The alternative was for investment and commercial bankers to take the railroads in hand, reorganize them, and choose able executives. Both alternatives are found, but generally speaking it was bankers' control that came in during the period 1890-93-97-1901. With this, the railroads entered the stage of financial capitalism, a subject that belongs to the next chapter.

A few lines did succeed in keeping or putting their own house in order and in maintaining themselves within the stage of industrial capitalism. The Chicago, Milwaukee, and St. Paul Railroad is an example of this, until it finally got into financial difficulties during the period 1905–25 and had to reorganize 1925–27. Generally speaking, it was managed by its owners in the early days—industrial capitalists, such as Philip Armour, E. S. Harkness, and William Rockefeller. On the whole it was a Rockefeller railroad and was therefore on the way out of industrial capitalism.

The railroads have been sinners but, on the whole, have been more sinned against. Legislators held up charters and privileges until their leaders were bribed. Executives of railroads milked the lines, especially the Erie Railroad, in some cases legally and in some cases illegally. Employees have been grossly inefficient and careless in handling freight and luggage, at great cost to the railroads and their patrons. The conductors took so many tips for themselves in lieu of fares for their lines that a system of double conductors had to be adopted. The employees generally participated in holding up the railroads—in 1917 during the emergency of a war—for a basic eight-hour day which would not so much limit their day as increase their pay for overtime. The practice of "feather bedding" arose, whereby employees were paid for work not done or for work that was not necessary. One estimate has put the extra cost to the railroads at one quarter of a billion dollars a year. The public welcomed the railroads for the service which they would bring. It welcomed them also as public cows which could be milked. Many individuals charged too much for land and supplies and many participated in legislative hold-ups for free rides. It was not enough to give special rates to clergymen and others. It was justifiable to give the conductor five dollars, as I have learned by conversation, to go from New York to Chicago. By the thousands, hoboes and bums have stolen rides on passenger and especially freight trains without any inclination on the part of the public to protest. Railroads have long had to provide their own detective and police agents.

"Everybody's property is nobody's property" was a feeling that prevailed. Some thought that whereas the railroads had received public grants of lands and exemption from taxes, they, as democratic owners of the nation, were entitled to something in return. Wherever the feeling began, the end was the same—free milk for all—in marked contrast to conditions and developments in England. And, added to all these misfortunes, was the public encouragement of the building of unnecessary and competitive lines.

The results involved in the rise, spread, and development of railroads have been numerous and far-reaching. The railroads, like the factories, were prime movers in the destruction of mercantile capitalism and the creation of industrial capitalism. No mercantile capitalist could just take on one or the other of these two new instruments of production. Moreover, while he might take on a factory as an exclusive job and specialize in its operation, he could not single-handed take on a railroad. Accordingly, we may say that the railroad, beyond any other business activity, led to the extension of corporations and widespread participation of ownership.

We recall that the sedentary merchant was largely responsible for organizing the metropolitan economic unit in a general way. He laid the foundations. The industrial capitalist carried metropolitan economy through its second and third phases of growth. The first of these phases in England was the Industrial Revolution and the second was the revolution in transportation. In America the order of these two was in reverse, but it was still the railroad that was largely responsible for the revolution in transportation. Without the railroad there could have been none of that intensive cultivation of business in the great American hinterland. Without the railroad there could have been no hurried development of the natural resources of inland continents. Without it the metropolis could not have tightened its hold and influence upon its own hinterland.

The railroads almost made over the iron and steel industries. They created a body of investment securities beyond any precedent. So important did these become that we have grown accustomed to think of them as one of the four big groups of securities—railroads, industrials, utilities, and governments.

Let us not forget in passing on to something else that the world was waiting for the railroad. Each town wanted to be on a railroad line. Communities that failed to be visited by the iron horse withered and saw real estate values crumple up. The railroad led the imagination of men off to the great beyond of travel and adventure and at home to the realm of business prosperity and personal wealth. Long live the railroad!

3. COMMERCIAL BANKING AND ITS RELATION TO BUSINESS

Commercial banks had been started by sedentary merchants for the purposes of mercantile capitalism as we have already seen. They relieved the sedentary merchants of one of their functions, that is, banking on behalf of their own business and on behalf of clients and friends. Such banks were useful to the merchants' own business, for example, in so far as they discounted bills of exchange and promissory notes given to them in return for goods sold to other merchants and to retailers.

The great era for the beginning of modern commercial banks was the late eighteenth and early nineteenth centuries. Without performing radically different functions, banks nevertheless were very much more necessary than ever before, because numerous enterprises in manufacture, transportation, and merchandising were starting up and, once these firms provided their equipment, they found themselves lacking in working capital. No such widespread need for working capital had ever before existed, so far as I can see.

The new factories, to take an important type of situation, had to purchase large quantities of raw materials and had to meet heavy payrolls. In a few months plenty of cash would be forthcoming through the sale of products, but in the mean-

SIR RICHARD ARKWRIGHT

CORNELIUS VANDERBILT, ABOUT 1850

time there was a dearth of funds. From various sources the manufacturer could borrow for sixty days and sixty days' renewal. A rich sedentary merchant partner of the manufacturer might supply the manufacturer with capital. We know that the merchants, Almy and Brown, of Providence, not only sold the output of their partner, Samuel Slater, but they advanced him the cash or goods as he required them, first to erect mills and then to meet current demands. In addition, a sales' agent, who might be a surviving sedentary merchant or a specialized commission agent under the régime of industrial capitalism, was commonly called upon to advance funds against the goods that would soon be sent to him for sale. The treasurer of the manufacturing company might adopt a third method by selling his firm's short-term notes, signed by himself, and that name might mean a lot to a retired merchant who was on the lookout for a safe short-term investment. The commercial bank offered a fourth means of raising working capital. It would discount the note of a manufacturer or railroad for sixty days or ninety days. Or it would from time to time discount the promissory notes received from purchasers of materials or the bills of exchange used in both domestic and foreign trade. Increasingly, however, these drafts were shifting in early nineteenth-century America from foreign to domestic bills of exchange.

Examples of the commercial banks that I have in mind are the Bank of North America (1781), the Bank of New York (1784), and the Massachusetts Bank (1784). All of these banks were, over the long run, conservatively managed and served their communities and governments well.

Such banks performed more services than just the providing of working capital, though that was their chief function. They also bought and sold gold and silver coins. A New England cotton manufacturer could get a few boxes of gold and silver coins to send to New Orleans for the purchase of cotton. The bank's charges would cover the cost of collecting, boxing, and carting to the steamer. The bank also exchanged paper money, often at a discount. It also gave drafts on its account in a corresponding bank; for instance, a Boston bank would sell to a local business man a draft on a Philadelphia bank for $1,000. There would be a small fee and then either a premium or discount according to the condition of the domestic exchange market. To the business man, the industrial capitalist, not the least service that the commercial bank could perform was receiving deposits and transferring credits from his account to that of someone else to whom he owed money.

The commercial banks of the last days of mercantile capitalism were formed by retiring sedentary merchants or by industrial capitalists who were anxious for banking service. Rich families interested in real estate welcomed the opportunity to buy stock in these banks. In general, there were two groups of stockholders—those who were looking for a long-term investment and dividends therefrom and those who were more concerned with getting loans. The latter might buy from one to ten shares and then might be elected as directors, but they were chiefly interested in borrowing. Indeed one of the early problems of such banks was to keep from loaning too much to directors.

Some banks, established early, did not make rapid adjustment to the new needs of industrial capitalism. For instance, the Massachusetts Bank which had been set up by mercantile capitalists continued far too long to cater to the dying group. Some of the newer banks that did see the future of industrial capitalism at once met the needs of the new manufacturers, railroad operators, and real-estate developers. In Boston the Shoe and Leather Dealers' Bank, formed in 1836, catered to the two local industries that formed it. In New York the Chemical Manufacturing Company, chartered in 1823, was next year allowed to use one-fifth of its capital in banking. The agent of the manufacturing company became the cashier of the bank. In 1844 a charter for the exclusive function of banking was secured. This bank was to become one of the most successful in New York, ranking in earning capacity with the First National of New York.

Although there is much more to be said about commercial banks—found in the many acceptable treatises—there is one general policy of such banks that is worthy of emphasis at this point. Throughout the period of mercantile and industrial capitalism these commercial banks were passive and not active in their relation to their clients. Borrowers came to them and received loans or were denied them. That was about all there was in the situation. The banks did not say they would loan on condition that a director of the bank became a director of the borrowing firm or on condition that this or that should be done. This and much more came about under financial capitalism, as we shall see in the next chapter.

4. THREE PHASES OF INDUSTRIAL CAPITALISM

In spite of all the study made in the field of business in the nineteenth century we know very little about the course of *administration* in the régime of industrial capitalism. What we need is a series of studies in various businesses such as manufacturing, railroading, wholesaling, and banking. The research should lie in the minutes, correspondence, and accounts of individual firms. Lacking such investigations we can do little more than surmise what happened. Anything that is written here on the subject is meant to be suggestive and tentative.

An initial difficulty in studying the history of private business administration during the period of about 1790–1890 lies in the diversity of the types of administrations that we encounter. On examining the situation in detail, we probably find three phases of development. And some of the phases might closely resemble types which might not themselves change very much in some industries.

The first phase of industrial capitalism saw an emphasis on production—ways and means of bringing forth manufactured goods, transportation services, and so on. The problems were partly physical, or machine, production and partly the organization and management of workers. In many instances, the

INDUSTRIAL CAPITALISM

heads of the firms were themselves technicians; in other cases, technicians were hired or trained. In general, there was an undersupply of the kinds of goods and services which were being offered. This involved a brisk demand and profitable prices.

The industrial capitalist got along very well at first even though he was an experimenter and, therefore, a speculator. His costs were low—water power and unskilled labor. Often he had a patent of monopoly of production. Or he was the only one in the field of manufacture, shipping, or railroading in his market. He was the pioneer in the business and had the able pioneer's enthusiasm and ability to contrive and make good. Competition with handworkers operating in their little shops or in a room in their homes presented no great problem to him on the economic side. On the human side, the industrial capitalist could say simply, "if you do not like our competition, come into our factory and work for us."

The second phase experienced a very different situation: the problem was not to produce enough goods or services at a remunerative price, but to sell them at any satisfactory price. In other words, the difficulty was oversupply at profitable prices. Costs were increasing as men turned to more expensive kinds of power—from water power to coal in the case of factories and from firewood to coal in the case of railroads. Labor, though it tended to be better adapted to the new technique and new discipline, was organizing to demand better working conditions and higher wages. Probably the impact of a second or third generation of family executives was unfavorable to administration. Patents were running out and therefore competition was becoming more keen. Moreover, the competition was changing from competing with handworkers or other antiquated groups (such as stagecoaches and horseback mail-carriers) to competition with producers using about the same new technique.

Even more severely competitive was the new type of business which comes into an industry after the first pioneering has been done. The new firm allows the old to make great expenditures on production technique. Then the new firm comes in, perhaps buying out a bankrupt concern, and puts all of its emphasis on distribution. It has none of the burden of invention or experimentation or adaptation. It can allow the older concern with a reputation already expensively established, to continue to produce most of its old wares without competition and to go ahead and pioneer in new products. The new firm will pick out certain old products (the patents for which have died out) to manufacture with the most improved machinery. These wares the new firm can often produce more cheaply than the old one can. Then it picks up and picks off as many new articles as can be garnered legally and produces them in the same extensive specialized way. Perhaps the new firm uses a little cheaper material and labor; certainly, it has no reputation to maintain. The new firm, like the young tree in the forest, is really fighting for a place in the sun.

The new firm in this second phase has an advantage in distribution, closely connected with its advantages in production. The cheaper commodity which it makes it can sell on a price basis. It may even reduce the cost of distribution by a series of devices, of which doing its own wholesaling or even retailing is the outstanding illustration. At this point we need careful and numerous studies in the history of marketing during the period 1840–90 and beyond.

During this phase the machinery which the pioneer firm had during the first phase to make for itself in its own workshop is being made complete for use by an outside machine shop devoted to the construction of machinery. The day was not far off when these machine shops were themselves to become highly specialized—one to make textile machinery, another guns, another locomotives, and so on.

Into the atmosphere of business competition on an increasingly specialized basis crept a general feeling of extreme individualism in human affairs. To be sure, individualism had been growing slowly since the late fourteenth century. By now, in the middle nineteenth century and later, it semed to have been near its height in the doctrines of biological evolution and class struggle. In short, ruthless individualism seemed to be fast becoming the natural order of the day and leaders of thought were accepting this competition as the normal or the ideal. The rank and file of men, seeing the price of goods being reduced, thought chiefly of the fact that this competitive system was increasing their real income. Subtle influences these, making for keen underhand or aboveboard methods of getting and holding business.

A race of competitors arose in business, the like of whom the world had never known before. Cornelius Vanderbilt illustrates the type in railroading. No man and no government could hold him back. He would not sue an opponent, he would wreck him through competition. He knew that his services were more important for society than the private selfish purposes of rival business men or venal politicians. Andrew Carnegie could make steel rails more cheaply than competitors could and enjoyed wrecking those competitors. Rockefeller would allow no corner stand or store to hold up his network of Standard Oil. He knew that he had something worth while. Petty dealers were flies to be swatted as he made his way to victory for himself and service to society. Make the most out of these, ye moralists and devotees of social ethics! The method bothers me as it does you, but I also think of the results and the advantage of rapid results.

There could be no better illustration of the second phase of industrial capitalism than Andrew Carnegie and no better introduction to the third phase. Carnegie shifted from railroading to the manufacture of Pullman cars, steel rails, and so on, for the use of railroads (and other products for other purposes). During the period about 1865–1901 Carnegie became the greatest ironmaster in America and one of the greatest in the world. And yet no one would think of him as a production man; he did not belong to the first phase of industrial capitalism. He did not make iron and steel but hired those who could and he bound them to him with chains of gold. Bessemer of England was his master production genius. Following the Bessemer process, he replaced dear iron with cheap steel. His great profits came from this service to growing America.

Carnegie's special contribution was to sell the products of his steel works, that is, to sell them in the larger sense of providing just the right product at the lowest cost and building up friendly relations with customers. It was no idle gesture when he called his big new plant after Edgar Thomson, the president of the Pennsylvania Railroad, one of his biggest customers.

The declared policy of Carnegie was to specialize, or to "concentrate," as he preferred to express it. "Put all your eggs into one basket, and then watch the basket," was an oft-repeated maxim. But at the very time that he urged this policy, he was developing diverse functions and integrating them effectively. He reached out for coal in Pennsylvania and for iron in Minnesota. He built railroads and docks, and operated steamships to serve his various concerns. In truth, he thought of the concentration on one product, not on one process. In his egg basket went iron and steel products, coal, coke, iron ore, limestone, railroads, steamships, docks, and so on. Competition drove him to buy so many eggs and such big eggs of diverse colors!

Carnegie could have been a shrewd financier, had he planned his work that way. As it was, he emphasized low costs and effective distribution. Any surplus cash he reinvested in plant equipment. He had no policy of building up a reserve against a crisis and indeed was somewhat distressed during the crises of 1873 and 1893. He was a true industrial capitalist, a captain of industry, who hesitated on the threshold of the financial phase of industrial capitalism. Had he not sold out to Morgan in 1901, in order to give away his wealth, he might have made the complete transition into the third phase. In truth, however, the Morgan purchase took the Carnegie Steel Company over into financial capitalism, thus precluding a full realization of the financial phase of industrial capitalism for this particular concern.

The third phase—financial—slips into the general picture of the development of industrial capitalism, as we have just seen it emerge in one particular instance. I am thinking of inside finance, not outside or bankers' finance. The firms threatened in the second stage with extinction must sooner or later develop inside financial strength or fail. Of course, an outside financial industrialist of great acumen and resources, such as Frederick H. Prince, might buy himself into a dying railroad or floundering meat-packing firm and give it new vigor and jack it up to the financial competence necessary for strength and survival. He might remain in control, leaving the management to others, or he might sell out and be gone, if general conditions looked unfavorable.

This phase of inside financial strength involves several things. Certainly, it includes a nice coördination of production and distribution so as to avoid oversupply. It involves careful attention to costs of production, distribution, and administration. It also includes the building up of financial reserves in one form or another which will enable the concern to meet any emergency. Policies are devised which distinguish clearly between longtime and short-time situations. Accounting becomes a technique of importance unequalled since the fifteenth century. The balance sheet sits down frequently with the statement of profit and loss as effective and equal partners.

Some firms, indeed in the aggregate a great many, saw that they would have to turn away from the chief policy of industrialists—operating on the basis of a high degree of firm specialization. A recombination of functions and even a combination of firms were devices adopted increasingly to maintain profits and stave off insolvency. It was to become clear enough finally that excessive competition is no more conducive to business health than to social well-being. We deal with this aspect early in the next chapter.

If a firm failed to attain this financial strength, one or two things happened. It might become insolvent and then disappear or arise again as a new firm to make competition for the others all the more keen. Or, it might be taken in hand by bankers, in other words, transferred into a régime of financial capitalism.

Thus we see that the choices were (1) inside financial efficiency within the system of industrial capitalism, (2) failure, or (3) (outside or bankers') financial capitalism.

5. MARKETING IN INDUSTRIAL CAPITALISM

The aim of production is consumption. Before we can consume we must distribute. In the childhood of the race a man shared the products of his hand with the members of his family and a woman divided the products of her hands with the same persons. This is sharing-distribution. When goods came to be made for sale there entered the other kind of distribution, namely, market distribution. This has become one of the most important studies in economics and business but historically little work has been done. It is helpful to keep in mind the village, town, and metropolitan markets, but these are only broad frameworks within which many particular developments have occurred. In the growth of the metropolitan market both mercantile capitalism and industrial capitalism have played their parts. Just now we are considering market distribution, or marketing, under the régime of industrial capitalism, 1790–1890.

During the period of about 1790–1840 the chief problem of the industrial capitalists—manufacturers, railroad operators, insurance underwriters, merchants, and so on—was to reorganize their business on the new production basis, that is, on the new basis of using power machinery. Only a little real pioneering was done on the purely marketing side. The system of marketing in use may be expressed as follows:

Producer or —— commission agent —— retailer
    importer   or wholesaler

The chief changes that occurred from the palmy days of mercantile capitalism were the substitution of the commission agent for the commission merchant and the rise of the specialized wholesaler as an important element. The reader will recall that the commission merchant was a sedentary merchant who also did a good deal of business as the agent of other merchants buying and selling for a commission fee. Although the wholesaling function was very old, the specialized wholesaler was relatively new. These two specialists—commission agent and wholesaler—were to develop in the East and gradually move westward in competition with one another. One or the other was to win because of the better services that he performed.

We have to account for the rise of the commission agent and the specialized wholesaler. First, as to the commission agent. Throughout the period of mercantile capitalism, the wholesaling function was performed by the sedentary merchant. Now, all that was happening was that some former sedentary merchants did nothing else except take goods on consignment to sell as best they could, or to buy goods for others on as favorable terms as possible. If the commission agent could get enough orders, he had an excellent business and dependable income, for the risk of loss was borne by someone else and he received about five per cent on the turnover. Examples of sedentary merchants changing to the commission agency are Henry Lee, Jr., of Boston, and Peter Remsen, of New York.

There are sundry circumstances to which we may ascribe the change from the business of an all-round sedentary merchant to that of a commission agent. Many sedentary merchants had found by experience that in periods of depression it was safest to do a commission business and probably longed for a chance to do no other kind of business. Many new manufacturers—factory operators—had come early in their careers to choose a former merchant to act as their agent and to handle all of their output. Now, at this point, other merchants found themselves shut out of handling the goods in question, at least on as favorable terms. They tended, therefore, to look for a similar commission from another manufacturer. The new transportation offered more ample and more regular services, better even than the old sedentary merchant, unless very prosperous, could provide. Accordingly, the commission agent could be more certain of finding ships to handle his wares. Commercial banks and private banks also helped the individual merchant to break away from his old group of mutual associates who took common risks in ventures and underwrote one another's own undertakings. English manufacturers found in 1815 that commission agents were helpful in dumping a surplus of goods accumulated during the long war. Manufactures were sent, for instance, to New York to be sold at whatever the market could afford.

Our period 1790–1840 witnessed the growth of a strong commission agency in America. The word "agent" became widespread at this time, being applied to a number of functionaries whether they were true agents receiving a fee and open to employment by any firm or whether they were really employees of one firm. Examples are ticket agents, freight agents, steamship agents, and to a slight extent insurance agents. At that time, the term "agent" lost its exact significance. To be sure of what any agent really is, we need to know the circumstances under which he operates.

The second period in the growth of marketing in America sees the wholesaler triumphant over the commission agent. In the East this occurred about 1840–90, in the West somewhat later. We often regard the manufacturer-wholesaler-retailer relationship as normal, while, as a matter of fact, it is just the typical relationship under industrial capitalism.

Whether goods were imported or manufactured at home, the commission agent handling them either in London or New York was not well equipped to distribute the goods to retailers. His business was in large amounts and he liked quick turnovers. The spirit of his work was to pass the wares through his hands as soon as possible. Of course, this opened a place for a specialized wholesaler, such as R. C. Williams and Co. founded in New York, 1811, and dealing in groceries and the Simmons Hardware founded in St. Louis, 1864. Retailers liked to buy their small orders in each line from one or two firms who knew their needs and who valued their orders. The rise of mercantile or credit agencies in the 1840's in America gave to a wholesaler a chance to sell to many scattered retailers with a feeling of security. The railroads made it possible to send out commercial travelers to promote business and take orders. This new method probably helped wholesalers more than commission agents, because wholesalers could stand the additional expense, while agents received only a small commission fee. The spread of advertising and the rise of the advertising agent doubtless aided the wholesaler as well as the retailer and manufacturer.

By about 1860 in America we observe that specialization had gone a long way. By that time there were the following specialized types and, of course, many more:

1. Wholesalers:	hardware	drugs
	groceries	clothing
	dry goods	wines and liquors
	hats and caps	
2. Retailers:	hardware	boots and shoes
	groceries	jewelers
	dry goods	liquors
3. Brokers:	real estate	note
	stock	cotton, tobacco, etc.
	merchandise	
	ship	
4. Agents:	credit	insurance
	real estate	intelligence (labor)
	transportation	
5. Local manufacturers:	blacksmiths	harness-makers
	carriage builders	shoemakers
	brickmakers	grist mills
		saw mills

In 1853 it was said that in New York City the tendency of retailers was ever toward more specialization—tailors' woolen goods, dress goods, cotton prints, plain cottons, piece silks, ribbons and smaller articles, hosiery, lace, perfumery, handkerchiefs, shawls, and even suspenders. Within the next decade, it was anticipated, there would be a store established to sell spool cotton and another store to sell corset laces! Of course, specialty stores and shops had grown up in the Middle Ages but were greatly multiplied in the nineteenth century and caused surprise in America which had not had much experience with them. Specialty stores really flourish in large towns and metropolitan centers.

The third period in the history of marketing under the system of industrial capitalism sees the partial elimination or absorption of either wholesaler or retailer or both. The time was about 1870–1930 and thus overlapped the earlier period and in some industries even went beyond the system we are dealing with (if the industry in question escaped the rival financial capitalism). The public came to be conscious of the need for reducing the costs of distribution. Coöperative distributive societies had been formed as early as the 1840's and began to be widespread in the 1870's. One manufacturer of shoes—W. L. Douglas and Company—established in 1876 a chain of retail stores, thus cutting out entirely the wholesalers of its product. Many small producers at the close of the period tried selling to the consumer directly through advertising. The increasingly high cost of living during the upward secular trend in business 1897–1920 seemed to stimulate the process of eliminating the wholesaler, whilst the downward trend since 1920 has helped him partially to regain his position.

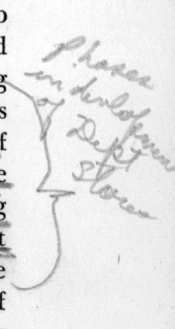

The department store played a notable part in impairing the position of the wholesale concern. We may stop briefly to note some of the main lines of development, which are indeed sorely in need of careful study. There were at least three big changes that a full story would need to record. First, there was the diversification of products and the departmentalization of store management. Second, there was the growth of multiple functions and their integration into an effective operating unit. Third, there was the formation of chains of department stores in the nineteenth century but chiefly in the 1920's. The first of these developments involved the growth, commonly, of a dry goods store or a clothing store (an Oakhall) into a big store with several departments. The sale of dry goods and clothing provided more profits or surplus than any other and accordingly the retailers of these two sets of commodities were commonly the progenitors of the department store. In New York, A. T. Stewart and Company, Lord and Taylor, and R. H. Macy and Company got their start in dry goods. On the other hand John Wanamaker began with men's clothing. Whichever was the nucleus, other departments were added gradually, such as leather goods, house furnishings, toys, books, and furniture. With the incoming of new groups of goods necessarily came a departmentalization of management and specialization of the work of individuals that meant much for the effective operation of the store. Gradually, the store of an owner and a few clerks came, as it grew, to be operated by a whole hierarchy of owner, general manager, department heads, advertising manager, accountant, cashier, floor walkers, cash girls, delivery men, and so on. Although such a growth actually began in some instances as early as 1850–70, still its main unfolding came in the period 1870–90. In the vanguard of development were Jordan Marsh and Company, of Boston, Marshall Field, of Chicago, and the other firms already mentioned.

The second development in the history of department stores, dependent on the first, is the multiplication of economic functions performed by the different units during the period 1870–90–1920. The very fact that one store was made up of six in one, or twenty in outstanding instances, gave the big new unit a special position. It could buy directly from manufacturers, thereby eliminating the wholesaler, not completely but in a threateningly large number of cases. It could import goods from abroad, through commission agents, through its own buyers ordering by cable, or through its own buying offices maintained abroad as in Paris and Tokio. In addition, during the period with which we are dealing, some leading department stores undertook to manufacture for themselves. This was notable in women's and children's undergarments, candies, drugs, and cosmetics. The practice continues chiefly to provide private brands to be sold in competition with national brands and in order to evade the price maintenance laws.

The department store arose to meet new needs. It was obviously a convenience to shop in various departments under one roof rather than seek out sundry stores on different streets. One account at a big store was more satisfactory than several in small stores. No doubt at first there were economies in the purchase and sale of goods and in general management. As time went on, however, these economies receded and department stores became generally identified not with low prices but with customer services. The downtrend of prices and business profits during the period 1866-97 gave a severe challenge to the specialized store and by the same token opened up opportunities to the larger unit that could employ men of greater ability and could offer inducements to customers, such as pleasant surroundings and even entertainment, to offset the appeal of bargains. In more recent years many department stores have partly returned to their appeal to the bargain instincts and economic necessities of their customers. One instrument in this appeal has been the bargain basement in which vast quantities of goods are sold at prices much lower than those prevailing on the upper floors. An additional feature is the automatic price reduction of goods for sale in the basement, so much per week until the wares are disposed of, somewhat reminiscent of the Dutch auction.

One very significant instance of the rise, prosperity, and final extinction of a wholesale business centers in the Claflin family. H. B. Claflin, when a young man, received $1,000 from his father to help him enter business. The father had kept a general store in a small town in Massachusetts. The son chose to open a retail dry goods store in Worcester. The store prospered from its opening about 1833 until 1843, when its owner, H. B. Claflin, left to try his fortunes in New York City. In the latter growing commercial center, he entered into partnership with others to form a wholesale dry goods firm. In 1890 the concern was incorporated as the H. B. Claflin Company, some of the stock being sold to employees and customers. The firm had grown with New York and had come to have a national distribution for its goods, both imported and domestic. It was one of the chief concerns in the United States handling New England fabrics. Probably it had already passed the point of its maximum strength when it was incorporated. It was naturally proud of the fact that it had passed through the crises of 1861 and 1873 without going into bankruptcy but not without having its feathers singed. The depression of 1893–97 was a hard blow to the Company and to its jobber customers.

The primary policy of this giant concern in a giant city was to grant liberal credits to retail firms. In the eyes of the credit manager these might appear to be good risks but frequently they were not. The retailers were expected to buy a large proportion of their goods from the Claflin Company and in turn they were not hard pressed for payment in years of little business. As time went on—the details are unknown—the firm reached out to influence or control other retailers, until in 1914 it owned, controlled, or influenced in varying degrees about thirty large retailers in various parts of the country. This was not a formal chain of stores but it had somewhat the effect of a chain. About 1902 the Claflin Company purchased the Defender Manufacturing Company, of New York, which is now remembered as a small concern. In addition, the Claflin Company or John Claflin—the son of the founder (who had died in 1885)—owned stock in manufacturing concerns outside of New York City. Of course, while all these developments were occurring in the United States, the firm continued to import foreign wares according to the needs of the market.

We might think that this was enough for one man to administer. In 1900, however, John Claflin formed the Associated Merchants Company to possess in whole or in part four large eastern department stores and one fur store. Next year J. P. Morgan and Company formed a syndicate to issue shares of the new company. On and on went Claflin: in 1909 he formed the United Dry Goods Company which bought four large de-

ANDREW CARNEGIE, ABOUT 1899

JOHN D. ROCKEFELLER, SR., 1895

partment stores outright and a controlling interest in Lord and Taylor (founded in 1826 in New York.) J. P. Morgan and Company purchased large blocks of preferred and common stocks. Of course, the firm was being driven by circumstances to control retail stores so as to find outlets for its goods—to keep going. We cannot help thinking of the old-time sedentary merchants who, for so long, maintained just such a ramified business. Here, in John Claflin, for about a generation of man's life we have a recrudescence of some of the multiple functions of the sedentary merchant. Whereas the sedentary merchant's central function was export and import, that of Claflin was wholesaling. Although the sedentary merchant performed more functions than Claflin did, his capital and sales turnover were infinitely smaller.

John Claflin was driven into the complicated web of wholesaling-manufacturing-retailing by the very competitive circumstances of his time. He might have met competition by remaining a wholesaler but at the same time opening up branch wholesale houses in Chicago, St. Louis, Minneapolis, Kansas City, and so on, perhaps even moving his main office to Chicago. He did none of these things. He was violating the genius of industrial capitalism by taking on these multiple functions, at least as some might say. On the other hand, as we might put it, he was adapting his firm to new conditions, indeed, putting it on a sounder competitive basis. By 1908 he had gone so far as to add to his lines of dry goods the following—toilet articles, women's clothing, laces, hosiery, novelty jewelry, and household furnishings. He was doing these things with little help from financial capitalists and indeed with no control from them, though he knew the elder Morgan well—they had been co-founders of an exclusive club. Perhaps, if he had been so controlled, he would have avoided trouble.

In 1914, three days before the Archduke and Archduchess of Austria were assassinated—thus starting the forces that led to the World War, the H. B. Claflin Company failed—to the great consternation of an already apprehensive business community.

The failure was caused not by a lack of earnings on the part of the wholesale firm and the two chains but by the accumulation of a large debt—$34,000,000—in the form of notes which had been too often renewed. These notes were issued by subsidiary firms and customers and backed by the Claflin Company. Assets were put at $44,000,000. Practically only the industrial capitalist, a few stores and factories, and commercial bank allies were concerned. Rather tardily, the commercial banks had offered temporary and partial assistance, but Claflin said that the matter was more serious. Claflin had given back to the business $4,353,000 to help save it, 1893–1913. Now, in 1914, he handed over all his personal assets on going into bankruptcy. Perhaps we would be right in saying that Claflin had really long needed the aid or control of financial capitalists. One weakness of the industrial capitalist is that he clings to an old central interest—a way of manufacturing, a product, or a location—and then builds up around that core. If the core should become rotten, then all else decays. Claflin had been advised by a colleague to give up wholesaling in 1903. His reply indicated that a sentimental regard for this part of the business would keep him from ever abandoning it.

By 1914 it was clear enough to many that certain developments had occurred which had made the Claflin Company's commercial position untenable. Manufacturers were selling more and more to retailers, especially department stores and chain stores, leaving the business of the wholesaler in dangerous exposure. New York was ceasing to be a national center for dry goods when those dry goods were being increasingly made in America and outside of New England. Moreover, as the West developed metropolitan centers, it produced its own wholesalers who could service the retailers of their own region better than could be done from New York City. Also, some of the Claflin stores were located downtown in New York at the very time the retail trade was moving uptown.

To close the story, we may say that the two chains of stores formed in 1900 and 1909 were in 1916 consolidated to form the Associated Dry Goods Corporation. One of the stores had been liquidated and at least one other was having difficulty. From 1901, when Morgan first helped float Claflin stock, down

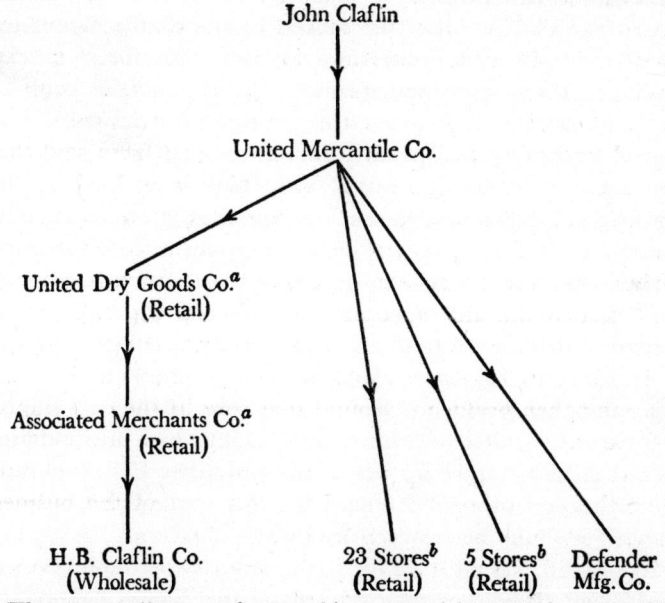

```
                        John Claflin
                            |
                            v
                    United Mercantile Co.
                   /    |    |    |    \
                  /     |    |    |     \
                 v      |    |    |      \
       United Dry Goods Co.ᵃ  |    |       \
           (Retail)       |    |    |      \
              |           |    |    |       \
              v           |    |    |        \
       Associated Merchants Co.ᵃ    |         \
           (Retail)       |    |    |          \
              |           |    |    |           \
              v           v    v    v            v
         H.B. Claflin Co.   23 Storesᵇ  5 Storesᵇ  Defender
           (Wholesale)      (Retail)    (Retail)   Mfg. Co.
```
(The arrow indicates stock ownership and partial or complete control.)

ᵃ These concerns were united in 1914 to form the Associated Dry Goods Corporation.

ᵇ These became the major part of the Mercantile Stores Corporation in 1914 and in 1919 the Mercantile Stores Company, Inc. This concern was given all the stock of H. B. Claflin Corporation (wholesale, formed in 1914), which it sold in 1917 for the benefit of the Claflin creditors.

THE CLAFLIN MERCHANDISING EMPIRE IN 1914

to 1915, when a Morgan partner became a director in the Associated Dry Goods Corporation, there was a tendency for the concern at least to flirt with financial capitalism. In 1912–13 the senior Morgan was under a cloud and in 1913 he died. Thus did one opportunity pass away. We might think that

Claflin was eager to do by himself what financial capitalists were everywhere doing—economizing, pruning, and integrating—but could not do these things effectively. The commercial banks were his faithful allies but they could not meet his real needs. We shall see that the most virile Claflin firm—the Associated Dry Goods Corporation—went over into financial capitalism in the period 1915-29.

An interesting analogy to the Claflin story during the régime of industrial capitalism is found in Butler Brothers. This is a wholesale firm operating seven large warehouses in as many cities. The firm goes back to about 1877 and was incorporated in 1887. It was well entrenched in the distribution of various wares, including dry goods, notions, drugs, books, cutlery, sporting goods, furniture, and crockery. Its success was threatened by the developing direct sale of manufactured goods to retailers. In 1927 it established two *voluntary* chains of independent retailers who handle its goods and receive valuable aids in sales and administration. These stores now number about 4,000 and account for a large minority of the sales of the company. In 1928 it added a chain of low-priced retail stores, now numbering 115 in various parts of the United States. In 1929 it added a chain of junior department stores—now 20 in all. In 1930 the company secured a shirt factory, the complete output of which it handles itself.

Clearly, Butler Brothers are reaching out to control outlets which might otherwise not buy from them. In the next chapter we shall see examples of retail stores forming chains to benefit from a central purchasing agency or wholesale department. Some of these chains have had considerable success. It remains to be seen whether success can come from the other side. Certainly, Butler Brothers are still operating within the circle of industrial capitalism.

Of course, the movement to eliminate the wholesaler was very complex and should be studied carefully by those specially concerned. One interesting example was found in the effort of the great Chicago packers to do their own wholesaling by establishing distributing plans of their own in well-located centers here and there throughout the country. Such a movement was greatly stimulated by national advertising on the part of the manufacturer.

As we look back over the history of wholesaling, we see that during the Middle Ages no specialized wholesalers were allowed to operate. Local law would not permit the specialization and business men were not interested in specializing. Then, in the early modern period, local law would permit but sedentary merchants saw no advantage in specializing. Finally, the functions of the sedentary merchant, including wholesaling, came to be split up and a contest arose between the commission agent and the wholesaler. The wholesaler won only to lose to the manufacturer as the nineteenth century drew to a close and to the retailer early in the twentieth century. Whether the current trend or ripple back to the wholesaler has any long-term significance remains to be seen.

Under the next system of private business capitalism, namely financial capitalism, the bankers financed many firms whose policies looked toward the elimination of wholesalers, for instance, large stores, chain stores, and groups of factories. This story belongs to another tale.

6. BUSINESS AGENTS AND AUXILIARIES

When industrial capitalists came into being, they often continued to use agents as mercantile capitalists had done before them. In many cases, the work of outside agents was drawn into the individual firm and there performed by specialized employees often organized in special departments. Such a shift was a more or less continuous process through the nineteenth century. Though continuous, however, the process was uneven and incomplete.

We may serve our purposes best by listing some of the most important agents, particularly of larger business units, notably corporations.

1. Selling agent—a commission agent who handles a part or all of the output of a producer in return for a percentage fee. This functionary is well illustrated by the New York City selling agent who has sold the output of New England textile mills for over a century. Frequently, he has advanced money to the mill-owner whose products he has handled. The early freight and passenger agents of railroads and ocean-going vessels constituted another, but less important, example of this class.

2. Purchasing agent—a similiar agent, who purchased supplies and raw materials for factories, railroads, and so on. Apparently this class was not so well developed nor so long lived as the selling agent.

3. Legal agent—a law firm, often retained by a corporation, that habitually takes care of the corporation's legal affairs.

4. General auditor—a firm of public accountants, which periodically makes an audit of the corporation's business and financial position.

5. Advertising agent—an expert in advertising who takes charge of part or all of a corporation's advertising for a commission fee.

6. Financial (or "fiscal") agent—commonly a trust company which may undertake either the whole duty of a treasurer of a corporation or part of the duties. In the former case it would look after receipts and disbursements, pay interest and dividends, and keep securities, mortgages, and deeds. In the latter case it would not be concerned with receipts and payments. In some instances the financial agent may be an investment banker. Jay Cooke and Company was such an agent for the Northern Pacific, and now Morgan and Company for the United States Steel Corporation. In the former case financial capitalism (in which the investment firm would have a measure of control) was dawning and in the latter well developed.

7. Registrar—a trust company or other bank which undertakes to keep strict account of the total number of a corporation's shares outstanding and the ownership of the same. Such an agent is a check against the treasurer of the corporation served.

8. Transfer agent—a similar concern which undertakes to

transfer ownership of shares from one person to another and to check its list independently against that of the registrar.

The strength of this group of agents lies in a combination of independence of any one principal firm or corporation, on the one hand, and more or less dependence upon the whole group of principals, on the other hand. Apart from the auditor, any one of these agents may be taken within the firm itself. And then also, any one of these agents may on occasion become an adviser or auxiliary.

Business associations may be regarded as coöperative agents of individual entrepreneurs and firms. In the Middle Ages, petty capitalists had their gilds by the hundreds. Mercantile capitalists made many of these over to suit their own purposes. In the seventeenth century these mercantile capitalists began to form chambers of commerce and in the eighteenth century trade associations. These two movements were greatly extended by industrial capitalists in the nineteenth century. The new associations have functioned in important ways, such as providing arbitration, presenting a united front to labor unions, requesting tariff protection, drawing up industrial codes, fostering coöperative research and advertising, seeking local improvement, and trying to hold up prices so as to prevent ruinous competition. Since economic historians have written much that is readily available, we may pass on without further reference, except to point out that under national capitalism efforts have been made, as we shall note more in detail later on, to give these associations new life—in Italy under fascism and in America under the New Deal. The American effort under the aegis of the Blue Eagle failed when the Supreme Court outlawed the NRA in 1935. To a minor extent, business associations, like individual agents, have been advisory or auxiliary to business firms. Rather obviously, however, this service could not go far in view of the highly competitive condition of business firms.

Business auxiliaries are professional advisers to business men. They serve all-comers and charge a fee. They have a fiduciary attitude to their customers and pride themselves on their special knowledge and integrity.

Petty and mercantile capitalists seem to have had no advisers, unless we regard Churchmen, astrologers, and patron deities and saints as such. In the ancient period Mercury was the god who presided over the destinies of traveling merchants and in the mediaeval period St. Nicholas did his best for the same group. Mercantile capitalists had commercial manuals at their service—such as arithmetics, accounting treatises, and books dealing with foreign towns, weights and measures, currencies, and laws—but these are very different from advisers.

For a number of reasons, advisers were necessary for the industrial capitalist. Above all, the industrial capitalist was a specialist in a wide market of many variables and unknowns. Also, there was growing up a common law in Britain and the colonies that needed study and elucidation from judicial cases. There was a rapid spread of companies in business which came under the common law and increasingly under statutory enactment. After 1720, when incorporated companies were under a statutory cloud in Britain, lawyers were required to advise business men how to form and manage joint stock companies, unincorporated, that is, how to operate beyond the pale of an unreasonable law. Within the framework of the business company there were gradually consolidated the rights of stockholders, bondholders, and general creditors, as well as the several old-time special corporation privileges as fictitious individuals and the servitudes inherent in creations of the state.

Apparently the first important advisers of industrial capitalists in America were lawyers. In two different ways were lawyers to influence business policy. First, they were chosen as directors of corporations and, secondly, they were retained and employed as legal agents and counselors. In the first capacity they entered into the discussion of business policy in general and were asked to make reports on certain legal aspects in particular. In the second capacity they represented the firm, particularly the corporation, in lawsuits and negotiations having a difficult legal bearing. To be sure, many industrial capitalists, following the tradition of the sedentary merchants, had the least possible to do with lawyers. The railroad and other corporations, however, could not get far along such a line. Every time a bond or other security was offered for sale, legal distinctions, that the capitalist found difficult, had to be made.

In Boston, New York, and Philadelphia corporation lawyers arose to rival and then to outshine the old-time general practitioner and leader in his community. This began almost with the rise of the Republic. By the 1840's considerable aggregations of such business lawyers had come into existence. They were to grow until, by the end of the century, giant law factories had taken root in the principal metropolitan centers across the country. To such organizations were attracted a large proportion of the best brains that went through the law schools. Within the walls of such legal offices grew up men of legal training, sharpened wits, broad culture, considerable wealth, and innate conservatism. The public came to look upon a corporation lawyer as a kind of enemy of the common man. Such a lawyer might become governor, congressman, member of the cabinet, and, of course, a shining light in the supreme court, but he could not become president of the United States, at least not after the Pujo Committee inquiry and report of 1912–13.

In Britain as in America, accountants followed lawyers as advisers to business firms. In London, Liverpool, and Edinburgh, accounting was well developed, while in America it was in genuine infancy. The growth of accounting in America has been slow in progress since the beginning of industrial capitalism. For a long time after the corporation came into existence in America, there was little thought of keeping financial accounts in order to check the work of executives on behalf of the stockholders. What obscured the cleavage of interest which later became pronounced was that in the early part of the nineteenth century the executives and directors and chief stockholders were the same persons. In the Boston Manufacturing Company the earliest audits were made by the directors or a committee of directors probably to check the treasurer. Later a committee of stockholders was appointed, and only much later were outside auditors brought in. The growth of cost accounting was slow, and, on the whole, had to wait till the stage of financial capitalism for full development.

So far we have considered accountants as inside employees and outside agents helping business units to keep accurate financial accounts. The outside accounting agents or public auditors also came to give advice to clients partly in the ordinary routine of an audit and partly when specially called upon by their clients. Questions on which they could be of great assistance concerned depreciation, obsolescence, reserves, and tax liabilities. In advising on tax matters the accountants came into conflict with lawyers. Outsiders have been much amused to learn how little law the accountants know and how little accounting the lawyers are conscious of.

Public accountants or auditors have had two origins which may or may not be as separate as they are distinct. In the first place there was the rise of efficient accounting out of mere bookkeeping which was carried on within the firm. This involves a knowledge of economic theory and a degree of professional pride and technical skill not found earlier. Then these attainments, along with a fiduciary attitude and a feeling for the public good, were developed in outside offices. John Heins (1836–1900), of Philadelphia, is a key man in this story in America. He was a great disciplinarian to whom some of the senior partners in the present firm of Lybrand, Ross Brothers and Montgomery owed not a little. The second line of growth came from abroad with the introduction of the firm Barrow, Wade, Guthrie and Company in New York in 1883. In 1890 came Price, Waterhouse and Company, also of London. The parent company in England had been accustomed to send its agents to America to audit accounts, particularly of railroads, on behalf of English stockholders. Then, it sent a resident representative and finally established a full-fledged office. The amount of auditing that this firm has done for railroads on the American continent is truly colossal, but of course government regulation and supervision have changed the picture greatly. In 1887 foreign-trained and American-trained accountants joined to form the American Association of Public Accountants. Let us recall the fact that these accountants were primarily agents but were often called upon to aid industrial capitalists by giving advice.

In treating of accountants after lawyers we have omitted engineering consultants who at least parallel accountants, possibly somewhat anticipate them, as advisers to American industrial capitalists. Engineers of various training had helped the revolutions in industry and transportation. They continued their work within factories and special machine shops, on railroads, and so on. Some engineers became so skilled in making over existing plants that they set up separate offices devoted to the business of giving advice as to how construction or reconstruction should take place.

Amos D. Lockwood (1811–84) was one of the earliest consulting engineers in America. He had been a cotton mill worker, then assistant superintendent in one of the Slater mills in 1832, and finally a partner operating a mill. In 1855 he was employed to reorganize the Pacific Mills in Lawrence. Other such tasks came to him, till in 1871 he set up in Boston an office of consulting engineers for the cotton industry. The firm he established still has an office in that city as well as elsewhere. Such engineering firms often act as the agents of business men, but frequently their sole contribution is advisory. I believe that they are most useful when they combine agency and auxiliary functions.

We may infer that the consulting engineer fitted into the highly competitive phase of industrial capitalism when one well-equipped industrialist found himself about as well off or as badly off in his productive machinery as his neighbor and rival. How to get ahead within the industry became the great object of concern. Hardly any price was too high to pay for advice as to how to use capital and labor more effectively in serving society.

I do not think that we have exhausted the subject of business auxiliary service to industrial capitalists even in outline. Certainly, commercial bankers have long given advice to industrialists. The latter have commonly thought that this advice was short-sighted and selfish and have accepted it only reluctantly. Advertising agents have also given advice that lay in the background of advertising. In the case of the Ayer Advertising Agency a market survey for one of its clients was made as early as 1879.

On the whole, we are inclined to think that industrial capitalists needed the service of many other kinds of counselors who had not yet come into existence, notably market counselors and office management counselors, to say nothing of labor relations and public relations counselors and advisers of general business conditions. These were to develop more under the system of financial capitalism but still were patronized by surviving industrialists. Now, in passing, there is one thought we must all have in mind: how can an adviser on the outside really help a man who is master of his own business? The outsider's experience is broader, his book learning greater, and his detachment more pronounced. The outsider rarely tells the insider anything he does not know in some form. What the outside counselor commonly does that is of greatest service is to corroborate the industrialist's judgment, suspicions, fears, and hopes. At times, the outside counselor helps break a deadlock over policy by giving support to one faction. Such a service is worth buying. Often the counselors will take on an expensive job of analysis and report, however, when in fact there is nothing in the industrialist's situation that can profit from such expenditure of time and money. This is the abuse of the system, however, not the normal use.

7. SECULAR TRENDS IN PRICES AND PROFITS

The business auxiliaries, with whom we have been dealing, were all the more necessary because of difficulties that arose through the ups and downs of trade. These were of two major types—the business cycle and the secular trend in business. The first is the familiar three to ten year gamut of prosperity, depression, and recovery. The second is made up of a group of such cycles and lasts about twenty-five years. The downward secular trend has cycles which are heavy with depression years, while the upward secular trend is buoyant with rich prosperous years. During the downward trend prices are falling and profits hard to make; what seems like prosperity is often accelerated turnover without profits. During the upward trend prices are rising and profits large and rewarding, till a war comes along and makes wages and profits disastrously high. The wage-earner spends his good fortune, but the capitalist, large and small, invests his and loses it in the next downtrend.

The first secular trend that industrial capitalists were confronted with extended from 1789 to 1815 in America and in this country was not so important for the new capitalism as it was in Britain where the Industrial Revolution was gaining strength in the manufacture of textiles and metals. In America, efforts were made to establish factories and a few succeeded, such as Slater's. Many patriotic endeavors, following the lead of Alexander Hamilton, were premature. Most of such efforts lacked technical skill and, when the permanent capital had been raised, not enough remained for operations. The Revolutionary and Napoleonic War was on in Europe and with it came heavy demands for goods. This was the last era of prosperity of the sedentary merchants and the dawn of industrial capitalism.

The period 1815–43 saw a downward trend in prices and profits. New industries could prosper but their prosperity was often at the expense of the old industries, especially those using hand techniques. But, above all, was the rapid withering away and drying up of mercantile capitalism—a process which we have already observed. Facilitating this change was the opening up, by the British, of unrestricted trade with India in 1813 and of trade with Canton in 1833. Henceforth, all British business men, not simply the East India Company as heretofore, could trade in those Oriental parts. Such fierce competition was not promising to Americans, particularly at a time when their own country was being opened up westward by steamship on rivers and lakes and especially by the ever-widening net of railroads.

The contrast in pictures is striking for this period 1815–43. On the one hand, the old mercantile capitalists are losing as also the old hand workers, stagecoach drivers, waggoners, and the like. On the other hand, a considerable measure of success was meted out sparingly to the new industries, especially textile and railroad. When depressions came, they were hard and long; but the new industries showed resilience in recovery. The depression of 1837–43 was probably more severe than that of 1783–89 and than the Massachusetts depression of 1640–48. When this downward trend, born largely of the reaction from the long preceding war, had come to an end about 1843, we find that mercantile capitalism was dead, except in far-western parts, and industrial capitalism was showing vigor that promised a triumph when general business conditions should improve. And thus it is generally, these long trends will hurry the exit of the old and *hasten* the entrance of the *new* system striving for mastery.

The period 1843–66 witnessed the upward surge of business, higher prices and greater profits, and also the supremacy of industrial capitalism. It saw the continuation of the western movement of people and capital, ideas and management. The world was going ahead materially as never before, at least so far as history records. Optimism was at its height. Englishmen led the procession, Americans hurried along, Frenchmen did their best, Germans dug more deeply into the soil and lit another forge, while the Russians prepared for another winter. Two banners were carried: one was "Freedom," the other "Plenty." Industrial capitalists had reason to be satisfied. They were chiefly small business men or, at most, medium sized. We know about those who attained unusual success: Slater in textiles, Baldwin in locomotives, Dennison in stationery, Cornelius Vanderbilt in steamships, and so on.

From 1866 to 1897 prices and profits again turned downward in reaction from war prosperity and business mismanagement during war periods. In Europe the period began in 1873, and, accordingly, from that year business was even worse in America. One of the deepest depressions on record, but one not complicated by government interference, reached across the years from 1873 to 1879 in America and from 1873 to 1886 in Britain. The new industries in America—flour, meat packing, and shoes—prospered, but the old industries—textiles, railroads, transatlantic steamships, and iron and steel—had a very difficult time. Protection and subsidies, higher and higher, were demanded and sometimes seemed not so much to protect an infant industry as to bolster up an old one. At a later date the talking point shifted to the protection of the standard of the worker.

Now, it was during this period that industrial capitalism was not only pressed sorely to survive but was presented with a rival—financial capitalism. Those firms which could themselves attain financial strength had little to fear, but the weak ones—notably the railroads—would go over, in fact did begin to go over during this period, to the new régime of financial capitalism. Again we see illustrated the capacity of a downward secular trend to injure or kill off, or at least to hasten the exit of an old system and to precipitate the incoming of a new one.

We are here chiefly interested in the course and the effects of the secular trend. Perhaps some day we shall all be studying the trend with great care—its pattern and its causal sequences. It is fundamentally a long-time shift in business administration which registers both internal situations and external factors. The inevitable war or group of wars, for instance, 1702–13, 1756–73, 1792–1815, 1854–70, and 1914–18, comes along and gives business a maximum of turnover and temporary profit. Then, at the close of the contest, come a reaction in feeling and a decline in volume of business and also in many prices. The changes are irregular, but finally the course of prices and profits is observed to be definitely downward. Business administration, which had become inefficient during success, has to reorganize. During the challenging downtrend, administration is improved and labor also. As prices fall, it becomes feasible to mine gold. Gradually, with prices at a low level and gold flowing in, there comes a breath of confidence. Imperceptibly, there arises a feeling that the worst is over, in fact that the uptrend has already begun. It has begun, for men are promoting, speculating, building, and rebuilding. They are using other people's money with the hope of making profits for themselves. National finances are put into better shape. Military equipment is perfected. Another war breaks out. Business is faced with fresh opportunities, and again its management disintegrates under a continuing and accentuated régime of easy profits. Again, business at the top of success is plunged over the cliff that leads irregularly to a deep valley below.

8. FLOW OF CAPITAL UNDER INDUSTRIAL CAPITALISM

The wealth that is created by man in the process called production is used for one of two purposes. First, in the form of consumers' goods (some fairly durable, others very ephemeral) it is used up by the producers and their families. Second, in the form of producers' goods (some fairly durable, others quite ephemeral) it is used by the producers to create more services and goods. Such wealth is the capital of our economic system. The flow to consumption must be continuous, though not necessarily constant. The flow to production is in effect very irregular and during a long downward secular trend almost ceases. Indeed, so large a proportion of the products of human effort goes into consumption during a downtrend that many persons have to use up some of their capital to supply themselves with necessities. But the flow continues. Wealth normally flows into one of its two channels. The flow of what we call "capital" may go on into its normal productive uses or it may be short-circuited into consumers' goods and be lost to capital.

In considering the normal flow of capital in its regular productive channel, we have distinguished three types called the usucapital (or autogenous) system, the direct putting-out system, and the indirect putting-out system. We may now reconsider these three types with reference to industrial capitalism.

The usucapital system always sees the possessor of the capital use it himself to yield an income. In pre-business days this was the only way. In petty capitalism the usucapital system was almost the only source of capital, except in the case of the traveling merchant. In mercantile capitalism the usucapital system gradually yielded some of its place to the direct putting-out and even, to a less extent, the indirect putting-out system. In industrial capitalism all three sources of capital are tapped but the direct and indirect putting-out systems predominate.

In industrial capitalism the small manufacturer or other producer may build up a capital out of wages and then his small store of capital may grow to large proportions by a process of plowing it back into the business. In such a case (and there were probably many small masters who became factory owners during the Industrial Revolution in this way), we have the usucapital system. But one of the dominant features of industrial capitalism is the large amount of capital required for power-machinery and other equipment. In other words, fixed capital takes on a stature that it had never before possessed. Such large amounts of capital were secured through partnerships and joint stock companies (unincorporated or incorporated). At first, mercantile capitalists were the most common investors. Thus, there was a flow of mercantile capital which had performed many functions into one industry, that is, one specialized economic function.

In the early part of industrial capitalism, not only was a partnership arranged by the persons concerned but a company was floated without external aid—in fact by a group of promoters. These persons would buy a large part of the securities; and, in the place of business of one of their number, subscription would be taken for the rest of the shares. Once the securities had been issued, they would be bought and sold, either through brokers or directly. If the sale was through brokers, it might be made on a public stock exchange, for example, on the New York Stock Exchange since 1792 or on a more closely organized exchange in New York since 1817. The amount of capital that went into the industrial capitalistic pursuits through the sale of securities was large, especially in banks, canals, railroads, and mining. In manufacture, individuals or partnerships predominated until perhaps about the 1890's.

The flow of capital was not simply within the country but from persons in one nation to persons or firms in another. British capital had entered American business in the seventeenth and eighteenth centuries through the financing of the colonial sedentary merchants from London, Bristol, and Liverpool. Under industrial capitalism, banks were the first private institutions in America to receive capital from England. In the period 1815–43 American canal stocks were bought by the British and also some railroad stock. In the next period, 1843–66, however, American railroads gained in popularity. Unfortunately some manipulators like Little, Drew, and Fisk discouraged the British. The Erie Railroad became the sport of such speculators in the field of industrial capitalism. Losses to investors at home and abroad were numerous.

The indirect putting-out system had risen in mercantile

capitalism, especially in the business of merchant bankers. It was to take deep root in the commercial banks founded by mercantile capitalists and the later crop of the same type of banks founded and used by industrial capitalists. The increasingly important function to be performed by these banks was to provide industries with working capital through the discount of promissory notes and bills of exchange. The industrial capitalists have never been happy, however, because they soon learned that commercial banks lending not so much their capital as deposits were forced to insist that all obligations be met promptly. This embarrassed, even threatened the independent position of many firms. On the whole, the policy of punctuality developed by commercial banks was an exceedingly wholesome influence in business. There were probably abuses, however, for it was charged that some banks pressed certain firms for repayment, whilst they were liberal, even generous, in their treatment of some of the competitors of these firms. In other words, it was said that the banks played favorites. That this did sometimes happen is in keeping with human weakness; that it was ever a very widespread fault has not been demonstrated.

Not all the banks that played a part in the indirect putting-out system were commercial. Increasingly, there has crept into the system an investment banking group which in a later stage—financial capitalism—was to become dominant. These banks arose in America after the War of 1812–15. S. and M. Allen and Company (1808–37) constitute an example. Beginning as a stationery store, the firm turned to handle lottery tickets, bills of exchange, and stocks. Starting in Albany, it came to have branches in the chief Eastern cities. We think back to the Fuggers for a close parallel, but, of course, the Fuggers were more mature and more wealthy. In the crisis of 1837 the firm went down into bankruptcy, as has been common with private bankers since the Middle Ages. In the period from 1837 onward, E. W. Clark and Company of Philadelphia carried on and developed the earlier methods and traditions; indeed, Clark had himself been an Allen partner. In 1857 this firm became insolvent and out of it came Jay Cooke and Company which was to do big things by way of helping to finance the North during the Civil War. After the War, this firm undertook to float railroad securities in a way almost as pretentious as had been followed in selling government securities. In the period 1869-73 Cooke and Company became tied up with a gigantic issue of stocks and bonds for the Northern Pacific Railroad. Attempting to do this on the eve of a financial crash and getting itself into the embarrassing position of being responsible for the management of the youthful line creeping from Duluth westward toward the Pacific, the firm had to close its doors in 1873.

These and other firms show that the new business of investment banker had arisen. Its functions were to buy and sell securities, to act as brokers for others, to underwrite, wholesale, and retail new securities, to hold up the values of such securities on a declining market, and to act as financial agent of the companies floated. Now, note that what such concerns did fundamentally was to provide industrial capitalists primarily with permanent or fixed capital. They might advance funds to help out in case of a depleted working capital position. But, throughout industrial capitalism, the investment banker, like the commercial bank, has been passive in his relation to his clients. After floating the securities, the investment banker kept hands off. There was to come a time, chiefly in the 1890's and under the leadership of J. P. Morgan and Company and Kuhn, Loeb and Company, when such aloofness was not politic and not desired by the companies receiving aid. The active participation of such bankers, often in harmony with the commercial banks, was to usher in the next or financial stage of capitalism.

In addition to commercial banks and investment bankers there were arising insurance companies which took the money of sundry members of the middle class and invested it against the day when lump sums or annuities would be paid at or following the death of individuals, or damage would be paid in case of marine accident or fire. In London the Amicable Society was established in 1706 and the Equitable in 1762 to write life insurance. The Philadelphia Contributionship, writing fire insurance, was chartered in 1752 and seems to be the earliest American business corporation still in existence. The Pennsylvania Company for insuring lives received its charter in 1812. Many other such concerns began under either mercantile or industrial capitalism and grew slowly. In all probability, private underwriters, for a long time, at least in marine insurance, were more important than the chartered companies. Such are further examples of the indirect putting-out system. In no case, apparently, did they ever become *actively* interested in the concerns in which they invested. That development came only in the stage of financial capitalism.

Trust companies provide a fourth illustration of the indirect putting-out of capital. The earliest examples of this nature in America seem to have been the Farmers' Fire Insurance and Loan Company, now the Farmers' Loan and Trust Company of New York, established in 1822, and the Massachusetts Hospital Life Insurance Company, which was established in 1818 and by at least 1823 was doing a trust business. The Pennsylvania Company, created to write life insurance, turned to the trust business in 1836 and after 1872 wrote no insurance. These trust companies seem to have had only a passive interest in the concerns in which they purchased equities or bonds. When trust companies changed to active participation, as they did later, they were helping to introduce financial capitalism, as we shall see in the next chapter. Just now, we are interested merely in the fact that commercial banks, investment bankers, insurance companies, and trust companies were part and parcel of the indirect putting-out system and, as such, were playing a part in industrial capitalism.

9. EFFECT OF INDUSTRIAL CAPITALISM ON INTERNAL ORGANIZATION

Inside of each firm there was someone responsible for this flow of capital with which we have been dealing. It might be the "boss" of a small firm or the treasurer of a large corporation. It is to officials and internal organization under industrial capitalism that we now direct attention.

Although the petty firm under industrial capitalism would not differ much from the petty firm under the older mercantile capitalism, still the typically large concern in each would vary a great deal and not least in internal organization. Under industrial capitalism the workers were inside the organization and not scattered about as under mercantile capitalism. Under industrial capitalism most of the functions hitherto performed by agents were performed by wage-earning employees and salaried officials. Under industrial capitalism the partnership of the older mercantile capitalism commonly became a corporation in the case of large units.

The greater size of the business unit and the growing predominance of corporations under industrial capitalism gave rise to more elaborate internal organization than ever before known to business and brought into being the conscious problem of the efficient management of capital and labor.

Discipline had been a problem under mercantile capitalism and it had never been solved completely. That fact was one reason why the system would not last indefinitely. Small scattered masters could not be depended on to produce goods in the style desired, at the time required, or without stealing some of the raw material handed out to them. Now, when these masters were all thrown together as employees under one roof or under one closely knit organization, they could be watched by foremen who had the power of dismissal in the case of dishonesty, malicious behavior, or incompetence. Since the workers had no other means of livelihood, unless they could find another job, there was pressure on them to work and act efficiently and coöperatively. Of course, this had actually been introduced in the central workshops of mercantile capitalist days, but now it was adopted generally—in factories, on railroads, in mercantile and banking institutions, and so on.

The central workshop of the mercantile capitalist régime had also introduced and developed the division of labor. This practice was taken over by factory operators and industrial capitalists generally and made one of the pillars of the new system. Among business firms under industrial capitalism there was firm specialization—one plant manufacturing watches, another guns, a third paper boxes; and within each firm one man performed indefinitely one small machine operation, while another started where he had left off. Never had there been such concentration of effort on such small bits of work, unless it was in the well-developed textile industry under mercantile capitalism. In order to accomplish this there had to be an elaborate organization of groups under foremen, and groups of groups under departmental managers.

Although a business unit under industrial capitalism was devoted to one purpose, such as making a clock or transporting goods, still there had to be a considerable division of employments within the firm. In practice, there were three divisions roughly indicated by production, distribution, and finance. This very analysis somewhat belies the statement that there was firm specialization. In fact, there never could be complete firm specialization. If you made a hat, you had to transport it to some small extent, and perhaps store it a day or longer, and then you had to sell it. And so, what we find is that, while the firm specialized in its general function before the world, there was a good deal of occupational diversification within the plant or—to use an old phrase—division of employments.

When business firms incorporated, there was a certain amount of formalism introduced into the situation. We may clearly recognize (1) outside legislators creating the charter or the law under which the charter was drawn up, (2) stockholders who owned the firm, (3) a board of directors, and (4) officials, such as governor and treasurer as commonly spoken of in the old charters or president and treasurer in the new. To be sure, all this goes back to the banking, commercial, and other companies created under the régime of mercantile capitalism, but now under industrial capitalism a corporation gradually became the normal external form of a business concern.

The board of directors would draw up the main lines of policy to be followed and the chief officials would manage the concern in accordance with those policies. Often, however, several of the officials were also directors; occasionally all of them were. And today there are these two types of internal organizations which we, as individual students, should study in the firms that come to our attention.

An industrial hierarchy came into being that compares favorably in elaborateness with that of the Catholic Church or the heavenly order, with its gradations down from the deity to the keepers of the Golden Gates. In thinking of this hierarchy we might keep in mind the following set-up as suggestive of something rather widespread:

President
General manager
Departmental managers
Foremen
Workers

In the new situation in which the industrial capitalist performs one main function through the many divisions of employment and labor on the inside, we find much to praise and much to blame. We like the cheapening of the products and the rising rates of pay of all classes of workers, but we do not like on the other hand the loss of independence on the part of the workers, the big aggregations of men and women where disaster involves catastrophe, the separation of owners, administrators, and workers, and the periodic loss of all employment through suspension of operation for one reason or another.

10. SOCIAL ENGINEERS

When the industrialist has completed his organization, developed his policies of operation, and then begun to manage the whole works, he has still left something undone. He is meeting the major needs of producing goods and services at low prices in a way that customers want them. This is perhaps ninety per cent of the whole task. Any class of leaders doing so good a job might well be considered as successful.

There is still ten per cent of the job that needs to be accounted for. This may be called social engineering—looking after the human element in the firm. A business man commonly finds his human problem at home, and often enough that home presents enough engineering for him. Much greater, however, is the human issue in his factory, railroad, warehouse, wholesale establishment, coal mine, or steamship line. The men are more than workers. Perhaps in their own homes they are bossed or neglected by wives and children. It is just too much to get no favorable treatment anywhere. The fraternal lodge is an outlet and the church too, but these are not daily influences. The public inn is of daily assistance but chiefly in the evening. And so the engineer, concerned with men, has a challenge to meet—to give the workers the treatment that they consider fair.

There are three principal lines of social engineering. The first one is to provide benefits which the men really need and which the employer sees will help them as workers. One of the oldest is medical aid. This was provided by Sir Ambrose Crowley in his hardware manufacturing plant in Northern England even before 1700—in the days of mercantile capitalism. Loan funds also prove helpful, though difficult to manage. Samuel Slater provided a Sunday school for his spinners right at the introduction of the factory system in America. Libraries, athletic clubs, dramatic clubs, glee clubs, and so on come under the category. Often such associations provide the lonely worker with the only active connection he has outside of his work.

A second benefit is a *just* wage. This raises the same vague problem as the Middle Ages wrestled with in just price. Certainly the wage must be just to the employee, employer, and customer. One solution has been to provide the worker with supplementary wages when his cost of living is high and to give him a bonus or a share in the profits when business is prosperous. In fact, while helpful, these devices are quite inadequate. The employee needs an annual income—one on which he can depend through the seasons and throughout his working life. Business has never reached the point, however, where it can undertake such responsibilities. Many business men do not like the methods referred to because they find that wage incentives do not make men work harder or better. In addition, while the workers share profits, they do not share losses.

The third device is management-sharing. There has been a thought that the fundamental trouble with the workers is not that their income is too small but that they are bossed too much. Give them a voice in the rules and execution of management and they will be content. There is no doubt that a few are pleased with this gift of power—vain souls who would otherwise be politicians, gang leaders, or promoters of clubs. The rank and file, however, see in this particular device little more than a friendly gesture. The employer sees that management-sharing is useful chiefly in an upward secular trend when his problem is not to get business but to get the effective coöperation of workers.

Although social engineering was practised in the days of mercantile capitalism, it was in the régime of industrial capitalism that it became an important aspect of business management. Robert Owen was the earliest social engineer of any prominence among the industrial capitalists. Since the story of Owen's life and work is so important and the sources of study so accessible, I recommend that all read his biography. Rising in the textile industry, Owen created benefits for his workers, shared profits, helped form coöperative societies, and so on. He let his social engineering engulf him to the point where he lost his footing in reality. He became a Utopian and turned against established religion. His life was not a failure, for he left a story of aid to fellow men. It is not necessary to be a cynic, however, to believe that he would have been of more use if he had put one single factory on an enduring basis and paid fair wages during his lifetime. The thousands who perform this major service to society are forgotten, while the Utopian extremist—part success and part failure—is long remembered.

In England the cocoa manufacturers have been prominent —Fry Brothers of Bristol, Cadbury Brothers of Bournville, and the Rowntrees of York. Joseph Rowntree (1836–1925), a Quaker like the Fry Brothers, introduced social benefits into his plant and advocated temperance reform. His son, B. Seebohm Rowntree, has carried on and extended the good work. In addition, he has written about poverty and the workers' lot in the town. His emphasis is upon the human factor in business. In his judgment much unrest has been due to a lack of "courtesy and consideration in industry."

One of the best known instances of social engineering is found in Port Sunlight, where soap and other products are made by Lever Brothers. Like Joseph Rowntree, W. H. Lever (1851–1925) entered his father's wholesale grocery business, only to turn to manufacture. His first location proving inadequate, he created a new village or port. His business was developed horizontally as factories were established or bought in various parts of the world and vertically as sources of supplies and distribution were acquired. The social engineering came out chiefly in the building up of the community of Port Sunlight with its houses, institutions, and generally favorable conditions for work and life.

On the Continent, there were and are many examples of social engineering. Among the older instances are the Krupp Works at Essen, Germany, the Le Creusot plant in France, and the great yeast factory in Delft (the Dutch Paradise). In America we have the Waltham Watch Company, Procter and Gamble, Endicott-Johnson, J. C. Penney, the Eastman Kodak, and many others. Hardly any efforts could exceed in interest the social engineering of Mr. Henry S. Dennison in his factory in Framingham, Massachusetts. In this plant, which manufactures chiefly stationers' goods, we find sundry benefits, profit-sharing, and management-sharing, born largely in the experiences of World War production.

During the World War there arose to prominence a Cape Cod artist by the name of Beneker who had a vision of workers and executives pulling together for a common good—victory in war and in peace. The specialty of this American Meunier was pictures of horny-handed men of toil who were hungry for a feeling of loyalty to some group or institution. He painted in high color hairy-chested men who did the spade and shovel work of production. To him they were engineers of the soil. Some employers had the same idea and bought his pictures. One firm in Cleveland employed him to paint its workers who in turn came to appreciate the compliment. The artist was made a member of the firm's industrial relations board. The War ended, the firm went into bankruptcy, and the effort slackened. Then death came to the artist and his pictures now languish in sundry places. Later in the days of the American New Deal, the idea of coöperation of master and men has been supplanted by the political concept of suspicion and strife. But let us not forget our artist friend who was a social engineer of rare creative capacity.

Another pictorial momento of social engineering during the War and post-War periods was the graph hung up in the offices and plants of certain American firms, showing how wages were to rise as production, sales, and profits rose. This was a profit-sharing which many of the workers appreciated and many executives held to be sound and just. Later, during the period 1933-37, government advisers thought they could work the scheme backwards and get increased sales and production by raising wages. This proved to be sharing distress and provided for a continuation of a low level of achievement. This government effort was social but not engineering.

Andrew Carnegie was a great social engineer but of a special type. No one would think of him as introducing profit-sharing or management-sharing into his plants. He believed in a competitive wage and fair treatment for his employees and lamented the Homestead Strike (1892) which proved to be a landmark in the distress of labor, or at least of trade unions, in the steel industry for a generation. His point of view was that poverty is a blessing, for it offers a chance for the individual to rise above obstacles; to the able worker, low wages matter little because soon he will be a foreman, superintendent, manager, or director. As the worker goes up into the ranks of management, he gets the reward of handsome profits.

But Carnegie would not leave the poor struggling worker without aid. He would provide libraries where technical and general information, useful to the worker and the citizen, could be found. This would be the greatest boon for the worker—again the worker who could rise to be a manager. Over $350,000,000 were given away by Carnegie to benefit his fellow men—for libraries, universities, pensions for teachers, research, publication, and peace. These gifts are monuments to be compared with the great steel business which he created.

In a sense, the climax of social engineering in American business is found in the work of the Rockefellers. The son was the active participant, and the father the willing supporter. An early example of the son's contributions is found in the affairs of the Colorado Fuel and Iron Company—a coal and iron concern which had been incorporated in 1892. Labor conditions in this firm had been bad and strikes serious. In 1915, after the Company had been victorious in a bitter strike, Mr. J. D. Rockefeller, Jr., introduced a company union which attracted wide attention at the time because of the prominence of the situation and because employee representation in management seemed to many persons a promising means of solving labor problems. Certainly, the strike had been and is no credit to our social order. The difficulty is obviously how to replace it with something better. Mr. Rockefeller has been responsible for a second bit of social engineering—the early use and encouragement of industrial relations counselors and public relations counselors. Above all, however, he and his family have supported the wholesale distribution of funds for purposes of education, research, and health, which redound to the advantage of rich and poor alike, in America and abroad. Here there is a close parallel in Rockefeller and Carnegie policies. The expenditure of the Rockefellers has apparently already exceeded six hundred million dollars. Most of this, we may assume, was derived from profits made in the American oil industry. The Rockefellers had been great industrial capitalists who later turned to financial capitalism. They have been *par excellence* social engineers. How far the strong religious influence of the Baptist faith has underlain their social work is hard to determine.

In America there has been written a whole chapter of efforts to establish private systems of insuring workmen against unemployment and of providing old-age pensions. In one country after another, however, private efforts in these directions have been abandoned or reduced as national systems of insurance and other benefits have been instituted. Industrial capitalists as a whole have been too slow or unable to act effectively and must now watch their workmen look more and more to another power for social engineering.

A cursory examination indicates that there are certain accompaniments of social engineering which are probably significant. Religion, especially Quakerism, has been associated with many efforts. Temperance runs parallel. A broad humanitarian feeling often is at the base of improved labor management. Some of the business leaders have had intellectual interests as deep as their business interests; indeed they might have been as successful in law, medicine, preaching, or teaching as in making profits in business. Often the accompaniment of social engineering is merely some changing circumstance. Strikes called the attention of Procter and Gamble to the need of labor reforms. The necessity of getting more work under the stress of war or under the opportunities provided by a sellers' market has been the impelling motive in many instances.

The merits of the work of the social engineer are very real. The most immediate result is better production—fewer strikes, less waste of material and time, and greater ease in getting things done, notably in improving methods of operation. The amelioration of labor conditions makes a worker a better man, quite apart from his being a better workman. This is high praise that needs no further comment. The social engineer himself becomes more proud of his job; his work beyond profits gives him an additional interest, incentive, and stake in life. To many a business man the chief merit is combating radicalism among workers by removing the causes of discontent, large and small. It is a well-known fact that the trade union leader cannot tolerate the social engineer: the model factory and village are like the cathedral from the lofty walls of which ascend sacred music and sweet incense which stifle the senses of the Prince of Discord.

Many a successful business man has regarded social engineering as a type of boondoggling in the midst of a serious job. He knows that he has other work to perform—to pay a going wage, meet his tax bill, and produce in competition with others who would drive him to the wall. Even he has a lingering sympathy with the whole effort, however, in so far as the social engineer tends to make the trade union and its bickerings unnecessary. In fact, he would go so far as to center most of the social engineering in a company union coöperating with a personnel manager.

To the outsider, there are four principal objections to an

emphasis on social engineering. First, great success comes chiefly through a genius who is rarely found in any walk of life and who in this case must be able to be a business man and social engineer at the same time. It is doubtful whether the office of social engineer can be permanently institutionalized. Second, there is a tendency that the firm which goes far in this direction will meet financial ruin. You will agree with this or deny it in accordance with experience and predilection. Third, most of the workers are not much interested in or affected by the whole movement. Fourth, the social scientist must see that ultimately the movement would lead to industrial feudalism in which the worker would be tied to his plant. In these days of fast autos and still faster airplanes, no one, except perhaps the philosopher, wants to be tied to anything. And, yet, a primary feeling has been growing that security in employment and good conditions of work are prime necessities in life. This may involve the return of status as a substitute for contract, or unfree status as a substitute for free status which men have possessed without enjoying, in one form or another, since the decline of mediaeval manorial-feudalism.

11. STRENGTH AND WEAKNESS OF INDUSTRIAL CAPITALISM

Hardly any two persons would agree on what the strong points of industrial capitalism were and what were the weak points. Indeed, we are still too near to the age of industrial capitalism and especially to the spirit and working of the system to pass a final judgment.

Industrial capitalism introduced a new emphasis upon producers' goods as against consumers' goods, thereby accentuating, of course, the secular trends in business. The new emphasis has been a source of strength in the world in so far as more wealth was henceforth to be devoted to production. This was to have important repercussions on the relation between capital and labor.

STRENGTH AND WEAKNESS

Among the elements of strength may be listed the use of power-machinery, the low prices of goods and services provided, the teaching of discipline to untamed souls, the utilization of the heavy-clod type of man, and the concentration of persons, economic power, and wealth. There was an advantage in firm specialization, for in no other way could progress be so rapid. As events were to prove, however, firm specialization had undisclosed areas of weakness as we shall see.

Now, there will be much difference of opinion as to concentration of persons, economic power, and wealth. The concentration of persons, while unfortunate from the standpoint of spreading disease, was helpful in calling attention to bad conditions of work and brought the workers to a consciousness of their common problems. The concentration of economic power gave the industrial capitalists a chance to have influence on public opinion and legislation that would cater to the needs of industrial capitalism in important ways. It did not take long to make England and France over into free-trade countries, and other nations later when it seemed that *laissez-faire* was the best policy for them to follow. By the same token, when it appeared that the less mature nations such as the United States, France, Germany, and so on needed protection, then the concentration of power was helpful in bringing about the desired results—more protection.

Some concentration of wealth is always helpful. The only uncertainty, as it seems to me, is how much concentration. In general, however, the people with some concentration of wealth possesses a leadership that it would otherwise not have. The rich man can afford to pioneer, support experimentation and exploration, and embark upon business, social, and cultural ventures that yield slow returns. Of course, he is our greatest collector of cultural objects which ultimately go to the use of the people.

Industrial capitalism soon displayed weaknesses to be marked down opposite its sources of strength. The loss of freedom in work itself was a heavy blow to the sensitive and the neurotic.

The loss of an alternative to the main employment in factory, railroad, or store was calamitous. Relief came only to those who could migrate to fresh lands.

One of the greatest weaknesses of industrial capitalism was specialization over a long period, particularly in old industries, as evidenced during the downward trend 1866–97. We shall consider this further in the next chapter. Akin to this was the severity of competition which the industrial capitalists liked so well but suffered so much from. The dog likes a fight even though he gets badly scarred. To be sure, biologically this contest may be wholesome but men have tired of it as they have seen that worker, administrator, investing capitalist, and nation, all suffer.

One of the subtle weaknesses of industrial capitalism is the failure to capture the interest, or appeal to the imagination, or enlist the sentimental regard of the average man. This can be illustrated by modern art. Apart from the portrait painter who receives fat fees for painting business men, and apart from caricatures of business men found in magazines, it is not the executive but the man who works with his hands that is given attention. The mansion of the rich factory operator or banker offers no picturesque corners to the artist's eye, while the ramshackle hovel of a drunken workman strikes a deep feeling in the artist's breast. Thus, sentiment is enlisted against big business. The artist, scholar, philosopher, and moralist is essentially a petty capitalist who is at best half workman; their tools vary but they are all struggling onward under difficulty; they have little sympathy with industrial capitalism. Meunier (1831–1905) somewhat exemplifies the group. He loved to paint and carve workers in the field, the factory, and the mine. He thought less of the ship at sea, bending to the wind, and more of the burden of the longshoreman unloading the cargo. An artist reproduces a synthesis of himself and his age. Meunier was over-sensitive, even maudlin; he was impressed with the weakness of himself, his kinsmen, and his fellow men under existing circumstances. There was something of the Oriental Christ in him—an acceptance of worldly defeat. Meunier was a thirteenth apostle—born to walk the rough seas of private business capitalism, without even reaching the port where he might have learned what economic systems really mean. Like most artists and scholars, he lived his life without making essential distinctions concerning business. He knew more about the sailor than the merchant, more about the miner than the mine operator, and more about the iron puddler than the great ironmaster. He was more interested in the workshop and the mill-race than in the office or the accounts. He painted and carved the scenes of the buttery and the stable without ever visiting the drawing room or riding in the carriage. He left in enduring form the concept of labor but not of business administration. And, yet, Meunier is a fact—a hard representative fact in business history.

On the side of industrial management itself there are weaknesses to record. In those firms organized as corporations, the industrial capitalist had a chance to develop industrial democracy in making his stockholders a responsible voting group, electing and rejecting directors at will. Instead, he killed every virile impulse to make this system work. True, he would have encountered difficulties but that is inherent in democracy. He himself undertook to be a director of too many concerns—industrial and charitable. He used his position to regiment his workers, after the manner of a patriarchal tribal leader, instead of building up a feeling that loyalty should and would go to the worthy employer. While he was strong in production and only a little less in distribution, he was weak in financial management. Those firms that did not correct such weakness within their own organization went over into financial capitalism—the subject of the next chapter.

Chapter VI

FINANCIAL CAPITALISM

The Money Middleman Influences or Controls Business

*Develop financial strength or expect control from outside;
Emphasize capital, reduce competition,
Integrate the functions of units and diversify;
Strengthen the promising units, abandon the weak.
Nations are instruments, not objectives.*

1. SEARCH FOR PROFITS BY TURNING AWAY FROM SPECIALIZATION

Industrial capitalism was long a system of firm specialization which also involved the division of labor and division of employments (personal specialization). As we have seen, the system worked well so long as it was competing with the lingering remnants of mercantile capitalism, especially small dependent masters using hand machinery and tools. There came a time, however, when the specialized business firms found increasing difficulties in making money. This occurred notably in the period 1866–97. It was gradually becoming obvious to many business men that they must do something other than merely compete a little harder. Many industrial capitalists did a good job in coördinating production and distribution and giving their business financial strength. Often part and parcel of this development was a turn away from specialization. Indeed, many saw that specialization was, in the long run, ruinous and, indeed, not a normal way of doing business on a large scale.

In the process of turning away from specialization there

were two series of efforts. The first was made by industrial capitalists and the second by financial capitalists. Many of the first series of efforts succeeded, as we shall presently see. Many of them failed, however, and that failure left no other possibility than leadership through financial capitalists—the government of the day being incapable of action in such matters. It is the task of the present section to set forth examples of the efforts made by industrial capitalists to save themselves from ultimate ruin.

There are at least four types of efforts made by industrial capitalists to increase profits. The first is the combination of unlike functions or operations. This is commonly found in small towns where a coal dealer will sell lumber, write insurance policies, and act as notary public. In Rhode Island up to the crisis of 1873 the Sprague family was engaged in a number of individual and distinct businesses that is truly remarkable. The Spragues had established a calico mill in Cranston, R.I., in 1811. The second generation, Amasa and William, showed itself enterprising and not too scrupulous. The third generation (of the same names) not only pushed ahead in business and politics but on many fronts. It was not enough for a Sprague (William) to be governor of his State and United States senator; he had also to be the chief shareholder and even executive in business enterprises. The kernel of the business empire was the spinning, weaving (apparently), and printing mills in Rhode Island, Connecticut, Maine, and South Carolina. In the last named, the Spragues also owned water power. In Providence, the brothers owned stock in five banks which, of course, helped finance the cotton mills by buying their paper. They owned a dominant interest in a steamship line operating between Providence and New York and doubtless thus carried many of their own cottons to the growing metropolis. In that great center they were partners of Hoyt, Sprague and Company which was apparently a textile commission agency handling the Sprague cottons. Thus, so far there is some dovetailing of functions, though little coherence of management.

On the outer fringes of the Sprague industry there were strange holdings. There was the street railway in Providence which operated horse cars and on the hills cable cars. There were timber claims in Maine, and possibly New Hampshire, with mills to cut up the logs. In addition, there were at least four metal factories, one for sheet iron, one for horseshoes, one for horseshoe nails, and one for moving-machines. How much undeveloped land was owned by the Spragues in the West is not clear.

The process seems to have been to take profits out of cottons and then diversify holdings, sometimes just as investment and sometimes as management obligations. In fact, authority had to be delegated. Control was impossible because of multiplicity of units and preoccupation of the owners with politics and horses. When the crisis of 1873 came along, this unwieldly estate, worth about nineteen millions and owing about eleven, was seen to be temporarily insolvent. A trustee (from whose grandson I have learned many facts) operated the holdings 1873-89, and some till 1927. The properties were gradually sold and the proceeds paid to the creditors to the extent of about thirty cents on the dollar. Above all is the towering monument to faulty policy and managerial inefficiency. The Spragues were trying to carry on the multiple functions of the old sedentary merchants in an era of specialization.

Another example, this time typical of the early West, is W. C. Ralston (1826-75) who had silver mines in Nevada, railroads near San Francisco Bay, and real estate, water works, a large palatial hotel, and a bank in San Francisco. When Ralston's body was found floating in the Bay, his heterogeneous empire fell apart as it should because from a management standpoint it was a monstrosity. It is true that Ralston's bank financed his mines and his railroads carried his ores and supplies, but still there was no administrative unity and no adequate control. As investments, his interests in divers concerns and industries were unsound because speculative and unseasoned. Ralston is now remembered by many as a typical example of the new rich of the Far West and as a devotee to gross and conspicuous expenditures.

A second type of effort to get away from the evils of specialization is found in a recombination of functions after the manner of the mercantile capitalist—the sedentary merchant. As we remember, this merchant managed the various functions in an integrated fashion. In other words, they were made to fit as cog in cog and belt on wheel.

American railroads began operations as carriers of freight and passengers. Even before the Civil War they reached out to own and control forests and coal mines so as to insure themselves of plenty of freight. Ultimately they were practically denied by federal law (1887) the right to engage in either the lumber or coal business. They also picked up and delivered freight, but were forced out of this business in favor of local draymen and carriers. Later, they purchased local electric lines and steamship lines but were forced to give them up. The government—that is, the people—feared monopolies.

The iron and steel industry actually succeeded in multiplying and integrating functions. Engaged primarily in smelting iron ore, the iron and steel manufacturers reached back to mine the ore and transport it to the furnaces. They even reached back to mine the coal used as fuel. They extended their operations on into the semi-finished or even finished iron and steel industry, such as the making of rails, pipe, wire, and structural parts. One of the leaders in this movement was Andrew Carnegie, perhaps America's keenest industrial capitalist.

Meat packers, at first concerned with slaughtering and the selling of meat, added several other functions. They bought up or established stockyards in key cities. They purchased and equipped their own refrigeration cars. They began to emphasize by-products, such as oleomargarine, hides and leather, fertilizers, pharmaceutical products, and soap. They added, as auxiliary to their marketing, canned goods, eggs, butter, and poultry. Some of these activities they were allowed to continue but not the marketing of products other than meat and meat derivatives. The opposition came from the wholesale grocers who saw themselves threatened. It mattered not that the packers could reduce the cost of distribution by utilizing unused space in their cars.

Oil refiners, under the leadership of the Standard Oil group, developed the marketing, even the retailing, of their products —kerosene, gasoline, and lubricating oil. They reached back to the production of the crude petroleum and to the steamships necessary to transport the crude oil. They went far in constructing pipe lines, at first for crude oil, now increasingly for gasolene.

A third type of effort to grow out of and away from specialization led to diversification of production. An example of this occurs in the history of retail stores in large cities. In the 1820's, in New York and Paris, stores came into existence which carried dry goods and later also house furnishings, some articles of clothing, and some novelties. Alexander T. Stewart's store in New York is an example. Gradually new departments were added until the department store, with which we are so familiar, was a reality. R. H. Macy and Company (1858), John Wanamaker (1861), and Marshall Field (1865) are outstanding examples of department stores, as we have seen above. Such department stores were really a number of specialty stores under one management. In this arrangement there were advantages to the customer, for he was offered a whole street or cluster of stores under one roof. He could deal with the whole group of departments through a single account. He came to feel, as responsibility and integrity grew in big-store management, that he was safer in dealing with a big store. As time went on, extra services were offered to him that he appreciated. On the side of the store, there were advantages in the purchases of goods, in advertising, and probably in management costs. In time of financial stress the large store was regarded by banks and others as too big a firm to allow to go into bankruptcy because of the repercussions involved.

Factories often took their start in the manufacture of a single commodity. The Dennison Manufacturing Company is an outgrowth of a business which began in 1844 in the making of boxes for jewelers. Later it added, one after another, tags, sealing wax, crêpe paper, baby pads, display paper, and so on. Ultimately it was making about 10,000 products. An effort to reduce these succeeded in eliminating only about 2,000. There was no reaching out to make paper; the only concern was paper products. Retail stores have been established by the Company in a few cities, but about as much for display and promotion as for sales. Other manufacturing concerns have had experiences similar to Dennison's.

A fourth type of effort at escape from the evils of specialization involves the common device of combination of *like* units. At first, perhaps only a gentleman's agreement between firms producing the same kind of commodity or service would be attempted. Then a formal association with definite limitations upon amount of output might be created. This failing, as it nearly always did, sometimes another association was attempted with penalties for failure to observe rules. If prices were kept high and output curtailed, an invitation was in effect given to others to start up new competing concerns. These might be bought up but this process became an expensive practice and in the long run would be fatal. Only some kind of common ownership of a large group of units and common management proved to be an effective solution in one instance after another. One corporation would try out a lot of competing units and "stabilize" the industry by dominating it.

The oatmeal industry illustrates some developments very effectively. In 1856 Ferdinand Schumacher, an immigrant from Germany, established an oatmeal mill in Akron, Ohio. The number of mills in Ohio increased and the industry spread. Within thirty years, it had grown past its newness and run into difficulty. The downward trend of 1866–97 increased its problems. There was a combination of over-production and low prices. Something had to be done.

In 1886 the Oatmeal Millers' Association was formed by 21 millers who sought to regulate sales and prices. The millers pledged their word to obey the rules agreed upon but failed to keep their pledges. In 1887 the Consolidated Oatmeal Company took its place as industrial savior. This was a regulated company of 13 mills. Schumacher was one of the leaders. Efforts were made actually to enforce the rules: rewards were paid to informers and fines were levied on the disobedient constituent companies. Still there were difficulties: some millers evaded the rules; new mills were established which it cost too much to buy. Moreover, State laws against monopolies threatened the whole affair.

In 1891 the American Cereal Company was created by 6 mills, one of them the Quaker Mill Company. The able Schumacher was the leading miller. At last, a unitary concern had been created with a central management of ability. One mill was closed, and, when another burned, it was not replaced. Effective policies were worked out—pushing of the chief brand, advertising, use of packages (since 1899), and, beginning in 1893, expansion abroad. In 1901 the name was changed to the Quaker Oats Company. In 1911 this Company purchased its chief rival—the Great Western Cereal Company, made up of 10 concerns and using the notable brands of Mother's Oats and Friends' Brand. In 1925 the Aunt Jemima Mills Company of Missouri was bought up, and later other firms also.

The chief lesson for us is that associations of small firms cannot always meet the needs of a sick industry. There are internal difficulties of control, and State laws against monopolies create external difficulties. The solution is the big combination, so hated and feared by consumers. Of course, we know that in the long run consumers do not profit from over-production or from prices below costs. The combination puts prices high enough to reward business men and laborers and to pay the owners of capital enough to induce them to loan or invest. From 1915 to 1920 the Quaker Oats Company had to fight its way through the courts, but finally the case was dismissed. The Company had made good its claim that it possessed only 49.5 per cent of the total business.

Such a device as this horizontal combination has been common in highly competitive industries at home and abroad. While in Europe such combination is welcomed by governments, in America it is very much feared and often prosecuted by the State or federal government, particularly if it seems to be a "dangerous" monopoly or in restraint of trade. Where prosecution has occurred, the result has sometimes gone against the combination, as in the case of the Northern Securities Company (northwest railroads, 1904) and the Standard Oil group (1911); sometimes against the government, as in the case of the United Shoe Machinery Company (1918), the United States Steel Corporation (1920), and the International Harvester Company (1927).

Industrial capitalists were feeling their way toward another order of business, or driving hard toward another system—one that would assure them greater profits and security. The public—particularly workmen and farmers—feared the business man's efforts to help himself. These classes had no sympathy with a policy to stabilize business. Indeed, they commonly acted as if they profited by industrial distress and bankruptcy. A little thought would show that such could not be the case. And yet the other extreme of monopoly and monopoly prices was alarming to those who were trying to make their meager incomes go as far as possible.

Here we are confronted with the battleground of prices. Always the struggle is going on and always the results are feared by both sides. No matter whether the prevailing solution is in the hands of business men or of politicians, there is no feeling that social justice is being done. In truth, we have no yardstick for prices. It means nothing—or not much—to talk of a just price. Always we want to know, "just" to whom? We are left with the old market price ever changing and ever pressing upon one group or another. No, there is really a third price—a monopoly price such as the price of aluminum fixed by the

Aluminum Company of America, and a fourth price—a government fixed price as in the case of railroad rates. I can see objections to all and find no disposition to accept any one of these for universal application. Prices are like morals and artistic values: they are beyond exact or permanent determination.

2. FINANCIAL CAPITALISTS

We have seen that industrial capitalists tried hard to save themselves from the disastrous results of a policy of specialization. They struggled toward higher profits but met nothing but discouragement from the government and several classes of the people. They knew well enough that they could not go on in a condition of excessive competition or on a basis of specialization. Where the industrial capitalists failed, however, the financial capitalists came in to succeed. While the former were almost exclusively concerned with America, the latter had European investors in mind as well as American. To the industrialist, business would not be worth while if there were no profit reward. To the financial capitalist business could not carry on, unless there was a continuous return to capital so that there could be a renewal of investments and loans and increased investments and loans for improvements and expansion. What the industrial capitalist attempted, but accomplished only partly, the financial capitalist carried through in a big way in a relatively short time, in America about 1873–1929. For instance, he substituted multiple economic functions for specialization of firms, consolidated units, curtailed competition, built up reserves, and reduced costs, all in the interest of dividends and, ultimately, of refinancing for more progressive operations.

Financial capitalists are the owners or administrators of institutions which carry on the indirect putting-out system in its second or active phase. In other words, financial capitalists are the business men who receive capital from a wide variety of persons and who, when putting this capital out on loan or investment, follow it up by securing influence or control over the borrowing business so as to insure dividends and interest on stocks, bonds, and notes. J. P. Morgan, Sr. (1837–1913), is the striking example of a financial capitalist. For nearly a generation Morgan rivalled kings and presidents as an object of interest, respect, and hate. We may well compare him with Jacob Fugger (died in 1525) and Baron James Meyer de Rothschild. Some would be inclined, I think less aptly, to put him down alongside of Cecil Rhodes, Sir Basil Zaharoff, and Sir Henri Deterding.

An extended examination of the origin of financial capitalism would include at least three distinct and separate inquiries. We recall the attainment of a financial aspect on the part of mercantile capitalism in Italy and Southern Germany about 1500 when great merchant-banking families dominated a good deal of trade, manufacture, and finance (private and public). This system, promising as it was, did not last long, partly because world trade and economic power shifted to Western Europe where a less advanced and less financial type of mercantile capitalism prevailed. Here was an adumbration, however, of the growth of the money power. A second inquiry should be made into the rise of promotional banks in Western Europe about the middle of the nineteenth century. A third inquiry is peculiarly American and centers in New York.

Before proceeding to the third inquiry, let us consider the second, even if in great brevity. When the new Europe rose from the ashes of Napoleonic conflagration, there were five Rothschild brothers ensconced in centers of great strategic importance—Frankfort, London, Paris, Vienna, and Naples. In many ways, Baron James Meyer de Rothschild (1792–1868) was the most significant for our purpose. His office was opened in Paris in 1812 and five years later the house of Rothschild Brothers was established there. This firm operated on its own capital and on deposits of clients who had faith in its future. It carried on a sedentary merchant's business of import, export, and wholesale, especially in staple raw commodities. It had ships on the Atlantic to carry its wares. It gained high fame for its loans to governments. And, most important for our purpose, it promoted the establishment of industrial and transportation concerns in France and elsewhere. Its first railroad interest was in a little horse-car railway taken over in 1832. By the 1840's it had large undertakings in French and Austrian railroads. It helped to build railroads in Belgium and Brazil.

Baron James was a mighty man of money. He was clever, industrious, and luxurious in his habits. Like the sedentary merchants of old, he was a friend of the arts—the host of the composer Rossini and the patron of the poet Heine. To some, he was a ruthless bully; to many, he was a suspected power behind thrones. Democrats and socialists feared him. Republicans saw in him the financial backer of Bourbons and Orleanists. Other Jewish bankers and promoters, such as the Pereire Brothers and the Fould Brothers, found in him a clever rival who could beat them at most of their games. The object of jealousy, fear, and hate, he saw his property destroyed and his life threatened in the Revolution of 1848. Uneasy lies the head that wears the crown (Louis Philippe) and uneasy lies the head that supports it (Rothschild).

The rivals of Baron Rothschild got together to form the well-known Crédit Mobilier (or business bank) formed to parallel the Crédit Foncier (or land bank). The Crédit Mobilier (the full title was General Company of Business Credit) was supported by the Pereire Brothers, the new Emperor Napoleon III, and numerous small investors who were eager for gain and anxious to check the international banking firm of Rothschilds. The bank was formed somewhat in accord with the theory of the socialist Saint-Simon (died 1825) who favored banks which in promoting industries would provide work and facilitate the material progress of men. How far the promotion was to be followed up by influence or control is for the students of Saint-Simon and his School to say. At any rate, the Crédit

Mobilier raised capital by selling shares, and it used this capital to reach out to construct or consolidate various business enterprises in France. It received deposits of all who would trust it, including the companies, notably railroads, in whose stock it had invested. Although it did a commercial banking business, its distinctive service lay in promoting industries and railroads.

Some of the rivals of the Rothschilds, notably the Pereire Brothers, planned to form a Crédit Mobilier in Austria. The Rothschilds moved faster and got a concession to establish the Credit Institute for Trade and Industry which was designed particularly to build and buy railroads in the Dual Monarchy. Numerous Crédits Mobiliers in various countries became the rivals of the merchant bankers.

The Crédit Mobilier in France extended its investments too far and, in fact, held securities from which there were no returns. It made the mistake of paying dividends out of capital. Its stock went down and down on the market and finally in 1867 the firm failed miserably. The next year Baron James died and in 1870 Napoleon lost his throne. A glorious era of grandiose political schemes and promising business ventures (including the Suez Canal) had come to an end.

The decade of the 1860's must have witnessed just about the last lingering flicker of mercantile capitalism, because, although the Rothschilds were to live on and prosper, they were to play their chief rôles as more or less specialized merchant bankers. In 1861 the house in Naples was closed. The home office in Frankfort has been far from vigorous. In 1938 the house in Vienna was seized. In passing, we may note that mercantile capitalism, operating through the Rothschilds, almost introduced financial capitalism to the exclusion of industrial capitalism.

The lasting fruit of the promotion idea was ripened in Germany where the Darmstadt Bank, formed in 1853, and many others of the same type were set up to do a combination of commercial banking and promotion banking business. In other words, they were to provide working capital and permanent capital for promising activities. In Germany these banks, long called "Crédits Mobiliers," held stock in numerous concerns and elected directors to represent their interests. They were in a sense active investment trusts with permanent stock holdings.

America escaped, or missed, the Crédit Mobilier, though it did have an institution that bore the name but was really a construction firm for the Union Pacific Railroad. We cannot help raising the question whether the French Crédit Mobilier was not the very type of institution which Americans should have developed in order to extend their settlement and business westward from at least the 1850's onward. France was to abandon it and England was to have only temporary experience with it during its earliest era of railroad building, except in foreign trade and finance.

There is good reason why Germany and the United States should have been the leaders in developing capitalism. Both countries were poor in investment capital and both had great need for growing fast and far. Both could produce large profits if their credit was upheld. The opportunity for financial capitalists lay in making capital go a long way as safely as possible.

Financial capitalists in America have operated through institutions of sundry types but of wide ramifications among the investors at home and abroad. Most of these institutions we are familiar with as separate entities and nearly all of them have already been mentioned. Here is a list of the outstanding types:

1. Commercial banks (since 1781 in America)
2. Finance corporations (largely since 1918)
3. Savings banks (since 1816 in America)

4. Investment bankers (usually partnerships, chiefly since 1850's in America)
5. Stock brokers (since 1790's in America)

JOHN PIERPONT MORGAN, SR., IN THE 1890's

6. Insurance companies (since 1752 in America)
7. Trust companies (since about 1823 in America)
8. Investment trusts (since 1889 but chiefly since 1917 in America)

It should be noted that not all firms belonging to these types became very vital parts of the nexus of financial capitalism. Some remain more or less in isolation and hold to a passive policy—in other words linger on in the abode of industrial capitalism.

Institutions such as these possessed much of the capital that flowed into business or had influence over it or actually controlled it. In isolation, such institutions would have had but little influence and less control over other business. I say this without forgetting how big and strong some of the individual units were and are. Capital was the cement and investment bankers the cement-mixers. Without the aggressive leadership of Jay Cooke and Company, J. P. Morgan and Company, Kuhn, Loeb and Company, Kidder, Peabody and Company, Lee, Higginson and Company, and sundry others, the new system could not have come into existence in America. Such investment bankers were the most active, flexible, constructive, and responsible in the group and still are. And the greatest of these was J. P. Morgan and Company.

Investment bankers participated in the origination and underwriting of securities, in some cases their wholesale or even retail distribution, handling the securities when floated, acting as financial agents for the companies on whose behalf the securities had been issued, and in general, willingly or not, standing as the sponsors of the companies in question. When a company was known as a member of the Morgan group, the public assumed that it was strong or was on the way to strength. Accordingly, this backing and sponsorship was of great financial aid. On the other hand, the lack of it might be a real handicap.

Among institutions, as among men, there is a tendency to form rival groups. This was prominent in Florence in the

Middle Ages and in Paris at the time of the Rothschilds. A similar situation arose in New York at the end of the nineteenth century. John Moody, who had an excellent opportunity to observe Wall Street, thought somewhat extravagantly of American business as divided between the Morgan and the

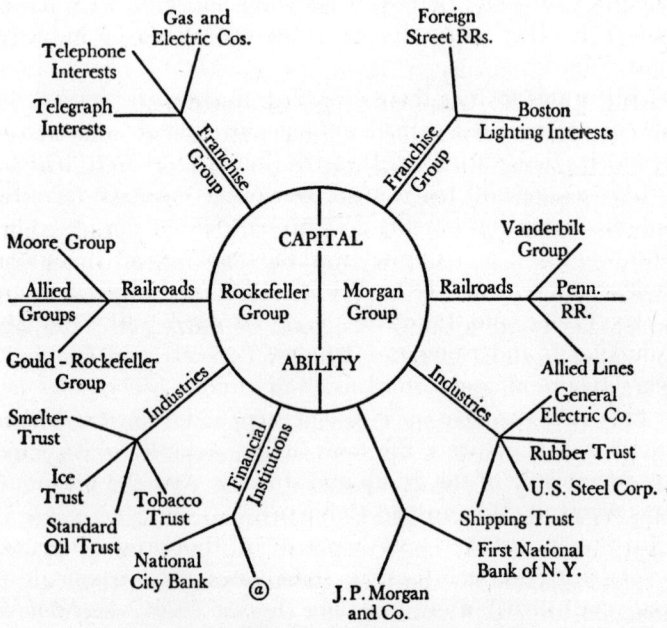

[Diagram: Two circles labeled "Rockefeller Group" and "Morgan Group" inside a larger circle marked CAPITAL / ABILITY, with branches extending outward.

Rockefeller Group branches:
- Franchise Group: Telephone Interests, Telegraph Interests, Gas and Electric Cos.
- Railroads: Moore Group, Allied Groups, Gould-Rockefeller Group
- Industries: Smelter Trust, Ice Trust, Standard Oil Trust, Tobacco Trust
- Financial Institutions: National City Bank, @

Morgan Group branches:
- Franchise Group: Foreign Street RRs., Boston Lighting Interests
- Railroads: Vanderbilt Group, Penn. RR.
- Industries: Allied Lines, General Electric Co., Rubber Trust, U.S. Steel Corp., Shipping Trust
- Financial Institutions: First National Bank of N.Y., J. P. Morgan and Co.]

ᵃ At a later date the Chase-Harris-Forbes Co. became a good opposite to J. P. Morgan and Co. in the investment field.

TWO DOMINATING COMBINATIONS IN
AMERICAN BUSINESS, 1904

Rockefeller interests. The Morgan firm had come up from an exchange and investment banking business, while the Rockefeller family was made up of John D. and William Rockefeller, and sons, and also business associates. It had arisen out of industrial capitalism—largely out of the oil industry. A second rivalry, also publicized by John Moody, was between the Morgan firm and Kuhn, Loeb and Company. The latter concern was a Jewish investment banking firm of rising prominence.

Every sizable city was by some supposed to have the two parties represented by banks, factories, or railroads. At times the two camps actually did battle for control of some individual concern, as in 1901 when Harriman, backed by Kuhn, Loeb and Company tried to get control of the Northern Pacific Railroad from Hill, backed by Morgan. It was this contest, with its repercussions from coast to coast, that aroused so much opposition to financial capitalism or Wall Street, as it was popularly called. So violent was the opposition to the growing control of the financial capitalists that a congressional investigation was made in 1912–13. The report of the Pujo Committee, appointed in 1912, is the most extensive treatise on financial capitalism in America. Of course, it is the usual one-sided partisan statement which no scholar would accept as it stands.

The investigation of financial capitalism in Washington 1912–13 was aimed at Wall Street domination or the power of the Money Trust. Journalists wrote passionately of the Money Trust and politicians rent the air in denouncing the power of the clique on Wall Street. A clever lawyer attained ephemeral fame by putting embarrassing questions to the financial leaders. A monster was created that it might be destroyed.

When Morgan was asked on the occasion of the investigation as to the source of his influence, he insisted that it was not wealth but confidence (in his ability and integrity). The nation sneered and the cynical raised their eyebrows. Of course, it was confidence and not wealth, for neither Morgan nor his partners had sufficient wealth to enable them to attain power. Their strength lay in the confidence that investors and financial institutions had in Morgan's ability and integrity. The rank and file of Americans, however, could not bring themselves to believe that a rich man could be honest and, much less, that his operations should redound to the advantage of the public. In the existing situation the public could have no understanding of, or sympathy with, an effort to put the nation's business on the sound basis of less specialization and less competition. Morgan and the other financial capitalists had come to understand the weakness of industrial capitalism through the issuing of securities and their sale at home and abroad. He and they had seen the whole business of investment bankers threatened by declining profits in the period 1866–97 and especially 1884–97, and by wholesale bankruptcies, notably 1890–97. To protect their clients it was necessary to do something.

Besides declining profits and bankruptcy there was irresponsible business administration. The executives of many corporations had become independent of the stockholders, except on the occasion of a crisis, and then it was too late for the stockholders to step in to save the situation. In New England, even before the Civil War, stock ownership had become so scattered and so much lodged in the dead hands of trustees, executors, guardians, and estate administrators that stockholders were in no position to check the administrators of a business. The government might do something but political theory was against action. Only the financial group could act and they did so through necessity. To be sure, they desired principally to save and develop their business of security underwriting and sale, but in doing this they were going to aid investors generally and indirectly the rest of the nation that could not thrive without a prosperous business. No such logic, however, could make headway among a people who chose their leaders from their own ranks.

Let us recount the benefits that ideally would come from financial capitalism. First, the owners of capital would get dividends or interest sufficient to justify the investments and loans they had made. Second, the financial capitalists would make more profits themselves by doing business for industries in which investors had confidence. Third, business would be less competitive, less specialized, and better provided with working capital through the sale of stock or bonds and therefore more independent of commercial banks which by their very nature had to call loans in a crisis. A wiser policy would come from the financial capitalists than purely local industrial capitalists (often apprentices in the trade, or technicians) were capable of. And in addition, business (and investors) were assured that, when necessary, the existing executives would be replaced by abler men, when and as often as it was necessary.

At this point we may give special attention to the various groups operating in close relation with investment bankers. In the inner circle there are the proprietors or chief owners of the financial institutions—Morgan, Schiff, Warburg, Baker, Storrow, and Windsor. A class of specialized partners, junior partners, is growing up. This is a most promising addition, if it does not come too late. Partners who specialize in the industries in which the firm is interested offer safe guidance in issuing securities and in reorganization. John M. Hancock, who calls himself "industrial banker," is an illustration of the type that is meant. Coming from the navy, he has been given new commands in manufacturing and merchandising firms. His work on behalf of the Jewel Tea Company and the Kroger Grocery and Baking Company should be remembered when the influence of investment bankers is being put in the balance.

There are the agents whom the financial firm employs, notably lawyers and accountants. One of the outstanding lawyers in the early days of financial capitalism in Wall Street was Francis Lynde Stetson (1846–1920). This able and unostentatious man of the law advised Morgan and others of the Morgan group on the legal aspects of organization and reorganization. His best efforts were used to keep out of the courts by conforming with the law. In the third circle there were business auxiliaries who gave advice to financial capitalists; for example, Ivy Lee gave advice to the Rockefeller group in public relations.

In the fourth circle were business administrators sponsored or chosen by financial administrators to do their work. With little appreciation of individual strength and diplomacy, these have sometimes been labeled "the henchmen of Wall Street." This class of business executives, occupying key places in the structure of financial capitalism, is extremely interesting. Its growth points to the possible development of a group of executives who would serve any master—financial capitalists, national capitalists, or perhaps even communistic capitalists. Sometimes the executives, summoned by financial capitalists, were drawn from the law, as for example Judge Gary and Myron C. Taylor of the United States Steel Corporation and Owen D. Young of the General Electric Company. Sometimes they have come from engineering as, for example, Gerard Swope and A. P. Sloan. Or they might be industrial apprentices as in the case of Ralph Budd, Eugene G. Grace, and F. E. Williamson. Once these executives have been chosen from the law, engineering, and so on, there is a question as to what policy they are to follow. Some investment bankers dictate that policy, while others, notably Morgan and Company, choose executives whose general policy is well known to them and who therefore can be left to operate with little or no actual control.

In the fifth circle there was a very important, though somewhat diverse, group of former industrial capitalists who bowed their heads for safety or who made friends and allies on Wall Street, State Street, or La Salle Street. Even George Westinghouse and James J. Hill were in danger of joining this class; some would say they did join it. When these one-time industrialists were able and adaptable, they became part and parcel of financial capitalism. When they proved incapable and noncoöperative, they were pushed out in favor of men who could better serve financial capitalism. In this case their places were taken by the fourth class of business administrators, that is, administrators of ability whose appointment was brought about by the financial capitalists and who looked to them for support.

With such a corps of officers and advisers, the general staff of investment bankers had great possibilities for success or failure. They used not cannon and airplanes but certain well-known devices, some held objectionable and others not. Merely sponsoring a firm is beyond criticism, but, when this extends to starving a rival until it fails, then the case is open to critical examination but possibly on inquiry not to objection. The system of interlocking directorates, the importance of which is probably somewhat exaggerated, whereby a banker or an ally would sit on as many as sixty or more directorates, helped check ruinous competition and helped support promising though languishing firms. The supreme weapon was the holding company—one corporation holding a majority or a sizable minority of stock in a subordinate company. This might be extended to several degrees. In this way an investment of a million dollars might in fact control an empire of a billion dollars, for example, of railroad property.

In order to further control without ownership, non-voting stock was devised, floated, and kept upon the market. In effect, this non-voting stock had been used by industrial capitalists, for instance, when they issued preferred stock without voting rights. But under the plan being considered the common stock would be divided into voting and non-voting shares. Both might be sold to the public, but the voting stock would not get far out of the hands of a few persons who could be depended upon to produce profits, that is, be efficient and honest. When the non-voting stock is used unfairly, it is objectionable. Of course, the buyer knows what he is paying money for. And, yet, it is near to a final judgment that ownership involves control, if the owner desires it. Governments do not always believe in this, for increasingly they are regulating control out of the hands of the owners, notably in the case of railroads and public utilities.

Before closing this section on financial capitalists, let me give one concrete example of how these capitalists work, so that the reader may observe the mode of operation and get something of the import of the system in a single case. Let us consider a New England medium-sized factory established in 1934. The stock was floated by a New York investment and brokerage house. The shares were sold in America, England, and South

Africa, in many instances to clients of the investment house. All the proceeds from the sale of the stock went into plant and working capital. The investment house was to receive, however, a percentage of profits, if and when earned, for a certain period, as promoter's profit. The executives of the manufacturing concern had planned the undertaking and had gone to the investment banker who in turn used his standing to float the concern.

All went along with fair promise and flags flying high till an accident, combined with a series of mismanagements in production, brought about a serious deterioration of product. This led to the loss of the market in a highly competitive industry, and this was followed by demoralization among the executives and depletion of working capital. Bankruptcy lay straight ahead.

The New York banker became alarmed. His own reputation was at stake and his chance for a promoter's profit was impaired. He gathered proxies and put them into the hands of one of his partners who was a director of the concern. With these proxies in hand, the director took virtual charge. He unseated the president and the production manager. He brought in an executive experienced in the industry as the new president. This executive was really a good public relations manager but proved to be a poor chief executive. He succeeded in producing a good product, but in attempting to win too wide a market he exhausted a large part of the supply of fresh working capital which the banker had provided through a small bond issue privately arranged. The banker followed the situation through weekly reports sent to him. One of his partners attended frequent directors' meetings. The new order, however, was proving to be little better than the old.

Again, an axe had to be wielded and drastic changes brought about. The new president was dropped and the former president—a marketing manager—was restored. Costs were reduced by this executive and the confidence of consumers was gradually regained. At last an even keel was attained.

Without the investment banker's aid, failure would have been complete. The commercial banks, which had been as much fooled by the substitute president as the investment banker, would loan no more capital; they could take no further risk of failure. After success was finally attained, suit was brought under the recent laws, that deprived the investment banker of his arrangements for a promoter's profit. The investment banker had earned fees for handling the stock, sought promoter's profit, got many headaches, but saved his reputation with his clients at home and abroad. Now that the sponsoring investment banker has been cut loose from the manufacturing concern, I fear for the future of the concern if ever it gets into production or other trouble again. As a creditor of this manufacturer, as a stockholder, as an executive, as an employee, as a wholesale or retail customer, or as a consumer of the product, I should feel a real loss when the government cut the bond that held the concern in the control of the investment banker.

3. FLOW OF CAPITAL

As water flows over the land, seeking the low places, so does capital flow into channels where it is profitable to go. One of these movements of capital is from one people to another. In early days this was from one people to another near at hand; nowadays, distance is not a limiting factor. The accompanying chart embodies a rough effort to depict some of the most significant channels along which capital has flown. Obviously, not all the lines have been drawn.

There are various ways in which capital flows. The very exchange of goods for goods embodies a flow of capital. We may regard the flow of raw materials, tools, machinery, and general equipment as most vital for the peoples concerned. Apply this to the accompanying chart. The sale of goods on credit involves a flow of wealth, including capital, as obviously does the loan of funds or the granting of general credits. The investment of funds in a country's economic activity illustrates a modern form of the flow of capital. The payment for services has been

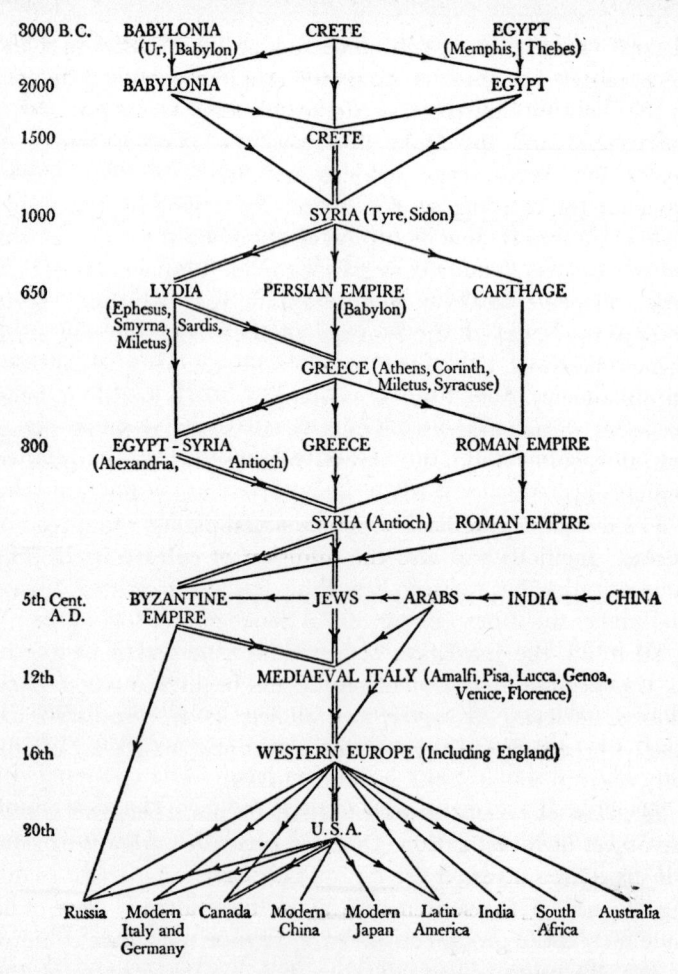

```
3000 B.C.   BABYLONIA          CRETE              EGYPT
            (Ur, Babylon)                         (Memphis, Thebes)

2000        BABYLONIA                             EGYPT

1500                           CRETE

1000                    SYRIA (Tyre, Sidon)

 650        LYDIA          PERSIAN EMPIRE         CARTHAGE
            (Ephesus,        (Babylon)
            Smyrna, Sardis,
            Miletus)
                        GREECE (Athens, Corinth,
                                Miletus, Syracuse)

 300        EGYPT - SYRIA      GREECE             ROMAN EMPIRE
            (Alexandria,  Antioch)

                        SYRIA (Antioch)   ROMAN EMPIRE

5th Cent.   BYZANTINE ——— JEWS —— ARABS —— INDIA —— CHINA
  A.D.      EMPIRE

12th                MEDIAEVAL ITALY (Amalfi, Pisa, Lucca, Genoa,
                                     Venice, Florence)

16th                WESTERN EUROPE (Including England)

20th                        U.S.A.

      Russia  Modern   Canada  Modern  Modern  Latin   India  South    Australia
              Italy and        China   Japan   America        Africa
              Germany
```

Under the "diffusion of business and capital" is included the migration of business methods, cultural institutions supporting business, goods used in production, and often business men themselves. Double lines indicate more important influences.

DIFFUSION OF BUSINESS AND CAPITAL

of great importance. For instance, during the Middle Ages and since, money has gone to Rome for religious services rendered by the Catholic Church. The hire of soldiers, for example, from Switzerland and the Duke of Hesse, was another source of capital flow in the early modern and in the modern period. Payment for carrying service, especially freight by water, has involved a steady flow of capital that has meant much to the Dutch, English, and Norwegian peoples. Plunder in war or piracy in peace has been more dramatic than weighty, except perhaps in the case of the Spanish colonies. With the migration of men, however, has gone a considerable quantity of capital—untold amounts from Europe to America. Much wealth, too, has been sent abroad in the form of gold, silver, and precious stones for safekeeping amid the threats of war and the inroads of depression.

The flow of capital has commonly accompanied the spread of business methods and also the diffusion of culture itself. The same ship that has carried these three has also freighted disease that makes the other gifts seem less beneficial on the whole.

All in all, the Jews have been the most persistent people in the transfer and migration of capital and business methods. The process, however, has never been allowed to be cumulative for long. The beneficiaries of Jewish contributions have periodically risen to rob and kill the benefactors.

The flow of capital to America has been studied and is still the object of investigation. Under mercantile capitalism, London capitalists invested the capital necessary for the first planting of some of the settlements, as we have already seen. The same mercantile group continued to finance American colonies by the extension of considerable credits. One reason for the American Revolution was to get rid of debts which Americans owed to this class in England. After the Revolution, the old type of credit was continued and a new one begun by merchant bankers, such as the Barings, who made loans and bought securities in America. American brokers and investment bankers, such as George Peabody, Junius Spencer Morgan, and

J. P. Morgan, Sr., developed the business of selling American securities abroad, especially in London. The movement continued unbroken till 1914, when there set in a general movement of capital in the other direction. Americans not only bought foreign securities but they made loans (especially 1923–29) and established branch factories, assembly plants, and warehouses abroad. It has been hard for America to enter the stage of adolescence in exporting capital, but maturity will eventuate.

The flow of capital that is perhaps most significant for our purpose is not international but inter-institutional. We have noted how capital has flowed from the owner direct to the user and then, centuries later, indirectly through a money middleman. When this indirect flow—the indirect putting-out system—changed from a policy of passive relations to active control, then financial capitalism was born.

The active rôle played by the financial capitalist is to be likened to that of the heart supplying the various parts of the body economic with the life blood of capital. The financial capitalist has been eager to help society but only through the avenue of profits—the profit system. When in his opinion a business situation has become inimical to profit-making, he has become hostile and shut off the supply of capital. Mind you the capital that he has shut off has not been his and the entrepreneur or concern that has wanted to use it has not been his. Here is a difficult position in which he has found himself. He—the financial capitalist—has had to make the decision, for otherwise just the ones concerned in a smaller and even more narrowly selfish way would make it. Such decisions might be wise or unwise; no matter which way the decisions of the financial capitalist should go, they might injure individuals, even though society as a whole might be benefited by the decision.

The position of the financial capitalist in the general money market has been vital. In this market there are four principal competing groups—(1) private business (such as railroads, manufacturers, mining operators, etc.), (2) farmers (singly or in coöperation), (3) speculators (in stocks, bonds, and commodities), and (4) the various governments at home and abroad. We have observed so far that the financial capitalists came to dominate the private business situation through various devices, including control of the flow of capital. Perhaps not a few of us would say, well, for better or for worse, financial capitalism in private business is about the best available system known to us. But how about petty capitalists, industrial capitalists, and (New Deal) national capitalists? Would the financial capitalists be acceptable to these groups? This question raises only a subjective issue which can be passed by.

During the 1920's the financial capitalists were responsible for the pouring of colossal amounts of capital into the speculative market. That is, if a speculator had, say, $250 in cash, he could easily buy $1,000 worth of securities or commodities by borrowing $750 through brokers. So much capital went in this direction that over-speculation occurred. The downward secular trend, begun in 1920 in the country, was precipitated on its course in the town in 1929 and a prolonged period of depression was ushered in. By federal statute, control over the amount of borrowing for speculative purposes is now vested in the Federal Reserve Board; that is, the Board fixes the amount of margin that the broker may allow in accordance with the Board's own notion of what the general situation requires.

Financial capitalists have been accused of ignoring the interests of farmers. Although this is not true if we take into account the fact that they help create a good market for farm products by keeping home trade and industry in good condition, still it is true in so far as they do not directly attempt to meet the needs of farmers. The establishment of the Federal Reserve Board in 1914 was partly designed to give to farmers reserve banks that would somewhat consider their interests. In 1916 the Federal Farm Loan System was created to help the farmers get long-time loans at rates little higher than business men paid. In 1923 the Federal Intermediate Credit System was set up to help provide the farmer with working capital. Thus, we have a rival political system for extending credit to the farming group, which industrial capitalists had neglected.

The government in years past has been glad enough to go to Wall Street for help in need and always must work in harmony with it, if it is to succeed. But, beginning with the extension of credit to farmers, there is growing up a national capitalistic system that is already spreading to public utilities and threatens to include railroads, insurance, banking, and some key industries. We shall come to this in the next chapter.

Just now we may consider where the capital comes from that flows through the hands of the financial capitalists. In order to save space we may list some of the chief categories of capital-owners. No effort has been made to avoid overlapping.

Owners of Capital
Which Flows Through the Hands of Financial Capitalists

1. Financial capitalists themselves.
2. Retired industrial capitalists who sell their business and reinvest.
3. Heirs who hold to preferred stocks, bonds, and selected common stocks.
4. Widely scattered holders of war bonds, 1917 and following.
5. Many who have mortgaged farms and homes for speculation.
6. Those who have drawn their savings from banks and insurance companies to speculate.
7. A large group of business executives who invest or speculate in securities, including the stock of their own companies. This latter practice has recently been made more difficult by federal law.
8. Middle-sized people who invest or speculate with current earnings, including politicians, lawyers, doctors, dentists, racketeers, and retailers.
9. Wage-earners who have money in the savings banks and leave it there, except in 1928–29 when they took it out to lose on the stock market.

10. Farmers who used their war profits of 1917–20 to buy oil stocks and real estate bonds, mostly worthless.
11. Charitable institutions with large endowments, such as colleges, hospitals, libraries, museums, homes for the young and the aged, and Churches.

The mechanism now in existence that is designed to facilitate investment and speculation in the United States is elaborate and widespread. Metropolitan and other brokers have offices in numerous towns, in which high-speed tickers give continuous information about the price of commodities, stocks, and bonds and also news affecting the market. Advisory services send out their daily or semi-weekly statements about the time to buy and sell. Financial journals seem to prosper in selling information and advice. The daily newspaper contains its financial pages or at least columns. The radio shouts out facts about the condition of the market so that even housewives hear about changes in prices and opportunities for investment and speculation.

The number of investors of capital in the United States has sometimes been put at nearly twenty million. Even if that number is twice too large, we still have a numerous class of persons who are playing with a weapon which they do not know how to use. All the greater is the responsibility on the shoulders of the financial capitalists—and the politicians who undertake to establish a national capitalistic system.

The question of responsibility in the flow of capital from owner to money middleman to user is one that has never been exactly settled. We might expect that the very rise of a class of money middlemen would signify service accompanied by some measure of consideration for both original lender and ultimate borrower. However that may be, at least when these money middlemen become financial capitalists on the assumption of an active rôle in the putting-out of capital, a high degree of responsibility is to be assumed. That is the point of the whole system. Indeed, financial capitalism rises and falls on a combination of efficiency and responsibility in the borrowing and lending of money. Doubtless the feeling of responsibility is one that comes partly through outside suggestion, and doubtless it registers in different financial capitalists in varying degrees.

One interesting example of the flow of capital occurred in the period from 1923 to 1929. Americans in all sections of the land were eager to buy foreign bonds, especially those bearing high rates of interest. Germans, Chileans, and others wanted the money, and American investors were willing to sell their own government's bonds bearing low rates in order to purchase foreign bonds bearing high rates. Should the investment bankers have floated such foreign bonds in New York, which, it was well known in many cases, did not provide funds for productive enterprises? At least it is clear to me that these bankers should have (a) warned the investing public and (b) curbed the amounts of the loans. But the fact is that many of these bankers did neither and indeed were themselves caught in the subsequent crisis holding some of the most worthless of securities. This indicates that it was their judgment rather than their lack of a feeling of responsibility that was at fault in the mad period engendered by the World War.

4. INDUSTRIAL INTEGRATION AND DIVERSIFICATION UNDER FINANCIAL CAPITALISM

When highly specialized industrial capitalists were threatened with ruin in a régime of severe competition, they turned to multiple functions carefully integrated and to a diversification of production and investment. This is precisely what the bankers advised, and, when they came into control, they commonly insisted that the firms still remaining on a specialized basis should abandon specialization. In other words, whether a firm survived in industrial capitalism or entered the system of financial capitalism, it tended to integrate or diversify or both. Those concerns that did not, such as in the tobacco, gum, and beer industries, held aloof for the reason that they still had an expanding market or could not readily take on additional functions.

Of course, there are many firms that have not gone over to, or come under, the system of financial capitalism. The Ford Motor Company, Swift and Company, the General Mills Corporation, and the Dennison Manufacturing Company are examples of firms that have held out or almost held out. Perhaps we should say at this point "Just wait and see what happens." Some of the smaller or medium-sized firms, however, seem to be finding an ally in the national government and may skip or miss financial capitalism.

The fact that firms under both industrial and financial capitalism tend to integrate and diversify seems to indicate that this course is an improvement over specialization, or, as I think, it is nearer to the normal growth of big business. Doing this is redressing the unbalance created by the Industrial Revolution.

The illustrations of the multiplication of functions and their integration into a well-rounded business as planned by financial capitalists are numerous and important. Let each of us make his own list and select his own examples. It would be helpful in doing this to go to the Pujo Committee Inquiry and Report, though of course the period covered is about a generation back. Let us take here just one group of firms, those identified with the House of Morgan. The United States Steel Corporation (or its component parts) was built up around the process of smelting iron ore and manufacturing a few standard products such as steel rails. Following the lead of certain industrial capitalists there were added to these coal-mining, iron-mining, transportation by rail and steamship, and so on. Most of these antedate 1901 and were merely carried to greater height after that year. Added to these have been more manufacture of finished parts and the making of cement. From the coal, iron, and limestone in the earth to finished rails, girders, pipe, wire, and plates is all a continuous process within the one firm.

The International Harvester Company, formed in 1902, illustrates the development of integration and the appearance of financial capitalism in the agricultural machinery business. In this industry there had arisen a fierce competitive situation. Hundreds of small firms had come into existence after the Civil War to promote some patented article. Failures were numerous, notably in the period 1884-1901. An effort was made by an industrial capitalist in 1890 to form a combine of about twenty companies, to be called the American Harvester Company. Because of public opposition and inside dissension, the effort failed. The largest company in the field was the McCormick Harvesting Machine Company, which was apparently strong in marketing organization. The second was the Deering Harvester Company, which had integrated production by adding to its agricultural machinery plant iron mines, a coal mine, and a smelting plant. The McCormicks considered the cost of doing likewise in the period 1897-1901, perhaps with the aid of Rockefeller money. In 1902, however, Cyrus H. McCormick and George W. Perkins, a partner in Morgan and Company, came together to provide for the merger of five large companies. The ostensible purpose was to check price-cutting, reduce the cost of distribution at home, and provide capital for the development of production and distribution abroad. Possibly the immediate drive, however, was to aid the ambitious and able McCormicks to get the integrated set-up which the Deerings, who were personally less promising as leaders for the future, had been able to devise. In other words, Morgan and Company helped the McCormicks rectify their great mistake—their failure to integrate.

The International was from the first strong in capital resource, wise in policy, and able in management. It bought up many large manufacturers, thereby rounding out its line of machines and tools so as to reduce cost of distribution. In recent years its sales of motor trucks and also of tractors have exceeded those of agricultural machinery. While at first the

Morgan influence was strong, it has in more recent years apparently become more or less nominal, but still the connection has remained. We might conclude that financial capitalists, so far, have put the agricultural machinery business on a sound footing and then withdrawn. Perhaps, some would say that they simply helped the McCormicks attain the financial phase of industrial capitalism. Since nothing is fixed, we may watch the situation change in the future, near or far.

We find in the manufacture of branded food products a good example of investment banker influence. On the one hand, there is General Foods sponsored by Goldman Sachs and Company and Lehman Brothers; and on the other hand, there is Standard Brands sponsored by J. P. Morgan and Company. Both of these firms are mergers of concerns which manufacture or prepare foods. And each of them grew up around one manufacturer who had developed a business in branded foods. The nucleus of General Foods was the Postum Company; the nucleus of Standard Brands was the Fleischmann Yeast Company.

In the confident period of the 1920's business men saw infinite possibilities in the future of their country. They got their cue from the rank and file and passed on their enthusiasm to the bankers. After the post-War depression of 1920–21–23 investment bankers were coming to look with increasing favor upon the merchandising (wholesale and retail) business and its securities. Merger was in the air as in the early years of the century. Great economies and stability were to be derived from consolidation of medium-sized units. The larger firms were to be able to secure unlimited funds from investors because of the supposed security that they offered in times of depression and the high earnings in times of prosperity.

The Postum Company became General Foods in 1929 and started out with high promise. Its specialties included cereals and drinks—Postum, coffee, Sanka coffee, and tea. Many other commodities were included or were to be added such as Jello, sea foods, and frozen foods. These goods were to be sold through the ordinary channels of trade to small unit stores, chain stores, and department stores. They were kept before the public by extensive advertising.

On the other hand, Standard Brands, also formed in 1929, was built up around yeast, baking powder, and coffee (later dated). (The General Foods coffee was not dated but was sold in sealed packages.) To these commodities were added other branded food products to make out a full line for bakers' use. But Standard Brands had one distinctive feature: it was based on the bi-weekly delivery system that the Fleischmann Company had worked out for its yeast. The light trucks that delivered the fresh yeast (and the dated coffee) to the retailers were at first designed to carry a wide range of products (perishable or semi-perishable) which the retailer needed and would like to have fresh or frequently delivered. Unused perishable goods could be taken back. The idea was a good one—freshness has a strong appeal to Americans, but the build-up of general grocery products around the fresh foods has been difficult.

General Foods and Standard Brands are both horizontal combinations of like concerns, the business of which could be integrated to reduce costs of distribution and to gain a competitive advantage. The two firms could induce the retailer to buy broadly from them and not just take one product—cereals, gelatin powder, baking powder, spices, tea, coffee, vinegar, etc. In the case of General Foods are found outstanding advantages in research, sales promotion, and finance (to say nothing of frozen foods), which the component parts of medium-sized concerns never enjoyed. In the case of Standard Brands consumers get fresher products and retailers get unprecedented service.

Investors received an opportunity of buying the securities of these two stabilized concerns operating in a stable industry. When Standard Brands was formed, there was drawn up a preferred list of persons, Republicans and Democrats, Catholics and Protestants, Jews and Gentiles, who were to buy the stock at thirty-two dollars a share, while the stock soon came to sell at forty-four dollars. In the investigation of 1933 this list came

INDUSTRIAL INTEGRATION AND DIVERSIFICATION

to be used by newspapers as an example of a heinous practice of building up a following in financial capitalism that would be inimicable to the public welfare. Disclosure of the identity of the favored individuals, however, disproved the fears. Although the individuals who had quickly sold their shares gained, the others who held suffered considerable loss (real or paper). The favored group was like that invited by political administrators to advisory gatherings, by the navy to the christening of a ship, or by politicians to a select banquet of those to feast here and hereafter.

Many large firms under the régime of financial capitalism have stressed diversification rather than integration. The Westinghouse Electric and Manufacturing Company manufactures many products for home and foreign consumption, including electric generators and motors, electric lamps, electric refrigerators, and steam and gas engines. The General Electric, an even larger concern, has a similar line of products. The number of parts which it has to keep in store for separate sale to customers is over one million. A firm like the Gillette Safety Razor Company (dating from 1901) was formed to make razors and blades. This business was dangerously threatened by rivals, especially when the patents lapsed. To meet the situation the manufacture of additional products was undertaken, such as knives, scissors, wire, and shaving cream.

Practically all large concerns keep part of their working capital in the form of cash and part in the form of securities. These securities may be government bonds or notes or the stock of other companies. Railroads have the practice of investing in the stock of other roads. The Great Northern and the Northern Pacific own all of the stock of the Burlington. The Delaware and Hudson Railroad Company has had large holdings of the New York Central; the Pennsylvania of the New Haven; and so on. Often these investments have had an ulterior purpose of control or influence in anticipation of some future realignment of railroad companies. Manufacturing companies have invested surplus funds in concerns which they would like to influence and from which they expect profits in the form of dividends. The Du Pont Company has formed a subsidiary, which it almost owns outright, to hold stock in the General Motors Corporation. The subsidiary owns nearly twelve million shares of the common stock of General Motors, which is over one quarter of the total. Primarily, this investment is by way of diversification of capital outlay—an important matter for a firm which, at least formerly, derived much of its income from war products. Another ulterior purpose may be to sell their products to General Motors. Provided no unfair advantage is taken of this situation, there can be no objection to it. Indeed, it is part and parcel of the general policy of financial capitalism to make such alliances as will enable the individual firms to prosper in normal times and survive in depressions.

It is a nice exercise to consider the comparative merits of integration and diversification. Which industries should adopt which device? Does integration provide a special advantage in a secular uptrend of business and diversification in a secular downtrend?

5. TRANSPORTATION AND COMMUNICATION UNDER FINANCIAL CAPITALISM

It was in railroad transportation that financial capitalism was born in America. It was born in the need which railroads and the holders of railroad securities felt for control in the interest of transportation and transportation profits. The need for outside control existed in the 1860's when Drew, Fisk, and Gould mishandled railroads, particularly the Erie Railroad. All of these men were industrial capitalists who, without being primarily interested in the operation of railroads, came to manipulate the finance of railroads. Associated with them in the popular mind was Cornelius Vanderbilt I, who nevertheless showed himself a great operator as well as financier of railroads. We shall not stop to consider how far Vanderbilt was also a manipulator of railroad securities. At any rate, Vanderbilt's son asked J. P. Morgan and Company in 1879 to sell a block of his holdings in the New York Central Railroad so as to remove part of the criticism of Vanderbilt's domination of the New York Central Railroad. The sale was actually made in England and Morgan became a director of the Railroad.

Morgan's second introduction to railroad financing came in 1886 when he reorganized the Philadelphia and Reading Railroad. He made the mistake of turning over control to the stockholders before they were ready to do an efficient job of management. The result was a second bankruptcy, this time in 1893.

Morgan's first *big* job in railroad affairs came in 1893 when he rescued railroads in the South and created the Southern Railroad system. By 1893 about one-third of the railroad mileage of the country was in financial difficulty owing to the general depression in business and to mismanagement. This was a great opportunity for investment bankers. During the period 1893–1901 the chief consolidations and reorganizations at the hands of financial capitalists occurred. Publicists came to talk about the great systems in accordance with financial participation and control. Sometimes the term "railroad empires" was used.

There came to be two of these railroad empires of great significance to us at this point because they illustrate the growth of financial capitalism. One of these was the Morgan empire ultimately made up largely of the following railroads:

Southern Railroad   Central New Jersey
Northern Pacific   Atchison
Great Northern   Erie
Burlington   Pere Marquette

A second and rival railroad empire and one that was never completed was the Harriman System, made up as follows:

Illinois Central
Union Pacific
Southern Pacific

Supporting Harriman, who had been and remained a broker, was the investment banking firm of Kuhn, Loeb and Company. Since these two banking houses were rivals in their railroad ambitions, it became customary to speak of them as rivals in all investment affairs, and of their rivalry as dividing the whole of the country into two great financial groups. Although there was a measure of truth in this, the cleavage lay chiefly in railroad affairs, and even there was not complete.

Out of the operations of Morgan and Company, Kuhn, Loeb and Company, and other such firms came larger railroad units, better equipment, more efficient operation, and more intelligent financing than ever before. While the *general* result of the operations of industrial capitalists such as Vanderbilt and Gould was to inflate the capital structure, the *general* result of the work of financial capitalists such as Morgan and Company was to deflate the capital set-up. Investment bankers were always conscious of the need to reduce capital to the point where dividends could be paid so as to enable the railroad to secure fresh funds at reasonable rates. To be sure, they have not always succeeded in accomplishing this result. Indeed, they have sometimes inflated capital with the hope and expectation that impending prosperity would bring high earnings and justify the excess capital.

The contributions of financial capitalists to the field of railroad transportation are worthy of extensive treatment. Lack of space permits nothing more than listing, as follows:

1. Financial capitalists have reorganized railroads in such a way as to reëstablish the credit of the lines, though they have not always been able to undo the inflationary work of preceding industrial capitalists.

2. They have cut down bonded indebtedness in many cases, but not enough to stand the strain of competition with automobiles and airplanes, the former heavily subsidized by the provision of excellent free roads.

3. They have generally appointed capable and honest executives.

TRANSPORTATION AND COMMUNICATION 275

4. They have rounded out companies by horizontal combination.

5. They have cut off unprofitable parts unless prevented by the government.

6. They have checked financial and operating abuses begun by former industrial capitalists.

7. They have enabled one company to aid another both in business and in finance.

8. They have sought to keep down costs so as to earn a profit, secure more capital, and improve the system.

9. They have tried to keep rates at the points where they would yield a maximum return.

Charges against financial capitalists in the field of transportation, especially railroad, may be summarized in part, as follows:

1. Reorganizations often not sufficiently drastic.

2. Too high fees for financier's services. We have no evidence concerning this that has any technical value.

3. Too high prices paid for units—in the light of subsequent hard times and technical changes.

4. Salaries of executives too high.

5. Wage rates too low—not a serious charge since 1917 so far as the brotherhoods are concerned.

6. Rates on railroad securities floated by bankers too high at times. The answer is that market rates prevailed.

7. Waste in receiverships.

8. Failure to respect public feeling, especially fear of monopoly.

To the railroad situation there is a parallel in steamship operation and ownership which, however, is less extensive than in the case of railroads. One of the chief examples is the formation of the International Mercantile Marine Company in 1902. At a time of superactivity in mergers, Morgan bought a number of lines—English and American—and consolidated them into a great concern which he thought would earn a profit. He failed to secure the Cunard Line, without which he could not possess the dominance necessary to control. French and, particularly, German lines offered further competition. He paid too much for his lines. He had not observed that steamship operation was a rare art and one that had few devotees in America. Hardly any amount of ownership would give him safe control in an international situation in which the national pride and prestige of foreign peoples would enter to frustrate his plans. And so this effort became one of Morgan's great failures. Also, but on a minor scale, came the buying up of coastal lines and their merger with the New Haven Railroad. Too much was paid for the lines and popular opposition forced the dissolution of the combine in transportation.

A presentation of the situation in communication would include the telegraph, telephone, radio, and television industries and companies. The reader might make an examination of these for himself. He would find himself studying the Western Union (1851, 1856), the American Telephone and Telegraph Company (1885), the Radio Corporation of America (1919), the International Telephone and Telegraph Corporation (1920), and so on. Let us here concentrate on the American Telephone and Telegraph Company.

At the head of the list of greatest American business corporations are the Metropolitan Life Insurance Company, the Chase National Bank, the United States Steel Corporation, and the American Telephone and Telegraph Company. It is the last-named that we are specially concerned with here. This Company has probably the largest number of stockholders in the country, most of them women, and no one stockholder owns (in 1937) as much as one per cent of the stock of the Company. Its chief business is to provide a long-distance telephone service, to hold together a number of regional telephone companies, and through a subsidiary company—the Western Electric—to manufacture almost all its special equipment. With over twenty million telephones in its system, now connected with all parts of the world, it obviously is a tremendously important link not only in the world's business but in the world's culture.

The history of the American Telephone and Telegraph Company illustrates how capitalists came in to make practical the telephone invented by Bell in 1876 and how the system resulting from their efforts has experienced changes in management and control. A recent government investigator has worked out five periods of control as follows:

1. Stockholder control, 1876–81.
2. Director control, 1881–1906.
    Stock was being more and more widely held and accordingly stockholders were not so effective in controlling the business.
3. Banker control, 1907–18.
    Ownership of stock passed from Boston to New York and large blocks came into the hands of a few bankers who obtained representation on the board of directors.
4. Federal government control, 1918–19.
    The World War brought this about.
5. Management control, 1919–present.
    The chief officials, who are not great holders of stock, have the confidence of the scattered stockholders who appreciate efficiency and dividends.

Let us note particularly the situation under banker control, 1907–18. During the years 1905–07 the American Telephone and Telegraph Company was turning from Boston to New York, looking for new money, and securing new banking support. Which group came out to meet the other is not very important in the face of the obvious welcome that each gave to the other. George F. Baker, Sr. (and associates), bought 50,000 shares of the Company's stock and became a director, as did his son after him. This stock ownership brought the Company into close relations with the First National Bank of New York to the benefit of both institutions. The purchase of stock by Waterbury, president of the Manhattan Trust Company, gave the Company another strong institutional root in the money market of America. When the Company sold a large bond issue to Morgan and Company in 1909, H. P. Davison of Morgan and Company became a director of the American Telephone.

To me it seems that the American Telephone and Telegraph Company is one of the best managed firms in the United States and that the choice of financial allies is one of the bits of evidence of efficiency and wisdom. Many of the charges of the government against the Company in 1937 were really evidence of efficiency and public service, objected to only by those outside the business field and by those radically opposed to private ownership whether successful and beneficial or not. Of all the charges against the Company, mostly captious and specious, there are only two to which I give a second thought. One is that the Company should not have continued to charge the old-time rates to customers and to pay the old high dividends to stockholders during the depression that began in 1929. The other is that the Company should *admit* banker influence (not control) and glory in its existence as an aid to the Company and a guarantee of advice which any management needs when its stockholders are scattered and mostly women. To me this banker situation is one that should give the stockholders confidence, as it should be a guarantee to the Company that its financial needs will be taken care of so as to provide for indefinite expansion of telephone service. The alternative to the influence of financial capitalists in this case is government control. The English experience with telephones is not reassuring on this score.

A full examination of financial capitalism in the fields of transportation and communication would point out the varying degrees of banker influence or control. Some American railroads have come under *control* of bankers, while in the field of communication some companies, like the American Telephone, have just entered the banking sphere of *influence*. Because of the public nature of the service that transportation and communication firms perform, many persons hold to the view that the national government should nationalize or socialize them. This is a subject that belongs to the next chapter and is inherently difficult to consider effectively. At this point, we might urge the thought that nationalization would mean more benefits for the workers and fewer for the users. The stockholders of bankrupt railroads would probably gain, while those of the American Telephone would probably lose. All in all, the flow of capital into the telephone business could not be more smooth, ample, or effective than at present. Whether the provision of capital could be made at a lower *total* cost is open to debate.

6. PUBLIC UTILITIES UNDER FINANCIAL CAPITALISM

By "public" utilities are meant chiefly water, gas, and electric services. While in Europe public utilities have been largely publicly owned, in America they have been almost wholly privately owned as well as operated. In a sense, they are no more public than railroads, telephones, telegraphs, and radio, or even theaters and department stores. Their operation, however, is continuously vital to the public, and they can function best by monopolistic arrangements. Accordingly, they come in for a heavy dose of public regulation, in America by means of State commissions.

A private company was planned to supply Boston with water in 1652. In Baltimore a company was formed in 1816 to make and distribute coal gas for street and house lighting. About 1880 electricity was generated for local lighting purposes. First of all, came the ways of creating the service and then the arrangements for providing it. If you will, first the inventor, then the business man. And so, this alternation has gone on from earliest times. New devices for making, transmitting, and using the services were taken up by the companies and made practical and useful.

The early companies were not ordinarily given the exclusive right to provide a service. Competitors arose, and rate-cutting resulted in hard feeling. Then, two or more companies were put together and called, say, the Union or the Consolidated Company. In New York City six gas companies were united in 1884 to form the Consolidated Gas Company. In Philadelphia the first holding company—the United Gas Improvement Company—was established in 1882. It was to develop various functions such as operating, engineering, and holding securities.

When the new source of light and power—electricity—came into commercial use after 1879, the gas companies were alarmed. These companies had tended to regard their position as secure and looked forward to the quiet enjoyment of income rather than to competition. Gradually, the policy was adopted of buying up the new electric companies and operating the two services side by side. This arose largely through holding-company activity beginning chiefly about 1890.

The period of the early growth of larger public utility firms or groups of firms covers the years 1882–90–1923. It includes the formation of the United Gas Improvement Company in 1882 and the North American Company in 1890. The latter holding company expanded greatly, till it had systems in and around Milwaukee, St. Louis, Cleveland, and Washington, D. C., with large security holdings in various companies even on the Pacific Coast. Certain hard facts were coming to be perceived. The alternating current, developed by the Westinghouse Company, pointed the way to larger central generating plants. Electricity could be carried long distances without heavy loss of power when the alternating current was used. It was obvious that there were great advantages in having fewer plants and more efficient central equipment. Moreover, it was expensive to operate many local plants in certain locations in large cities where rents were high and transportation congested. In addition, there was the fact that water power which was available only in a few places could be carried long distances to supply many communities in the form of alternating electric current. Well, here was a duty and an opportunity.

There was no great public interest in investing in public utilities till about 1923. Investors and speculators had focused attention on industrials, railroads, governments, and municipals. Investment bankers paid little attention to public utilities because the public had little interest in them. It was to meet this lack of public investment interest that the General

Electric Company, which wanted to sell equipment for the new central plants, established in 1904 a subordinate financing company called the Electrical Securities Corporation. This concern was interested primarily in giving financial and engineering service to public utilities. It has now grown into the gigantic Electric Bond and Share Company, the model of a maze of holding companies, which, however, in this case operates no public utility in America.

During the World War, one of the great problems was to get coal. Only essential industries could obtain a supply. This meant that many industrial establishments had difficulty in keeping their own electrical generating equipment in operation. Accordingly, many turned to the public utility companies for part or all of their power. These public electric companies had, of course, to be supplied with coal in order to provide public necessities. Naturally, the public utilities liked the idea of signing up new customers, especially large factories, which would be heavy and responsible users. This addition of industrial to domestic customers created many problems. It pointed to the need of more central plants, more powerful generators, and the linking up of contiguous systems to provide continuity in case of local breakdown and to spread the load which then tended to fluctuate beyond any past experience.

The World War and subsequent industrial prosperity made domestic service expensive and consequently many families had to do without maids. (A similar situation prevailed during the depression that began in 1929 but for another reason—the lack of an income to employ maids.) This meant unprecedented demands for labor-saving appliances in the homes. Americans love gadgets; the weakness was met by the manufacturers of electrical devices. Of course, these appliances used increasing amounts of current.

The period 1882–1923 saw the technical foundations of a vigorous public utility development laid deep in the American soil. It also saw industrial capitalists come to the front to promote the growth. Sometimes these industrial capitalists operated unitary companies and sometimes holding companies. Without being dominated by bankers, they were aided by financial houses. We think of the Duke concern in the South, the Foshay array in the West, and the Insull group in and around Chicago.

Foshay operated in and out from Minneapolis where he crowned his achievement by a commanding tower in the business district. He bought up public utilities in the Northwest and in scattered areas from Alaska to Central America. He had plans for the development of a light and power system in northern Vermont when his firm went into bankruptcy and he to prison. He had scorned the banks and bankers. His great achievement was to have built up a corps of security salesmen who avoided brokers and stock exchanges. Security offices were maintained in over a score of cities in the United States. Foshay salesmen cut out the middleman and middleman profits by selling stocks directly to their clients. Unfortunately, the bait held out—the high dividends that were being paid continuously —proved to be just gilded pills. Dividends had been paid out of capital. The bankruptcy of Foshay somewhat helped to undermine confidence and precipitate panicky conditions in 1929.

The period 1923–29 was the high plateau of public utility promotion. Although the world, unnoticed, was slipping into a downward trend, the light of business endeavor was experiencing its brightest flicker. Foreign trade, domestic manufacture, transportation, the development of airplanes (symbols of high and irresponsible progress) were all flowering at once. This was at the very time that a popular political administrator declared that we should have no more depressions because we had investment trusts and the Federal Reserve System to level off and control excesses of investment. This New Era displayed many signs of insanity.

During the period 1923–29 there were built up a number of public utility groups, more and more centering in electricity, which suggested to many observers the growth of business principalities in the national state. The five of these groups near the top were roughly as follows:

1. Morgan-Drexel-Bonbright-National City group:
    (a) American Superpower Corporation, 1923
        Holding company with no bonds
    (b) United Corporation, 1929
        Holding company, investigated in Washington 1933
        No bonded debt
2. Insull group:
    Insull Utility Investments, Inc., 1928
    Investment trust, bankrupt 1932
3. Electric Bond and Share Company, 1929:
    Holding company; grew out of General Electric subsidiary
    More concerned with giving financial and engineering service. Controls operations only abroad
4. Chase-Harris-Forbes group:
    (a) Associated Gas and Electric Company
        Holding company—insolvent in 1932
    (b) Public Utility Investing Corporation, 1917
        Investment trust
    (c) United Founders Corporation, 1929
        Controls other investment trusts, not confined to utilities
5. Goldman Sachs group:
    (a) Central States Electric Corporation, 1912
        Investment trust, acquired by bankers
        Holding stock in North American Company and in investment trusts holding public utility securities
    (b) Atlas Corporation, 1929
        Investment trust holding many other trusts and a wide range of securities

Only a small part of the total story is told by this list. The first and third groups seem to be pretty well entrenched. The second went out of existence and with it the fortunes of many persons and families. The other two have already experienced difficulties and changes.

Samuel Insull, who was the organizing genius of the Insull group, had come up the utility ladder. Without being an engineer, he knew the technical needs of the industry, particularly for better equipment and consolidation into bigger units. He consolidated one company with another, using holding companies for his purpose. In order to accomplish his ends, he brought the investing banking firm of Halsey, Stuart and Company into his plans and made a member of this Company a director in the central or top holding company. When at the pinnacle of his career, with companies having assets of four billion dollars, 600,000 investors, and 72,000 employees, he feared the activities, as it is said, of Cyrus S. Eaton, of Cleveland. This man, long interested in public utility operation and an investment banker himself, was dominant in the investment trust called Continental Shares, formed in 1926. This concern invested heavily in Insull companies and caused Insull to fear for his own position. Accordingly, Insull bid in as much of his own stock as he could and thereby ran the stocks up to a price all out of line with the earning powers of the companies. Then, Eaton sold out to Insull in 1930 at the high price. Insull was victor, but he owed the commercial banks for the money he had borrowed in order to buy the stocks. Business conditions were going downward fast late in 1931. All values were sinking. The banks demanded repayment of the loans. Insull held utility stock but it was sliding fast on the market. Bankruptcy (1932), flight, trial (1934), and lonely death abroad (1938) closed this story. The contest had been between the Londoner (Insull) and the Nova Scotian (Eaton) on American soil. Eaton survived (or almost did so), just as the house of the Paris Brothers survived the John Law promotions in 1720. Like Law, Insull had been guilty only of the great crime of mismanagement.

People talked of the Power Trust as they had of the Money Trust in 1912. It was a silly phrase but it expressed journalistic efforts. There were large groups of utility companies—twenty have been listed—but they hardly held together as a Power Trust.

The modes of controlling the groups were various. They need but to be listed: non-voting stock, trust voting agreements, interlocking directorates, holding companies, and investment trusts. Some of these were, of course, mixed up with the others. But it was clear enough that a strange bewilderment of holding companies and investment trusts had been created partly by industrial capitalists (with the aid of bankers) but chiefly by the financial capitalists. Here was a new feudal régime based on the control of securities. Here was a capitalistic nexus which needed readjustment but like the scrambled egg was hard to disentangle.

The public utilities illustrate first the specialization of industry and then the combination of functions and the diversification of products. The combination of functions and the diversification of products had begun under industrial capitalism and were greatly extended and expanded under financial capitalism. The far-seeing industrial capitalists began to observe the economies of combination and diversification and the opportunities for profit. They were handicapped by the lack of capital and managerial ability. When the bankers came in, they were handicapped by a lack of managerial ability and knowledge of the industry.

Important as are the details of public utility services and functions, we are compelled in the interest of space to abbreviate our treatment of them. We may deal with the subject under three headings, as follows:

(1) Diversification of services and products of public utilities:
    Light—gas and electricity
    Power—electricity and steam
    Transportation—street railway and interurban lines
    Heat and cold—gas, electricity, and steam
    Storage—electricity and steam
    Commodities—water, toluol (in war), etc.
(2) Combination of economic functions by public utilities:
    Manufacture—gas, electricity
    Transportation—gas, electricity, water, passengers, light
        freight

Commodity production—coal, water
Storage—own products
    sundry goods for customers
Possession production—all of their own products by wholesale or retail

(3) Combination of industries with public utilities:
Public utilities and coal
Public utilities and paper manufacture
Public utilities and aluminum manufacture
Public utilities and petroleum

For their part in the public utility combination and diversification, as worked out by, or facilitated by, holding companies and investment trusts, the financial capitalists received a good deal of blame. It was said that they charged too much for floating the securities, made a promoters' profit out of speculation, and boosted the price of securities unduly. It is said that they often issued too many bonds in comparison with stock, and too much preferred stock when compared with the common, simply that they might themselves control the companies they formed, through the ownership of common stock. It is commonly believed that the complicated network of companies could serve no combination of useful and honest purposes. It is certain that the investment bankers put together companies that had no geographical contiguity—no physical or engineering advantage. It is probable that the top companies, when sore pressed during 1929-33, drew heavily upon the subordinate companies. That this levy was beyond the services rendered in supplying advice, management, engineering service, and capital is hard to prove or disprove. The financial capitalists worked too hard and too rapidly during the period 1923-29. They competed too strenuously for properties and paid too much, though few equalled the industrial capitalist, Samuel Insull, in this respect. Finally, having the speculative section of the public with them in 1923-29, they forgot the reactions that might come in a depression when deflated stockholders, impoverished consumers, and volatile intellectuals would unite to condemn with hindsight what they had failed to denounce with foresight.

There is no point in blaming the bankers for not understanding the implications of the growth of the industrial business acquired during the period 1917-29. Few saw that the two classes of customers—domestic and industrial—required separate handling. This failure was common among the public utility operators, the public utility commissions, the politicians, and the financial capitalists. The *domestic* consumers are fairly steady in their requirements, and companies catering to them can have a relatively heavy bonded debt—75 to 80 per cent. The *industrial* consumers, however, experience heavy seasonal and cyclical ups and downs. In the depression, a public utility company catering to them could pay no heavy charges on bonds. Such companies should either have no bonds or carry high reserves. These reserves should be built up out of income from high rates during prosperity. It is unsafe to encourage industrial users by giving them low rates during prosperity.

The whole public utility industry began to go over into national capitalism in 1933 and especially in 1935 when the public utility holding companies came in for revamping in accordance with a rather drastic piece of legislation, which, however, will probably be good for the industry in the long run. The unscrambling of the systems is already under way. In addition, the federal government is carrying on the construction of power facilities on the Tennessee River, the Colorado, and the Columbia. The power generated, it will sell at wholesale to privately owned and operated utilities as to municipally owned utilities. It will aid municipalities to construct or buy public utilities. Behind all this is the design to reduce rates to consumers. Of course, there is a question as to whether the taxpayer will not be really subsidizing the consumer and whether the industrial user will not be burdened to help the domestic consumer group which has more votes with which to pay for favors.

7. MERCHANDISING UNDER FINANCIAL CAPITALISM

During industrial capitalism the manufacturer had a dominant position. He sold his wares through commission agents or increasingly through wholesalers. The wholesalers sold to retailers. Even before industrial capitalism began to decline seriously, this modern trinity of manufacturer, wholesaler, and retailer began to disintegrate. The functions had to be performed but the alignment of the firms was changing. And in this change the lead was frequently taken by wholesalers and retailers.

As in manufacture or industry, so in merchandising, the specialization of function was given up in favor of multiple functions carefully integrated. Those firms that were early and successful in such a change long remained in industrial capitalism; that is, they developed financial competence and could keep out of the circle of financial capitalism. R. H. Macy and Company, the Great Atlantic and Pacific Tea Company, and Woolworth exemplify this competence and maturity within the field of industrial capitalism. And, yet, even they had to abandon the early emphasis on specialization of function. All three perform the function of wholesaling and retailing and the first and second manufacturing also. Perhaps such firms are in a stage of transition over into financial capitalism.

Although financial capitalists, led by investment bankers, have not been active in merchandising as they have in manufacture, railroading, communication, and public utilities, nevertheless they have played a part. There are at least three types of situations into which investment bankers have stepped in the reorganization of merchandising firms. The first is connected with bankruptcy and is illustrated by the action of J. P. Morgan and Company in the organization of the Associated Dry Goods Corporation in 1916. It will be recalled that the Claflin combine of wholesale-manufacture-retail got into difficulty in 1914 and that, of the four major parts surviving, the Associated Merchants Company and the United Dry Goods Company were the most promising. The Morgan firm had issued securities for the first and bought securities of the second. By 1915 both chains were in difficulty. In 1916, it brought the two chains of department stores together as the Associated Dry Goods Corporation. Its work consisted in facilitating an exchange of securities of the two companies for those of the new Corporation and following up this public pledge of confidence by partial control through the continuing representation of a Morgan partner as director. In 1929–30 the influence or control of investment bankers was extended with the increase in the number of their representatives on the board of directors of the chain. Four directors were chosen to represent four investment banking houses—Morgan and Company, Lehman Brothers, Lazard Frères, and Kidder Peabody. Moreover, these four were made members of the executive committee of the Associated, the other two being the president and a vice-president. For many years, John Claflin, whose father had established the original firm in New York City in 1843, had fought against the idea of banker control and tried to make adjustments which would save his wholesale business. We cannot help feeling that, if in 1901 Morgan and Company had been brought in, the old combination of wholesale-manufacture-retail would have been put on a sounder basis and might have survived. The continued support that commercial banks gave to Claflin may have postponed the inevitable and made it worse.

A second type of situation into which the investment banker steps, namely, assistance to a large owner of a concern to retire, is illustrated by the reorganization of the Kroger Grocery and Baking Company by Lehman Brothers. In 1883 B. H. Kroger began the retail grocery business which grew in his hands to be an important chain for the sale of groceries, bakery products, and meats. At the present time, the chain operates over 4,100 stores and many warehouses and factories. In fact, about 15 per cent of all goods sold by the chain is manufactured in its own plants. In 1927 Kroger, who was president, wished to begin the process of his withdrawal, for he was no longer young. Lehman

Brothers were employed to recapitalize and to sell much of the stock. Kroger reduced his holding of stock at a very favorable time and became chairman of the board of directors. Then, during the period 1927–29, smaller chains were purchased in anticipation of great things to come. The year 1930 saw the concern badly disorganized—suffering from indigestion—and losing money. Lehman Brothers felt some responsibility, and at once one of their partners stepped in to help reorganize the whole firm. This partner had specialized in merchandizing and was incisive in his methods. He made the Kroger lawyer the president of the firm and let many executives go, promoting some of the most promising that were kept. Many stores were closed. All were knit together more effectively. A more conservative accounting system was adopted. Budgeting of operations was introduced for each store. Soon there was a new spirit and with the revival of business confidence came profits.

The partner of Lehman Brothers who was the guiding hand in the reorganization stated that there were three degrees of banker activity in such a situation. First, the banker selected new managers; second, he assisted and participated in management; and, third, he stood by, offering his advice and coöperation where necessary.

The third general type of situation is the promotion of a new concern by the investment banker who thinks that the new firm will benefit society and therefore its stockholders and who expects that in the promotion he will himself profit. Many abuses lie here but, if the banker accepts his responsibilities and sticks with the newly established concern, I see no objection to the procedure.

The success of many merchandising concerns in the depression of 1920–23 suggested prosperity for the group in the future. It seemed promising to take medium-sized chains of stores and put them together to form large chains with better opportunities for operating efficiency. Let us take two examples. In the one case Merrill, Lynch and Company, investment bankers, promoted in 1926 the formation of the Safeway Stores, Inc., as a holding company in the retail grocery trade. In the other case, Lehman Brothers planned and organized in 1928 the Hahn Department Stores, Inc., a chain of large stores covering a wide area.

The Safeway Stores, Inc., was a holding company formed to buy up several subsidiary chains of grocery and meat stores largely in the Far West and in the Southwest. The total number of stores in the combined chain is now over 3,200. The success of the retailing venture was great, but the success of the promotion was probably greater. The investment bankers probably gained through the issue of preferred stock in large amounts, trading in the stock on the market, and probably from the appreciation of the common stock which sold no lower than $203 a share in 1926–28 and even rose to $790 a share. When one share was split into five, the price reached over $201 for a new share or over $1,000 per original share of common stock. Suppose during the subsequent depression the sponsoring house of investment bankers had left the chain to take care of itself. Even though no dishonesty be involved, such a policy of abandoning a sponsored concern would tend to discredit investment banking and financial capitalism, for it accentuates the element of profits from dealing in securities and minimizes the responsibility to security-holders. There are some scholars who regard this as typical financial capitalism. I regard it as the abuse not the use of the system. Such an occurrence, though this is not an example, arouses men's minds against the whole régime of the financial capitalist.

The Hahn Department Stores, Inc., was a chain of department stores (called the Allied Stores since 1935) which was first calmly conceived as an undertaking and then feverishly executed as a project. One member of the firm of Lehman Brothers, interested in retailing, secured the services of two bright young students of the subject. They were asked to investigate the possibilities of establishing a new chain of department stores. The report was favorable. Certainly some of the department stores were decidedly profitable and economies seemed to be possible in the purchase of goods for several stores through one organization. The report became a plan and the plan an undertaking. Mr. Lew Hahn, the managing director of the National Retail Dry Goods Association, was chosen to head the new firm. Stores were bought to the number of about 27, now 53. The fair prospects of current sales of a hundred million dollars a year were said to have been expanded to ten times that amount in the enthusiasm of planning and promoting.

The policy of Lehman Brothers was better than the execution. The man chosen president was essentially a publicity manager rather than a store executive. Too much was paid for some of the stores. And most serious, perhaps, was the fact that the wrong stores were put together: the fact that some were of one grade and some another impaired the chief part of the whole plan, namely, the centralized buying of goods.

It is noteworthy that Lehman Brothers have maintained their interest in, and connection with, the chain they formed. The Lehman group—Lehman Brothers (investment bankers) and Lehman Corporation (investment trust) have largely unconsciously developed a special interest in merchandising, but of course they do not confine their activity to this field. At least four of the partners hold directorships in at least eleven big merchandising units which include tens of thousands of stores and do hundreds of millions of dollars of business every year. The advice that investment bankers of such expanding experience can give to merchandising firms should be helpful. The leadership that these bankers can give in the floating of merchandising securities should be invaluable. It may be that we have here an adumbration of a growing specialization among investment bankers generally.

Financial capitalists owe to society the duty of faithful service: they can serve society by service to investors and business men. What benefits investors and business men benefits others as well. Merrill, Lynch and Company of New York and Childs, Jeffries and Thorndike of Boston have specialized in financing merchandising companies; and Lehman Brothers have made merchandising firms one of their chief interests. Such policies have tended to create the confidence that goes with special knowledge. The maximum service would be more nearly approached by continuous support of their special interests in depression as in prosperity.

In passing, there is the thought that, in the next great depression, investment bankers may be called in to organize and reorganize chains of small stores and chains of department stores. It will be at this point that the test will come as between the investment bankers who have specialized to a greater or less extent on the one hand and the non-specialists on the other hand. Of course, there will be the further test whether financial capitalists can be wise in policy and expert in the choice of executives in the merchandising field.

8. USE OF AGENTS, AUXILIARIES, AND BUSINESS TOOLS UNDER FINANCIAL CAPITALISM

The use of agents and business tools began on a large scale under mercantile capitalism and the use of auxiliaries under industrial capitalism. All of these aids to business were further developed under financial capitalism and made to serve fresh purposes.

We have specially noted the services performed by lawyers, engineers, and accountants in the régime of industrial capitalism. The great service of accountants had been in financial accounting whether inside the business firm or on the outside as auditor. Now, under financial capitalism, the accountant was to add cost accounting to his laurels, to say nothing of his work in matters of corporation and income taxes. Costs have been tender spots from the early days of mercantile capitalism, and sedentary merchants were forced to keep cost records. But in the present century the matter of costs has taken on new significance with the development of scientific management and cost accounting. The pressure came from the disastrously competitive conditions which the industrial capitalist (of financial mold) and especially the financial capitalist wanted to meet by closer control of costs. To the financial capitalists the issue was often to discover which plant or mine was a high-cost producer and which was low-cost. The former would often be closed in favor of the latter. Or, in some cases, reform would be instituted. While both public and private business units emphasize cost accounting in order to reduce costs, only private business has the ulterior motive of increasing profits. Most progress has been made in manufacturing, mining, and railroad operation; least has been made in farming. Merchandising lies in between. We get further evidence of the recency of the growth of cost accounting from the fact that the National Association of Cost Accountants (American) was formed only in 1919.

Cost accountancy is carried on within the firm or is an agency service performed by public accountants. When the public accountants are also asked to give advice, they are acting as business auxiliaries or counselors.

Business auxiliaries have prospered under the régime of financial capitalism. Let us consider only four groups—office management counselors, market consultants, public relations counselors, and industrial relations counselors. The growth of all four has been within the period of financial capitalism, though surviving industrial capitalists have also played an important part in the movement.

Office management saw but little change during the régime of mercantile capitalism. It was only when units began to grow very large under industrial capitalism that improvements were noted. These were along the lines of better accounting, the use of the card index, and loose-leaf devices generally, and the application of machinery to various office jobs. America led the way in much of the progress. The period began with the use of the typewriter and card index not much before 1890. If the growing size of business units started the movement, competition continued it. The office had to keep up with progress in the scientific management of production. When financial capitalism came in, there was a demand for good office practices so that control from above could be more strict and effective. In order that executives (whether industrial or financial capitalists) might check up on and improve their office management, outside experts were called in. Commonly these experts are found within the same advisory concern as consulting engineers. Probably the period of chief growth in America was 1910–29.

While considering the subject of office management, we may cast our eyes over the subject very broadly. A large part of the work of office management is statistical and is in the hands of statisticians and accountants. As we look back, we see at least the following steps or contributions made in office work.

Contributions to Office Management

1. Development of reckoning in business: change from Roman numerals to Arabic numerals (in Italy 14th century)
2. Records: change from tally to parchment or paper (12–13th century)
3. Bookkeeping: single entry rivalled by double entry (in Italy 14th century)
4. Specialization in office work: bookkeeper and cashier—in mercantile capitalism (in Italy 12–14th century)
5. Mercantile manuals (1340, especially 1481 ff.)
6. Clerk, or secretary, of the corporation (16th century)
7. Economic statistics (late 17th century)
8. Actuarial work, only in insurance (late 18th century)
9. Engineering—exact data (19th century)
10. Office equipment (late 19th century)
11. Business statistics (19th century)
12. Cost accounting (late 19th century)
13. Office management consultants (early 20th century)
14. Books on office management (after 1900, and in America 1917 ff.)

Market consultants arose chiefly in the period 1917–29 in New York and other metropolitan centers. In the secular downtrend, which became pronounced in towns and cities beginning in 1929, they have held their own with great difficulty.

Public relations has been a theme of growing importance in America since 1901, when so many persons were shocked by the Hill-Harriman contest for the Northern Pacific Railroad and the resulting panic. Various large firms came to employ publicity managers. Apparently Mr. W. J. Cameron is such an official in the Ford Motor Company. Lawyers, and journalists were chosen to guide public opinion or were retained as advisers. Beginning in 1915, Ivy Lee was adviser to John D. Rockefeller, the Pennsylvania Railroad, the Bethlehem Steel Company, and other large firms. He was a true business auxiliary and, though much criticized, seems to have exerted a beneficial influence on both business and the public. Another such counselor is Edward L. Bernays who had been publicity manager for various musicians. His distinctive services have been given to the federal government, business firms, and trade associations. Often we read sizable news items on important matters of business inspired by such counselors. In fact, such auxiliaries are becoming almost necessary adjuncts to business education—in rather too close proximity to propaganda.

The relation of the business man to his employees has been of great importance during both industrial and financial capitalistic régimes. Many industrial capitalists could not avoid strikes. Some of them instituted many benefits and employed special managers to consider relations with their employees. It was not until 1922, however, that we find industrial relations counselors functioning. In that year a firm of New York lawyers began to work on industrial relations with the financial aid of J. D. Rockefeller, Jr. About thirty persons were concerned with the work which involved a study of employee stock ownership, profit sharing, vacation with pay, unemployment compensation, and pensions. This effort led in 1925 to the formation of Industrial Relations Counselors, Inc., who are open to consultation on a cost basis.

It is an interesting fact that no financial counselors have come into being, so far as I know. Counseling was done, of course, but it was by banks and lawyers. Financial capitalists were in a position to furnish all the expert advice to their clients and dependent firms, that was required. To be sure, there are general business consultants and others who give advice that has an important bearing upon financial management but there seem to be no specialized auxiliaries for this purpose.

Business tools, which have had a continuous growth through the centuries, have also progressed under financial capitalism. Investment journals have multiplied. Investment services, beginning with Babson's in 1904, have increased in number and size. Manuals (Poor's, Moody's, Rand-McNally's, etc.), giving information concerning the firms whose securities the public wishes to invest in, have grown in number, size, reliability, and general usefulness. The larger firms, especially those that have come into the central circle of financial capitalism, occupy the most prominent part of the news and space devoted to business information. To be sure, there is great variation from the frequent and extensive releases of information by the United States Steel Corporation to the sparse array of facts given out by the Aluminum Company of America.

It is obvious that, as business becomes big and intricate, it becomes so difficult to administer that experts, outside experts, are necessary. When financial capitalists try to control business and at the same time sell securities to the public, they need the help of agents, auxiliaries, and business tools. Some think that the need for such helps to business will be partly obviated by government control.

9. SECULAR TRENDS AND FINANCIAL CAPITALISM

The advisers of business, whom we have been considering, had constantly in mind the business cycle of three years or of ten years but rarely thought of the secular trend in business, though Benner who began his studies in the 1870's had the general idea and even attempted to mark off the ups and downs in a chronological table. In this present chapter we are interested in only three of the trends, namely, 1866–97, 1897–1920, and 1920 onwards.

The period 1866–97 saw a downtrend in prices and an increase in the difficulty of making profits. In Europe the period covered the years 1873–97. On each continent the downtrend followed a great war or series of wars. We can deal with the movement only briefly. An incisive effect of the downtrend was a series of bankruptcies and threats of bankruptcy, especially in older industries. Salvation from bankruptcy, or the recovery after bankruptcy, was often or commonly due to a change of policy by industrial capitalists. The blessing of disaster for them was the lesson learned about specialization. They learned from experience that in a severely competitive régime, after initial technical advances had been made, it was wiser to turn to multiple functions, carefully integrated, diversification of products, and horizontal combination. Such changes occurred in the steel industry, large stores, and railroads. Coupled with this change in policy were shifts in management in the direction of economy and efficiency. Where such changes did not occur, business units, at least in the older industries, tended to get into the hands of financial capitalists.

During the period of 1897–1920 a great upturn in business came about and with it some of the largest profits ever made in American business. The drive during this period was not the avoidance of loss but the securing of gain. To this end, financial capitalists became increasingly active and their policy became the building up of large and strong units which could produce cheaply, be certain of supplies, and occupy a strong position in the market. Their objective was achieved chiefly by integration, diversification, and horizontal combination. Their greatest activity came during the boom periods of 1900–03, 1904–07, and 1915–20, which, of course, they helped to create. The first is sometimes called "merger prosperity," the second "corporate prosperity," and the third "war prosperity." During the whole period there were many threats to prosperity, such as the Northern Pacific panic of 1901, the rich man's panic of 1903, the financial panic of 1907, the money trust investigation of 1912-13, and the brief war depression of 1914-15. In spite of these threats to prosperity, business remained buoyant and tended to grow in inefficiency and a feeling of security. The great triumph of big business and of bankers came during the World War. The threats to big business had loomed large through the political fire that had swept the country under Woodrow Wilson who set out to give to small business a New Freedom. It soon became evident, however, that only big business could have any chance of winning the War.

The downtrend of the period from 1920 onwards (we might argue for the period 1920-51-54) was introduced by the sharp reaction from war conditions. We may outline succeeding movements briefly as follows:

1920-22 Primary post-war depression
1923-29 Recovery (notably in building) and boom on stock market
1929-32 Secondary post-war depression, in both town and country
1932-37 The Hoover recovery, which was checked by bank failures, was supplanted by New Deal artificial recovery, especially in consumers' goods

During the prosperity of 1923-29 the investment bankers and other financial capitalists reached their greatest heights, far beyond the attainments of 1900-03, 1904-07, and 1915-20. Remember that this prosperity, chiefly in the town, occurred in a general downtrend. The long World War had built up many needs in country districts and, especially, in the towns. Prominent among these were needs for houses and other buildings, automobiles, and agricultural equipment. A great deal of capital had been saved by the people—about eighteen million persons—who had invested in federal bonds. A government had come into power that personified capitalism: some economists have called this period the "Coolidge prosperity." The financial capitalists, under the lead of the investment bankers, stimulated the flow of capital by issuing foreign bonds to eager American buyers. They went on and on, issuing bonds and stocks of American companies, notably, holding companies and investment trusts. Prices kept going higher and getting out of line with a reasonable expectation of income. The answer commonly given to such a fear was that perhaps the normal rate of income in America would in the future be little above two per cent. Above all, many business men reflected, God was in his heaven and the Republicans in Washington.

The year 1929 marked a climax in investment securities available for purchase through brokers on the exchange. For the year 1884 the Dow-Jones averages were based on 11 stocks made up of 9 railroads, one steamship, and the Western Union. In 1897 the 12 "industrials" included one steamship company, and 2 gas companies. In 1914 the 12 industrials included only one gas company. In 1916 the 20 industrials were all really industrial, except the American Telephone and Telegraph and the Western Union. By 1928 the 30 industrials were truly industrial. In 1929 public utilities were given a prominent place as a separate group alongside of industrials and railroads, being made up of first 18 and then 20 utilities, including the American Telephone and Telegraph. From that time onward, the investor and speculator have daily or hourly followed the course of the averages of these three groups—the trinity of the market place. In this trinity the father, the railroads, is giving way to the son, the public utilities, in the weighing of changes in the security markets.

On March 7, 1929, Paul M. Warburg, investment banker in the firm of Kuhn, Loeb and Company, warned the country of impending danger not only to speculators but to the whole country. He did not oppose the craving for the ownership of securities or the satisfaction of new wants, but he feared the dangerous purchase of stocks on margins at prices that were inflated beyond reason. Some saw the writing on the wall and withdrew from speculation. Most people, however, continued to play with the fire. This was true even during the summer of 1929 when production was falling off in ominous fashion.

The scene now shifts to London where on September 20, 1929, Clarence C. Hatry and associates surrendered their persons to the authorities and exposed their deeds to an astonished world. England was shocked, but America, while it covered its eyes from the lightning, soon went on its way into the deluge. But let us look at Hatry, for he was a financial capitalist performing in London in such a way as to make us wonder whether he was not holding up the glass of fashion to Wall Street.

Hatry was a small but well groomed man of middle age who was persuasive in speech and, radiating confidence, disarmed the natural suspicion of banker and industrialist alike. With a good secondary school education and a pretentious social life, he walked among business leaders with ease. Full of energy and persistent, he formulated his plans for reorganization and for new firms. Fate had dropped down a great promoter in a great era of promotion. A clerk in an insurance office in London, then an insurance broker, and finally a director of an old insurance company at twenty-five, he showed his skill at reorganization, and then in the formation of the Commercial Bank of London, later the Commercial Corporation of London, a financing corporation which went into bankruptcy in 1923. Not to be kept down for long, Hatry went ahead with other concerns, in part, as follows:

Corporation and General Securities, Ltd.
Austin Friars Trust.
British Glass Industries, Ltd.
Jute Industries, Ltd.
Drapery Trust (dry goods chain).
Steel Companies of Great Britain, Ltd.
Allied Ironfounders, Ltd.

Hatry aroused discouraged British industrialists and inspired the little band of financial capitalists in London. He began to show the British what financial capitalists could really do if they formed bigger business units and rationalized industry. But he made mistakes. He paid too much for the firms he brought together, he built up a complex, even maze, of firms with intricate inter-firm relations. He kept on promoting when the foundations of business were cracking at the bottom. Finally, he forged municipal bonds as security for loans to save his various concerns. The result was disaster to himself and a loss to investors, large and small, and a warning signal to capitalists wise enough to heed it.

The day after Hatry went to jail, prices dropped in New York but recovered. Following were the most dramatic moves in 1929:

Oct. 3—Year's worst break to date. Front page headlines.
Oct. 19—Loss in security prices, 5 to 20 points.
Oct. 28—Stampede—drop of 14 billion dollars' value.
Oct. 30—Rockefellers announced they would purchase good common stocks.
Nov. 1—Foshay utilities in receivership.
Nov. 6—Stocks off 5 to 66 points.
Nov. 12—New rush to sell. New lows.
Nov. 13—Rockefellers place an order for one million shares of Standard Oil of New Jersey at $50 a share.
Dec. 20—Drop of 1 to 20 points. Fresh bear raid.

The market for securities and commodities went up and down, but chiefly down, especially in 1931 until the bottom was reached and recovery begun on July 8, 1932. The disaster to values caused men to jump out of top windows and forced governments to resign and nations to go off the gold standard.

Before the bottom was reached, occurred the affair of Ivar Kreuger, the Swedish financial capitalist who shot himself in Paris on March 12, 1932. Nothing so dramatized the financial spree of the times, because few men had ever held a financial umbrella over so many countries. In 1911 Kreuger had formed the Kreuger and Toll Company in Stockholm. This concern was designed to invest, manage, and finance. It came to hold stock in the Swedish Match Company which operated in over half the principal countries of the world through its subsidiary the International Match Company, and also in pulp and power, mining, real estate, and banking companies in Sweden. It loaned large sums to governments in return for the privilege of manufacturing, importing, and selling matches. It floated companies, merged various concerns, and bought and sold securities. Through a wholly owned company in Holland it held a wholly owned investment company in America—the Swedish American Investment Corporation, formed in 1925, rather fittingly in Delaware. This concern owned securities of companies located in Sweden and elsewhere. Prominent Americans were on its board of directors, men who were directors of dozens of other firms. Doubtless these were useful in floating a large issue of preferred stock in America, the proceeds of which were to be used apparently almost wholly for investment in Sweden. It was so arranged that, while prosperity ruled, control lay wholly in the hands of Kreuger.

Kreuger was a typical financial capitalist in that he had wide interests. He was unique, however, in his geographical spread. This was part of his technique—to play one country off against another—and not least to get American money to finance ventures abroad. Few were so disarming in conversation because so candid: he was fond of putting *all* of his cards upon the table. Under the trying circumstances of the times, only such a man as he could have lasted so far down into the depths of depression. To save himself, he finally forged Italian government bonds as security for a loan. Had the market turned upward he might have paid off the loan and redeemed and destroyed the bonds. When the forgery was discovered, however, all was lost. Financial capitalism was being buried under a heavy cloud of ill-fame.

The enemies of private business capitalism have said "this is the end." Attention to historic changes bids us see that wars have made business administration weak and then have caused secular downtrends in prices and business profits. In this weakened condition, mercantile, industrial, and financial capitalism have been supplanted each by a new system. Whether financial capitalism will be given one more trial, in modified form, or is permanently submerged by national capitalism is not entirely clear. It may be that, after long years of deflation and unemployment, men will cry out "let us have some credit inflation, let the financial capitalists make private capital flow freely once again, even if losses do occur, for it is more wholesome to lose even large sums with men everywhere employed, buildings going up, and public debts going down."

We are reminded of abuses by various groups in history. Romans fed Christians to the lions and enjoyed the sport. Catholics burned Protestants. Spaniards robbed and killed American Indians. Anglo-Saxons cheated, robbed, and slaughtered Indians. Northerners destroyed Southern property. The universities of Oxford and Cambridge degenerated in the eighteenth century. Nazis plunder Jewish property and take away from Jews ordinary human rights. The offenders have survived, and, reforming, have again performed their normal duties. Presumably, Germans and financial capitalists will live to write another chapter in their history, though they can never eliminate the stained pages already numbered. Economic, religious, political, and educational institutions have on record pages that are pure white, bloody red, and foul black. Whirl them on the disc of time, and they are all equally drab and gray.

10. MISTAKES AND CRIMES IN BUSINESS

In this book we are primarily interested in the uses not the abuses of business. Many readers do not share this preoccupation; in fact, the rank and file even of scholars are more prone to dwell upon the business crook than upon the upright executive. We may assume that the same individuals prefer devils to saints; to them the stories from divorce courts are more interesting than the announcements of celebrations of fifty-year anniversaries of marriages. In truth, there is more involved in business irregularities than mere perversion: it is part of the constant problem of the honest executive to eliminate the dishonest man from business and to check the action of dishonest customers, politicians, and racketeers on the outside.

No effort is made here to cover the whole subject. Some distinctions, however, can be offered for further study. With this in mind I have included a diagram not to express finality but rather to suggest differences and proportions. I hope that every reader will make a better one. As we study the diagram here offered for consideration, we should note that the two upper parts deal with mistakes and crimes in business, while the lowest deals with ideas and rules of the non-business world. The cross sections of the triangle represent both the ideals on various levels and the volume of the breaches. The volume is pure guesswork.

In studying this diagram, note that the two upper segments of the whole triangle are superimposed upon the base of non-business mistakes and crimes. Between the business and the non-business areas there is a constant interchange of ideas and ideals. The offerings are reciprocal. This fact keeps the segments of human activity and values in constant interplay. No judgments about business irregularities have any value unless they recognize this fact.

The smallest group of breaches of ideals and rules is the topmost in the diagram. I cannot actually prove that the breaches of the *letter* of the law are fewest in number, for there are from the nature of the situation no statistical data. The number of laws is great but those directly applying to the average firm is small; and business is continuously anxious to avoid the sullied reputation of the criminal. Nevertheless, crime is committed in business and the criminals are dealt with according to their deserts. Witnesses to this fact are Foshay in America and Hatry in England. Kreuger in Sweden, Stavisky in France, and Musica-Coster in America took the processes of justice into their own hands and shot themselves. The memories of such men live

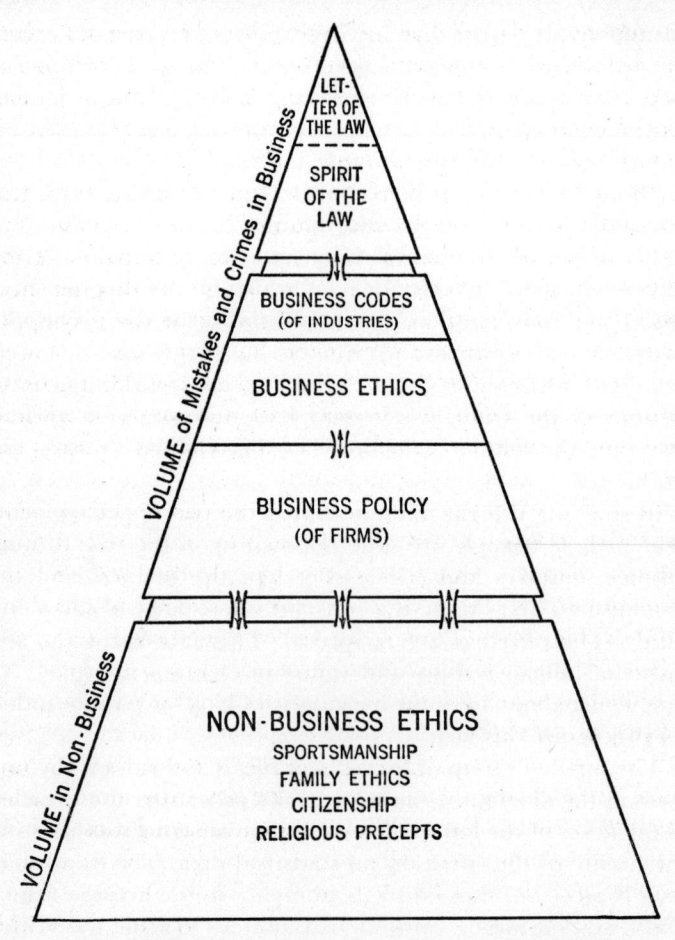

```
                    /\
                   /  \
                  /LET-\
                 / TER OF\
                /THE LAW  \
               /-----------\
              /   SPIRIT    \
             /    OF THE     \
            /      LAW        \
           /--------------------\
          /   BUSINESS CODES     \
         /    (OF INDUSTRIES)     \
        /--------------------------\
       /      BUSINESS ETHICS       \
      /------------------------------\
     /       BUSINESS POLICY          \
    /          (OF FIRMS)              \
   /------------------------------------\
  /          NON-BUSINESS ETHICS         \
 /              SPORTSMANSHIP             \
/                FAMILY ETHICS             \
                 CITIZENSHIP
              RELIGIOUS PRECEPTS
```

(Left side labels: VOLUME of Mistakes and Crimes in Business; VOLUME in Non-Business)

MISTAKES AND CRIMES ESPECIALLY IN BUSINESS

A tentative effort to show by a diagram both rules and ideals, and the approximate volume of deviation therefrom.

long in the annals of the public. Indeed, it is only from such crimes that some persons become conscious of the existence of big business.

It should be clearly stated, and never forgotten, that business has commonly had its share of law-breakers for whom no excuse can be offered. Those who have broken the *letter* of the law have been guilty of theft, debauchery, and the taking of human life—as relentless and ruthless as the actions of American settlers in competition with the Indians.

All men break the *spirit* of the law, and therein lies both general freedom and individual advantage. No legal penalty ordinarily arises, and the moral issue seems to be a matter of the conscience of the individual. One formula for obeying the letter but breaking the spirit is "conforming with the law." The subtleties of procedures are worked out by corporation counsels and other lawyers. After 1720 in England the law frowned upon business corporations, but lawyers soon were advising business men how to enjoy the advantages of corporations by using unincorporated joint stock companies. Under the American securities and exchange law of 1934 it was made difficult and expensive to float securities in the old way and to sell through the old channels. Gradually, firms have learned to sell their securities directly to investors, commonly in large blocks to insurance companies. Thus, many of the new disabilities of the legislative enactment have been avoided.

If the laws were equitable, evasions of the spirit would involve a prick of conscience and widespread condemnation. Legislators are often neither wise nor honest, however, and thereby make the breaking of the letter of the law little more than a pastime. Cornelius Vanderbilt I is quoted as saying substantially that "you cannot run a railroad according to the law," and, if anyone knew, he did. National prohibition in America further illustrates the point. From our present viewpoint, those who broke the spirit of the law merely kept burning the torch of freedom. There is a moot question as to whether a law which deprives a man of inherent and fundamental property rights is not contrary to the supreme social law of survival; to take property away is often equivalent to taking life away. Property and life came before the state and are not to be taken, except in the most unusual and necessary situations.

Often when the business man is accused of crime, he is meeting a racket carried on by his critics. Politicians have been the most greedy and persistent of racketeers. Let us consider them or their analogs through the ages. Mediaeval barons insisted on a share in the profits of business. Nomads in Asia and Africa collected a tribute in lieu of plunder. Kings imposed forced loans on merchants in return for real or nominal protection. Modern political leaders have required financial assistance from business men in meeting party expenses. Municipal and State leaders have been more hungry and less scrupulous in America than any other class of politicians. The churches (and we may add to a less extent schools and colleges) have had their own racket or game of applying leeches. Possibly a measure of racketeering arises from the resurrection of classical forms and patterns which modern students are required to learn from teachers. In charity, forms of influence are used in the modern period: a storekeeper in a small town *has* to contribute to about every religious denomination and then to the Salvation Army. Judges in New York, from Barnard's day onwards, have levied their toll before handing out justice. Of course, this is an ancient device of courts and is writ indelibly into the history of justice. France has made a contribution to racketeering—this time on the inside—in the form of the sit-in and the sit-down strikes and other kinds of sabotage. These are gems from the intellectual world of labor leadership. Throughout early history the robber or pirate, armed and without mercy, has been a power on the outskirts of business, sometimes near the inner recesses. In America this class of person is called the "gangster." He operates in the wilds of metropolitan cities where life is roughest and toughest and stakes are highest. To all of these enemies of business, there are only three possible answers—submission, resistance, and compromise. One or another course is followed according to circumstances. The business man must both carry on his business and meet his problem of defence. He hires detectives, private police, lawyers, and lobbyists. Occasionally petty capitalists resist to the death. Then our venal judges and our juries with doubtful records let off the criminal. Such are the frills of the non-business world, the roses with thorns that the business man has to enjoy. One of the distinctive contributions of democracy is the multiplication and variation of these racketeers.

The picture changes as we dig down into the pyramid or triangle. When industries such as shoemaking, retailing, and trucking make rules, the members have to take notice, for the enforcers of the rules are ever at hand—right in the trade. Petty capitalists have been the greatest formulators of ethical codes in the world's history. The two great groups of ethical codes created by petty capitalists in the Middle Ages were (1) the customary law of traveling merchants, called the Law Merchant, and (2) the regulations promulgated by gilds and, where allowed by town magistrates, having the effect of law. In France these gild regulations ran current, with varying fortunes and success, until 1791. In the period beginning in the 1770's in England and increasingly after the Civil War in America, national trade associations have arisen to develop and make rules for their group—as well as to procure other advantages for the constitutent members.

A great number of codes are available for study over a long period. They deal with honest trading, fair competition, and price regulation. Misleading advertising, commercial bribery, and manipulating the market are proscribed, and efforts are made to prevent consumers from continuing unfair practices. The leading men and firms in the industries in question, however, often refuse to join such associations or subscribe to such codes. The reason is that the codes are broken in underhand ways and are in many respects so far below the better practices of the leaders that the leaders feel that they would lose prestige by the connection.

In a highly competitive society, where a wide and intricate market exists, the effective regulation of an industry is one of the most difficult problems. Efforts have been made, for instance in open-price trade associations, to hold prices up to a place where dividends may be earned—unfortunately even for the poorest managed concern in the group. Then, at once some firms begin to chisel the price level, offer unusual discounts, or supply special services for buyers. Of course, the pressure arises on the buyer's side as well as on the seller's. Similarly, among very good people—even teachers and preachers—coöperative societies are formed to chisel into the price level of the district in the purchase of oil, coal, and other commodities. Many individuals boast that they never buy certain goods at retail, always at wholesale and therefore at a lower price. And so goes the eternal round of struggle to earn a living or make the income go a little farther. In this struggle, the Jews have been somewhat more persistent and successful than their gentile cousins and accordingly have received not a little blame for their pains.

Beneath the area of business codes is business ethics. This is the unwritten idealism of the whole business group. It is the voice of conscience and the finger of right directed to business activities. It deals with elementary situations and is elastically applicable to new and changing scenes. Business men agree that they should not malign a competitor and should not depreciate his wares, though they may amply praise their own. They agree that the skirts of business should be kept clean in the face of the non-business world. In a general way, they also agree that fairness should prevail between the component parts of a business—the creditors, stockholders, executives, employees, customers, and neighbors. Business ethics is a reservoir of clear water which may be drawn upon to build up the codes of industry. It is a lake upon which the individual firm can sail its ship into the harbor of Good Policy.

Of all the irregularities in the triangle the most serious is the breach of good business policy. This is a matter of the action of individual business men and firms. It leads to loss of profits and to final failure. A live firm can reform a bad practice but it commonly cannot survive a very bad policy. Let us consider some examples. The adoption of a short-term point of view where a long-term policy of development or growth is needed and the disregard of the rights or feelings of the public or of employees are instances. Often a business concern believes itself firmly established and beyond serious competition when it is enjoying great success; in reality, it is allowing serious competition to develop right under its very eyes. Charging too high prices or aiming at too much of the total amount of business are policies that bring their own nemesis. The nepotism of executives and the disregard of stockholders' rights are cankers that eat deep into the vitals of many a business firm.

If business policy were all-wise, the world would be somewhat different. The attainment of wisdom (balance, long-time point of view, and justice) would soon be disrupted by the lack of wisdom outside of business. Complete reform would be attained only by the simultaneous growth of wisdom in business and non-business areas. This is but the idle dream of one who is addicted to social narcotics; it belongs to academic circles and debating societies rather than to the realm of reality in a changing society.

When we proceed from the middle of the triangle into the base, from business into non-business, we enter a world that is at once different and yet the same. The non-business world with its ethical concepts and precepts is made up of business men and others acting in non-business situations. There is in this non-business world an absence of material profits but there is a similar dominance of pursuit of some advantage which an individual may secure for himself, such as a reputation for being a good loser, a strict observer of divine decree, a kindly father, or a loyal supporter of an institution for helping others. In between the two worlds, there is an exchange of ideals and methods and an interplay of ideas and procedures, resources and attainments.

The world of non-business is constantly sitting in judgment upon business, and this is all to the good. But the opinions of the non-business world must be accepted with care, for they sometimes have no application or meaning. For instance, when a firm charges the market price even if that be high, or pays the market wage even if that be low, it is playing the game of business according to the accepted ethical code and within the law. To be sure, it may be following a bad policy, but that is generally not clear. The judgment expressed very often that advertising is frequently a waste of effort and money is correct so far as it goes. It matters little to society whether we use one tooth paste or another, but it is important that private competitive business be maintained even when and where some general losses are incurred. In short, much advertising is the price we pay for the advantage of private business capitalism. Urging the sale of goods, services, or securities even beyond the needs of buyers is no offence, ethically or legally, though it may involve bad policy. Whether bad policy is to be the final judgment is commonly obscure to both business executive and independent observer.

The non-business group often blames business for taking advantage of changing conditions. For instance, well-meaning persons criticize John Jacob Astor for buying securities and lands in a crisis or depression. In truth, they should praise him for coming to the rescue of the sorely pressed. The rank and file of men buy when prices are high and sell when they are low. It is the policy of a shrewd man to sell when prices are high and buy when they are low. This is good policy, for it yields profits, and it checks the worst evils of fluctuations. It often leads to the creation of big fortunes, however, which represent the superior judgment of one man over another. In such a case, the non-business judgment against the business man is wrong on every count: the latter makes no breach in the law, industrial code, business ethics, or good business policy. When one speculator buys up the good securities of another speculator at a low price, the world chuckles. But when a rich man like Thomas Guy (1644–1724) buys up scrip from poor sailors or when a well-to-do investor like William Scully buys up scrip of veterans returned from the Civil War, we do not smile but frown. Feeling that there is something wrong, we blame Guy and Scully, whilst we should put the finger of accusation on the governments responsible for the issuance of the scrip.

It is difficult to pass a judgment as to the relative volume of irregularities of the various types of capitalism. The petty capitalist has been conspicuous for the multiplicity of trade codes and for his persistence in breaking them. All through his experience there have been breaches of rules concerning quantity, quality, and prices. Breaches of the assize of bread and ale, forestalling, regrating, engrossing, and, in our day, also deception concerning quality, and in addition a good deal of shortchanging, and underweighing are conspicuous examples.

Mercantile capitalism saw both the control and the exploitation of small masters. In most cases the system not the individual capitalist was at fault. Such evils as were involved in shifting burdens onto other groups were somewhat easier to bear than nowadays, owing to the fact that many of the workers concerned had alternative modes of livelihood.

Industrial capitalists, notably during the period 1843-73, stand oftenest at the bar of justice to answer for the crimes of promotion, getting rich quickly, and excessive competition. They have been young men, so to speak, eager to earn a fortune, and careless of their procedures. George Hudson, the English railroad king, is a good example. Promoter of a bank, many railroads, docks, and industrial companies, he pushed England ahead by leaps and bounds. Honest little fellows who never did a thing of importance, good or bad, found fault with his methods. They were technically right and he was egregiously wrong, but he was the imperfect instrument of the progress of a nation and a people. In America, Daniel Drew, James Fisk, and Jay Gould showed themselves to be masterful in the pursuit of gain in the wrong way. They were picturesque scoundrels who were near to being amoral—the product of an age that was as short as it was unsavory. Industrial capitalists they were, though their distinctive operations lay in financial manipulation. They were of service to business in consolidation of small units—chiefly in the case of Gould—and in rousing the public to a need for higher conduct in business.

Financial capitalists have been the big ogres of recent American journalists and politicians. In spite of their great services, they have promoted reorganizations simply for the profit that comes from selling securities. Some of them have sold securities when the more conservative of their profession have known that no interest or dividends were likely to be forthcoming or when the principal was unsafe. In many of their promotions they have paid too high a price for the concerns they have bought. The reader may classify these charges as they appeal to him or according to the diagram presented at the beginning of this section. But let us never forget that financial capitalists serve society in a superb fashion: they guide funds into productive enterprises and try to direct these enterprises along productive channels. They do imperfectly what national capitalists can do with difficulty and communistic capitalists hardly at all. They make free men plan new enterprises and remodel old, they lead men to shift their activities in accordance with their increased powers and new opportunities, they support public improvements out of current taxes, and they give laborers work.

National capitalists, whom we shall consider at length in the next chapter, have bought votes by using other people's money. They have rigged the market for government bonds. They have taxed an industry to build up competitors to wreck it. They have threatened and made war in order to remain in power. They have crushed a class in order to get funds and jobs for their own supporters. They have perverted education and culture. They have brought about the social inversion of the individual. And then, crime of crimes, they have hypothecated the welfare of the future for a weak-kneed solution of current problems.

Brevity may grant us the favor of some opinions stated but not urged. Large units have fewer irregularities to their credit, but these few are necessarily more serious. The business methods of the Occident have been preferable to those of the Orient (and of Asia Minor and Syria). We run no risks in urging the superiority of good policy over good codes or good laws. Policy is dynamic and prophylactic. If business policy were all-wise, there would be no need for business ethics, codes, or laws, except perhaps to protect business against the non-business group.

Unhappy lies the head of the moralist, for he must try to fit parts that do not match. Some observations, however, may be expressed that point to larger truths but may be left without elaboration.

1. Business is the daily exercise of the primeval instinct to survive. With such a descent, it naturally does well by itself.

2. The profit motive is a prolific mother of deformed children, but there are other wombs with ugly offsprings such as vanity, bad disposition, lack of courtesy, political ambition, moral principle, and religious zeal.

3. Confuse not the mistakes of the business man with his intentions.

4. Business gives a man risks, lets him make mistakes, and rewards him according to his rectitude, ability, and luck.

5. Fortune dances with a man but once, while integrity and ability are companions that are neither fickle nor unfaithful.

6. The evil deeds of business men are carved in stone; their good deeds are recorded in invisible ink.

7. There is much merit in making a dollar for one's self and ten for others.

8. An unprejudiced archangel would decide that business men are both sinned against and sinning.

9. Business is for some a playground, for others a battle-ground or a conquered city fit for plunder, but for a larger number it is a field to be plowed, sown, and harvested.

10. For those who have no undertakings and no major responsibilities, it is easy to be virtuous and critical. The yellow dog successfully barks at the heels of the work horse without being able to drag the plow.

11. It is not necessary to be a cynic to record that there is little gratitude, fairness, justice, or intelligence put into the formation of public opinion concerning business, particularly in an era of economic difficulties.

11. STRENGTH AND WEAKNESS OF FINANCIAL CAPITALISM

The system of financial capitalism was at its height in America about 1901–12, 1914–20, and 1923–29. It was accepted because of what it offered to business and therefore to society. Let us judge the system with its normal uses not abuses in mind.

Financial capitalism, at its best, encouraged people to save and speculate and invest. It made the owner of capital feel that there was a group of leaders—a financial general staff—looking out for his interests. In the presence of irresponsible executives in corporations under the régime of industrial capitalism, the investing capitalist felt somewhat hopeless even before the time of the Civil War. Now, the owners of securities could be scattered and yet have a business administration that would be in their interest. Accordingly, a certain portion of the total productive yield would go back into the business of the country to maintain a progressive economic order. In addition, financial capitalists, as never before, were spreading the ownership of securities, aided by the sale of World War bonds. The people—farmers and workers as well as others—were becoming the owners of private business. Unfortunately, the plan was better than the execution, for the people did not know how to buy good securities and the financial system did not in practice provide the necessary guidance, except indirectly through savings banks and investments trusts which the rank and file of investors thought were not sufficiently lucrative.

The financial policy that financial capitalists were inviting business firms to adopt or were forcing upon them was in general sound and a real improvement over what had commonly existed under industrial capitalism. A distinction was made between long-time and current conditions. The former was made as safe as possible by the reduction of bonded indebtedness. The latter was improved by building up out of earnings or out of new securities, if necessary, a surplus to be used as working capital. Accordingly, a firm could more readily escape the dangers of crises and depressions. Bonds would not have to be refloated in a downward secular trend or in a depression and commercial banks would have no chance of embarrassing a firm in case a loan had to be called to meet the needs of depositors.

The business policy of financial capitalists was no less well adapted to the needs of the time. It included cutting costs—of management, capital, and labor. Of course, there went with this a raising of the reward of top men of ability who in America have rarely been paid too much, although popular belief runs to the contrary view. The business policy of financial capitalists also included a reduction in cutthroat competition which in the long run benefited no one except the speculator. It involved a shift from specialization to multiple functions well integrated, to diversification of production and investment, and to horizontal combination.

Financial capitalists were realists. Their best leaders—such as J. P. Morgan, Sr.,—insisted on solvency and liquidity. Going through the wringer of the bankruptcy courts was like a surgical operation; it held out the greatest promise of healthy recovery. It released the real capital assets and the best administrative abilities for fresh tasks.

In a sense, above all else, financial capitalism was international. This was part of its realism. The financial capitalist was no more fooled (in general, though the practice has often broken down) by the enthusiasms of patriotism than he was by the mistaken hopes of industrial capitalists that they could sell what they would like to produce. The very mention of international bankers causes a virtuous democracy to recoil with horror. A well-meaning Catholic priest denounced Wall Street in 1936 as made up of international bankers—the kind of charge made against the Jews in Germany. Yes, financial capitalists like ministers of the gospel, scholars, and labor leaders have an international point of view that transcends nationalism. Pulling together, these might attain sanity.

It is an easy error to think of financial capitalism as a speculator's paradise. We may condemn speculation in stocks, bonds, commodities, and real estate as unproductive and predatory if we will, though I think this attitude is superficial. Still, the whole matter has nothing to do with financial capitalism as such. Speculation is found under mercantile, industrial, financial, and national capitalism. Compare the excesses of 1720 (mercantile capitalism), 1873 (industrial capitalism), and 1933 (national capitalism). These years all witnessed liquidity bubbling over under comparable circumstances.

Of all the forms of capitalism that have ever existed, financial capitalism has come in for most denunciation. The probable reason for this is partly that it prevailed at a time of greatest interest in social reconstruction and partly that it promised the preservation of a private business system that many considered diseased and decrepit. It is clear enough that financial capitalism has had its weak points and some of these we shall examine.

The financial capitalist has a minor weakness that at times leaves him fatally vulnerable. Often, he is too trustful of those with whom he operates. He looks them in the eyes and fails to see that they have their hands on daggers. Accustomed to doing business by word of mouth—in conversation or over the telephone—he accepts the word and does not examine the bond. American investment bankers loaned money to Kreuger and Toll without examining the government bonds offered as collateral. Of course, for one bogus bond there are a thousand bona fide contracts entered into by word or by nod.

The actual management of private business under the influence or control of financial capitalists has not been so promising as the policies that have been adopted. This charge does not mean that, in time, adequate management could not be provided, but that actually events have moved rapidly and little maturing has been possible. Be it noted in this connection that financial capitalism has had the shortest span of life of all the private business systems of capital up to date.

Under the head of mismanagement by financial capitalists are several items. The charge has often been made that when units were brought up and consolidated there was over-capitalization. The New Haven Railroad is still suffering from this condition.

In the lush and sunny days of the upward secular trend, 1897–1920, and even on to 1929, too little thought was given to costs of property and resulting capitalization. In the case of railroads the old policy of a heavy funded debt was inherited from industrial capitalists in many instances and not always remedied. In the long run far more serious than this charge of over-capitalization is the inability of financial capitalists (or of kings and presidents) to find able lieutenants—business administrators to manage factories, stores, and steamship lines. Good scholars, good preachers, good artisans, and good farmers are as sands on the seashore as compared with good administrators. These must have energy, rationality, judgment concerning events, insight into character, and tenacity—a combination that the human race is not very prolific in producing. As the units of business have grown in size, the problem of management obviously has become more difficult and more serious for financial capitalists. Apprenticeship to business, legal training, engineering, and now school of business training have been doing their best, but the volume of first-rate administrators remains distressingly small.

I cannot help feeling that the separation of policy and management—the policy-formulation by financial capitalists and the actual management by salaried executives—is in some cases dangerous. Business policy is not really capable of very generalized formulation. Much of it arises out of actual management and much of it should be formulated by the heads of the units. Well, you say, let Wall Street give the executives of factories, stores, public utilities, and railroads a good deal of latitude. In most instances, that is already done and yet the subtle dependence, such as we see in political administration to a much higher degree, enters in to sap the best efforts of the average executive, actually operating on the firing line of business.

The financial capitalists have helped many individual firms survive the downward secular trends, but they are powerless (1) to help those industries, like railroads, that have to face unfavorable technological and tax situations, and (2) to prevent the recurrence of secular trends. The answer is probably that it is better not to try to do either, but in the meantime financial capitalists find their citadel stormed by enemies.

The vanity of power and preference for bigness stick out all over many financial capitalists. The same weakness that the general, the bishop, the college president, and the head of an academy shows is found in the financial capitalist. The leader habitually comes to think himself a great man. At this point some of the highest attributes of greatness that may linger on fly out of the windows of the soul and leave the hollow mockery of a man.

By circumstance, financial capitalists have constituted the general staff of private business and this private business group includes directly very little agriculture. The farmer has not seemed a good risk or at least far behind industry, transportation, and merchandising. Out of this neglect of agriculture comes opposition to financial capitalism not only of a whole class of farmers but of whole regions in which agriculture sets the standards of thought and especially emotion.

If financial capitalists have made farmers their enemies through neglect, they have made others enemies through positive action. Executives have had to be killed off because they could not deliver the goods. Labor has had to be given a lower rate of pay so that it could be given work to do and an income. It does not matter that this is the most helpful service that can be done to the workman and his family: workers themselves and especially their leaders are obsessed with the rate of pay to the neglect of the real annual income that under existing circumstances is available. Of course, I recognize that this subject has two sides and requires more extensive treatment than can be given here.

Financial capitalists are in an exposed position in so far as they have great economic power, and in so far as they are few in number. The public is ignorant of the main purposes of financial capitalism and of its real service to society. Industrial capitalists surviving here and there are hostile to the money power. National capitalists—politicians and social reconstructionists—

see in the financial capitalists their chief rivals to economic power.

No one knows what the fate of financial capitalism really is. The system has played a great part in Germany and the United States. It has maintained a foothold in France and in Great Britain chiefly in foreign trade. It is a plausible view that, when the existing national capitalistic effort has made sufficient mistakes, financial capitalism will have an opportunity to function, at least once again in a more restricted area than before. This may coincide with the beginning of the next secular trend which will be upward and possibly will come in the early 1950's.

In the meantime let us consider a constructive policy for financial capitalism in America.

1. Let financial capitalists coöperate with the federal government in monetary and credit affairs in prosperity and in depression.
2. Meet the developing regionalism in the United States by furthering the decentralization of financial capitalism in Federal Reserve cities somewhat after the pattern of the Federal Reserve System. The industrialist Hugo Stinnes made such an attempt in Germany but his methods were too autocratic.
3. Aid promising consumers' and producers' coöperatives, if they do not threaten socially desirable private business units already provided for.
4. Work with trade unions that have leaders who will develop responsibilities along with power.
5. Form a semi-public institute for the control of the business practices of the members and for the widespread dissemination of information about past and current business that would be useful to all leaders and to some of the general public. Let this institute discipline its own members for the infraction of its own rules. In the formation of such an institute, attention should be given to Lloyd's of London which is made up, however, of underwriters of insurance rather than of securities.
6. Demand that the young incoming financial capitalists be vocal and not just strong silent men, for it is hard to make even widespread knowledge and known truth prevail in a democracy.

7. Let financial capitalists rejoice in the name "financial capitalist" and develop a little courage in the face of their fellow citizens; let them present themselves to investors and clients with the same openness that commercial bankers require from their borrowers.

8. In working out all policies, remember the human aspect of business in order that current social and economic gains may not be wiped out by political reactions.

9. Develop and declare policies concerning farmers, workmen, management, financing, speculators, and investors.

10. Let the investment banker make clear what his position is, for instance, that he floats the security of a certain firm, stands by or with the firm, has a partner on the board of the borrowing firm or acts as a trustee for its securities, and that he regards the industry in question as one of his special fields of operation. As an investor, I should like to know that Morgan, Stanley and Company stood behind (of course without guarantee) this railroad, Lehman Brothers that chain of stores, and so on. In making more secure the task of investment, the banker would perform a much greater real service to society than the politician or the social worker can ever perform.

11. Let investors form State and national associations to fight for the interests of security holders as against workmen, politicians, and business management.

Chapter VII

NATIONAL CAPITALISM

Political Instead of Financial Control of Private Capital

Power for government, security for its supporters;
Keep big business, encourage small.
Brook no rivals in financial control;
Socialization must come slowly and remain incomplete.
Reward producers according to their contribution.

1. MEANING OF NATIONAL CAPITALISM

In successive chapters, we have considered at length four species of capitalism under the headings of petty, mercantile, industrial, and financial. All of these belong to the genus of private business capitalism. There is one more example of private business capitalism, namely, national capitalism, which is indeed the subject of the present chapter. This new and growing system is exemplified by fascism, naziism, and the American New Deal. Differing from the first two in political methods, the third—the New Deal—has the same essential economic objective—the preservation of a core of private property in times that are difficult and in the face of the danger of losing all private property to the alternative system of communism.

Obviously we are confronted at this point with a new category—public capital—which at the risk of anticipating a later treatment of the subject, we may stop to consider briefly at this point. Public capital comes in to *supplement* private capital in the system of national capitalism, but it comes in to *supplant* private capital in the system of communistic capitalism. Of course, in this latter system capital also reigns supreme, though it is owned by the state and the proceeds of industry are designed to be shared among the people according to human needs.

In the interest of clarity, the whole set of ideas underlying the evolution of capitalism, as presented in this book, will be expressed in tabular form as an introduction to the subject of national capitalism. In this table we should note the duality of the *use* of capital and the *flow* of capital. Together, these constitute the reality of capitalistic effort that runs through the history of mankind.

Dualism in the Evolution of Capitalism

Use of capital (business administration)	Flow of capital (investment)

1. Pre-business capitalism
   a. Collectional economy
   b. Cultural nomadic economy
   c. Settled village economy
	1. Private capital
	   a. Usucapital

2. Private business capitalism
   a. Petty capitalism
   b. Mercantile capitalism
	b. Direct putting-out

	c. Indirect putting-out: passive
c. Industrial capitalism d. Financial capitalism	d. Indirect putting-out: active
e. National capitalism	2. Public capital: supplementing private capital
3. Public business capitalism Communistic capitalism	3. Public capital: supplanting private capital

National capitalism, as has been pointed out, is that form of capitalism in which the still dominant private business capital is *supplemented* by public business capital. Under this system capital and credit will be increasingly provided and directed into certain economic channels by the government. Some socialization is involved but it will probably be far from complete) and will not necessarily destroy the private business capitalism that remains.

One of the central parts of the national capitalistic system is the use by the national government of its power to command capital and credit so as to control private business according to its own policies. The system of national capitalism is in part designed to supplant *financial* capitalism. It rather naturally allies itself with petty capitalists and some industrial capitalists. So far as I know, the old-time mercantile capitalists have disappeared from the American scene and are therefore not available as allies of the new régime.

A fundamental purpose, an underlying drive, of national capitalism is to redress the weakness of financial capitalism. The demand for the new order comes from small business men, farmers, and permanent wage-earners (including some preachers and teachers), not from all of the members of each but from the rank and file.

The means whereby the main purpose is served is political action. The personnel in charge is threefold (a) politicians, (b) political and military administrators, and (c) civil and military servants. The first will determine policy and the others execute it. Thus, the dangerous cleavage of policy-formulators and managers, found in financial capitalism, will be continued and accentuated. The course of national capitalism is bound to be paved with bumps caused by contests between the two groups. The age-old problem will remain, namely, how to get the masses to do an honest and efficient day's work. It is open to question whether the new leaders can be more effective than mercantile, industrial, or financial capitalists. The probability is that they will ultimately use force and kill liberty.

There seem to be five principal parts to the introduction of national capitalism. First, there is the curbing of financial capitalists. The internationally minded financiers, including all

Jews in some lands, are to be shorn of their fleece. In America, laws were passed during the years 1933–35 to regulate commercial banks, investment banks, and the stock exchanges in the direction of less control by financial capitalists and less profitable speculation. Whether in doing all this reformers have impaired the liquidity of the capital market remains to be seen.

Second, the national government develops the tax power to the extent required to meet its needs and incidentally hits as hard a blow as may be at financial capitalism. So far does taxation go that it becomes confiscatory in the case of the very rich, and, in the case of people in high middle positions, enterprise is checked. There is a tendency to maintain only the old enterprises under a policy of high taxation. The politicians are partly conscious of this but are unable to avoid excesses.

Third, the national government uses its income and its credit (based chiefly on the activity of private business capitalists) to assist classes which the financial capitalists neglected or did not get around to help. These are principally the petty capitalists and the many industrial capitalists who did not attain financial strength. The small farmers would come under the head of petty capitalists and the large commercial agriculturists under the head of industrial capitalists.

Fourth, the national government tends to use its income and its credit to create work or to stimulate fresh production so as to employ men out of work. In this effort to look after the unemployed it develops a more discriminating attitude to workers, classifying them according to age, employability (health), and skill. There is a tendency to segregate the aged, infirm, and disabled for special and long-time treatment. The private capitalist finds himself taxed to support these various groups but still he knows that his own business, directly or indirectly, is helped by the fact that these groups have money to spend.

Fifth, the national government begins to socialize or hurries to make up for lost opportunities in this direction. In America, the public utilities have come in for early attention, not so much at the hands of local as of federal authorities. The provision of electricity from water power, which is to be sold to municipal plants or privately owned utilities, is already under way. The fact that many private utilities have left themselves open to charges of misuse of their opportunities and the fact that they have been allied with financial capitalism makes an early attack upon them logical and fairly easy. How far socialization—ownership or operation or both—of productive units will go is the question. It is likely to include railroads, coal mining, some insurance, and the manufacture of munitions.

One of the most significant instances of socialization occurred in Great Britain where in 1937 provision was made for a new régime in coal mining. This was done, mind you, by a Conservative government in the interest of several groups. The owners, between 4,000 and 5,000 persons and estates, were to be deprived of their rights to the coal or royalties therefrom. The owners were to be compensated, however, and, in view of the fact that this has been a sick industry, they may not fare badly. The operation of collieries is left in private hands but under government control. The government actually expects that uneconomical firms, especially small ones, will have to be forced to amalgamate. The present marketing arrangements will be continued for a period. Special consideration is to be given to domestic consumers of coal, and this may prove to be significant. The purposes of the action are to bring greater efficiency into the industry by closing submarginal mines, to gain strength in the export market of the world, and to provide better working conditions. The only aspects of the new policy which financial capitalists would not have adopted in the past are the regulation of the industry on behalf of the domestic users of coal and the turning aside to improve labor conditions in the mines.

In my opinion, national capitalism is very different from state socialism, of which there has been no clear example in history. To be sure, there have been local socialistic communities held together by religious bonds, but these are different from state socialism and have generally been temporary. In a régime of state socialism, the nation would own all the capital and the workers would share according to their contributions. If once established, state socialism would go one of two ways. Either it would accept a dictator and be made into national capitalism (as the only economically feasible way out) or it would go over into communistic capitalism. It is difficult to imagine that, in a democratic socialistic state, the workers (the only citizens) would long defer voting themselves what they want and thereby introduce communistic capitalism. At best, state socialism would be but a step to something else.

In Russia, communistic capitalism was established by Lenin in 1917. This was a system of sharing the income from the nation's productive capital according to the needs of the people. It was found, however, that, as hundreds have said and written, the workers would not work efficiently or honestly unless forced to do so by the danger of starving or at least by having to do without what they wanted. The system of Lenin (and Marx) was overturned by Stalin and a graduated reward established. This seems like the entering wedge to a shift to socialism or to national capitalism. The firing squad has been tried on men in lowly positions and in high places as a substitute for the rule "no work no pay" but even in Russia this method is drastic. One conception of the Russian situation is found in the following aphoristic stanza.

Let the state own and operate all essential industries;
Divide the gross income according to human needs.
The difficulty of business efficiency is heightened;
If you slip, you go over to national capitalism or to chaos.

We sometimes see three groups of nations listed as follows:

1. Democracies—Great Britain, United States, France, Belgium, Netherlands.
2. Fascist—Italy, Germany, Portugal, Japan, Brazil, Spain.
3. Communist—Russia, China, Mexico.

MEANING OF NATIONAL CAPITALISM 329

We might all raise the question whether the democracies, being each divided internally into two camps, will not soon split and go each into one of the two other groups—communist or fascist (national capitalist). The years that lie ahead may witness great shifts of position. Those nations now in number one group may switch to two, those in two to three and those in three to two. If so, group two is to be the winner, but, it is to be hoped and expected, much sobered and chastened.

We have put the United States down as a national capitalistic state and also now (1938) as a democracy. The apparent

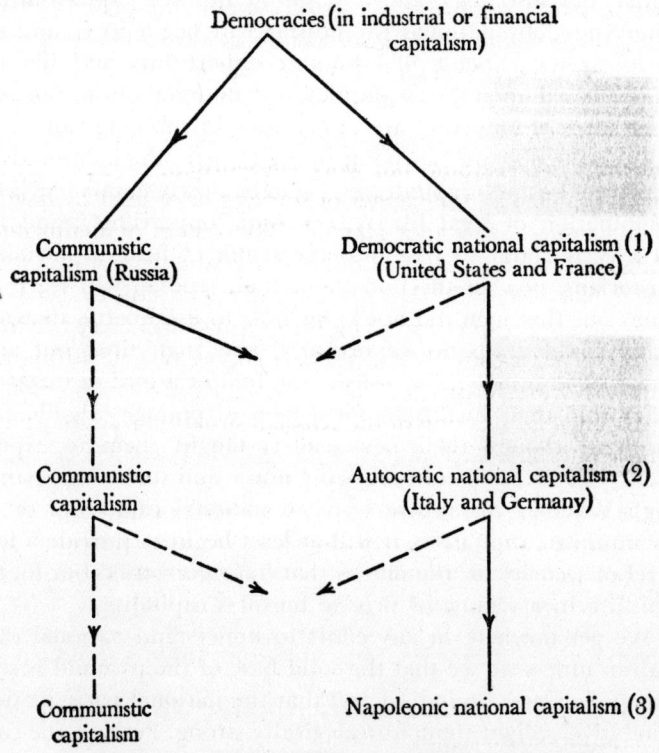

```
                Democracies (in industrial or financial
                              capitalism)
                    ↙                    ↘
      Communistic                    Democratic national capitalism (1)
      capitalism (Russia)            (United States and France)
           │                                    │
           ▼                                    ▼
      Communistic                    Autocratic national capitalism (2)
      capitalism                     (Italy and Germany)
           │                                    │
           ▼                                    ▼
      Communistic                    Napoleonic national capitalism (3)
      capitalism
```

RECENT POLITICAL AND ECONOMIC CHANGES
IN NATIONAL RÉGIMES

contradiction will be cleared up by the preceding diagram.

The outstanding questions for the present are whether the United States and France will step over into autocratic national capitalism, whether Russia will enter the same system completely, and whether the autocratic national capitalism will develop into a Napoleonic type which will engulf the world in war.

As we look back into history, we seem to see that pre-business capitalism provided security for the rank and file, that private business capitalism provided legal liberty, economic opportunity, but insecurity, and now public business capitalism (as adumbrated by national capitalism) will begin to restore security at the expense of economic opportunity and liberty. This is based upon the assumption that national capitalism and some form of autocracy are inseparable in the long run.

From the obscure viewpoint of the present, the halcyon days of private business capitalism *seem* to be slowly numbered. The combination of legal liberty, economic opportunity, and insecurity is about to pass into the realm of historic memory. Historians, now in the nursery of their studies, will learn to point out that men did not know how to use liberty, that too many could grasp no opportunity, and that, tired out and afraid of insecurity, they sought the fold of a lord—a dictator. They sold their birthright for a mess of pottage (a gallon of gasolene) though their new leaders taught them to expect plenty, leisure, and culture (swing music and surrealistic painting). Whether the future leads to national capitalism or to communistic capitalism, it will at least begin to provide a low level of security for the masses that have been tried but found wanting in a régime of private business capitalism.

We get nowhere in any effort to understand national capitalism unless we see that the solid base of the pyramid is still private-business capitalism and that the national participation is relatively slight though strategically strong. Perhaps the conception may be indicated graphically.

From this diagram it is apparent that all historic forms of private business capitalism, except mercantile capitalism, survive to this day. From this diagram it should be clear that private business capitalism is the cow that still gives the milk out of which government butter and cheese are manufactured. It follows that government activity is still based upon private business administration. It is not at all clear, however, whether private business can flourish under government control of

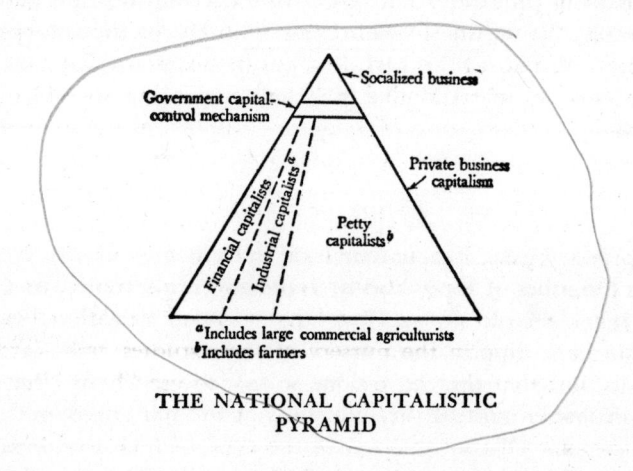

Socialized business
Government capital-control mechanism
Financial capitalists *a*
Industrial capitalists *a*
Petty capitalists *b*
Private business capitalism

a Includes large commercial agriculturists
b Includes farmers

THE NATIONAL CAPITALISTIC PYRAMID

capital and credit and the heavy drainage of private business income to support socialized or public production and the many growing consumers' benefits that can be paid for only out of taxes. One of three things must happen: civilization will go down into the dust of the past; or communistic capitalism will be tried as a desperate remedy; or business men will lead or support a revolt, which suffering humanity will follow, in the direction of autocratic national capitalism away from the democratic variety.

It is only fair to ourselves to note that there are different attitudes that we as students may take. Perhaps the following are the three most important. We may hold that the swing to national capitalism is a fundamental turn in the course of capitalism, in which there have been many turns in the past. Earlier changes were revolutionary also and caused much perturbation. Or, we may hold that national capitalism, as is said of fascism, is the last stand of "capitalism." This is the wishful thought of many theorists. Again, we may believe that recent developments (1922–1932–present) reflect merely temporary and passing conditions that prevail in a secular downtrend in business. This again is wishful thinking, but of the conservative not the radical thinkers. Perhaps in the pages that follow there is some material that will help us in making up our minds.

2. EARLY ADUMBRATION OF NATIONAL CAPITALISM

No big system like national capitalism rises wholly fresh from the ashes of the past. In rebuilding themselves, cities use and re-use the old stones. How far the leaders of national capitalism have dipped down into the chest of old records is unknown, but that they have done so to some extent is clear to me. Probably most of the influences of the past, however, are unconscious. Of course, many of the events which we liken to the outgoing of financial capitalism and the incoming of national capitalism are mere sequences which have not yet been discovered by scholars and therefore could have little or no influence upon leaders.

There is ample precedent for the hostility of one capital system to another. Petty capitalism fought hard in mediaeval towns to prevent submergence in the slowly developing mercantile capitalism. Mercantile capitalism in turn struggled, though less manfully, against the incoming industrial capitalism. And, finally, industrial capitalism had to bow before financial capitalism, which like every new system had something constructive to offer. What is new now is not just a change in private business capitalism but a change from business control to political control. Politicians take the place of financiers in the formulation of business policy and political administrators take the place of business executives in the management of those industries and firms that are socialized.

Relief of the poor, the distressed, and the "forgotten" (the cruelest and truest epithet ever hurled at men out of slavery) has been a charge upon society from ancient days. At the time of the Caesars it was bread and circuses that had to be provided. In the Middle Ages the rich towns and gilds provided grain at low prices and pageants and miracle plays without cost. In the sixteenth century, when the old private means of relief by monasteries, gilds, and so on were breaking down, city magistrates on the Continent and the government in England, learning from the experience of those cities, undertook to give to the poor a measure of relief on a subsistence basis. The first choice was to force the able-bodied to work or go off to the colonies (in the seventeenth century) but, barring that, such relief as was necessary was provided out of taxes. During the whole early modern period there was a tendency to emphasize alternately indoor and then outdoor relief, but the relief was there. Under Lloyd George, in the twentieth century, relief on an outdoor basis was put on a higher level, at least so far as the feeling of the poor was concerned. But still in England there is a stubborn refusal to mix relief for the unemployed and the restoration of business prosperity.

Germany undertook in the 1880's a scheme of social insurance, under the leadership of Bismarck, that was designed at once to help the poor and to stave off a movement toward socialism. The system grew until an intricate network of dependence upon the state was created that is a source of weakness and of strength.

In America relief has been on a subsistence basis by private, municipal, and State organizations. Some business firms have had funds to help relieve unemployment, but their inadequacy became apparent in the period 1929-33. Free land had helped a few well-to-do artisans and a great many farmers in the East who had been on the edge of bankruptcy or distress. In the present century this source has dried up, at least on a frontier basis, but not on a basis of scattered subsistence farms in almost every State.

The imposition of taxes, even heavy taxes on the well-to-do, is an ancient and necessary device. We all have had to learn "to pay unto Caesar" so that Caesar might buy support for his political and military schemes. The Industrial Revolution helped to bear this burden, but thereafter the standard of public benefits and relief rose so high that the tax burden overtook capacity to pay. In addition, we have the mingling on a dangerous basis of two practices—one taxation for the support of the government and the other taxation for social reform. The old dictum that taxes should be levied in accordance with ability to pay has become confiscation. In the Middle Ages the Jewish pawnbroker was periodically fleeced; now all rich are regarded as sheep to be shorn. When they resist, they are called tax-dodgers by those who dodge taxes through their political influence on election day.

In America, government has been a ruthless thief of private fortunes. It dispossessed the Loyalists after the Revolution. It freed the negro slaves during the Civil War and without compensation to the owners. It robbed the brewer and the distiller during the period of prohibition. It took the gold of citizens in 1933 and 1934 without their consent and at less than the new market price. Now, it is said to be running down public utilities privately owned to a point of serious impairment of the rights of stockholders. Of course the government (Republican and Democratic) has just been doing what private business was doing to competitors under industrial capitalism. And, in all our cities and in some of our towns, men are being held up and robbed or are being forced to pay tribute to gangsters and racketeers. To the cynic it seems amusing that a government which robs on a wholesale basis should be so jealous of little fellows carrying on a retail trade in "thine and mine." At times this interference has been in the direction of

EARLY ADUMBRATION OF THE SYSTEM 335

assistance to consumers and debtors and at times in the direction of protection or encouragement of small masters (including farmers). In the Middle Ages town laws tried to give advantages to small master artisans. In the seventeenth century Colbert tried to revive their early position of dominance in manufacture by assisting their gilds on a national basis. In the United States aid has been given to farmers in the form of free lands and protection in the holding of their property even against the just claims of creditors.

The governments of nations have been ready to help some business men against others in the interest of the nations concerned. Charters of liberties and privileges have been given to foreign groups of traders and to domestic groups. Patents of monopoly have been given to traders, manufacturers, and politicians primarily for their own advantage and secondarily for the public good. Bounties and subsidies have been given to farmers, ship-operators, and railroad companies. The governments of the past have bravely stepped in, why should not ours, following the same tradition?

National capitalists go back to the protectionists and even the mercantilists for their methods and their emphasis on nationalism. What a composite national capitalism, for example the American New Deal, appears to be—a bit of Jefferson's emphasis on the small producer, especially the farmer, a fair amount of Jackson's opposition to chartered banks, a lot of the nationalism of Alexander Hamilton and Tench Coxe, and a heap of the sentimental regard of the ward politician for the poor and the unfit.

Governments have had some small influence upon business through the use of capital and credit. They have purchased shares in early trading companies since the sixteenth century. England and France bought large blocks of shares in the Suez Canal and England a large holding in the Anglo-Persian Oil Company. The early American States owned shares in banks, canal companies, and railroads. The federal government received a handsome return from its holding of stock in the first

Bank of the United States. The Reconstruction Finance Corporation, established by a Republican administration in 1932, bought its way into many American banks, largely through preferred stock ownership. The same Corporation has been active in other directions and undoubtedly has played a brilliant part in holding up weak firms.

Such items of adumbration of national capitalism suffer from their sporadic and occasional nature. There is one example that puts much together and stands on a hill as if to say "here is what national capitalism can do when the time is ripe." I refer to the System of John Law, in effect in France 1716–20. The Scottish adventurer Law, who had robbed men of their money at gambling and matrons of their virtue, came to France with a constructive plan for the restoration of prosperity through a commercial bank. At first privately owned, the bank later became public property. At first passive in its administration, it became active in its reaching out to control business thereby anticipating financial or national capitalism by about two centuries. The chief means of influencing business was through a great trading company which ultimately came to have a monopoly of all French colonial commerce, and a monopoly of the minting of coins and collecting of certain taxes at home. In the best manner of Wall Street, the price of the shares of this company was boosted and then maintained. A boom was engineered and trade was increased. Expectations ran high in Paris, London, and Amsterdam. The bubble broke and politicians supporting Law were left worse off than before, as was France also. Some business men had been left outside of the System, however, and were available to carry on, as before the experiment. Only shrewd speculators gained, unless *we* in our day remember the example and profit by it. When the System was slipping, the same political power was used to bolster up the edifice as had been used to build it up. Even the might of a Bourbon, however, could not hold up the System of a controlling bank and a monopolistic trading company, the value of whose stock was inflated far beyond the expectation of reasonable and customary returns. There can be little doubt that under national capitalism there will be many such crashes as was adumbrated by the fall of Law's System.

3. FORCES MAKING FOR NATIONAL CAPITALISM

The new régime of national capitalism was not acceptable in Law's time. Mercantile capitalism had laid no foundation on which it could be permanently built. Like Roger Bacon and John Wycliffe, John Law was ahead of his time. Industrial capitalism and financial capitalism were to lay the kind of base on which national capitalism could build. If anyone who reads this statement does not understand it, let him read or reread Chapters V and VI above.

It was dissatisfaction with such industrial capitalists as lingered on but primarily with the system of financial capitalism in control of general business, that brought about the demand for the changes that national capitalism introduced. Let us make no mistake. The unfortunate results of our economic system were there. I do not blame the leaders any more than the rank and file who got winded in the race and could not keep up. The fact is that whole groups were in distress. The middle class—the petty capitalists—could not keep out of debt whether in the town or the country. The permanent working class was distressed in depressions and in old age.

Thinkers who carry off to their study room the things they see, hear, and read about, now enter the picture. They see the evils and concoct the remedies. Commonly they have the weakness of their strength: they provide logical remedies which fit beautifully into their own thinking or wishing. The greatest of these in modern times was Karl Marx. He offered scientific socialism—an unplanned growth of business into ever larger units, a competition that would leave but a few big firms, and an opportunity for socialization that a democratic state could easily grasp. The financial capitalists checked this development but encountered difficulties of their own in the downtrend beginning in 1920.

Publicists and teachers, not always thinking for themselves, took up the plausible views of Marx and others. Agitators, commonly not themselves good workmen, championed the theories they heard about, with the idea of improving the race and benefiting their own positions. And so the thoughts of dimly lighted studies went flickering on into the groping world.

Next came the politicians. When men cannot earn a living otherwise, they often turn to politics. The politicians heard the cry of the agitators, heard the lessons of the teachers, read the columns of journalists, and wondered about the thoughts of the original social philosophers. It is part of their duty to listen to pleas of their followers and, if they seek reëlection, to yield themselves to what is expected of them.

Historically it is the clergy that have the honor of knocking first at the door of government for benefits and exemptions. The business men came next as a class. And now, in our day, the workers arrive in serried ranks for justice to themselves. Petty capitalists march aloof but in parallel formation.

There was no *great* danger to the nation in the demands of special groups so long as those groups remained small. When the franchise was opened to the lower middle class and to the proletariat, then there was danger that these classes would ask for more than the nation could afford.

When to middle class democracy was added proletarian democracy, then government itself was threatened. The new voters, notably in American States and municipalities, sold their votes to the highest bidder—the one who offered most. Indeed, the political ideal came to be and still is to sell the vote to only one side. The favorable aspect to all this was that the poor and needy at last had champions who offered them something this side of heaven. The bad side is that these champions could encourage the electors to expect too much—to kill the goose that lays the welcome eggs. As usual, politicians listened to the demands for relief of the workers and of petty capitalists. They knew the theories of social philosophers and others. They arrived at a solution which was a compromise—national capitalism. This system, as has been said, keeps private business capital as the base of the pyramid, while it puts government at the top. Financial capitalists are dissatisfied. Social philosophers of extremist views are infuriated when they find their logical straight lines diverted by practical considerations. It seems that The Day of scientific socialism, already postponed by financial capitalism, is to be further delayed by national capitalism.

4. FASCISM

The earliest rounded experiment in national capitalism was begun in Italy in 1922. The start was made in Italy because that country was the first capitalist state to feel the pinch of the secular downtrend in business following the World War. Fascism is the system of a small group of determined persons who take the fasces (bundle of rods surrounding an axe) as their emblem. These fascists would save Italy from the evils of a class war in which socialists, communists, and anarchists constituted the more active part.

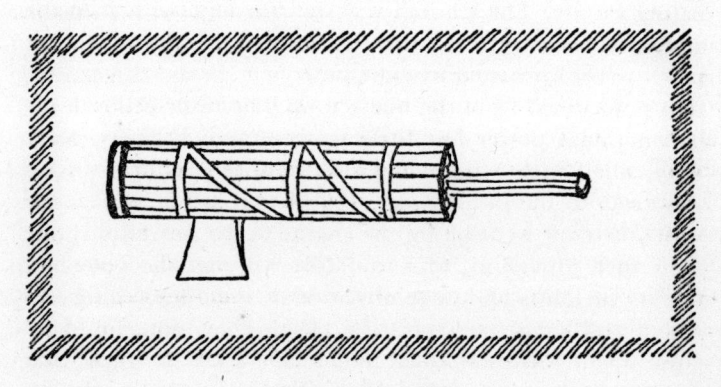

ITALIAN FASCES

Italy was born in a formal way only in 1870. It remained, however, a group of provinces, the leaders of which were trying to create a nation but without great success. The people were backward in education and sanitation. Sicily was infected with brigands. The government railroads were unsafe for baggage unless watched. The industries were dependent upon foreign firms for coal, iron, and capital. Industrial capitalism was making headway in the North, but elsewhere petty capitalism prevailed. Through certain German banking syndicates, capital and capitalistic control was making headway but slowly.

When the World War broke out, Italy deserted its allies Germany and Austria to join the side which was thought to be the winner. Italy fought half heartedly and at least on certain occasions distinguished itself by rapid flight. This was a repetition of centuries of experience. Why should Italians not return as rapidly as possible to their sunny skies and leave wars to those who wanted them? This was more rational than the rest of the world, but it did not make for prestige. How much of the inability of the government to drive forward towards the enemy was due to communists and other such in the ranks is not clear.

The inglorious war was followed by a dangerous peace. The king was an amateur archeologist. The parliament was a debating society. The Church was shot through with formalism and agnosticism. The nobility, landowners, and industrial capitalists were threatened by extreme policies of social reconstruction proclaimed from the house tops. The trade union leaders had nominal power but little sense of responsibility. Strikes were called with a frequency that showed how little thought was given to the public weal. Trains were left in the country, while the crew went off on the engine to the nearest station.

In 1922 Mussolini, who would be a leader—first of revolutionary socialists and later of national capitalists, marched on Rome and soon overthrew the existing government. A new government was established and a new political organization was planned—the so-called corporate state. The government was to be made up of a monarch or nominal head, a dictator who was the leader of the dominant party, a Grand Council composed of leaders of that party, and a lower house made up of representatives of thirteen national gilds. These representatives were imposed upon the gilds by fascist leaders. There was no place for numerous political parties, for trade unions, or for free and open discussion of the new régime. After long preparation, this constitution was put into full effect in 1938.

The dominant party was Mussolini's Black Shirts or Fascists. These Fascists are a triumphant group of men who willed themselves into power. Their symbol is the ancient Roman fasces, the instrument carried by the lictor as a mark of the authority of the magistrate and a sign of punishment to be meted out to the obstreperous. The Fascist party is supported by the rich propertied classes, the petty capitalists, professional classes, and many workmen who have become tired of their leaders and the overhanging anarchy. The spirit of the party is to create a strong Italy based on a will to power, high birth rate, and private business capitalism. The business man is encouraged by the Fascists to earn profits so that the state may have a large share in the form of taxes.

During the period 1922-35 fascism had a great deal of success. It was conciliatory to the Church, left the Jews alone, and injured the feelings of only insignificant foreign powers. It embarked upon constructive programs in sanitation, agriculture, industry, hydro-electric power, and military preparations.

During the period from 1935 to the present, however, there have been signs of action that is largely destructive. The conquest of Ethiopia was costly and inglorious. The conquered territory is so far a doubtful asset. In 1936 the Spanish War was begun at the suggestion or at least with the support of Mussolini. The expulsion of Jews entering Italy since 1918 was decreed in 1938.

Fascism has elements of strength. It has established a kind of unity in Italy hitherto lacking. It has created an enthusiasm which has made the Italian people forget their economic distress. It has put an end to strikes and inculcated a high degree of morality among the petty capitalists. It has learned to produce more wheat, develop water power, get control of some oil supplies, and manufacture motor cars and airplanes that are efficient. It has encouraged industrial capitalists to produce and to profit.

On the other hand, there is unmistakable evidence of slowly creeping financial weakness. Italy remains poor in capital, deficient in large fortunes, and without a reserve of gold. A nation lacking raw materials is being urged to increase the birth rate beyond the point of subsistence, the idea being that the surplus persons will migrate to the colonies of Libya and Ethiopia. Moreover, the meager resources of the country have gone into the preparation for war and left the people suffering both economically and politically. The professional class has been injured by the pressure put upon freedom of thought and expression.

For many years foreign prophets have looked over the borders for signs of bankruptcy. There are signs but the symptoms are not yet pronounced. This means that the day of reckoning will be all the more severe when it finally comes. The workers have been kept at home and not allowed to migrate to foreign lands but have been put on expensive tasks of draining swamps to produce wheat at a time when wheat is selling for almost less than it costs the American farmer to produce it. Many of the workers have been used, not in a socially useful fashion but by way of preparing for a war which may never come. Late in 1938, an Italian fascist editor concocted this amazing mixture: "Italy—the agrarian, proletarian, pacific, industrious, and legionary state—is uncrushable."

Italy has solved many of her problems that were severe under a régime of industrial capitalism and under the influence of foreign capitalists. But, for every problem solved, a fresh problem has been created. The politician is doing his best in Italy not through catering to the people's needs but by imposing on the people what he thinks the people should have. For a final

5. NAZIISM

The German pattern of fascism is naziism. As in Italy so in Germany, the movement and the régime are called after the dominant party—the NAtional-SoZIalisten. The symbol is the cross-like swastika which may indicate that people are on

NAZI SWASTIKA

the run, especially foreign enemies and domestic Jews. The economic counterpart of the political naziism is national capitalism. Private business capitalism is at the base of the German national pyramid.

Naziism rose out of German experience. The German Empire was newly formed in 1871 out of old and stable local States. It had a spectacular climb upward during the period 1871-1914 both economically and culturally. On the economic side, Germany developed very rapidly a financial capitalism that was the wonder of all who had eyes to behold it. With little investment capital, Germany reached out for world markets and world power. By combining its five great joint stock banks into consortia, centering in the Imperial Bank, German business men were able to promote manufacture, mining, and transportation at home, and trade and shipping in all foreign lands. Using French capital, German banks helped finance local French industry at a profit to themselves. Using a little Italian capital, secured by control through slight ownership of well-placed securities, German firms could control not a little of Italian trade. Using English capital and credit, German business men competed with Englishmen in the four quarters of the world.

Success came to Germans but went to their heads. It is the curse of fate that Germans should keep rising only to fall again. There have been over 1,500 years of such experience. Germans have rolled back the Latins, only to be pushed back in turn. And so with the Slavs. Wealth comes only to be lost. The World War undid all and more than had been built up in a generation.

From 1914 to 1923 Germany labored under the stress first of war and then of currency depreciation. It is difficult to decide which was the harder to bear. In the era of depreciation certain business men, notably Hugo Stinnes, got titles to properties which they later paid for in depreciated currency. In so far as the Jews did this, they were laying up trouble for themselves.

From 1923 to 1933 Germany tried to keep an even keel under circumstances of national exhaustion and national humiliation. The prosperity of 1924–29, based on borrowing, was followed by depression and unemployment. Liberalism was a fine but disgustingly impotent system. Near at hand, smoldered the fires of communism ready to break out when the time was fully ripe.

In 1933 Germany, like other countries, was in the depth of the depression and ready for any plausible change in government. The question was whether it should be toward communism or fascism. Hitler helped Germany to decide in favor of the latter. Then, in one blast after another, Hitler bid defiance to the enemies of Germany, dispossessed the Jews of office and business, rejected the Treaty of Versailles, and withdrew from the League of Nations. He was in favor of dividing up large estates for the use of small farmers but he has never done this, at least not on any large scale. He at once gave attention to increasing employment, whether privately or on public works. What remained of the control of financial capitalists was overthrown in favor of control through his own government. Business men were encouraged to make profits so that he might increase the taxes on their enterprise. Foreign trade and monetary exchange were tightly controlled in order to maintain a balance of trade and in order to import the chief necessities of German life, especially war materials.

Naziism was not born in the momentous year of its struggle to power 1932–33. For over ten years it had been in the process of formulation by Hitler and several others. In 1920 and 1922 it drew up a platform and in 1923 attempted to seize power. It was the deep depression and widespread unemployment of the period 1929–33, however, that held the ladder for the Nazi leaders. The party of the Social Democrats, that had been slowly growing in strength, was supplanted by the party of National Socialists. In both cases the term "Social" or "Socialist" means little more than "National Progressive" means in America. Both Social Democratic and Nazi parties were supported by the lower middle class of entrepreneurs, professional groups, and artisans. We might assimilate them to the petty capitalists whose régime had long since had its day; but, whereas the Social Democrats leaned heavily on industrial workers, the National Socialists drew much of their power from the lower middle class that had been dispossessed of property and self-respect during the inflation period following the War. Also, whereas the Social Democrats were democratic in politics, the National Socialists were autocratic.

Under Naziism German courage and self-respect were restored. All men were employed. Strikes and threats of communism ceased. Party strife ended because there was only one party recognized. Private business was told to go ahead and that it would receive every assistance. Farmers were encouraged and home-making and home life were glorified.

Weakness soon developed. Germany was still Germany—poor in raw materials and in native investment capital. The depletion of the War and the post-War period was accentuated by non-productive enterprises, civil and military. The gold reserve was dangerously small. Jews were deprived of their high posts in public life and in the professions and in many instances, especially in the case of large storekeepers, found that their ordinary business had to be abandoned. Beginning in 1939 Jews were to be excluded from retail, handicraft, and other businesses. When Jews were mistreated, many Germans, especially debtors, felt that their cause was winning. As the Jews were dispossessed and in many cases forced to emigrate, they were compelled to leave some or all of their capital behind them. The theory was that Germany would lose nothing if it kept the capital, forgetting, as did the peoples of the Middle Ages, that ability to create capital is more important than the capital itself in the long run. Taking but one specific example of the situation created by the exodus of Jews, we can say that liquidity on the Berlin stock market has been impaired by the loss of Jewish speculators and Jewish brokers.

The dearth of foreign raw materials, such as non-ferrous metals, petroleum, cotton, and rubber continued. The experiments with substitutes were expensive and sometimes failures as in the case of Vistra, which was designed to take the place of cotton. Business was really much hampered by being turned aside to prepare war materials and by restrictions on foreign exchange and foreign imports. It was further hampered by the call of so many men to the colors. High taxes increased the costs of production and checked sales abroad. Corporations were forced to invest all or part of their surpluses in government bonds rather than build up reserves or improve equipment. Almost every business man, in fact every citizen, has something to be thankful for in Germany and also something to complain about. Here we see a danger in national capitalism in so far as a double-headed opposition to the government may arise partly economic and partly political.

We may summarize a few results of the Nazi régime as follows:

1. The petty and industrial capitalists are anchored.
2. Financial capitalists (especially Jews) are excluded.
3. Farmers are helped though regimented.
4. Costs (except taxes) are kept low.
5. Freedom of entrepreneurs yields to control by politicians.
6. Labor is honored but held bound.
7. Labor receives benefits but lower real wages.
8. Plenty is sacrificed to power.
9. Final day of financial reckoning is postponed in preparation for war.

In the case of Germany as of Italy we might find much to admire and little to complain of, if there were not the military preparations to support. It may be doubted whether either of these countries provides a normal example of the course of national capitalism. Or, perhaps war really is a normal part of a national capitalistic régime. Certainly both Germany and Italy have done battle for their policy of anti-communism in Spain. Cynics say that they were really trying out their new military equipment there—airplanes, guns, and tanks.

National capitalism is a phase or aspect of nationalism. In Germany this has become even more irrational than it is in most countries. Perhaps this is prophetic of the future everywhere. From one, learn all. From the example of Germany learn what will everywhere happen under national capitalism. The antagonism to Jews, a policy to bring about favorable psychological and economic results, has led to the creation of a doctrine of racial purity—the theory of the Nordics. Emphasis on this leads to a self-righteous attitude to all that the kingdom of the Nordics stands for. This in turn leads to a belief that all non-Nordics are enemies and are plotting war against the one nation of pure bloods. In the long run this means periodic war. Now, to a certain extent, war is a function of competitive private business capitalism. To a much greater extent war might become a function of national capitalism. Or, on second thought, should we really associate this aggressiveness and childish worship of the national ego with the early growth of the system of national capitalism? We must wait for the answer.

6. THE AMERICAN NEW DEAL

The tradition is that America gives to the poor man a new deal. This has really never been the case. What America has done to immigrants and natives is to give them a chance to become entrepreneurs first as petty capitalists and then as industrial or financial capitalists but only on condition that they work hard, plan carefully, save, and reinvest. Those who will not play such a game become permanent workers, enter politics, become reformers, and so on. But now, beginning in the depths of a business depression, the common man, the forgotten man, is really to get a new deal. How full history is of such efforts! The same type of ambitious leaders arise and the same longing and pitiful souls reach out for something they cannot grasp. The god of things funny and pathetic must be a cynic.

The New Deal has this one big circumstance in common with fascism and naziism: there is a great unemployment problem which, unless solved, may lead to communistic capitalism. It also has a group of professional classes, the least efficient members of which are not receiving what they think should be their reward. But America has one problem of its own—a large group of producers of raw materials who were loaded with debt and then found themselves with an income reduced through the fall in the price levels of the world market. In all your thinking, keep in mind these three potentially revolutionary classes: permanent workmen, professional classes, and small farmers. The inefficient in each group are the first to suffer and the last to pick up when depression ceases. Society just does not appreciate them at their own valuation of themselves and will not come to their rescue except under compulsion.

If this were a history of the New Deal rather than a sketch of a few essentials, we should go back to the Interstate Commerce Act of 1887 or beyond. We should note especially the beginning that Wilson made with his New Freedom. We should not fail to note that the Republicans created the Federal (Rural) Intermediate Credit System in 1923 and the Reconstruction Finance Corporation in 1932. Two points stand out in thus briefly skipping over events. One is that the World War stopped reform and retribution in 1917 and another war may do the same once again. The other is that both of the old political parties have taken steps in the direction of national capitalism.

We may attempt a brief and partial statement of the working of the New Deal. In March, 1933, when Roosevelt became president, all intelligent citizens held their breath but rather felt that there would be no recurrence of the depression. It is still an open question whether such was the case. Undoubtedly, Roosevelt could have seized full dictatorial power, if he had had the will. It is a thought that some have indulged in that he missed his opportunity. At any rate, there soon came a series of actions that reversed the experiences and views of American business men, high and low, and violated all classical economic theory. For the various new deals, read the federal laws and regulations for the period beginning in 1933.

Much of the gist of the New Deal can be dealt with under six headings, namely, what was done for

1. Big business units in trouble,
2. Small business men, farmers, and home-owners,

3. Professional men,
4. Permanent workmen,
5. Medium-sized and large business units in sound condition,
6. Investment capitalists.

Big business units in trouble are exemplified by the railroads, metropolitan banks, and a few industrial concerns. Loans were made to these in one form or another on a fairly conservative basis. Assets were required as collateral but they were often such as a bank would not accept in normal business times. There can be no general criticism of the work that was done by the Reconstruction Finance Corporation to meet immediate situations which threatened to spread disaster. This same Corporation, however, is beginning to go beyond its original scope: it is beginning to go from a passive to an active attitude, in other words, to develop control, just as the financial capitalists found they had to do in order to attain their major purpose of restoring health and strength. When this governmental agency goes so far as to tell commercial banks where to lend, it is taking a step that may lead far. Already, it has insured specific loans made by banks. For instance, in one case a bank loaned at 2 per cent, and the R.F.C. charged ½ of one per cent for insuring the loan. This is in line with the work of the Federal Deposit Insurance Corporation which insures deposits up to $5,000 in those banks which come into the scheme. In all this work of the government in using its credit on behalf of big business and banks, we can discern a preference for aiding industrial capitalists and not financial capitalists.

The heart of the New Deal beats most lively on behalf of the second class. Here lay the core of the New Freedom of Wilson. Here is an effort to revive petty capitalism. Here is a resurrection of official Catholic economic policy that has existed for over a millennium. Here is the deeply imbedded political aspect of national capitalism, for in this group of small business men, farmers, and home-owners, lies the chief support that may be counted on in a civil or a foreign war. This group votes and fights.

The second group—petty capitalists—found itself in bad shape when values were tumbling during the period 1929-33. It held on grimly but was ready for drastic action, when the New Deal sprang to the front to assume leadership. The National Recovery Administration was designed to help business, perhaps small business, but proved to be unconstitutional, unwieldy, and un-American. With it disappeared in 1935 the symbol of the Blue Eagle, a possible emblem for the New Deal. A promising future organization for assisting the small business man is a Federal Intermediate Business Credit Bank.

AMERICAN BLUE EAGLE

The Agricultural Adjustment Administration of the New Deal aimed at aiding the farmer partly by raising prices through a process of limiting production. It, too, proved to be unconstitutional and had to be abandoned. The Federal Security Administration loans money to tenant farmers. The Home Owners Loan Corporation of 1933 was authorized to loan money to owners of homes which were mortgaged. In general, the dollars that were owed had been reduced in value and loans had to be made to help people meet their obligations. This looks much better than it is, because in many cases it has been impossible to meet even the new and reduced obligations. Often the holder of a title to property has no shred of claim to an equity on the basis of the prevailing price level. By 1938 the federal government owned about one-third of farm mortgages and nearly one-sixth of urban mortgages. During the next severe depression there may be a move to cancel part of this debt to the government.

It is a plausible view that the system which increases the tax burden put on petty capitalists (including professional classes), largely for the benefit of the lower grades of permanent wage-earners, tends to introduce fascism in America. It is a likely formula, based on German experience, that when sufficient farmers, artisans, storekeepers, and professional men have lost their property, they will be ready to follow a fascist leader who will help them regain it. Lovers of democracy may well pray for a speedy return of prosperity, perhaps even led by financial capitalists.

Professional men got jobs in Washington and elsewhere. Lawyers and teachers and others were given work or they were transferred from posts that were badly paid to others more remunerative. Just what will happen if their services are ever dispensed with on a large scale is an unpleasant thought. Certainly, they are being carried beyond the age of adjustment to new work.

For workmen there were sundry services. Young men with dependents were provided with a wage if they joined the Civilian Conservation Corps. In the various rural parts, where the units were located, they performed jobs often of the greatest value in forest preservation, flood-control, and the like. They constitute a semi-military organization that the chief executive could count on for some physical support. The Public Works Administration provides for permanent improvements that involve the use of labor and materials. The Works Progress Administration provides chiefly work that can be improvised and hurried to meet the needs of waiting men. A national insurance plan was provided for old age and against unemployment; although inadequate at present, the system probably will be remade in a satisfactory fashion. Trade unions were given encouragement to demand higher rates of pay and even a yearly wage. Higher rates were obtained in many cases but the greater resultant cost actually cut down employment. The net result was that workmen have been worse off than ever in many industries. A national minimum wage and maximum hour law on a regional basis was provided to curb sweatshop employment and the hiring of workers at a rate below subsistence. The result will probably be to exclude from all employment the unfit (submarginal worker) and to make the minimum wage the maximum.

Under the New Deal in America, as in France under Blum,

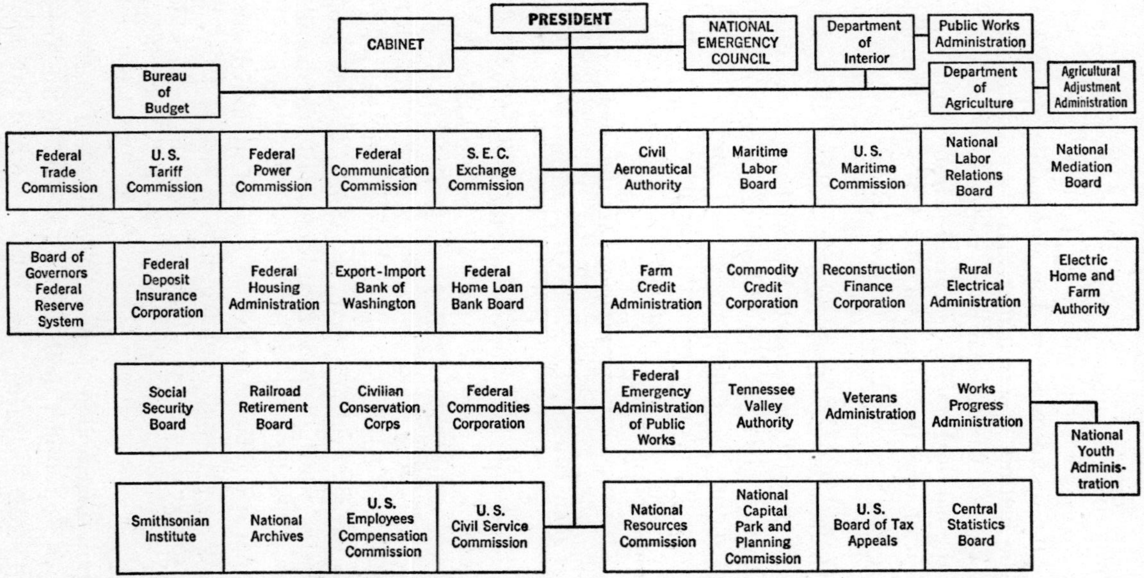

Based on a chart put out by the United States Information Service, September 1, 1938. Modifications have been introduced. The chart is obviously incomplete.

AMERICAN NATIONAL ADMINISTRATION

the sit-down strike flourished. It was not frowned upon by President Roosevelt nor put down by the Governor of Michigan where the sit-downs occurred in automobile plants. Many citizens who had not observed that strikes are a threat to the state now realized whence may come the power that may disintegrate the national state based upon private capitalism. In the election of 1938 the friends of sit-downs were repudiated and in 1939 the Supreme Court outlawed the sit-down in clear terms.

The fifth class, business firms in good standing, owing their strength to industrial capitalists of financial ability or to financial capitalists, is given the task of bearing a large part of the burden of aiding the other persons and corporations. For them there are high wages and strikes, high taxes, uncertainty of property rights (since the devaluation of the dollar), and the encouragement of radicalism at home and abroad. On the other hand, trade treaties and a higher purchasing power on the part of their customers are offered to them to use as best they can.

The investing capitalists—for instance, those who have retired from life's burdens or widows who have only stocks or bonds to live on—are being made to travel a rough and barren course. To be sure, the loss of business came in to check dividends before the New Deal began, but now it is high costs that prevent firms from paying dividends—that condition known as "profitless prosperity" which the New Deal is only mildly responsible for. The bondholder is worse off, for rates have been scaled down so that it is difficult to live on interest from high-grade bonds. This affects small capital-owners as well as large, for they have to take a lower rate of interest from the banks which hold their savings because the banks get less on the bonds they hold.

We obtain some notion of the relative situation of different classes when we consider their income position. In the American steel industry in 1937 the stockholders received only about one-sixth of the income that the employees received. The two groups are numerically about equal. In the case of a large number of American railroads, the contest for meager income is between bondholders and employees. In the case of a few railroads, the contest for the crumbs of income is between executives and workmen. Of course, in the case of railroads the determining factor is not simply the New Deal but also, in part, the downward secular trend in business and the easy prosperity of the new and rival forms of transportation. Clearly, the influence of the New Deal is to raise wages and taxes. Since much of the tax levy goes to help the workmen, the contest between the owners of property and the wage-earners is clear cut. It was the depression that brought class antagonism into American consciousness but it has been the New Deal politicians who have fanned the flames and thrown onto the fires the most inflammable materials.

There is much to be said for the New Deal, especially as a temporary measure. It has made the unfortunate feel that they have a friend—President F. D. Roosevelt—it matters little that he is personally ambitious and a spendthrift. The New Deal has put a check upon another extreme—the commercialization of the earlier period. It has erected an immediate bulwark against communistic capitalism. And, if carefully managed, it might provide a precedent and a mechanism for bridging the gaps in employment that occur from time to time. Some of its reforms, when toned down by administrators and modified by subsequent legislation, will prove of lasting value.

On the whole, the weaknesses of the New Deal have made a greater impression than the points of strength, especially if we think of the New Deal as a permanent régime. The New Deal tends to ever-increasing taxation and costs and therefore to inflation. It tends towards public financial bankruptcy on a private business basis (and therefore ultimately to communistic capitalism). It tends toward war, because in dire straits of unemployment it will create jobs for men by expanding the army and navy, and it may bring about a war in order to divert attention from a domestic difficulty. It endorses the mad consumptive habits of a section of the people instead of inculcating habits of thrift and careful management. It encourages the self-pity which has been the curse of the post-War age with its belly-aching songs and tales. The stoicism of the common man is being transmuted into a whining complaining attitude of defeat. The New Deal encourages cultural anarchy by helping individuals to do the work they are interested in rather than the work they are qualified for or the work that is in demand. In the long run, the New Deal would corrupt democracy and necessitate its abolition. It is the tammanyization of the people on a national basis. It tends to oust opponents as enemies and it seeks scapegoats for the misdeeds of others. In Germany and Italy the Jews have been the scapegoats and in America financial capitalists. The New Deal retards business progress by raising costs, creating hard feeling, and making property uncertain. Mistakes of economic policy are not corrected because of the political aspects, as was the case also in the mediaeval Church. Moreover, mistakes are magnified greatly by being made national. Politicians bid for votes by offering benefits to voters without regard to ultimate economic or social results. This is a substitute for private-business capitalism which requires efficiency and honesty and checks up periodically on the question whether this or that benefit can be afforded or justified by prevailing conditions.

Some critics have thought that they could sum up the New Deal by saying that it was strong in the heart and weak in the head, that its objectives were good but its methods bad, and that, in general, it was going in the wrong direction—toward endless consumption and destruction rather than work and production.

It may be that the final historical verdict that will be most unfavorable to the New Deal will be concerned with the effort to control world prices. So long as prices were going up, and then going down, the American president could have some apparent influence when he ordered them to rise and then to recede. But when they finally turned in the direction not desired, the policy of "do it we will" became a bit absurd. The beginning of wisdom of an administrator is to know the limitations of his own position. A prophet tried to make a mountain come to him, a king bade the tides to stay back, and a president willed the prices to move with his wand. But the mountain, the tides, and the prices submitted to no command except the laws of their own nature.

The first phase of the New Deal involved aid to the middle class. It had been adumbrated in Wilson's New Freedom and embodied in the changes of Roosevelt's first administration. The second is developing benefits for the workman. This is almost the special contribution of Roosevelt. It is not clear how far this will go or how genuine it is. There may be a third phase which will involve war and a resulting denouement.

There is an interesting point raised by the New Deal's treatment of the unemployed. In 1933 the issue was whether the British system of a virtual dole (all that was left of a national insurance system), on the one hand, or work provided at a rather low level of wages, on the other hand, should be adopted. Politicians stoutly bought votes by proclaiming the dignity of labor; work was to be provided and full citizenship (voting and jury service) retained by all recipients of public jobs and outdoor relief. The debasing elements of the British system were to be avoided! Many Americans who then thoughtlessly adhered to this view have since changed their minds, for now it appears that the worker is being taught habits of bad work or no work at all. Although some good results have come from his pick and shovel, many of the works of his untrained hands must be done over again. Without adequate supervision and without any special knowledge, many a workman has been taught simply how to lean on his hoe at the public expense.

In the endless elbowing of classes for social esteem, the American New Deal tends to produce a slight shift. Let us look at the matter broadly and also with special reference to the subject at hand.

Social Classes in Order of Popular Esteem

Ancient China	Ancient Egypt	Mediaeval Germany	United States (before 1929)	National Capitalism	Communistic Russia
Officials	Priests	Warriors	Business	Officials	Officials
Farmers	Warriors	Peasants	Professional	Professional	Professional
Artisans	Peasants	Business	Officials	Business	Workmen
Business	Business		Farmers	Farmers	Farmers
			Workmen	Workmen	

By "officials" is meant public officials, without any prejudice as to whether they are politicians or public administrators. In 1929–30 American business men lost courage and prestige. Public officials filled the vacancy caused by the collapse of their leadership. Where business men have stood high, there has been a broad spread of well-being. Professional men seem to occupy a place of considerable stability but not of dominance. They may hold a balance between private business men and public officials. Certainly fresh work has been created for accountants and lawyers.

It may be that we shall not step from national capitalism to communistic capitalism. There may be an escape from the third phase of national capitalism and its aftermath, by the establishment of a balanced national capitalistic system. This might involve a modified democracy. Only those who produced would share and only according to their contributions. Unemployment would be reduced by birth control—in one generation. All citizens would be educated to management in life and work rather than just in cultural and recreational enjoyment. We can hardly attain economic and political stability; perhaps we do not want it, for it means stagnation, but we may attain balance between nations young and old, rich people and poor, investors and business executives, able managers in work and infantile performers in life's various tasks, and finally between economic producers and cultural contributors.

7. THE SECULAR TREND IN BUSINESS AND THE GROWTH OF NATIONAL CAPITALISM

We recall that there is a theory of the secular trend of business: that business goes up about a quarter of a century and then down for a little longer period. Then the process is repeated. Some day the theory may be corroborated or restated. Just now it is at least interesting.

During the period of 1897–1920 business was prosperous, not with even pace but more or less continuously. The crises were financial and the ensuing depressions short and far from severe. Financial capitalism ruled the day. The politicians growled under both Theodore Roosevelt and Woodrow Wilson. The World War restored such prestige as business men had lost during the period 1912–17. After the War there was continued prosperity till 1920 when the change came. During this period of business prosperity all classes shared in the income, especially business men, farmers, and workmen. Much of the income was invested in equipment. America seemed to have found the secret of eternal prosperity and became the envy of the world.

In 1920 the long downtrend began. The war demand had ended and first war materials and then raw materials were a glut on the world market. Down went the price of farm products and with it sank the heart of the American farmer who found himself burdened with debt and deprived of income. During the period that began in 1920, we shall probably find the same type of ups and downs as we found in previous secular downtrends such as 1815–43 and 1866–97. Perhaps there is also an analogy with downtrends in the periods 1764–89 and 1713–40. All of these periods followed great wars.

The pattern of the downtrend seems to be something like this:

1. Primary post-war depression
2. Recovery

3. Secondary post-war depression
4. Recovery
5. Tertiary post-war depression

The first depression is likely to be short but severe, whilst the other two are likely to be long and hard. We may find drastic measures taken during any one of the depression periods, leading to a certain amount of recovery real or false.

The John Law episode in France lasted from 1716 to 1720. It seems to have followed the primary post-war depression (1714–16) in which landlords, business men, and government were greatly depressed and near bankruptcy. It led to the crash of 1720 which, of course, was wider than the French empire and in some form might have come without John Law's interference. It is interesting to note that the American New Deal came in the secondary post-war depression and has survived the end of its own recovery, or initial recovery, period. That is, the New Deal has lasted as a kind of recovery agency or accompaniment (whether as cause or not is not yet to be stated) from 1933 to 1937.

In the present downtrend, beginning in 1920, the primary post-war depression hit both town and country. Recovery quickly came to the towns but not the country and an unparalleled prosperity lasted especially from 1924 to 1929 in the towns. How much of this was due to America's liberal loans to speculators and foreign peoples is not clear. Then came the depression of 1929–32 or 1929–33. The Republicans prefer the earlier, the Democrats the later period.

What is absorbingly interesting is the fact that the drop in farm income beginning in 1920 and in town income following 1929 came at a time when the appetite for consumable goods was at the highest in history. The automobile was the ambition of every man and the cry had gone up "two cars for every family." Some persons have regarded the depression of 1929–32 as primarily an automobile depression. This is, of course, untrue because the depression arose in other countries where no autos used up the national income.

Also, as business declined and employment was greatly reduced, population kept on increasing. There was about the same pressure of young men and women every year for jobs. Thus we see that, while the secular trend in business and therefore income was downward, the secular trend in consumption and in population was up. Thus, the hardships were very severe.

In social affairs there is a circle of events which display distressing tendencies to go around of itself for a certain period —a vicious circle, if you will. First, we find real distress caused by unemployment, prolonged and severe, beginning with the secondary post-war depression. Then, measures are taken in democratic countries to meet the need of the unemployed which actually create further unemployment. Then, the democratic régime gives way to an autocratic form of national capitalism. This régime, when threatened still further by unemployment, builds up a war machine to employ distressed workmen. At this point, the Napoleonic national capitalism enters and the world will do well if it escapes the slaughterhouse. Between this drift to chaos, led by the politicians, on the one hand, and an effort of business men to pull back into constructive production of goods through human labor, on the other hand, is a great struggle. We cannot discern the victor.

Here is a thought that may bring comfort to many. Once the downtrend in business is over, sometime in the early 1950's, then the whole national experiment in capitalism may cease and we may go back to financial capitalism. The West and South would say "no," the labor group would say "no," the intellectuals would say "no," but all might acquiesce in the prosperity involved. If financial capitalism came back, would financial capitalists be wise enough to keep an even keel and avoid a future reaction?

The whole point is that national capitalism, including fascism 1922—naziism 1933—and the New Deal 1933—was in reality a manifestation of indigestion in the financial capitalistic system and an episode in the dislocations following a great war.

8. FLOW OF CAPITAL UNDER NATIONAL CAPITALISM

Few subjects are more important than the flow of capital. We have already noted how changes occurred in the past. First, the owner put his capital out directly to the user when he was not going to make it the basis of his own business. Later, he entrusted it to a money middleman who in turn put it out to the user. At first, the money middleman was passive and then active in this putting out. When he became active, financial capitalism was born. We may illustrate the flow of capital as follows.

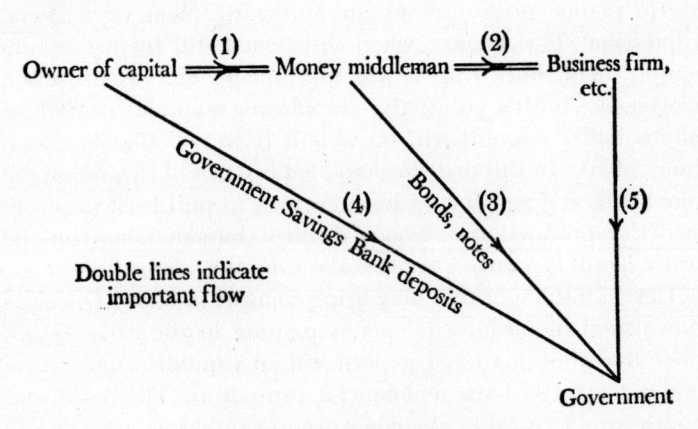

Owner of capital =(1)=> Money middleman =(2)=> Business firm, etc.

(4) Government Savings Bank deposits
(3) Bonds, notes
(5)

Double lines indicate important flow

Government

THE FLOW OF CAPITAL UNDER FINANCIAL CAPITALISM

Under this system the most important flow is along routes (1) and (2). No. (2) involved both purchase of securities and control of business. No. (3) was becoming increasingly important during the World War, but represented little influence

FLOW OF CAPITAL 363

and no control. No. (4) was a minor factor from 1910 onward. No. (5) involved an important purchase of government securities but this purchase led to no influence or control.

When national capitalism got under way, changes occurred in the flow of capital. The following diagram will be of assistance in observing these changes.

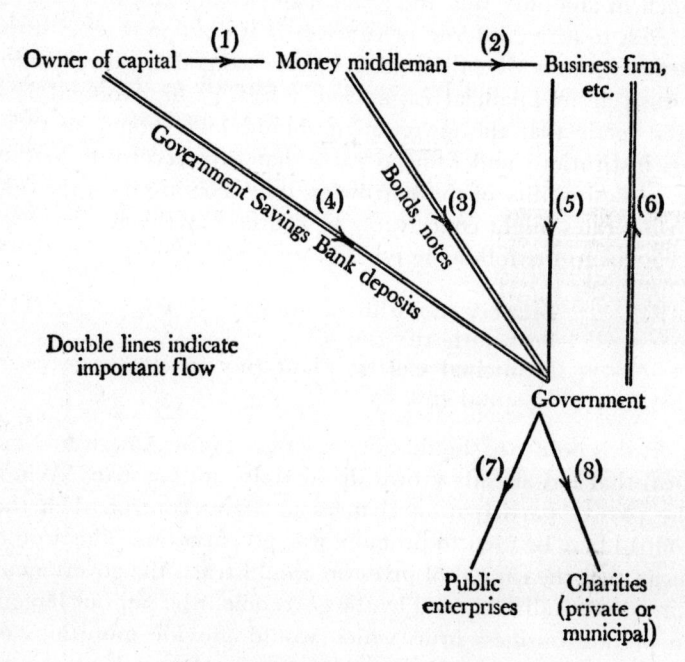

```
                (1)                    (2)
Owner of capital ───▶ Money middleman ───▶ Business firm,
                                              etc.
        ╲         (4)    ╲ (3)      │ (5)    ║ (6)
         ╲Government Savings Bank deposits
          ╲       Bonds, notes

Double lines indicate
important flow
                                         Government
                                      (7)╱    ╲(8)

                                      Public    Charities
                                    enterprises (private or
                                                 municipal)
```

THE FLOW OF CAPITAL UNDER
NATIONAL CAPITALISM

Under the new system, the source of capital is still the people, whether of large or small income. The flow along route 2 is being short-circuited by a greater flow along (3) and (4). Many investors, large and small, prefer to entrust their capital to the government in the belief that this course involves less risk. Such persons, often hating national capitalism, are doing much to make that system possible. Number (4) promises some day to be of real importance. The big new route is (6). This is the capital loaned to private business, invested, for instance, in the form of preferred stock.

There is at least a question as to the course route (6) is going to take. In general, it will flow as indicated, but will it grow much in amount? Will the government change from a passive interest to active interest or control? If it does go through this metamorphosis, it will be largely repeating the growth from industrial to financial capitalism. Already the proposal has been made that the government should loan money to various institutions and firms at rates that vary according to the social desirability of the borrowing unit. For instance, the following rates might conceivably be charged by the government for loans to the following types of concerns:

Brewery (no. 6 in diagram)	6%
Port authority (no. 6)	5%
Municipal electric plant (no. 7)	4%
Hospital (no. 8)	3%

At this point we should note a danger to the American New Deal that has already grown up in Italy and Germany. When the passive participation changes to active control, then the control may be used to promote war preparations. This would mean that the capital of investors would reach the government directly or indirectly and by the government be put out largely to private business firms which would provide munitions of war or services used in war. We surmise that if laws should be passed to force all corporations to invest a certain part of their surplus in government bonds, then this would soon undermine such private business capitalism as remained. *All* our resources might be forced into war preparations. It is not a happy thought that whether we look in the private business direction or the public business direction we see war as a function of the system of capitalism. The condition is no better in the case of communistic capitalism unless perchance that system were universal, as Trotzky would like to have it. But even then the ingrained "will to revolt" would split the Trotzkyites and bring about fresh war.

9. STRENGTH AND WEAKNESS OF NATIONAL CAPITALISM

It was a common judgment at the time that the adoption of national capitalism (1922-33) staved off communistic capitalism. Although this is still believed by many, there is no proof of it. Trouble there would have been, and perhaps bloodshed, but serious revolution is doubtful. Still this is a possible point.

There is no doubt that national capitalism has checked the worst excesses of financial capitalism, particularly along the line of speculation. There is no doubt that it has aimed at aiding petty capitalists and industrial capitalists. How far this effort has been important for the long run remains to be seen. Certainly America's NRA was a complete failure.

National capitalism, having a national basis, aids regions long neglected. Industrial and financial capitalism skimmed here and skinned there according to their purposes. When one region was exhausted or used up, capitalists passed on to the next. National capitalists (politicians and others) will take from favored regions to help backward regions in the interest of general national strength.

National capitalism has produced many useful public works such as better bridges, public parks, overhead railroad bridges, schools, bath houses, and apartment houses. Much as there is to criticize in these matters still a great deal of benefit has accrued to the people. The cost, however, has been high and a balanced judgment as to the value for the outlay is yet to be made.

Some would say that the chief lasting benefit of national capitalism is the socialization of a limited number of businesses such as public utilities. This may prove to be the case, but the successes will vary according to the country undertaking the enterprises. The hydro-electric in Canada is a success, though there is little excuse, apart from buying up votes, for the relatively low rates to household consumers. If a clear and equitable accounting were made in most cases of productive public undertakings, it would probably appear that private enterprise could do all the government could do and more at lower *total* cost for the service.

Socialization may actually assist private business capitalism if it is turned largely in the direction of sick industries, that is, old industries which are highly competitive, purely routine, entirely standardized, or bled by social circumstances. There are many instances of this already, such as the British coal mines and American canals.

One of the greatest tasks for a national capitalistic government is to control business. Conceivably, it is easier to control corporations than individuals but that is not clear over a long period. The making of laws would be comparatively easy, the making of wise laws rather difficult, and the making of laws that could be enforced without unjustifiable hardships practically impossible. One great difficulty is the impossibility of establishing a uniform accounting system that is fair to all concerned. Lawyers think this easy but accountants know that it cannot be done.

We may assume a certain amount of control possible but we can have little enthusiasm for that control. Anyone who has had real contacts with the civil services of various countries and with regulated industries knows that the breath of the government may be as blighting as that of the dragon of old. The hand of the law sweeps across the activity of men only to foster mildew and blight. The American railroads seem to be illustrations of this point. "First regulate, then destroy, then save" may be a maxim of national capitalists. To be sure, this would not apply wholly to American railroads, for industrial capitalists misused and robbed the railroads in gallant rivalry with the workers and the public.

The creation of ever increasing numbers of regulators of

human activity—persons living on the backs of the genuine workers—is a serious matter. These people, such as civil servants, are a fixed charge on industry and therefore create a further rigidity that produces great difficulty in depressions.

The one rock that will split many a politician will be the use of credit. The politician's training is not such as to give us any assurance that he is by disposition prone to conserve. Certainly, his position as the tool of voters will tend to accentuate his willingness to spend other people's money. This is a very prosaic matter and the road of disaster may be long but it is straight and its decline is faster toward the end.

The costs of control, of social benefits, of providing work, and of supporting war preparations, and war, and war aftermath already has put a heavy burden on the industrious part of society. Any system such as national capitalism which accentuates such a burden is dangerous. To take from the strong and give to the weak may be good politics but it is ultimately hard on all classes. There are two broad classes—those that build up and those that eat up. In general, to take from the former and give to the latter is just breeding downward.

There is every reason to believe that politicians, political administrators, and civil servants will make just about all the mistakes that industrial and financial capitalists have made and then some of their own. They will take control from owners, kill by taxation, cause first inflation and then a crisis. They will stop some speculation and then rig the market themselves, and though they will stave off the great day of reckoning, they will not prevent its arrival.

It was a common criticism under industrial capitalism that owners and administrators were frequently separated and that under financial capitalism this separation was extended by one degree. Under national capitalism the owners (the people) would be separated from the policy formulators (the politicians) and they from the executives (political administrators). All this is essentially the same as under financial capitalism, except that the politicians care little for making ends meet and the political administrators are likely to degenerate into automatons. The situation would be improved somewhat if security-owners were closely organized so as to defend their rights.

Between the two classes of (1) politicians (policy formulators) and (2) political and military administrators (managers) there is little sympathy. There is a suggestion of struggle for power. History would seem to indicate that either the politicians or the political administrators who build up a civil and military service will attain dictatorial power. But, while the first dictator might create a more sound national capitalistic state that democracy could hold to, the second dictator might overthrow national capitalism in favor of communistic capitalism. Whatever the particular direction of affairs, the new tyrant is not the private capitalist but the public capitalist—the political tyrant who is bred and nurtured under proletarian democracy and soon graduates into fascism or bolshevism. To many, the only choice lies between these two extremes. Financial capitalism may soon look good to us again.

It remains to be seen whether national capitalism is but a brief transition in the affairs of men. We observe the tendency for stages to be briefer and that is ominous.

10. THE PHILOSOPHY OF CAPITALISM

The total set of circumstances and logics that surround a system constitutes the basis of that system. The orderly presentation of these circumstances and logics provides the philosophy of the system. Perhaps, in the interest of brevity, we may merely enumerate some of the major points in that philosophy.

1. Capitalism depends on saving from consumption a part of the goods produced. This requires administrative ability in both high and low places.

2. There are two processes that must continue side by side —the use and the flow of capital.

3. In the use, there are three principal types: the pre-business, private business, and public business capitalism.

4. In the flow there are also three principal types—usucapital (from income to capital goods), direct putting-out, and indirect putting-out systems.

5. In the indirect putting-out system (operated by money middlemen), there was a vital shift in the nineteenth century from passive investment to active investment, involving continued control on the part of the money middlemen.

6. Changes in these types of use and flow of capital and in their interrelation make up the great capital systems of history, especially: Petty capitalism
Mercantile capitalism
Industrial capitalism
Financial capitalism
National capitalism

7. In all systems of capitalism, even in communistic capitalism, there must be a replacement of the capital used and a net addition (to cover losses, depreciation, and obsolescence), if we are to assume a progressive society. The part of the net addition that takes care of losses is called profit and is inherent in the use of capital and essential to its continuous flow.

8. Under all types of capitalism there is a set of "costs" that must be met for the use of: land
labor
administration
capital (profits and interest)

9. Circumstances determine the reward of each according to general conditions which can be but little changed in the long run by any public planning.

10. The entrepreneur may be a body politic but this fact does not change the essential distribution of costs. Effective accounting under communistic capitalism would not differ much from that of private business capitalism if it were fairly done. Though intangible assets would disappear, cost values would be essential and the surplus account vital.

11. Production cannot continue without the coöperation of all the agents—induced to act through a sense of fair treatment.

12. The key position rests with the man who undertakes to use capital and who must be rewarded with profits. In the long run, if he does not prosper, the rest cannot.

13. This entrepreneur can never have complete knowledge of conditions he is to be confronted with and accordingly runs risks and incurs losses. These losses must be reckoned on the business as a whole and over a considerable period.

14. In the ebb and flow of conditions there is a pattern, rather hard to discern, first, of a long uptrend of prices and profits during which there is thrift and a heavy investment in fixed capital in anticipation of an indefinite continuation of prosperity, and then of a long downtrend during which all is reversed. During this down-period the prevailing system of capitalism is threatened, perhaps undermined, and the way is prepared for a new system.

15. As one system of capitalism follows another, we observe that each system seems to be shorter lived than its predecessor.

16. The ultimate system that some thinkers can see is communistic capitalism which, in a sense, is somewhat of a return to petty capitalism though on a group basis. The fear is that with the return of a new type of petty capitalism would come all the immature cultural associations of the historic petty capitalism.

17. There is much that points to an instability of either private or public business capitalism. Man has many sides to his nature. He has many ways of spending his time such as eating and drinking, learning, amusement, sexual pursuits, idleness, crime, search for health, contemplation, worship, and earning a living.

18. The great problem becomes one of deciding how a man is to get an income whereby he can satisfy several of these interests. Private capitalism has assumed that, if an able-bodied man would not work, he should not ordinarily share. This has driven him to some sort of effort useful to a wide group.

19. The economic drive upon men has been systematized far beyond the capacity of many individuals to stand. It remains

uncertain what the next step is to be. The *temporary* means of meeting a downtrend in business is to shorten hours and let up on economic effort. This increases costs and threatens profits without which enterprise fails and likewise the ability of the government to gain support for its various activities. A *permanent* solution may come unnoticed through the extension of security and other benefits to unemployed laborers and submarginal farmers, leading to their loss of a free status in society and consequent removal from a capitalistic society for which they are not equipped by nature. History has close analogies for this realistic development.

20. Any kind of capitalism will work, but the best, if we accept the framework of modern times, assume able leadership, and allow time to learn how to function normally, has been financial capitalism which offers most for the two sides of capitalism—the use of capital and the flow of capital. The world may give it another chance to function at the close of the present downward trend in business (beginning in the 1950's?).

21. The basis of capitalism is struggle amid dangers, primarily for a material reward but secondarily for a higher cultural reward for an increasingly large number. As capitalism has progressed, the welfare of more persons has been provided for. As these persons taste of advantages, they want more; and in depressions, like hungry offspring, threaten the breasts of supply.

22. Under the various forms of capitalism, man struggles upward, always seeking results and using the method of trial and error. He learns by doing and does by learning. He continues those earlier processes that we may call "biological." The biological survival of the fittest becomes the economic survival of the fittest. A large part of what man has in physique and in brain power has come through the challenge of getting a living. Just how much has been added by the tasks of administrative business on an increasingly large scale is unknown. This addition to man's equipment might well be studied in the progression from petty capitalist to mercantile capitalist

to industrial capitalist to financial capitalist to national capitalist.

23. In recent generations, there has been a return to the mediaeval tendency to challenge the system of using capital to get a living. This challenge has been excessive and seldom has clearly aimed at any one type of capitalism. On the other hand, also in recent generations, there has arisen a philosophy of becoming, of effort, of struggle in a medium of many variables, that gives to the user of capital and to the owner and controller of capital a high place. This philosophy is pragmatism, which should be studied by all who are interested in the evolution of capitalism. They will find in it a system of thought that is more satisfying than the time-honored philosophies of idealism and realism, which in a changing world of real men and situations leave us so much suspended in an atmosphere that we associate with other altitudes or with unrealistic elaborations of the real. For those timid souls to whom respectability can come only through a philosophical system, pragmatism offers much: it enables them to emphasize materialism as a safe basis for man to rest upon and to follow an evolutionary course in this world of matter and mind that looks forward and points onwards to ever better things.

READINGS

GENERAL TREATISES ON CAPITALISM

Barnes, Harry E. *An Economic History of the Western World.* New York, 1937.
Benn, Ernest J. P. *The Confessions of a Capitalist.* London, 1925.
Brentano, Lujo. *Die Anfänge des modernen Kapitalismus.* München, 1916.
Commons, John R. *Legal Foundations of Capitalism.* New York, 1924.
Espinas, Georges. *Les Origines du Capitalisme.* Bibliothèque de la Société d'Histoire du Droit des Pays Flamands, vol. vii and vol. ix. Lille, 1933 and 1936.
Hauser, Henri. *Les Débuts du Capitalisme.* Paris, 1927.
Hobson, J. A. *Evolution of Modern Capitalism: A Study of Machine Production.* London, many eds. 1897 onward.
Hyma, Albert. *Christianity, Capitalism, and Communism: a Historical Analysis.* Ann Arbor, 1937.
Marx, Karl. *Capital: A Critical Analysis of Capitalist Production.* German ed. 1867; first English ed. 1887.
Pirenne, Henri. *Les Périodes de l'Histoire Sociale du Capitalisme.* Bruxelles, 1914.
Robertson, H. M. *Aspects of the Rise of Economic Individualism. A Criticism of Max Weber and His School.* Cambridge, 1933.
Salvioli, G. *Le Capitalisme dans le Monde Antique.* Paris, 1906.
Sayous, A. E. (ed.). *L'Apogée du Capitalisme.* French translation of Sombart's *Kapitalismus* with a study of Sombart's life, scholarship, and ideas.
Sée, Henri. *Modern Capitalism, Its Origin and Evolution.* London, 1928.
Sombart, Werner. *Der moderne Kapitalismus.* 2 vols. Leipzig, 1902. Various later editions.
———. *The Jews and Modern Capitalism.* London, 1913.

Sombart, Werner. *The Quintessence of Capitalism: a Study of the History and Psychology of the Modern Business Man.* London, 1915.
Strieder, Jacob. *Zur Genesis des modernen Kapitalismus.* Bonn, 1903.
Tawney, R. H. *Religion and the Rise of Capitalism.* New York, 1926.
Weber, Max. *General Economic History.* New York, 1927.

CHAPTER I

Beard, Miriam. *A History of the Business Man.* New York, 1938.
Bennett, H. S. *Life on the English Manor: a Study of Peasant Conditions, 1150–1400.* New York, 1937.
Gras, N. S. B. *A History of Agriculture in Europe and America.* New York, 1925.
———. *An Introduction to Economic History.* New York, 1922.
Lipson, E. *Economic History of England.* Vol. I. *The Middle Ages.* 7th ed. London, 1937.
Pirenne, Henri. *Economic and Social History of Medieval Europe.* New York, 1937. Tr. by I. E. Clegg.
Rostoftzev, M. I. *A Large Estate in Egypt in the Third Century B. C., a Study in Economic History.* University of Wisconsin Studies in the Social Sciences and History, no. 6, 1922.
Seebohm, F. *The English Village Community.* London, 1883. 4th ed. New York, 1926.
Walter of Henley's Husbandry, Together with an Anonymous Husbandry, Seneschaucie, and Robert Grosseteste's Rules. London, 1890.
Xenophon. *The Oeconomicus.* Ed. by A. H. N. Sewall. Cambridge, England, 1925.

CHAPTER II

Ancient Period
Babylonian Legal and Business Documents from the Time of the First Dynasty of Babylon Chiefly from Nippur. Ed. by H. Ranke and A. Poebel. 2 pts. Philadelphia, 1906–09.
Burn, A. R. *Minoans, Philistines, and Greeks, B. C. 1400–900.* London, 1930.

Byrne, A. H. *Titus Pomponius Atticus.* Bryn Mawr College, 1920.
Calhoun, G. M. *The Business Life of Ancient Athens.* Chicago, 1926.
Daremberg, C., and Saglio, E. *Dictionaire des Antiquités Grecques et Romaines.* Paris, 1873–84. Articles on Negotiator, Mercator, Publicanus.
Frank, Tenney. *An Economic History of Rome.* 2d ed. rev. Baltimore, 1927.
———. *An Economic Survey of Ancient Rome.* 4 vols. Baltimore, 1933–38.
Harper, R. F. *The Code of Hammurabi, King of Babylon about 2250 B. C.* Chicago, 1904.
Heitland, W. E. *Agricola: a Study of Agriculture and Rustic Life in the Greco-Roman World from the View of Labour.* Cambridge, 1921.
Rostovtzev, M. I. *Social and Economic History of the Roman Empire.* Oxford, 1926.
Schoff, W. H. *The Periplus of the Erythræan Sea: Travel and Trade in the Indian Ocean by a Merchant of the First Century.* London, 1912.
Zimmern, Alfred E. *Greek Commonwealth; Politics and Economics in Fifth-Century Athens.* 4th ed. Oxford, 1925.

Mediaeval Period
Ashley, Sir William J. *An Introduction to English Economic History and Theory.* Vol. I. *The Middle Ages.* London, 1888.
Bovill, E. W. *Caravans of the Old Sahara.* Oxford, 1933.
Byrne, E. H. Commercial Contracts of the Genoese in the Syrian Trade of the Twelfth Century. *Quarterly Journal of Economics,* vol. xxxi (Nov., 1916), pp. 128–170.
———. *Genoese Shipping in the Twelfth and Thirteenth Centuries.* Cambridge, Mass., 1930.
Grant, Christina P. *The Syrian Desert; Caravans, Travel and Exploration.* London and Toronto, 1937.
Gras, N. S. B. *Industrial Evolution.* Cambridge, Mass., 1930.
———. *An Introduction to Economic History.* New York, 1922.
Hoover, C. B. The Sea Loan in Genoa in the Twelfth Century.

Quarterly Journal of Economics, vol. xl (May, 1926), pp. 495–529.
Krueger, H. C. The Routine of Commerce between Genoa and Northwest Africa during the Late Twelfth Century. *The Mariner's Mirror,* vol. xix (Oct., 1933), pp. 417–438.
———. Wares of Exchange in Twelfth-Century Genoese-African Trade. *Speculum,* vol. xii (Jan., 1937), pp. 57–71.
Larson, L. M. (ed.). *The King's Mirror.* New York, 1917.
Lipson, E. *Economic History of England.* Vol. I. *The Middle Ages.* 7th ed. London, 1937.
Major, R. H. *India in the Fifteenth Century, being a Collection of Narratives of Voyages to India.* Hakluyt Society. London, 1857.
Nussbaum, F. L. *A History of the Economic Institutions of Modern Europe; an Introduction to Der moderne Kapitalismus of Werner Sombart.* New York, 1933.
Pirenne, Henri. *Economic and Social History of Medieval Europe.* New York, 1937. Tr. by I. E. Clegg.
Reynolds, R. L. Merchants of Arras and the Overland Trade with Genoa in the Twelfth Century. *Revue Belge de Philologie et d'Histoire,* vol. ix (June, 1930), pp. 495–533.
———. Genoese Trade in the late Twelfth Century, particularly in Cloth from the Fairs of Champagne. *Journal of Economic and Business History,* vol. iii (1930–31), pp. 362–381.
Salzman, L. F. *English Trade in the Middle Ages.* Oxford, 1931.
Thompson, J. W. *An Economic and Social History of the Middle Ages (300–1300).* New York, 1928.
———. *An Economic and Social History of Europe in the Later Middle Ages (1300–1530).* New York, 1931.
Unwin, G. *The Gilds and Companies of London.* London, 1908.

Modern Europe and America
Ardouin-Dumazet. *Les Petites Industries Rurales.* Paris, 1912.
Bédollierre, E. de la. *Les Industriels Métiers et Professions en France.* Paris, 1842.
Clark, V. S. *History of Manufactures in the United States, 1607–1860.* Washington, 1916; New York, 1929.
Gras, N. S. B. *Industrial Evolution.* Cambridge, Mass., 1930.

Keir, M. *Manufacturing Industries in America.* New York, 1920. Chapter IV, "The Unappreciated Tin-Peddler."
Kropotkin, P. *Fields, Factories and Workshops; or Industry combined with Agriculture and Brain Work with Manual Work.* London and New York, 1912.
[Phillips, Sir R.] *Description of the Plates, Representing the Itinerant Traders of London in Their Ordinary Costume; with Notices of the Remarkable Places Given in the Background.* London, 1804.
Schmoller, G. *Grundriss der allgemeinen Volkswirtschaftslehre,* vol. i, Leipzig, 1908, pp. 450–454 (list of books and articles).
Tryon, R. M. *Household Manufactures in the United States, 1640–1860.* Chicago, 1917.
Wright, R. *Hawkers and Walkers in Early America.* Philadelphia, 1927.

CHAPTER III

Beardwood, Alice. *Alien Merchants in England, 1350–1377: Their Legal and Economic Position.* Mediaeval Academy of America. Cambridge, Mass., 1931.
Buchanan, D. H. *Development of Capitalistic Enterprise in India.* New York and Toronto, 1935.
Edler, Florence. *Glossary of Mediaeval Terms of Business, Italian Series, 1200–1600.* Mediaeval Academy of America. Cambridge, Mass., 1934.
Ehrenberg, R. *Capital and Finance in the Age of the Renaissance: a Study of the Fuggers and Their Connections.* London, 1928. Tr. by H. M. Lucas.
Gras, N. S. B., and Larson, Henrietta M. *Casebook in American Business History.* New York, 1939.
Gras, N. S. B. *The Early English Customs System.* Cambridge, Mass., 1918.
Hauser, Henri. Le Parfait Négociant de Jacques Savary. *Revue d'Histoire Économique et Sociale,* vol. xiii (1925), pp. 1–28.
Lane, F. C. *Venetian Ships and Shipbuilders of the Renaissance.* Baltimore, 1934.
Malden, H. E. (ed.). *The Cely Papers, Selections from the Correspondence and Memoranda of the Cely Family, Mer-*

chants of the Staple A. D. 1475–1488. Camden Series, 3d ser., vol. i (1900).

Peragallo, E. *Origin and Evolution of Double Entry Bookkeeping*. New York, 1938.

Porter, K. W. *John Jacob Astor, Business Man*. 2 vols. Cambridge, Mass., 1931.

———. *The Jacksons and the Lees: Two Generations of Massachusetts Merchants, 1765–1844*. 2 vols. Cambridge, Mass., 1937.

Power, Eileen E. *The Paycockes of Coggeshall*. London, 1920.

Power, Eileen, and Postan, M. M. *Studies in English Trade in the Fifteenth Century*. London, 1933.

Richards, G. R. B. *Florentine Merchants in the Age of the Medici: Letters and Documents from the Selfridge Collection of Medici Manuscripts*. Cambridge, Mass., 1932.

Roover, Raymond de. La Formation et l'Expansion de la Comptabilité à partie double. *Annales d'Histoire Économique et Sociale*, nos. 44–45 (1937), pp. 171–193, 270–298.

Salzman, L. F. *English Trade in the Middle Ages*. Oxford, 1931.

Sapori, A. *La Crisi delle Compagnie Mercantili dei Bardi e dei Peruzzi*. Florence, 1926.

Scott, W. R. *The Constitution and Finance of English, Scottish, and Irish Joint Stock Companies to 1720*. 3 vols. London, 1910–12.

Sieveking, Heinrich. *Genueser Finanzwesen mit besonderer Berucksichtigung der Casa di S. Giorgio*. 2 vols. Freiburg, 1898–99.

Sombart, W. *The Jews and Modern Capitalism*. London, 1913.

———. *The Quintessence of Capitalism: a Study of the History and Psychology of the Modern Business Man*. London, 1915.

Staley, J. E. *The Guilds of Florence*. London, 1906.

Strieder, Jacob. *Jacob Fugger the Rich, Merchant and Banker of Augsburg, 1459–1525*. New York, 1931. Tr. by Mildred L. Hartsough.

Unwin, G. *Industrial Organization in the Sixteenth and Seventeenth Centuries*. Oxford, 1904.

Westerfield, R. B. *Middlemen in English Business, particularly between 1660 and 1760*. New Haven, 1915.

CHAPTER IV

Denucé, J. *Inventaire des Affaitadi Banquiers Italiens à Anvers de l'Année 1568.* Antwerp, 1934.

DuBois, A. B. *The English Business Company after the Bubble Act, 1720-1800.* Commonwealth Fund. New York, 1938.

Edler, Florence. "The Van der Molen, Commission Merchants of Antwerp: Trade with Italy, 1538-44," in *Medieval and Historiographical Essays in Honor of James Westfall Thompson.* Chicago, 1938.

Ehrenberg, R. *Capital and Finance in the Age of the Renaissance: a Study of the Fuggers and Their Connections.* Tr. by H. M. Lucas. London, 1928.

Gras, N. S. B. *An Introduction to Economic History.* New York, 1922.

Gras, N. S. B., and Larson, Henrietta M. *Casebook in American Business History.* New York, 1939.

Guiraud, Louise. *Jacques Cœur.* Paris, 1900.

Heaton, Herbert. *Economic History of Europe.* New York and London, 1936.

Heckscher, Eli F. *Mercantilism.* 2 vols. London, 1935.

[Hoare, H. P. R.] *Hoare's Bank: A Record 1673-1932.* London, 1932.

Johnson, E. A. J. *Predecessors of Adam Smith: the Growth of British Economic Thought.* New York, 1937.

Packard, Laurence B. *The Commercial Revolution, 1400-1776.* New York, 1927.

Porter, K. W. *John Jacob Astor, Business Man.* Cambridge, Mass., 1931.

———. *The Jacksons and the Lees: Two Generations of Massachusetts Merchants, 1765-1844.* Cambridge, Mass., 1937.

Postan, M. M. Private Financial Instruments in Medieval England. *Vierteljahrschrift für Sozial- und Wirtschafts-Geschichte,* vol. xxii, no. 1 (1930), pp. 26-75.

Sieveking, Heinrich. *Georg Heinrich Sieveking, Lebensbild eines Hamburgischen Kaufmanns aus dem Zeitalter der französischen Revolution.* Berlin, 1913.

Smith, Adam. *An Inquiry into the Nature and Causes of the Wealth of Nations*. London, 1776.

Strieder, Jacob. *Studien zur Geschichte kapitalistischer Organisationsformen*. 1st ed., 1914. München and Leipzig, 1925.

Unwin, George. *Industrial Organization in the Sixteenth and Seventeenth Centuries*. Oxford, 1904.

CHAPTER V

Appel, Joseph H. *Living the Creative Life*. New York, 1918. Can be purchased at Wanamaker's, New York.

Ashton, T. S. *Iron and Steel in the Industrial Revolution*. London, New York, and Manchester, 1924.

Benson, A. L. *The New Henry Ford*. New York, 1923.

Berdrow, Wilhelm (ed.). *Krupp: A Great Business Man Seen through his Letters*. New York, 1930.

Best's Insurance Reports (Fire and Marine Edition), 1899–

Best's Insurance Reports (Casualty and Surety), 1914–

Best's Life Insurance Reports upon All Legal Reserve Companies, 1906–

Buck, N. S. *The Development and the Organization of Anglo-American Trade, 1800–1850*. New Haven, 1925.

Clark, V. S. *History of Manufactures in the United States*. 3 vols. New York, 1929.

Cole, G. D. H. *Robert Owen*. Boston, 1925.

Ford, Henry. *My Life and Work*. In collaboration with Samuel Crowther. New York, 1923.

Fortunes Made in Business: A Series of Original Sketches, Biographical and Anecdotic, from the Recent History of Industry and Commerce by Various Writers. 3 vols. London, 1884–87.

Fuller, R. H. *Jubilee Jim; the Life of Colonel James Fisk, Jr.* New York, 1928.

Gras, N. S. B. *The Massachusetts-First National Bank of Boston, 1784–1934*. Cambridge, Mass., 1937.

Gras, N. S. B., and Larson, Henrietta M. *Casebook in American Business History*. New York, 1939.

Hendrick, B. J. *The Age of Big Business*. New Haven, 1921.

———. *The Life of Andrew Carnegie*. 2 vols. New York, 1932.

Holyoake, G. J. *The History of Co-operation.* London, 1908.
Hutchinson, W. T. *Cyrus Hall McCormick.* 2 vols. New York and London, 1930–35.
Jenks, L. H. *The Migration of British Capital to 1875.* New York and London, 1927.
Kropotkin, P. *Fields, Factories and Workshops; or Industry Combined with Agriculture and Brain Work with Manual Work.* London and New York, 1912.
Larson, Henrietta M. *Jay Cooke: Private Banker.* Cambridge, Mass., 1936.
Leverhulme, William H. L., 2d Viscount. *Viscount Leverhulme, by His Son.* Boston, 1927.
Lewis, Cleona. *America's Stake in International Investments.* Washington, 1938.
Mantoux, P. J. *The Industrial Revolution in the Eighteenth Century: an Outline of the Beginnings of the Modern Factory System in England.* New York, 1927.
Minnigerode, M. *Certain Rich Men: Stephen Girard—John Jacob Astor—Jay Cooke—Daniel Drew—Cornelius Vanderbilt—Jay Gould—Jim Fisk.* New York, 1927.
Moody's Industrials, 1917–
Moody's Industrials and Public Utilities, 1916.
Moody's Manual of Railroad and Corporation Securities [some changes of contents], 1900–24.
Moody's Public Utilities, 1917–
Moody's Railroads, 1916–
Moulton, Harold G. *Financial Organization and the Economic System.* New York and London, 1938.
Neff, John U. *The Rise of the British Coal Industry.* Studies in Economic and Social History. 2 vols. London, 1932.
Northrop, H. D. *Life and Achievements of Jay Gould, the Wizard of Wall Street; Being a Complete and Graphic Account of the greatest Financier of Modern Times.* Philadelphia, 1892.
Olmsted, D. *Memoir of Eli Whitney.* New York, 1846.
Pearson, H. G. *An American Railroad Builder, John Murray Forbes.* Boston and New York, 1911.
Pinner, Felix. *Deutsche Wirtschaftsführer.* Charlottenburg, 1925.

Poor's Bank, Government, and Municipal Volume: Investment Trusts, Real Estate, Mortgage, Finance and Insurance Companies [some variations in title], 1930–
Poor's Industrials, 1910–
Poor's Public Utilities, 1913–
Poor's Railroads, 1868–
Pyle, J. G. *Life of James J. Hill.* 2 vols. Garden City, 1916.
Roll, Erich. *An Early Experiment in Industrial Organization.* London, 1930.
Smith, A. D. H. *Commodore Vanderbilt: an Epic of American Achievement.* New York, 1927.
Stidger, W. L. R. *Henry Ford, the Man and His Motives.* New York, 1923.
Swift, Louis F. *The Yankee of the Yards: the Biography of Gustavus Franklin Swift.* Chicago, 1927.
Thornton, H. J. *The History of the Quaker Oats Company.* Chicago, 1933.
Ure, A. *The Philosophy of Manufactures.* London, 1835.
Usher, A. P. *The Industrial History of England.* Boston and New York, 1920.
Westerfield, Ray B. *Money, Credit and Banking.* New York, 1938.
White, B. *The Book of Daniel Drew: a Glimpse of the Fisk-Gould-Tweed Régime from the Inside.* New York, 1911.
Williams, Iolo A. *The Firm of Cadbury, 1831–1931.* New York, 1931.

CHAPTER VI
(See also works cited in Chapter V)

Adams, J. T. *Our Business Civilization.* New York, 1929.
Arnold, Thurman W. *The Folklore of Capitalism.* New Haven and London, 1937.
Baker, J. C. *Executive Salaries and Bonus Plans.* New York and London, 1938.
Berle, A. A., Jr., and Means, G. *The Modern Corporation and Private Property.* New York, etc., 1932.
Brandeis, Louis D. *Other People's Money.* New York, 1914.

Campbell, E. G. *The Reorganization of the American Railroad System, 1893–1900.* New York, 1938.
Corey, Lewis. *The Decline of American Capitalism.* New York, 1934.
——. *The House of Morgan: A Social Biography of the Masters of Money.* New York, 1930.
Corti, Count Egon Caesar. *The Reign of the House of Rothschild, 1830–1871.* New York, 1928.
Edwards, G. W. *The Evolution of Finance Capitalism.* London and New York, 1938.
——. *International Trade Finance.* New York, 1924.
Gordon, Robert A. Ownership by Management and Control Groups in the Large Corporation. *Quarterly Journal of Economics,* vol. lii (May, 1938), pp. 367–400.
Gras, N. S. B., and Larson, Henrietta M. *Casebook in American Business History.* New York, 1939.
Haney, L. H. *Business Organization and Combination.* 3d ed. New York, 1934.
Hauser, Henri. *Germany's Commercial Grip on the World.* New York, 1918.
Jones, Eliot. *The Trust Problem in the United States.* New York, 1921.
Kennan, George. *E. H. Harriman.* 2 vols. Boston, 1922.
Kuczynski, R. R. *American Loans to Germany.* New York, 1927.
——. *Bankers' Profits from German Loans.* Washington, 1932.
Larson, Henrietta M. *Jay Cooke: Private Banker.* Cambridge, Mass., 1936.
Life Insurance Companies doing Business in the State of New York, Testimony taken before the Joint Committee of the Senate and Assembly of the State of New York to Investigate and Examine into the Business and Affairs of. 7 vols. Albany, 1906.
Money Trust Investigation. Investigation of Financial and Monetary Conditions in the United States . . . before a Sub-Committee [Pujo] *of the Committee on Banking and Currency.* Washington, 1913.
Moody, John. *The Masters of Capital: a Chronicle of Wall Street.* New Haven, 1921.

Moody, John. *The Railroad Builders: a Chronicle of the Welding of the States.* New Haven, 1919.
——. *The Truth about the Trusts: a Description and Analysis of the American Trust Movement.* New York, 1904.
Riesser, Jacob. *The German Great Banks and Their Concentration in Connection with the Economic Development of Germany.* Washington, 1911.
Ruggles, C. O. *Problems in Public Utility Economics and Management.* New York, 1938.
Vergeot, J. B. *Le Crédit comme Stimulant et Régulateur de l'Industrie.* Paris, 1918.

CHAPTER VII

Chase, Stuart. *Government in Business.* New York, 1935.
Donham, W. B. *Business Adrift.* Boston, 1931.
Fay, Charles R. *Co-operation at Home and Abroad: a Description and Analysis, with a Supplement on the Progress of Co-operation in the United Kingdom (1908–1918).* 2d ed. London, 1920.
Gras, N. S. B., and Larson, Henrietta M. *Casebook in American Business History.* New York, 1939.
Heaton, Herbert. *The British Way to Recovery.* Minneapolis, 1934.
Hitler, Adolf. *My Battle.* Boston, 1933. Also as *Mein Kampf.* New York, 1939.
Hubbard, L. E. *Soviet Trade and Distribution.* London, 1938.
James, William. *Pragmatism.* New York, 1907.
Kallen, H. M. *Individualism: An American Way of Life.* New York, 1933.
MacDonald, William. *The Menace of Recovery: What the New Deal Means.* New York, 1934.
Persons, Warren M. *Government Experimentation in Business.* New York, 1934.
Ramsay, M. L. *Pyramids of Power: the Story of Roosevelt, Insull and the Utility Wars.* Indianapolis and New York, 1937.
Rogers, J. H. *Capitalism in Crisis.* New Haven, 1938.
Roosevelt, Franklin D. *On Our Way.* New York, 1934.

Schuman, F. L. *The Nazi Dictatorship: a Study in Social Pathology and the Politics of Fascism.* 2d ed. New York, 1936.
Sullivan, L. *Prelude to Panic: the Story of the Bank Holiday.* Washington, 1936.
Welk, W. G. *Fascist Economic Policy.* Cambridge, Mass., 1938.
Wunderlich, Frieda. Germany's Defense Economy and the Decay of Capitalism. *Quarterly Journal of Economics,* vol. lii (May, 1938), pp. 401–430.

SUGGESTED STUDIES

1. Free and unfree status in the development of business.
2. Cultural nomadic economy as the beginning of effective capitalism.
3. Comparison of the capital equipment of cultural nomads with that of settled villagers.
4. Strength and weakness of manorial management. Was there a manorial policy?
5. Whether big business began with the temple, monastic, or manorial estates.
6. The administration of an outstanding mediaeval bishop, particularly of the thirteenth century.
7. The preparation for business during pre-business capitalism.

8. An inquiry into the beginnings of private business—in ancient Egypt, Babylonia, Crete, or elsewhere.
9. Certain ancient cities as business centers—Antioch, Athens, Miletus, and Alexandria.
10. List of important kinds of capital found among ancient peoples, for example, Babylonian canals, Cretan ships, and Greek workshops.
11. Contributions of Jews to European business, 1200–1500.
12. The influence of the Arabs on European business during the Middle Ages.
13. The history of the traveling merchant.
14. Business of the pawnbroker during the Middle Ages.
15. Analysis of craft codes of petty capitalists in mediaeval town economy.

16. The shift from the traveling to the sedentary merchant.
17. The shift from petty to mercantile capitalism.

18. The extent to which sedentary merchants developed in the ancient period.
19. Whether the sedentary merchant was the only type of mercantile capitalist.
20. The history of apprenticeship in business (as distinct from the handicrafts) and of school training for business up to about the 1850's.
21. Analysis of partnership during the Middle Ages.
22. Business agents and agency during the mediaeval and early modern periods.
23. The functions of the senior partner in mediaeval Italian cities.
24. Business in mediaeval Florence.
25. Business in Venice from the twelfth to sixteenth century.
26. History of a Hanseatic merchant.
27. The types of control of one man over another, with special attention to business control.
28. The influence and control of the sedentary merchant over manufacture, fishing, lumbering, and mining.
29. The industrial entrepreneur in the régime of mercantile capitalism—his functions and the reasons for his existence.
30. Why Northern Europe used the regulated company during the period 1200–1500, while Southern Europe used it very little.
31. The brief promise of a financial capitalism in late mediaeval Italy.
32. The internal organization of early corporations.
33. Adam Smith's understanding of business in his own day.
34. The relation between mercantile capitalism and mercantilism.
35. The specialization that occurred in the régime of mercantile capitalism—in transportation, storage, and banking.
36. The business boom in Europe about 1716–20.

37. The life and writings of scholars of the Italian Renaissance (such as Conrad Peutinger) in so far as they affect business.
38. Bradford's *Plymouth Plantation* as business history.
39. The career of Stephen Girard as a business man.
40. A critical examination of the contributions of sedentary merchants to the Industrial Revolution.
41. Examples of surviving mercantile capitalists in smaller communities and in the Orient.

42. Significance of the use of the word "agent" in industrial capitalism.
43. The New England type of industrial capitalist.
44. The early policy and management of railroad executives in America.
45. Study of that phase of industrial capitalism in which one firm competed with another which had about the same equipment.
46. Financial phase of industrial capitalism.
47. The extent to which Saint-Simon would follow up investment by control.
48. The policy and management of George Hudson, British railway king.
49. Competition between the commission agent and the wholesaler in America, 1815–66.
50. The history of a wholesaling firm of considerable age in some district.
51. Career of Jacob Little as a market operator.
52. Analysis of the business policy, management, and social engineering of Andrew Carnegie.
53. Comparison of the careers of Vanderbilt, Carnegie, Rockefeller, and Hill.
54. History of a telephone company in some region.
55. History of the Foshay business, or the Insull utilities.

56. History of accounting during the régime of industrial capitalism.
57. Integration as developed (1) in the financial phase of industrial capitalism and (2) under financial capitalism.
58. Activities of social engineers in some region.

59. Business prosperity in France, 1840–70.
60. The history of financial capitalism in Germany, 1853–1914.
61. History of an investment banking house in America.
62. History of the competition between investment bankers and commercial banks in America.
63. The behavior of operating executives under the régime of financial capitalism.
64. The growth of financial capitalism in Great Britain in both foreign and domestic business.
65. Influence of financial capitalism on accounting.
66. Critical examination of the Pujo Committee report.
67. Detailed history of Clarence C. Hatry's business career.
68. The growth of financial industrialists, industrial financiers, and industrial bankers as business administrators.

69. Comparison of current national capitalism and ancient Egyptian national economy.
70. Study of the regulatory, relief, and other activities of governments during business crises and other difficulties before the incoming of national capitalism.
71. Comparison of the New Freedom of Wilson, New Era of Coolidge, and New Deal of Roosevelt.
72. History of the Reconstruction Finance Corporation.
73. The influence that national capitalism is likely to have on metropolitan economy.

74. Analysis of the attitudes and policies of petty, mercantile, industrial, and financial capitalists.

75. Analysis of the economic groups in some community—capitalists (petty, industrial, financial, and national) and permanent workmen.
76. Correlation of the growth of town and metropolitan economy with the types of private business capitalism.
77. Classification of the large nations of today under the headings of industrial (Great Britain), financial, national (Italy, Germany, United States), or communistic capitalism (Russia).
78. Analysis of the peoples of the world, using the two-fold classification of business and non-business peoples.
79. Study of the neglect of management by economists.
80. Effect on business of the opposition of intellectuals, churchmen, and reformers.
81. The factors underlying the formation of sundry classes of persons—policy-formulators, managers, temporary workmen, and permanent workmen.
82. Why certain persons cannot become good business administrators.
83. Specialization vs. non-specialization as a normal business policy.
84. The view that business is the chief defender of biological principles.
85. The position of business men in society in ancient, mediaeval, and modern times.
86. Comparison of the social service of business men seeking profits with that of non-business men seeking income.
87. The history of business and the history of humanism as parallel growths.
88. Whether business men have always operated in a buyers' market (barring short periods of great prosperity). Consider the opening of world trade, the Industrial Revolution, and the scientific management of capital and labor (early 20th century).
89. How and why races and nationalities differ in their aptitudes for business.

90. The flow of capital in general or during some phase of history.
91. The history of business promotion.
92. The study of some secular trends in modern business in some one nation. Consider 1660–1713(?), 1713–64, 1764–1815, 1815–66, 1866–1920, and 1920–.
93. History of commercial manuals since the fourteenth century in Europe and America.
94. Kinds of secular trends in business—ease of management and profits, inventions, freedom from political control, etc.
95. History of industrial codes in American business.
96. History of business auxiliaries in the United States.
97. Rackets that business men have had to face.
98. History of office management in America.
99. The organizations which are of service to investors in the United States.
100. The history of stocks and bonds, 1500–1850.
101. The adaptation of inventions for commercial use.
102. History of private contractors in Europe (since 1500) or in America (since 1763).
103. History of salaried executives.
104. History of accounting under some system of capitalism.
105. Rise of the commercial lawyer (corporation lawyer class).
106. History of a great law firm, showing its special business interests and chief legal contests.
107. History of a great accounting firm.
108. History of a consulting engineering firm.
109. Rise and progress of market consultants.
110. Rise and progress of industrial relations counselors and public relations counselors.
111. Work of the business historian as an employee in American firms.

112. Experience and success of the economist in American business.
113. Analysis of a number of recent and current speeches made by business men, economists, and politicians, so as to place the speakers in the capitalistic stage to which they severally belong.

INDEX

Associations, 31, 41, 74, 103, 104, 140, 209, 228, 243, 244, 296, 309, 322. *See also* Chambers of commerce, Companies, regulated, Gilds, Livery companies, Lloyd's association.
Astor, John Jacob, 73, 169, 312
Athens, 30, 31, 60, 386
Auditing, 118. *See also* Accountants, Accounting.
Auditors, 50, 208, 209, 212, 293
Augsburg, 72, 87, 134, 144, 145, 153, 154, 166, 167
Auxiliaries, business, 48, 50-51, 63, 65, 209-214, 215, 255, 293-297, 391

Babylon, Babylonia, 27, 30, 260, 386
Bailiffs, 20, 21, 22, 79
Baker, G. F., Sr., 255, 277
Bakhtiári, 10-11
Balance of trade, 126, 127, 133, 345
Bankers, industrial, 255, 389
Bankers, international, 317. *See also* Financial capitalists.
Bankers, private, 144. *See also* Bankers, investment, Merchant bankers.
Bank (first) of the U. S., 336
Banking, 77, 105, 120, 157, 165, 166, 169, 387
Bank of Amsterdam, 149, 150
Bank of Barcelona, 149
Bank of England, 87, 138, 140, 149
Bank of New York, 187
Bank of North America, 87, 149, 187
Bank of St. George, 87, 149, 150
Bankruptcy, 44, 134, 161, 183, 191, 194, 202, 203-204, 221, 230, 240, 245, 249, 254, 268, 273, 282, 284, 288, 298, 317, 334, 342, 355, 360
Banks, commercial, 86, 87, 106, 118, 137, 143, 147, 148-151, 169, 183, 186-189, 196, 204, 206, 214, 220, 221, 222, 223, 242, 250, 253, 255, 259, 264, 284, 297, 299, 317, 322, 326, 335, 336, 344, 350, 389
Banks, bankers, investment, 105, 183, 222, 223, 250, 251, 254, 256, 257-258, 259, 261, 266, 270, 273, 274, 280, 285, 288, 290, 291, 293, 299, 300, 318, 322, 326, 389
Banks, savings, 250, 316, 354
Barcelona, 105, 149
Bardi, 80, 87, 118, 133, 134, 145
Baring Bros., 261
Barter, 47
Belgium, 100, 182, 248, 328
Beneker, G. A., 230
Benner, Samuel, 297
Bermuda Company, 107
Bernays, E. L., 296
Bezant, 78
Bills of exchange, 42-43, 55, 77, 142, 143, 146, 149, 165, 167, 176, 186, 187, 221
Blacksmiths, 9, 34, 36, 100, 177, 179, 198
Blue Eagle, 351
Boinebroke, Jehan, 72, 97-99
Bonds, 58, 130, 140, 148, 222, 255, 263, 264, 265, 266, 271, 274, 287, 299, 300, 302, 303, 314, 316, 318, 354, 355, 362, 363, 391
Bonus, 228
Bookkeepers, 19, 110
Bookkeeping, 114-119, 163, 295. *See* Accounting.
Bookkeeping, double-entry, 72, 83, 91, 155, 295
Boston Manufacturing Company, 103, 179, 212
Boston, Mass., 76, 84, 151, 168, 169, 173, 176, 188, 196, 200, 211, 213, 279
Bottomry loan, 55
Boulton and Watt, 102, 179, 180, 181
Bourgeois, 30, 104. *See* Middle class.
Bourse, 129. *See* Stock exchange.
Branch banks, 144
Branch office, 84, 146, 166, 221
Branded foods, 269
Brands, trade, 201
Braund, Wm., 140, 167, 177
Bremen, 30, 41
Bristol, 72, 76, 100, 127, 176, 220

INDEX

Abacus, 52, 116
Accommodation partnership, 57, 81, 106
Accountants, 50, 79, 80, 89, 102, 114ff., 200, 211-213, 255, 293, 295, 358, 366
Accountants, public, 208, 294
Accounting, viii, 35, 62, 128, 161, 290, 294, 366, 369, 389, 391
Accounting, cost, 21, 212, 293, 294, 295
Accounting, double-entry, 21, 116-119, 128
Accounting, single-entry, 21, 115-116, 295, 366
Accounts, 20, 21, 22, 33, 49, 50, 71-72, 84, 140, 155
Actuarial work, 295
Administration, ix, xi, 18-23, 25, 28, 32-33, 72, 91, 121, 126, 132, 134, 158, 159, 180, 189, 194, 217-218, 240, 254, 255, 256, 303, 316, 319, 324, 331, 333, 336, 357, 367, 368, 369. *See also* Control in business, Management, Policy.
Advertising, 65, 113, 137, 199, 200, 209, 242, 309
Africa, 6, 9, 11, 34, 41
Agents, 19, 21, 33, 48-50, 65, 67, 68, 74, 77, 79, 80, 91, 117, 129, 135, 175, 188, 197, 198, 207-209, 224, 293-294, 369, 387, 388. *See also* Brokers.
Agents, advertising, 208, 214
Agents, commission, 167, 187, 195, 197, 207, 208, 288, 388. *See* Commission fee, Commission merchants.
Agents, financial, 136, 208
Agents, mill, 173
Agents, protective, 50, 184, 308
Agents, purchasing, 208

Agents, selling, 173, 187, 208
Agents, transfer, 208-209
Agreement, gentleman's, 243
Agricultural Adjustment Administration, 351, 353
Agricultural Revolution, 131-132, 164
Agriculture, 13-18, 22, 24, 58, 63, 65, 72, 108, 124, 131, 162, 268, 299, 320, 326. *See also* Settled village economy.
Agriculture, capitalistic, 3
Alexandria, 57, 119, 260, 386
Allen and Company, S. and M., 221
Almy and Brown, 102, 164, 178, 187
Aluminum Company of America, 297
American Telephone and Telegraph Company, 276-277, 300
Amsterdam, 30, 121, 138, 140, 145, 147, 167, 336
Anarchism, 339
Antioch, 119, 260, 386
Antwerp, 30, 129, 136, 137, 145, 158, 167, 181
Apprentice, apprenticeship, 36, 52, 71, 73, 89, 162, 255, 319, 387
Arabs, 5ff., 38, 52, 119, 143, 152, 155, 170, 260, 386
Arbitration, 101, 209
Arkwright, Sir Richard, 102, 179-180
Armour, Philip, 184
Artisans, craftsmen, x, 29, 35, 46, 60, 63, 94, 100, 111, 125, 152, 170, 177, 319, 333, 345, 358. *See also* Handicraftsmen, Workmen.
Artisans, traveling, 45. *See also* Tinkers.
Asia, 11, 41
Asia Minor, 8, 11, 41, 119, 314
Associated Dry Goods Corp., 205-206, 288, 289

Champagne, 55, 97
Chapman, Peter, 45
Chapmen, 45, 46
Cheques, 145
Chicago, 184, 200, 203, 206, 282
Chicago, Milwaukee, and St. Paul RR., 184
Child, Sir Francis, 144-145
China, Chinese, 27, 30, 52, 59, 72, 170-173, 260, 328, 358
Church, The, xi, xiii, 17, 22, 23, 24, 25, 35, 40, 51, 54, 55-56, 58, 59, 75, 88, 122, 126, 134, 135, 143, 148, 152-154, 157, 169, 226, 227, 261, 265, 308, 340, 341, 350, 356
Civilian Conservation Corps, 352, 353
Civilization, 13, 23-26, 30, 35, 51, 61, 104, 108, 114, 331. *See also* Culture.
Claflin Company, H. B., 201-206, 288
Claflin, John, 202ff., 289
Clark and Company, E. W., 221-222
Classes, social, 14, 24, 25, 367
Clerks, 49, 68, 73, 79, 80, 83, 89, 295
Climate, 29
Clothiers, 95, 99, 100, 102
Coal mining, 327
Codes in business, 306, 309, 312, 315, 391
Cœur, Jacques, 135, 159
Coffee house, 80, 140
Colbertism, 124, 335
Collectional economy, 4, 9, 15, 23, 24, 25, 88, 324
Cologne, Köln, 30, 41, 103
Colonies, 101, 133, 261, 342
Colonists, 90, 91
Colonization, 79, 85, 87, 111, 138
Combination in business, 104, 239, 243-245, 270, 275, 285, 286, 298, 317
Commendation partnership, 57, 81, 106
Commercial manuals, 72, 210, 391. *See also* Pegolotti.
Commission fee, 48, 50, 78, 80, 89, 196, 198, 208

Commission merchants, 80, 102, 174, 195-196
Commission, sale on, 158-159
Communication, 77, 276-279, 288
Communism, xii, 23, 85, 323, 339, 340, 344, 345, 346, 347. *See* Capitalism, communistic.
Companies, holding, 280, 285, 286, 291, 300
Companies, joint stock, 74, 86, 103-114, 116, 126, 133, 137, 159, 161, 219
Companies, regulated, 41, 42, 49, 59, 74, 80, 103, 104, 106, 126, 133, 164, 244, 387
Companies, subsidiary, 109, 272
Compass, 52
Competition, xii, 29, 61, 98, 185, 190, 193, 209, 236, 238, 243-245, 246, 254, 255, 258, 266, 268, 274, 279, 293, 309, 311, 313, 317, 388
Consolidation, 273, 284, 313. *See* Mergers.
Consumers, 37, 47, 75, 93, 96, 121, 287, 327, 331, 335, 366
Consumers' goods, 63, 218, 219, 234, 299
Consumption, 8, 11, 61, 160, 195, 219, 356, 361, 368
Conti, Nicolò, 43
Contract, 1, 3, 25, 29, 35, 49, 234
Contractors, 134, 136, 391
Control (or influence), bankers', 183, 194, 247, 269, 277, 278, 289, 290, 297, 323, 340, 345, 350, 388
Control, birth, 358
Control, government, 297, 323, 325, 333, 345, 347, 350, 363, 364, 366, 367
Control in business, 2, 3, 9, 27, 28, 29, 59, 67ff., 75, 84, 88-92, 120, 121, 122, 128, 141, 152, 156, 158, 160, 165, 166, 169, 174, 202, 206, 238, 240, 244, 256, 257, 262, 266, 289, 295, 318, 322, 356, 387
Control, pre-business, 9, 15, 17, 18, 21, 22, 24, 25, 33, 70
Cooke and Company, Jay, 208, 222, 251

INDEX

Brokers, 33, 35, 48-49, 78, 198, 220, 222, 250, 261, 263, 282, 300, 301, 346
Bruges, 30, 44, 84, 103, 129
Bulmer, Sir Bevis, 137
Business, big, 64, 65, 109, 162, 236, 297, 299, 302, 323, 349, 350, 386
Business cycle, viii, 215, 287, 297
Business historian, 33, 391
Business history, vii, 49, 237, 390
Business history, beginning of, 30, 33
Business men, private, x-xiii, 3, 7, 22, 25, 27, 28-29, 34-35, 110, 279, 338, 358, 359, 361, 364, 392. See Entrepreneurs.
Business men, retired, 39, 40, 53, 57, 87, 89, 148, 151, 264
Business, origin of, 37-38
Business, private, 2, 3, 27-30, 53, 315, 316, 318, 320, 321
Business, public, 2, 28. See Capitalism, public-business.
Butler Bros., 206
Byzantium, Constantinople, 21, 72, 119, 143, 260

Calvinism, 152-153
Canada, 78, 128, 260, 363
Canals, 105, 138, 181, 220, 335
Canon law, 142, 145
Canynges, Wm., 72, 76, 176
Cape-merchant, 110
Capital, 1ff., 27, 29, 39. See also Capital goods, Capitalism.
Capital accumulation, 2, 3, 7, 52ff., 85, 87, 91, 134
Capital, autogenous, 32. See Usucapital system.
Capital, confiscation of, 331, 334
Capital, fixed, 219, 222
Capital, flow of, vii, viii, 2, 52-58, 78, 85-88, 163, 218-223, 251, 259-266, 279, 300, 324, 362-365, 368-369, 371, 391
Capital flow, direct putting out, 32, 53ff., 58, 59, 85-86, 219, 324, 369
Capital flow, indirect putting out, 86, 87, 219, 220-221, 223, 246-247, 262, 324, 369
Capital goods, 2, 4, 5, 6, 8, 10, 11, 13, 21, 23, 26, 30, 53
Capital, migration of, 10. See Capital, flow of.
Capital, origin of, 57-58
Capital, public, 323, 324. See also Capitalism, communistic, Capitalism, public-business, Communism.
Capital, use of, vii, viii, 2, 324, 371
Capital, working, 187, 221, 222, 255, 258, 264
Capitalism, agrarian, 3
Capitalism, business, 25, 28, 51, 88, 133-134, 155
Capitalism, communistic, 2, 26, 314, 323, 324, 328, 329, 330, 331, 332, 348, 355, 358, 364, 365, 369, 370, 390
Capitalism, definition of, vii, 1, 2, 28
Capitalism, philosophy of, 368-372
Capitalism, pre-business, vii, 1-26, 28, 29, 88, 92, 324, 330, 368, 386
Capitalism, private-business, vii, xiii, 26, 92, 207, 312, 323, 324, 325, 326, 330, 331, 332, 339, 341, 343, 346, 348, 354, 356, 364, 366, 368, 369, 370, 390
Capitalism, public-business, vii, 92, 324, 368, 370
Capitalism, stages of, 2, 3
Captain, ship's, 72, 76, 77, 80, 81, 83, 89, 107
Caravan, 6, 41, 42, 49, 50
Carnegie, Andrew, 192-193, 231, 241, 388
Carpenters, 177, 179
Carrier, common, 76, 98, 159, 181
Carthage, 27, 30, 119, 260
Cashiers, 19, 79, 80, 89, 102, 150, 188, 200, 295
Central workshops, 81, 93, 97, 98, 99, 102, 177, 180, 225, 386
Chain stores, 64, 84, 204-205, 206, 207, 289, 290ff., 322
Chambers of commerce, 209

INDEX

Coolidge prosperity, 299, 389
Coöperation, 5, 13-18, 24, 82, 88, 108, 157, 181, 199, 209, 211, 228, 229, 230, 263, 290, 310, 321, 369
Coördination, 22, 183, 238
Corporations, 65, 79, 105, 150, 175, 185, 207, 208, 209, 224, 225-226, 254, 307, 316, 346, 354, 364, 366
Costs, 27, 48, 122, 123, 124, 190, 194, 228, 242, 258, 270, 293, 294, 317, 319, 347, 355, 356, 366, 369, 371. *See* Expenses.
Counselors, financial, 296-297
Counters, 103, 104
Counting-house, 71, 72, 75, 77, 78, 79, 129, 140, 145
Court of arbitration, 42. *See also* Arbitration.
Coxe, Tench, 159, 173, 335
Cradock, Matthew, 73, 107, 112-113, 114
Crafts, 32. *See also* Artisans, Handicraftsmen, Handicraft system.
Credit, 43, 54, 67, 117, 119, 144, 149, 161, 250, 259, 261, 264, 314, 326, 331, 335, 344, 367
Credit instruments, 141ff. *See also* Bills of exchange, Bonds, Drafts, Notes, circulating, Notes, demand, Notes, promissory.
Crédit Mobilier, 248-250
Creditors, 21, 24, 40, 126, 142, 183, 310, 335
Credit, sales, 54
Crete, Cretans, 38, 260, 386
Crimes in business, 304-315. *See also* Foshay, Hatry, Kreuger.
Crises, 149, 193, 255, 266, 312, 316, 367
Crisis of 1720, 138, 318, 336, 360
Crisis of 1837, 221
Crisis of 1861, 202, 359, 389
Crisis of 1873, 193, 202, 240, 318
Crisis of 1893, 193
Crisis of 1901, 296, 299
Crisis of 1903, 299
Crisis of 1907, 299
Crisis of 1929, 282, 302

Crisis of 1933, 318
Crowley, Sir Ambrose, 100-102, 179, 227
Crusades, 41
Cultural nomadic economy, 4-13, 25, 28, 324, 386
Culture, viii, 60, 148, 155, 160, 162, 235, 261, 276, 314, 330, 356, 358, 370, 371. *See* Civilization.
Custom, 5, 38, 81, 88

Darien Company, 138
Darmstadt Bank, 249
Debtors, 24, 40, 142, 164, 335
Debts, 55, 142, 151, 304, 319, 337, 348
Defoe, Daniel, 127
Democracy, 309, 317, 321, 328, 331, 338, 352, 356, 358, 368
Dennison Mfg. Company, 217, 230, 243, 267
Department store chains, 289
Department stores, 199-206, 242, 279
Deposits, bank, 77, 87, 146, 147, 149, 166, 188, 362, 363
Depreciation, 212, 369
Depression, 10, 12, 26, 161, 215, 216, 263, 269, 272, 278, 286, 287, 290, 291, 293, 299, 312, 316, 317, 344, 345, 348, 349, 351, 359-360, 361, 371
Dictators, 368
Diffusion, viii, 27, 51, 143, 260, 261
Directors, 118, 140, 189, 212, 226, 231, 237, 273, 289, 290, 303
Discipline, 98, 99, 190, 235
Distribution, market, 183, 191, 193, 194, 206, 225, 237, 238, 268, 270. *See* Marketing.
Diversification, 43, 122, 161, 173, 193, 242, 271-272, 285, 286, 298, 317
Dividends, 183, 246, 249, 254, 272, 274, 282, 314
Dole, 357. *See also* Relief, social.
Douai, 72, 97, 98
Drafts, 55, 143, 188
Drapers, 31, 35, 68, 74, 75, 94, 96, 101, 106, 129
Drew, Daniel, 220, 272, 313

Droit d'aubaine, 44
Drunkenness, 101
Du Pont Company, 272
Dyers, 36, 99

East India Company, Dutch, 106, 113
East India Company, English, 106, 107, 133, 140, 146, 216
Economic history, economic historians, viii, 33, 41, 68, 86, 107, 209
Education for business, 296. *See also* Schools of business.
Effusion, viii, 51, 143
Egypt, 11, 19, 27, 260, 358, 386, 389
Electric Bond and Share Company, 281, 283
Employment, division of, 22, 25, 225, 226, 238. *See* Labor, division of.
Engineers, engineering, 178, 213, 256, 280, 281, 286, 295, 319, 388, 391. *See also* Social engineering.
Engrossing, 60, 313
Entrepreneurs, x, 83, 139, 209, 345, 347, 348, 369, 370. *See* Business men, private.
Erie RR., 184, 220, 272
Ethics, 152, 306, 309, 310, 315
Exchange, commodity, 80
Exchange, mercantile, 129-130, 136, 145
Exchange, monetary, 126, 188, 345
Exchange of goods, 1, 2, 3, 4, 11, 22, 25, 28, 31, 32, 34, 76, 141
Exchange, stock, 130, 220, 282
Expenses, 21, 22, 41, 57, 117, 123, 183. *See also* Costs, Outgo.
Exploitation, 2, 37, 151-152

Factories, industrial, 93, 99, 100, 102, 173, 174, 180, 185, 203, 204, 207, 208, 225, 227, 229, 236, 240, 243, 253, 262, 281, 289, 319
Factories, mercantile, 80, 96, 103
Factories, specialized, 64
Factors, 50, 67, 68, 72, 73, 80, 89, 90, 95, 98, 103, 110, 140, 143, 159, 160.

See Agents, Agents, commission, Supercargoes.
Fairs, 42, 43, 55, 73, 77, 97, 132, 142
Family, 5, 11, 13, 14, 15, 16, 25, 40, 58, 83, 84, 88, 107, 144, 147, 160, 162, 166, 190, 306
Farmers, x, 63, 64, 79, 120, 156, 262, 263, 264, 265, 294, 316, 319, 320, 322, 326, 331, 333-334, 335, 345, 346, 347, 349, 350, 358, 359, 371
Farmers, tenant, 351
Fascism, 323, 328, 332, 339-343, 345, 348, 351, 361-362, 368
Federal Deposit Insurance Corp., 350, 353
Federal Farm Loan System, 263, 321
Federal Intermediate Business Bank, 351
Federal Intermediate Credit System, 263, 349
Federal Reserve Board, 263
Federal Security Administration, 351
Feudalism, 24, 35, 75, 155, 234. *See also* Manorial-feudal system.
Field, Marshall, 200, 242
Film, moving picture, 9-11
Finance, viii, 85, 101, 175, 225, 237, 247, 250, 275, 322
Finance corporations, 250
Finance, private, 173
Financial capitalism, xiii, 85, 88, 166, 174, 183, 189, 194, 205, 208, 212, 214, 217, 221, 222, 232, 238-322, 324, 326, 327, 332, 337, 339, 343-344, 359, 361, 362, 364, 368, 369, 371, 387, 389, 390
Financial capitalists, 204, 206, 239ff., 246-259, 264, 285, 286, 297, 299, 301, 303, 304, 316, 317, 318, 320, 321, 322, 325, 326, 331, 339, 345, 347, 348, 350, 354, 361, 367, 372, 389, 390. *See also* Bankers, investment.
Financial Statements, 50, 116, 119
Financiers, industrial, 389
First National Bank of New York, 188, 252, 277

INDEX

Fishing, 74, 84, 90, 91, 112, 120, 130, 131, 158, 166, 387
Fishmongers, 31, 64
Fisk, James, 220, 272, 313
Fitz Neal, Roger, 21
Flanders, 68, 70, 96, 146
Flemish Hanse of London, 41, 103
Florence, 31, 60, 72, 87, 97, 98, 118, 128, 141, 145, 167, 251, 387
Forces, causal, 51-52, 151-157, 337-339
Ford Motor Company, 267, 296
Foremen, 33, 62, 101, 225, 226, 231
Forestalling, 60, 313
Forgotten man, 333, 348
Foshay, W. B., 282, 302, 305, 388
France, French, 29, 70, 73, 135, 146, 148, 152, 168, 178, 182, 248, 249, 250, 309, 321, 328, 329, 330, 335, 344, 352, 360, 389
Frankfort, 46, 247, 249
Freedom, 1, 19, 25, 51, 158, 235, 307, 325, 330, 335, 391
Free trade, 67
Freight, 76, 82, 176, 181, 184, 261
Frescobaldi, 118, 134
Fugger, Jacob, 89, 100, 134, 141, 146, 247
Fuggers, 72, 83-84, 87, 144, 145, 154, 166, 221
Fullers, 32, 34, 99
Functions, economic, 67, 75-79, 165, 174, 240, 241, 246, 266, 267, 288, 298

General Electric Company, 256, 271, 280-281, 283
General Foods, 269-270
General Mills Corp., 267
General Motors Corp., 272
Genoa, 37, 40, 44, 49, 57, 58, 91, 97, 105, 116, 149, 150
Germany, Germans, 29, 68, 103, 134, 146, 166, 168, 182, 235, 247, 249-250, 260, 266, 276, 304, 317, 321, 328, 329, 333, 340, 343-348, 356, 358, 364, 389, 390
Gild merchant, 31, 35, 103

Gilds, 27, 31, 32, 33, 35, 59, 60, 71, 74, 87, 88, 111, 126, 129, 133, 145, 171, 309, 333, 335, 341. *See also* Livery companies.
Gilds, craft, 32, 35, 95, 103, 170, 209
Gillette Safety Razor Company, 271
Girard, Stephen, 73, 147, 169, 388
Gisze, George, 104
Glut of market, 121, 161, 359
God's penny, 42
Gold, 42, 124, 137, 138, 140, 141, 156, 187, 218, 261, 302, 342, 346
Goldman Sachs and Company, 269, 283
Goldsmiths, 87, 144-145, 146, 167
Gould, Jay, 272, 274, 313, 314
Government Savings Bank, 362, 363
Gray, Wm., 76, 176
Great Northern RR., 271, 273
Greece, 20, 27, 55, 119, 260
Gresham, Sir Thomas, 129, 135-136, 159
Groceries, 47, 198, 229, 289, 291
Grocers, 35, 64, 68, 74, 94, 129, 242
Gypsies, 9

Haberdashers, 68, 74, 94, 95, 107, 112
Hahn Department Stores, 291-292
Hamilton, Alexander, 154, 215, 335
Hancock, John, 73, 166, 169
Hancock, John M., 255
Handicraftsmen, 36, 59, 69, 70, 71, 72, 90, 346
Handicraftsmen, dependent wholesale, 96, 102
Handicraftsmen, retail, 69, 70, 90, 93-94
Handicraftsmen, wholesale, 46, 70, 82, 94
Handicraft system, dependent wholesale, 90, 99
Handicraft system, retail, 93
Handicraft system, wholesale, 93, 100, 121, 169, 177
Hanseatic League, 41, 103-104
Hardware, 64, 101, 198
Harriman, E. H., 253, 273-274, 296
Hatry, C. C., 301-302, 305, 389

INDEX

Heins, John, 212
Henley, Walter of, 20
Hill, J. J., 253, 256, 296
Hitler, Adolf, 345
Hoare, Sir Richard, 145-146
Holland, Dutch, Netherlands, 29, 104, 105, 106, 111, 113-114, 146, 153, 168, 303, 328
Home-owners, 349, 350, 351
Home Owners Loan Corp., 351
Hoover recovery, 299
House-builders, 31, 35, 64
Hucksters, 37, 45, 61, 64
Hudson, George, 313, 388
Hudson's Bay Company, 146, 161
Humanism, xi-xiii, 154, 160, 390

Income, 21, 22, 25, 52, 54, 87, 122, 320, 328, 348, 360, 370, 390. See Profits.
Income from capital, 7. See Dividends, Interest, Profits.
India, 27, 43, 103, 161, 170, 260
Indians, American, 29, 47, 108
Individualism, 59, 191-192, 314
Industrial capitalism, xiii, 92, 118, 151, 157, 170, 174, 175-237, 238, 249, 252, 254, 269, 288, 293, 294, 303, 316, 318, 324, 331, 332, 334, 337, 340, 342, 364, 365, 367, 369, 389, 390
Industrial capitalists, xi, 92, 164, 204, 227, 232, 236, 239, 245, 246, 255, 256, 263, 266, 267, 268, 272, 281, 286, 293, 294, 296, 298, 301, 313, 317, 319, 320, 325, 326, 331, 340, 342, 347, 348, 350, 354, 365, 366, 367, 372, 388, 389, 390
Industrial entrepreneurs, 71, 95, 99, 100, 102, 387
Industrialists, financial, 194, 389
Industrial masters, 69, 70. See also Handicraftsmen, Masters, small.
Industrial relations, 93
Industrial relations counselors, 232, 294, 296, 391
Industrial Revolution, 103, 107, 132, 164, 169, 172, 177, 178, 181, 182, 185, 215, 219, 267, 334, 388, 390
Industry, 92-103, 120, 133, 158, 263, 306, 309, 320. See Manufacture.
Industry, sick, 327
Inequality, social, 14-15
Inflation, 300, 304, 337, 345, 367
Influence, bankers'. See Control, bankers'.
Inheritance, 13, 14, 87
Inns, innkeepers, 44, 49, 64, 80, 227
Insull group, 283
Insull, Samuel, 283-284, 286, 388
Insurance, 65, 74, 78, 79, 82, 90, 105, 122, 140, 166, 174, 177, 195, 198, 222, 223, 232, 251, 264, 301, 307, 321, 327, 352
Integration, 67, 87, 193, 199, 238, 241-242, 266-271, 288, 298, 317, 389
Interest, 56, 78, 87, 122, 124, 254, 314, 354, 369
Interlocking directorates, 257, 285
International Harvester Company, 245, 268-269
International Mercantile Marine Company, 275-276
Inventions, inventors, 279, 391
Inventories, 21, 22, 83, 115
Investment, viii, x, 39, 40, 41, 46, 54, 68, 81, 106, 162, 166, 173, 185-186, 187, 221, 246, 247, 249, 259, 265, 271, 272, 303, 316, 317, 344, 346-347, 350, 354, 359, 362, 363, 364, 369, 388. See Capital, flow of.
Investment manuals, 297
Investment services, 297
Investment trusts, 251, 285, 286, 292, 300, 316
Investors, x, 140, 236, 292, 300, 302, 307, 322, 391
Ironmongers, 35, 68, 94, 100, 101, 129
Italy, Italians, xi, 29, 68, 70, 78, 96, 116, 143, 146, 158, 159, 166, 168, 169, 178, 209, 328, 329, 339-343, 344, 347, 356, 364, 387, 390

Jackson, Patrick Tracy, 102-103, 179

INDEX

Jamestown, Va., 109-110
Japan, 260
Jews, 27, 38, 47, 56, 58, 78, 130, 143, 147, 152, 153, 170, 248, 253, 260, 261, 304, 310, 317, 326, 334, 341, 343, 344, 345, 346, 347, 356, 386
Journeymen, ix, x, 36, 53, 70, 71. See Workmen.
Justice, social, 98, 131

King's Merchant, 72, 136
King's Mirror, 38-39
Kreuger, Ivar, 302-303, 305, 318
Kroger Grocery and Baking Company, 255, 289-290
Kuhn, Loeb and Company, 222, 251, 253, 274, 300

Labor, ix, 1, 4, 16, 28, 29, 35, 36-37, 48, 52, 120, 180-181, 190, 198, 218, 224, 231, 232, 233, 234, 237, 308, 317, 320, 327, 347, 352, 357, 361, 369, 390. See Workmen.
Labor, division of, 3, 98, 99, 177, 225, 238. See Employment, division of.
Labor, hours of, 102
Labor relations counselors, 214
Labor unions, 209
Laissez-faire policy, 235
Land, 1, 13, 15, 18, 28, 29, 39, 40, 180, 369
Land, natural resources, 52
Landlords, 19, 20, 21, 23, 24, 25, 36, 41, 42, 57, 58, 69, 134, 155, 167, 340
Law, John, 150, 284, 336-337, 360
Law merchant, 42, 59, 88, 309
Lawyers, 42, 50, 59, 110, 132, 210-211, 212, 255, 256, 264, 290, 293, 296, 297, 307, 308, 352, 358, 366, 391
Leader, 19
Lee, Henry, Jr., 159, 168, 196
Lee, Ivy, 255, 296
Legislation, 64, 287, 307, 349, 366
Lehman Bros., 269, 289, 290, 291, 292, 322
Lenin, 2, 328
Levant Company, 103

Lever Bros., 229
Liberalism, 344
Little, Jacob, 220, 388
Liverpool, 176, 181, 211, 220
Livery companies, 74, 95, 101, 103, 111, 129
Livestock, 4ff.
Lloyd's association, 79, 140, 141, 321
Loans, 40, 42, 46, 54, 55, 56, 86, 87, 97, 101, 111, 136, 142, 146, 149, 227, 246, 247, 255, 350, 351, 360, 364
Lockwood, Amos D., 213
Lombards, 56, 58, 78, 80
Lombe, Thomas, 102, 164, 178, 179
London, 30, 31, 36, 41, 44, 49, 68, 69, 70, 73, 79, 80, 87, 94, 95, 99, 100, 101, 103, 107, 108, 110, 111, 112, 121, 127, 128, 129, 137, 138, 140, 143, 144, 145, 146, 147, 149, 151, 164, 167, 169, 176, 178, 211, 220, 223, 247, 261, 262, 301, 321, 336, 337
Loss, 118, 369, 370
Lottery tickets, 221
Lübeck, 41, 103
Lumbering, 74, 84, 387

Macy and Company, R. H., 200, 288
Malynes, Gerald, 122, 123, 126, 133, 139, 159
Management, viii, 1, 2, 3, 4, 5, 6, 7, 11, 16, 18, 22, 23, 25, 28, 29, 32-33, 43, 52, 53-54, 72, 74ff., 79, 83, 101, 107, 110, 128, 134, 166, 172, 178, 179, 183, 199, 201, 218, 224, 237, 239, 240, 244, 268, 273, 277, 284, 286, 297, 298, 317, 318, 319, 322, 333, 356, 358, 388, 390, 391
Management, manorial, 386
Management, scientific, 293, 294, 390
Managers, x, 132-133, 161, 226, 231, 233, 290, 296, 325, 358, 368, 390
Manor, 19ff., 32, 79, 109, 114, 126, 386
Manorial economy, 23
Manorial-feudal system, 24, 25, 31, 63, 158, 234. See also Feudalism, Manor.

INDEX

Manufacture, 4, 8, 9, 32, 51, 63, 70, 74, 79, 80, 84, 92-103, 105, 125, 126, 162, 166, 172, 174, 186, 229, 247, 267, 269, 282, 285, 288, 294, 327, 335, 387. See Industry.

Manufacture, centralized, 93. See also Central workshops, Factories, industrial.

Marco Polo, 72

Market, 18, 27, 61, 81, 94, 96, 102, 121, 131, 156, 163, 177, 195, 263, 265, 267, 348, 367, 390

Market consultants, 294, 295, 391

Market counselor, 214

Marketing, viii, 101, 158, 172, 173, 195-207, 258, 327

Market place, 30, 34, 35, 130

Market survey, 214

Marx, Karl, 2, 28, 180, 328, 337, 338

Massachusetts Bank, 187, 188

Massachusetts Bay Company, 106, 107, 112

Masters, industrial, 62, 97. See also Handicraftsmen, Masters, small.

Masters, small, 33, 52, 61, 70, 71, 81, 94, 96, 97, 98, 121, 129, 158, 169, 224, 238, 313, 335. See Handicraftsmen.

Meat packers, 241-242

Mecca, 42, 50

Medici, 72, 83, 84, 97, 118, 119, 133, 141, 145, 155, 166

Memphis, Egypt, 30, 260

Mercantile capitalism, 61, 67-174, 176, 177, 185, 186, 188, 195, 216, 223, 224, 228, 238, 247, 249, 261, 293, 294, 295, 303, 313, 318, 324, 331, 369, 386

Mercantile capitalists, 60, 209, 210, 220, 241, 325, 371, 388, 389. See also Merchants, sedentary.

Mercantile treatises, 72, 210, 391. See also Pegolotti.

Mercantilism, imperial, 124

Mercantilism, national, 120ff., 127, 180, 187

Mercantilism, urban, 60

Mercator, 33

Mercers, mercery, 31, 33, 35, 46, 68, 74, 75, 94, 104, 106, 129, 178

Merchandising, 186, 270, 288-293, 294, 320

Merchant Adventurers, 96, 103, 104, 133

Merchant bankers, 87, 141, 144-145, 147, 148, 149, 150, 154, 155, 159, 162, 167, 168, 170, 177, 221, 247, 249, 261

Merchant prince, 173. See also Merchants, sedentary.

Merchant Staplers, 103, 104, 176

Merchants, sedentary, viii, 40, 62, 66, 67-81, 81ff., 121ff., 176, 187, 196, 203, 207, 215, 220, 241, 247, 293, 386, 387, 388. See also Mercantile capitalists.

Merchants, traveling, 6, 8, 31, 34, 35, 36, 37-44, 48, 49, 50, 54, 55, 56, 57, 61, 67, 68, 69, 70, 73, 74, 81, 86, 93, 103, 117, 119, 129, 136, 143, 152, 170, 210, 386

Mergers, 268, 269, 298. See Consolidation.

Merrill, Lynch and Company, 290, 292

Metropolitan centers, 63, 68, 101, 128, 132, 139, 177, 185, 199, 204, 211, 295, 308

Metropolitan economy, 93, 125, 127-132, 156, 158, 176, 185, 195, 389, 390

Meunier, C., 236-237

Middle class, 30, 31, 50, 163, 223, 337, 338, 345, 357. See Bourgeois, Business men, private.

Middlemen, 282. See also Money middlemen.

Migration, 1, 4ff.

Mills, 64, 100, 136, 164, 178, 198, 213, 244

Mining, 74, 84, 105, 130, 131, 158, 166, 220, 240, 294, 327, 387

Misselden, Edward, 120, 123, 126, 133, 159, 180

Money, 24, 32, 34, 36, 40, 42, 44, 46, 54, 55, 57, 76, 77, 78, 81, 97, 101,

INDEX

124, 126, 134, 142, 143, 144, 149, 314, 321, 367
Money-barter economy, 76, 141, 142
Money-changers, 77, 147
Money-lenders, 40, 147
Money-lending, 40, 69
Money market, 262
Money middlemen, 86, 87, 262, 265, 362, 363, 369
Money, paper, 187
Money power, 168, 247, 320
Money Trust, 253, 284, 299
Monitor, 102
Monopoly, 29, 74, 112, 121, 126, 154, 162, 163, 190, 241, 244, 245, 279, 335, 336
Morgan empire, 273
Morgan, J. P., Sr., 205, 253, 255, 262, 269, 276, 317
Morgan, J. P., and Company, 202, 203, 208, 222, 251, 253, 256, 267, 268, 269, 273, 274, 277, 283, 288, 289
Morris, Robert, 109, 135, 159, 166
Mortgages, 351
Mun, Thomas, 120, 123, 126, 159, 180
Mussolini, Benito, 340-341

Naples, 84, 145, 147, 166, 247, 249
National capitalism, xiii, 26, 88, 209, 287, 323-369, 389, 390
National capitalists, 263, 264, 304, 314, 318, 320, 372, 390
Nationalization, 278-279. See also Socialization.
National Progressives, 345
National Recovery Administration, 351, 365
Naziism, 323, 343-348, 362
Negroes, 29, 47
New Deal, 64, 162, 209, 230, 263, 299, 323, 335, 348-358, 360, 362, 364, 389
New Era, 282, 389
New Freedom, 299, 349, 350, 357, 389
New York, 114, 169, 184, 188, 197, 200ff., 208, 211, 220, 239, 242, 247, 252, 266, 279, 289, 292, 295, 302

New York Central RR., 182, 271, 273
Nikitin, 43
Nomads, 4ff., 308. See also Cultural nomadic economy.
Nomads, pastoral, 6ff., 18
Norfolk husbandry, 72, 131, 164
North American Company, 280, 283
Northern Pacific RR., 208, 222, 253, 271, 273, 296
Norway, 38-39, 103
Notary, 33, 35, 49
Notes, circulating, 77, 147
Notes, demand, 145, 149
Notes, promissory, 54, 142, 146, 150, 186, 187, 204, 221

Obsolescence, 212, 369
Office management, 294-295, 391
Office management counselors, 294, 295
Officials, pre-business, 19ff. See also Bailiffs, Reeves, Seneschals.
Oppenheimer, Franz, 12
Organization, internal, viii, 224-227, 387
Organization of business, 11, 255, 275, 301, 314
Orient, 44, 168, 170
Outgo, 21, 22. See also Costs, Expenses.
Owen, Robert, 228-229
Ownership, 13, 15. See also Property right.

Pacioli, Luca, 72, 116
Paper, commercial, 150, 151. See also Credit instruments.
Parcel post, 138
Paris, 30, 55, 138, 147, 200, 242, 247, 252, 336
Partners, 21, 33, 39, 40, 43, 50, 67, 74, 119, 129, 146, 255, 289
Partners, junior, 83, 84, 85, 89, 90, 103, 146, 160, 166, 255
Partners, senior, 84-85, 89-90, 120, 141, 145, 166, 387
Partnership, 39, 42, 46, 49, 54, 56,

INDEX

57, 59, 65, 81-85, 86, 104, 106, 133, 135, 172, 175, 178, 219, 220, 250
Partnership, industrial, 102
Partnership, temporary, or one-venture, 82, 85, 105, 106, 115, 116, 128, 165, 387
Partnership, terminal, 84-85, 86, 118
Passengers, 82, 83, 181, 285
Patents, 179, 190, 271, 335
Paterson, Wm., 138
Patron of business, 37
Pawnbroking, 58, 64, 77-78, 145, 147, 334, 386. See also Lombards.
Paycocke, Thomas, 95, 96, 99, 100
Peabody, George, 261
Pedlars, 31, 35, 37, 44-48, 61, 64, 138, 170
Pedlars, wholesale, 47
Pegolotti, 80, 133
Peirce, John, 107, 111, 114
Pennsylvania Company, 223
Pennsylvania RR., 193, 252, 271, 296
Pensions, 101, 232, 296
Peruzzi, 87, 118, 134, 145
Petty capitalism, 27-66, 71, 72, 86, 115, 118, 122, 125, 152, 153, 154, 156, 170, 324, 332, 340, 350, 369, 370
Petty capitalists, 69, 70, 105, 114, 117, 128, 129, 158, 166, 175, 176, 209, 210, 263, 308, 309, 313, 325, 326, 331, 337, 338, 339, 341, 342, 345, 347, 348, 351, 365, 371, 386, 389, 390. See Handicraftsmen, Masters, small.
Petty capitalists, sedentary, 33-37
Petty capitalists, traveling, 37-48
Peutinger, Conrad, 153-154, 388
Philadelphia, 82, 87, 149, 169, 211, 212, 279-280
Philadelphia Contributionship, 223
Phoenicia, Phoenicians, 27, 38, 104
Piece wage, 35, 70, 96, 102, 172
Pirates, 37, 41, 50, 137, 261
Pirenne, Henri, 37, 73
Plane of living, 162
Planning, 72, 369
Plantation, 19, 109

Plymouth Company, 106, 107, 111, 112
Pole, Sir Wm. de la, 72, 136
Policy, business, viii, 32-33, 38-39, 43, 62, 72, 74ff., 120ff., 126, 128, 150, 159, 166, 172-173, 178, 179, 182, 193, 255, 268, 298, 306, 311, 312, 315, 317, 319, 325, 333, 356, 367, 388, 390
Policy, financial, 122
Policy, manorial, 386
Politicians, xiii, 287, 305, 308, 320, 322, 325, 326, 335, 338, 342, 347, 355, 356, 358, 361, 365, 367, 368, 392
Poverty, 32, 53, 229, 231
Power, electric, 285
Power, machine, 158, 178-179, 219, 235
Power over men, 9, 12, 52, 66, 120, 124, 129, 132, 154, 156, 235, 321, 347, 368
Power Trust, 284
Pragmatism, xi, 372
President, 226, 292
Price, just, 54-55, 122, 154, 227, 245
Price, market, 24, 29, 54-55, 95, 102, 121, 123, 132, 154, 160, 162, 177, 183, 190, 201, 235, 243, 245-246, 298, 309-310, 311, 333, 334, 348, 351, 356-357, 370
Priests, clergy, 17, 20, 35, 38, 40, 53, 153, 156, 338, 358, 390
Prince, Frederick H., 194
Privilege, commercial, 67. See Monopoly, Patents.
Producer's goods, 218, 234
Production, 11, 17, 18, 25, 28, 52, 61, 63, 103, 121, 123, 158, 173, 183, 190, 191, 194, 195, 218, 225, 230, 237, 238, 242, 268, 286, 294, 317, 326, 331, 351, 356, 361, 369
Production for use, 28
Professional classes, 63, 65, 160, 341, 342, 345, 348, 349, 350, 351, 352, 358
Profits, viii, ix, 2, 28, 29, 31, 35, 51, 53, 81, 83, 93, 111, 113, 118, 119,

INDEX

120, 123, 135, 138, 155, 173, 183, 193, 194, 215, 218, 238, 245, 254, 258, 262, 265, 269, 275, 294, 298, 303, 311, 341, 345, 369, 370, 371, 390, 391
Profit-sharing, 228, 296
Progress, economic, social, x, 11, 22, 23-24, 25, 96, 151
Prohibition, 63, 307, 334
Proletariat, 65, 338, 342, 368. *See also* Workmen, permanent.
Promoters, promoting, 136-138, 218, 220, 228, 258, 259, 301, 313
Promotion, 132, 248, 270, 282, 290, 291, 302, 314, 391
Property right, 307, 323. *See also* Ownership.
Providence, R. I., 102, 164, 178, 187, 239, 240
Publicans, 134
Public opinion, 120, 235, 296
Public relations counselors, 214, 232, 294, 296, 391
Public utilities, 105, 186, 257, 264, 279-287, 288, 300, 319, 326-327, 334, 365
Public Works Administration, 352, 353
Pujo investigation, 253, 267, 389
Punctuality, 221

Quaker Oats Company, 244

Racketeers, 42, 305, 308, 309, 334, 391
Railroads, 105, 174, 181, 182-186, 190, 192, 194, 195, 208, 211, 212, 216, 217, 220, 222, 225, 227, 236, 240, 245, 248, 250, 253, 257, 262, 264, 271, 272-276, 279, 280, 288, 294, 298, 300, 307, 313, 319, 335, 340, 350, 355, 366, 388
Ralston, W. C., 240-241
Real estate, 65. *See* Land, Landlords.
Reconstruction Finance Corp., 336, 349, 350, 353, 389
Recreation, 16
Reeves, 15, 20, 21
Reform, social, 334

Regions, regionalism, 321, 365
Registrar, 208, 209
Regrating, 60, 313
Regulation, public, 279, 309
Relief, social, 333, 389. *See also* Dole.
Religion, xi, 16-17, 22, 107, 108, 111, 113, 114, 152-153, 229, 232, 304, 306
Renaissance, 153-154
Rent, 18, 41, 57
Reserves, 194, 212, 246, 287, 347
Respondentia loans, 55
Retail, 75, 76, 84, 165, 171, 222, 242, 251, 269, 291, 310, 334, 349
Retailers, 37, 45, 195, 197, 198, 199, 202, 264, 270, 288
Retailing, specialized, 36, 75, 76
Revolutions in business, 69
Rigidity in business, 367
Risk, 29, 33, 40, 56, 78, 82, 105, 140, 141, 157, 165, 177, 196, 259, 315, 370
Rockefeller group, 231-232, 252, 255, 268, 302
Rockefeller, John D., Jr., 231-232, 296
Rockefeller, John D., Sr., 252, 296, 388
Rockefeller, Wm., 184, 192, 252
Rome, 30, 31, 37, 119, 134, 261
Roosevelt, F. D., 349, 354, 355
Rothschilds, 147, 247
Rotterdam, 30, 82
Rowntree, B. Seebohm, 229
Russia, Russians, 2, 23, 29, 43, 92, 103, 128, 161, 260, 328, 329, 330, 358, 390
Russia Company, 104, 106, 107

Sabotage, x, 308
Saddlers, 69, 70, 96
Safeway Stores, Inc., 290-291
St. Godric, 45
St. Ives, 45
St. Omer, 40
Saint-Simon, 248, 388
Salary, 48, 133, 275
Salem, 76, 176
Salters, 35, 74, 129

Sandys, Edwin, 110, 111
San Francisco, 240
Santo Stefano, 43
Saturday afternoon, 71
Savary, Jacques, 73
Schools of business, 163, 319. *See also* Education for business.
Scriba, Giovanni, 49
Scribes, 35, 49-50
Sea loans, 55, 56. *See* Commendation partnership.
Secular trends, viii, 26, 183, 199, 201, 215-218, 297-304, 320, 321, 359-362, 391
Secular trends, downward, 26, 183, 201, 215, 218, 219, 236, 243, 254, 263, 272, 282, 295, 298, 299, 303, 317, 319, 332, 338, 343, 355, 359-361, 370, 371
Secular trends, upwards, 199, 215, 218, 228, 298-299, 319, 359
Security, 5, 19, 23, 26, 39, 122, 234, 245, 299, 371
Security, social, 26, 326
Security underwriting, 254
Sedentary merchants, types of, 68. *See* Merchants, sedentary.
Self-sufficiency, 2, 3
Seneschals, 19, 20, 22, 25
Serfs, 19, 25, 89
Settled village economy, 4, 6, 11, 13ff., 18, 22, 25, 28, 52, 61, 324, 386
Settlement of peoples, 1, 6, 7, 13, 14-15, 23
Sewell, Samuel, 84
Shareholders, 106. *See* Stockholders.
Sharing of management, 101, 228. *See also* Social engineering.
Sherley, James, 111, 112
Shihsheng, Mr. Lien, 170-173
Ship-building, 82, 83, 113
Ships, 39, 40, 43, 44, 49, 50, 55, 75, 76, 79, 81, 82, 89, 101, 103, 135, 140, 155, 159, 165, 248
Ship's husband, 140
Shoemakers, 32, 34, 36, 45, 60, 198
Shopkeepers, 31, 33, 34, 35, 36, 37, 42, 43, 48, 54, 69, 70, 129, 165, 170

Shops, 53, 61, 64, 71, 98, 100, 144, 171
Slater, Samuel, 102, 178, 180, 187, 217, 227
Slaves, 9, 19, 20, 25, 81, 89, 334
Smith, Adam, 28, 124, 139, 169, 180, 387
Smyrna, 119, 260
Smythe, Sir Thomas, 73, 90, 107ff., 114, 166
Social democrats, 345
Social engineering, 101, 227-234, 389
Socialism, 85, 327-328, 333, 337, 339
Socialization, 323, 325, 326-327, 331, 337-338, 365, 366. *See also* Nationalization.
Sombart, Werner, 40-41, 57, 58, 151, 153
Southern RR., 273
South Sea Company, 101, 140
Spain, Spaniards, 29, 36, 114, 148, 153, 154, 156, 261, 341, 347. *See also* Barcelona.
Specialization, 60, 98, 162, 167, 169, 170, 174, 175ff., 191, 198, 210, 220, 225, 235, 236, 238ff., 246, 254, 255, 266, 288, 292, 293, 295, 298, 317, 387, 390
Speculation, 58, 132, 137, 218, 240, 263, 264, 265, 316, 317-318, 326, 367
Speculators, 138-140, 190, 220, 263, 280, 300, 312, 317, 322, 336, 360
Spicer, John, 45
Sprague family, 239-240
Stability, 358
Stalin, 2, 328
Standard Brands, Inc., 269-270
Standard of living, 123
Standard Oil, 192, 242, 245, 252, 302
Staplers, 176. *See* Merchant Staplers.
Statistics, statisticians, 295
Statistics, business, 295, 300
Status, 1, 2, 3, 11, 25, 26, 234, 371, 386
Steelyard in London, 49, 104
Stetson, F. L., 255
Stinnes, Hugo, 321, 344

INDEX

Stock exchange, 130, 220, 282
Stockholders, 104, 109, 118, 150, 183, 188, 210, 211, 212, 213, 225-226, 237, 239, 254, 259, 276, 277, 279, 286, 310, 311, 316, 322, 334, 368
Stock market, 264, 346
Stock, non-voting, 257, 284
Stocks, 58, 130, 140, 220, 222, 255, 257, 263, 264, 265, 271, 272, 275, 285, 286, 291, 297, 300, 302, 312, 316, 321, 335, 337, 362, 391
Stocks, preferred, 109, 112, 257, 264, 286, 291, 303, 336, 364
Storage, 4, 76-77, 104, 286, 387
Storekeepers, x, 31, 33, 34, 35, 36, 37, 43, 47, 48, 54, 62, 69, 72, 129, 165, 170, 346, 351
Stores, 61, 64, 140, 221, 236, 298, 319
Stores, department, *See* Department stores.
Stores, general, 33, 35, 201
Stores, retail, 46, 76, 89, 105, 121, 161, 242
Stores, specialized, 35, 199
Strikes, 231-232, 233, 296, 342, 346, 354
Success, 29, 40
Sun Fire Office, 137, 140
Supercargoes, 68, 72, 76, 79, 80, 81, 83, 117. *See also* Agents, Factors.
Supervision, 102
Swastika, 343
Sweatshops, 352
Sweden, 101, 113, 114, 150, 302-303
Swift and Company, 267
Syracuse, Sicily, 119
Syria, 119, 260

Tallies, 50, 101, 142, 295
Taverners, 35, 75
Taxes, 137, 185, 212, 233, 293, 319, 326, 334, 336, 341, 345, 346, 347, 351, 355, 367
Thebes, Egypt, 30, 260
Theft, 22, 50, 101
Time utility production, 28
Tinkers, 45, 46, 64
Tokio, 200

Tools of business, 293, 297
Town economy, 21, 30, 40, 93, 125, 128, 130, 158, 175, 386, 390
Towns, 6, 8, 19, 24, 25, 30, 31, 34, 35, 41, 42, 49, 51, 59, 60, 61, 62, 66, 68, 69, 70, 75, 88, 98, 125, 130-131, 152, 165, 182, 199, 239, 265, 309, 333
Trade, principles of, 42
Trade union, 231, 233, 321, 340, 341, 352
Transportation, 4, 76, 82, 105, 157, 174, 176, 181-186, 198, 248, 272-278, 280, 282, 285, 320, 387
Travelers, commercial, 198
Treasurers, 19, 20, 25, 87, 102, 107, 110, 133, 173, 187, 208, 226
Trimalchio, 101
Trust companies, 208, 223, 251
Turnpikes, 105, 174
Tyre, 30, 119, 260

Unemployment, 232, 296, 333, 345, 348, 357, 358, 361, 371
United Gas Improvement Company, 279-280
United States Steel Corp., 208, 245, 256, 267, 297
Ur, 30, 260
Usselinx, Willem, 107, 113-114, 153
Usucapital system, 7, 85, 219, 324, 369. *See* Capital, autogenous.
Usufacture, 93
Usury, 24, 56, 142, 145, 148

Vanderbilt, Cornelius, 182-183, 192, 217, 272-273, 274, 307, 388
Venice, 44, 72, 116, 149, 150, 158, 167, 181, 387
Vienna, 147, 247
Villages, 15. *See also* Settled village economy.
Vintners, 31, 35, 74, 75
Virginia, 81, 91, 162
Virginia Company, 86-87, 106, 107-111, 112

Wages, 37, 84, 97, 122, 124, 155-156, 215, 219, 228, 231, 233, 275, 312, 320, 347, 352, 354, 355, 357
Wall Street, 252, 253, 255, 256, 264, 301, 317, 319, 336
Wanamaker, John, 200, 242
War, 24, 30, 50, 134, 136, 154-155, 159, 184, 203, 216, 218, 222, 230, 261, 266, 281, 298, 299, 314, 342, 344, 345, 346, 347, 348, 349, 350, 355, 359, 362, 364, 367
Warehouses, 96, 97, 109, 140, 165, 206, 227, 289
Warehouses, common, 76-77
Wealth, 32, 44, 53, 63, 66, 72, 91, 101, 120, 129, 132, 133, 135, 154, 160, 165, 169, 186, 218, 219, 235, 253, 259, 261, 312, 342
Weavers, 32, 95, 99
Welsers, 72-73, 145, 154
Western Union, 276, 300
West India Company, Dutch, 107, 113-114
Westinghouse Electric and Mfg. Company, 271, 280
Wheelwrights, 177, 179
Whittington, Dick, 73
Wholesale, 43, 75, 77, 83, 94, 105, 122, 165, 173, 189, 203, 206-207, 222, 248, 251, 269, 310
Wholesalers, specialized, 195, 196, 197, 198, 199, 200, 201, 207, 227, 242, 288, 289, 388
Wilson, Woodrow, 299, 349, 350, 357, 359, 389
Winchcombe, John, 99-100
Woolworth, 64, 288
Work, ix, xii, 24, 27, 36, 71, 101, 229, 235, 328, 358, 367. *See* Labor.
Workmen, ix-x, 9, 35, 36, 37, 48, 50, 62, 63, 89, 90, 94, 95, 99, 101, 155, 159, 163, 166, 175, 177, 189, 216, 226, 227, 228, 230, 232, 236, 237, 245, 279, 296, 310, 313, 314, 316, 320, 322, 325, 326, 328, 337, 338, 341, 342, 348, 352, 354, 355, 357, 358, 359, 366, 367. *See* Artisans, Bookkeepers, Cashiers, Clerks, Journeymen, Labor.
Workmen, permanent, 66, 349, 350, 351, 390
Works Progress Administration, 352, 353

Xenophon, 20